Living the Life of the Lifegiver

Printed for
Remnant Publications
by
Pacific Press Publishing Association
Boise, Idaho
Oshawa, Ontario, Canada

Cover art by Harry Anderson

Living the Life of the Lifegiver

This edition published 1995

ISBN 1-883012-56-2

The bracketed numbers at the foot of each page co-ordinate this edition with the pagination of the standard hardback printings.

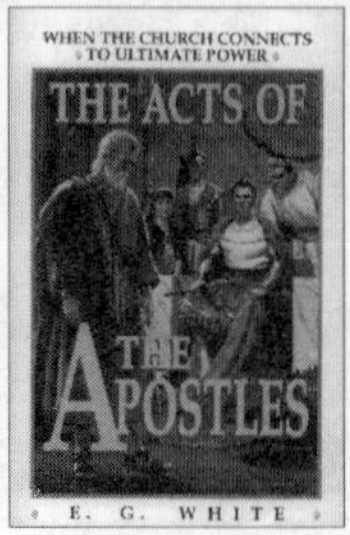

What makes this set so popular? The Results!

Lifechanging Results

The Bible Study Companion Set *$39.75

All five books together covering Genesis to Revelation — from the beginning of the universe through human history and on into our future. This set truly enriches your life with a better

Patriarchs and Prophets

Where did the human race come from? Why do bad things happen to good people? Why are babies born sick, and why do so many hard-working people never seem to get ahead? If God is good, why doesn't He prevent sadness and heartbreak? And if He is all-powerful, why doesn't He do something about evil and sickness? These questions and many more are answered in this remarkable book. Patriarchs and Prophets has brought peace and hope to millions throughout the world. *US$7.95

Prophets and Kings

Beginning with King Solomon, this book recounts the stories of great men and women of the Bible who lived from his reign to the first advent of Jesus Christ. Here you will read of Elijah, Daniel, Isaiah, and Jeremiah, among others–and you will find the lessons God would have us all learn from their lives. *US$7.95

The Desire of Ages

This book is about the Man who stands at the center of all human history. No one else has had such a profound influence on the people of this planet as Jesus Christ. *US$7.95

The Acts of the Apostles

This book is about power–ultimate power. The awesome power of the Holy Spirit, and what He can do in human lives when we surrender to be used by Him. When Pentecost came upon the early church, what God's people accomplished was miraculous. And all that the apostles did, God wants to do again through us today. *US$7.95

The Great Controversy

The world is on the verge of a stupendous crisis. Here is the authoritative answer to the confusion and despair of this tense age. Revealing God's ultimate plan for mankind, The Great Controversy may be the most important book you'll ever read. *US$7.95

A Note From the Publisher

Living the Life of the Lifegiver brings together in one volume, two classic Christian books previously published as *Thoughts From the Mount of Blessing* and *Christ's Object Lessons*.

Although the page numbering of the two books in this volume is consecutive, their chapter numbers and page headings have been preserved as in the original versions.

Contents

Thoughts from the Mount of Blessing

Christ's Object Lessons

Thoughts from the Mount of Blessing

Introduction

The Sermon on the Mount is Heaven's benediction to the world—a voice from the throne of God. It was given to mankind to be to them the law of duty and the light of heaven, their hope and consolation in despondency, their joy and comfort in all the vicissitudes and walks of life. Here the Prince of preachers, the Master Teacher, utters the words that the Father gave Him to speak.

The Beatitudes are Christ's greeting, not only to those who believe, but to the whole human family. He seems to have forgotten for a moment that He is in the world, not in heaven; and He uses the familiar salutation of the world of light. Blessings flow from His lips as the gushing forth of a long-sealed current of rich life.

Christ leaves us in no doubt as to the traits of character that He will always recognize and bless. From the ambitious favorites of the world, He turns to those whom they disown, pronouncing all blessed who receive His light and life. To the poor in spirit, the meek, the lowly, the sorrowful, the despised, the persecuted, He opens His arms of refuge, saying, "Come unto Me,...and I will give you rest."

Christ can look upon the misery of the world without a shade of sorrow for having created man. In the human heart He sees more than sin, more than misery. In His infinite wisdom and love He sees man's possibilities, the height to which he may attain. He knows that, even though human beings have abused their mercies and destroyed their God-given dignity, yet the Creator is to be glorified in their redemption.

Throughout all time the words that Christ spoke from the mount of Beatitudes will retain their power. Every sentence is a jewel from the treasure house of truth. The principles enunciated in this discourse are for all ages and for all classes of men. With divine energy, Christ expressed His faith and hope as He pointed out class after class as blessed because of having formed righteous characters. Living the life of the Life-giver, through faith in Him, everyone can reach the standard held up in His words.

1
On the Mountainside

More than fourteen centuries before Jesus was born in Bethlehem, the children of Israel gathered in the fair vale of Shechem, and from the mountains on either side the voices of the priests were heard proclaiming the blessings and the curses—"a blessing, if ye obey the commandments of the Lord your God:... and a curse, if ye will not obey." Deuteronomy 11:27, 28. And thus the mountain from which the words of benediction were spoken came to be known as the mount of blessing. But it was not upon Gerizim that the words were spoken which have come as a benediction to a sinning and sorrowing world. Israel fell short of the high ideal which had been set before her. Another than Joshua must guide His people to the true rest of faith. No longer is Gerizim known as the mount of the Beatitudes, but that unnamed mountain beside the Lake of Gennesaret, where Jesus spoke the words of blessing to His disciples and the multitude.

Let us in imagination go back to that scene, and, as we sit with the disciples on the mountainside, enter into the thoughts and feelings that filled their hearts. Understanding what the words of Jesus meant to those who heard them, we may discern in them a new vividness and beauty, and may also gather for ourselves their deeper lessons.

When the Saviour began His ministry, the popular conception of the Messiah and His work was such as wholly unfitted the people to receive Him. The spirit of true devotion had been lost in tradition and ceremonialism, and the prophecies were interpreted at the dictate of proud, world-loving hearts. The Jews looked for the coming One, not as a Saviour from sin, but as a great prince who should bring all nations under the supremacy of the Lion of the tribe of Judah. In vain had John the Baptist, with the heart-searching power of the ancient prophets, called them to repentance. In vain had he, beside the Jordan, pointed to Jesus as the Lamb of God, that taketh away the sin of the world. God was seeking to direct their minds to Isaiah's prophecy of the suffering Saviour, but they would not hear.

Had the teachers and leaders in Israel yielded to His transforming grace, Jesus would have made them His ambassadors among men. In Judea first the coming of the kingdom had been proclaimed, and the call to repentance had been given. In the act of driving out the desecrators from the temple at Jerusalem, Jesus had announced Himself as the Messiah—the One who should cleanse the soul from the defilement of sin and make His people a holy temple unto the Lord. But the Jewish leaders would not humble themselves to receive the lowly Teacher from Nazareth. At His second visit to Jerusalem He was arraigned before the Sanhedrin, and fear of the people alone prevented these dignitaries from trying to take His life. Then it was that, leaving Judea, He entered upon His ministry in Galilee.

His work there had continued some months before the Sermon on the Mount was given. The message He had proclaimed throughout the land, "The kingdom of heaven is at hand" (Matthew 4:17), had arrested the attention of all classes, and had still further fanned the flame of their ambitious hopes. The fame of the new Teacher had spread beyond the limits of Palestine, and, notwithstanding the attitude of the hierarchy, the feeling was widespread that this might be the hoped-for Deliverer. Great multitudes thronged the steps of Jesus, and the popular enthusiasm ran high.

The time had come for the disciples who had been most closely associated with Christ to unite more directly in His work, that these vast throngs might not be left uncared for, as sheep without a shepherd. Some of these disciples had joined themselves to Him at the beginning of His ministry, and nearly all the twelve had been associated together as members of the family of Jesus. Yet they also, misled by the teaching of the rabbis, shared the popular expectation of an earthly kingdom. They could not comprehend the movements of Jesus. Already they had been perplexed and troubled that He made no effort to strengthen His cause by securing the support of the priests and rabbis, that He did nothing to establish His authority as an earthly king. A great work was yet to be accomplished for these disciples before they would be prepared for the sacred trust that would be theirs when Jesus should ascend to heaven. Yet they had responded to the love of Christ, and, though slow of heart to believe, Jesus saw in them those whom He could train and discipline for His great work. And now that they had been long enough with Him to establish, in a measure, their faith in the divine character of His mission, and the people also had received evidence of His power which they could not question, the way was prepared for an avowal of the principles of His kingdom that would help them to comprehend its true nature.

Alone upon a mountain near the Sea of Galilee, Jesus had spent all night in prayer for these chosen ones. At the dawn He called them to Him, and, with words of prayer and instruction, laid His hands upon their heads in benediction, setting them apart to the gospel work. Then He repaired with them to the seaside, where in the early morning a great multitude had already begun to assemble.

Besides the usual crowd from the Galilean towns, there were great numbers from Judea, and from Jerusalem itself; from Perea, and from the half-heathen population of Decapolis; from Idumea, away to the south of Judea, and from Tyre and Sidon, the Phoenician cities on the shore of the Mediterranean. "Hearing what great things He did," they "came to hear Him, and to be healed of their diseases; and...power came forth from Him, and healed them all." Mark 3:8, R.V.; Luke 6:17–19, R.V.

Then, as the narrow beach did not afford even standing room within reach of His voice for all who desired to hear Him, Jesus led the way back to the mountainside. Reaching a level space that afforded a pleasant gathering place for the vast assembly, He seated Himself upon the grass, and His disciples and the multitude followed His example.

With a feeling that something more than usual might be expected, the disciples had pressed about their Master. From the events of the morning they gathered assurance that some announcement was about to be made in regard to the kingdom which, as they fondly hoped, He was soon to establish. A feeling of expectancy pervaded the multitude also, and eager faces gave evidence of the deep interest.

As they sat upon the green hillside, awaiting the words of the divine Teacher, their hearts were filled with thoughts of future glory. There were scribes and Pharisees who looked forward to the day when they should have dominion over the hated Romans and possess the riches and splendor of the world's great empire. The poor peasants and fishermen hoped to hear the assurance that their wretched hovels, the scanty food, the life of toil, and fear of want, were to be exchanged for mansions of plenty and days of ease. In place of the one coarse garment which was their covering by day and their blanket at night, they hoped that Christ would give them the rich and costly robes of their conquerors.

All hearts thrilled with the proud hope that Israel was soon to be honored before the nations as the chosen of the Lord, and Jerusalem exalted as the head of a universal kingdom.

2
The Beatitudes

"He opened His mouth, and taught them, saying, Blessed are the poor in spirit: for theirs is the kingdom of heaven." Matthew 5:2, 3.

As something strange and new, these words fall upon the ears of the wondering multitude. Such teaching is contrary to all they have ever heard from priest or rabbi. They see in it nothing to flatter their pride or to feed their ambitious hopes. But there is about this new Teacher a power that holds them spellbound. The sweetness of divine love flows from His very presence as the fragrance from a flower. His words fall like "rain upon the mown grass: as showers that water the earth." Psalm 72:6. All feel instinctively that here is One who reads the secrets of the soul, yet who comes near to them with tender compassion. Their hearts open to Him, and, as they listen, the Holy Spirit unfolds to them something of the meaning of that lesson which humanity in all ages so needs to learn.

In the days of Christ the religious leaders of the people felt that they were rich in spiritual treasure. The prayer of the Pharisee, "God, I thank Thee, that I am not as the rest of men" (Luke 18:11, R.V.), expressed the feeling of his class and, to a great degree, of the whole nation. But in the throng that surrounded Jesus there were some who had a sense of their spiritual poverty. When in the miraculous draft of fishes the divine power of Christ was revealed, Peter fell at the Saviour's feet, exclaiming, "Depart from me; for I am a sinful man, O Lord" (Luke 5:8); so in the multitude gathered upon the mount there were souls who, in the presence of His purity, felt that they were "wretched, and miserable, and poor, and blind, and naked" (Revelation 3:17); and they longed for "the grace of God that bringeth salvation" (Titus 2:11). In these souls, Christ's words of greeting awakened hope; they saw that their lives were under the benediction of God.

Jesus had presented the cup of blessing to those who felt that they were "rich, and increased with goods" (Revelation 3:17), and had need of nothing, and they had turned with scorn from the gracious gift. He who feels whole, who thinks that he is reasonably good, and is contented with his condition, does not seek to become a partaker of the grace and righteousness of Christ. Pride feels no need, and so it closes the heart against Christ and the infinite blessings He came to give. There is no room for Jesus in the heart of such a person. Those who are rich and honorable in their own eyes do not ask in faith, and receive the blessing of God. They feel that they are full, therefore they go away empty. Those who know that they cannot possibly save themselves, or of themselves do any righteous action, are the ones who appreciate the help that Christ can bestow. They are the poor in spirit, whom He declares to be blessed.

Whom Christ pardons, He first makes penitent, and it is the office of the Holy Spirit to convince of sin. Those whose hearts have been moved by the convicting Spirit of God see that there is nothing good in themselves. They see that all they have ever done is mingled with self and sin. Like the poor publican, they stand afar off, not daring to lift up so much as their eyes to heaven, and cry, "God, be merciful to me the sinner." Luke 18:13, R.V., margin. And they are blessed. There is forgiveness for the penitent; for Christ is "the Lamb of God, which taketh away the sin of the world." John 1:29. God's promise is: "Though your sins be as scarlet, they shall be as white as snow; though they be red like crimson, they shall be as wool." "A new heart also will I give you.... And I will put My Spirit within you." Isaiah 1:18; Ezekiel 36:26, 27.

Of the poor in spirit Jesus says, "Theirs is the kingdom of heaven." This kingdom is not, as Christ's hearers had hoped, a temporal and earthly dominion. Christ was opening to men the spiritual kingdom of His love, His grace, His righteousness. The ensign of the Messiah's reign is distinguished by the likeness of the Son of man. His subjects are the poor in spirit, the meek, the persecuted for righteousness' sake. The kingdom of heaven is theirs. Though not yet fully accomplished, the work is begun in them which will make them "meet to be partakers of the inheritance of the saints in light." Colossians 1:12.

All who have a sense of their deep soul poverty, who feel that they have nothing good in themselves, may find righteousness and strength by looking unto Jesus. He says, "Come unto Me, all ye that labor and are heavy-laden." Matthew 11:28. He bids you exchange your poverty for the riches of His grace. We are not worthy of God's love, but Christ , our surety, is worthy, and is abundantly able to save all who shall come unto Him. Whatever may have been your past experience, however discouraging your present circumstances, if you will come to Jesus just as you are, weak, helpless, and despairing, our compassionate Saviour will meet you a great way off, and will throw about you His arms of love and His robe of righteousness. He presents us to the Father clothed in the white raiment of His own character. He pleads before God in our behalf, saying: I have taken the sinner's place. Look not upon this wayward child, but look on Me. Does Satan plead loudly against our souls, accusing of sin, and claiming us as his prey, the blood of Christ pleads with greater power.

"Surely, shall one say, in the Lord have I righteousness and strength....

In the Lord shall all the seed of Israel be justified, and shall glory." Isaiah 45:24, 25.

"Blessed are they that mourn: for they shall be comforted." Matthew 5:4.

The mourning here brought to view is true heart sorrow for sin. Jesus says, "I, if I be lifted up from the earth, will draw all men unto Me." John 12:32. And as one is drawn to behold Jesus uplifted on the cross, he discerns the sinfulness of humanity. He sees that it is sin which scourged and crucified the Lord of glory. He sees that, while he has been loved with unspeakable tenderness, his life has been a continual scene of ingratitude and rebellion. He has forsaken his best Friend and abused heaven's most precious gift. He has crucified to himself the Son of God afresh and pierced anew that bleeding and stricken heart. He is separated from God by a gulf of sin that is broad and black and deep, and he mourns in brokenness of heart.

Such mourning" shall be comforted." God reveals to us our guilt that we may flee to Christ, and through Him be set free from the bondage of sin, and rejoice in the liberty of the sons of God. In true contrition we may come to the foot of the cross, and there leave our burdens.

The Saviour's words have a message of comfort to those also who are suffering affliction or bereavement. Our sorrows do not spring out of the ground. God "doth not afflict willingly nor grieve the children of men." Lamentations 3:33. When He permits trials and afflictions, it is "for our profit, that we might be partakers of His holiness." Hebrews 12:10. If received in faith, the trial that seems so bitter and hard to bear will prove a blessing. The cruel blow that blights the joys of earth will be the means of turning our eyes to heaven. How many there are who would never have known Jesus had not sorrow led them to seek comfort in Him!

The trials of life are God's workmen, to remove the impurities and roughness from our character. Their hewing, squaring, and chiseling, their burnishing and polishing, is a painful process; it is hard to be pressed down to the grinding wheel. But the stone is brought forth prepared to fill its place in the heavenly temple. Upon no useless material does the Master bestow such careful, thorough work. Only His precious stones are polished after the similitude of a palace.

The Lord will work for all who put their trust in Him. Precious victories will be gained by the faithful. Precious lessons will be learned. Precious experiences will be realized.

Our heavenly Father is never unmindful of those whom sorrow has touched. When David went up the Mount Olivet, "and wept as he went up, and had his head covered, and he went barefoot" (2 Samuel 15:30), the Lord was looking pityingly upon him. David was clothed in sackcloth, and his conscience was scourging him. The outward signs of humiliation testified of his contrition. In tearful, heartbroken utterances he presented his case to God, and the Lord did not forsake His servant. Never was David dearer to the heart of Infinite Love than when, conscience-smitten, he fled for his life from his enemies, who had been stirred to rebellion by his own son. The Lord says, "As many as I love, I rebuke and chasten: be zealous therefore, and repent." Revelation 3:19. Christ lifts up the contrite heart and refines the mourning soul until it becomes His abode.

But when tribulation comes upon us, how many of us are like Jacob! We think it the hand of an enemy; and in the darkness we wrestle blindly until our strength is spent, and we find no comfort or deliverance. To Jacob the divine touch at break of day revealed the One with whom he had been contending-the Angel of the covenant; and, weeping and helpless, he fell upon the breast of Infinite Love, to receive the blessing for which his soul longed. We also need to learn that trials mean benefit, and not to despise the chastening of the Lord nor faint when we are rebuked of Him.

"Happy is the man whom God correcteth:... He maketh sore, and bindeth up: He woundeth, and His hands make whole. He shall deliver thee in six troubles: yea, in seven there shall no evil touch thee." Job 5:17–19. To every stricken one, Jesus comes with the ministry of healing. The life of bereavement, pain, and suffering may be brightened by precious revealings of His presence.

God would not have us remain pressed down by dumb sorrow, with sore and breaking hearts. He would have us look up and behold His dear face of love. The blessed Saviour stands by many whose eyes are so blinded by tears that they do not discern Him. He longs to clasp our hands, to have us look to Him in simple faith, permitting Him to guide us. His heart is open to our griefs, our sorrows, and our trials. He has loved us with an everlasting love and with loving-kindness compassed us about. We may keep the heart stayed upon Him and meditate upon His loving-kindness all the day. He will lift the soul above the daily sorrow and perplexity, into a realm of peace.

Think of this, children of suffering and sorrow, and rejoice in hope. "This is the victory that overcometh the world, even our faith." 1 John 5:4.

Blessed are they also who weep with Jesus in sympathy with the world's sorrow and in sorrow for its sin. In such mourning there is intermingled no thought of self. Jesus was the Man of Sorrows, enduring heart anguish such as no language can portray. His spirit was torn and bruised by the transgressions of men. He toiled with self-consuming zeal to relieve the wants and woes of humanity, and His heart was heavy with sorrow as He saw multitudes refuse to come to Him that they might have life. All who are followers of Christ will share in this experience. As they partake of His love they will enter into His travail for the saving of the lost. They share in the sufferings of Christ, and they will share also in the glory that shall be revealed. One with Him in His work, drinking with Him the cup of sorrow, they are partakers also of His joy.

It was through suffering that Jesus obtained the ministry of consolation. In all the affliction of humanity He is afflicted; and "in that He Himself hath suffered being tempted, He is able to succor them that are tempted." Isaiah 63:9; Hebrews 2:18. In this ministry every soul that has entered into the fellowship of His sufferings is privileged to share. "As the sufferings of Christ abound in us, so our consolation also aboundeth by Christ." 2 Corinthians 1:5. The Lord has special grace for the mourner, and its power is to melt hearts, to win souls. His love opens a channel into the wounded and bruised soul, and becomes a healing balsam to those who sorrow. "The Father of mercies, and the God of all comfort…comforteth us in all our tribulation, that we may be able to comfort them which are in any trouble, by the comfort wherewith we ourselves are comforted of God." 2 Corinthians 1:3, 4.

"Blessed are the meek." Matthew 5:5.

Throughout the Beatitudes there is an advancing line of Christian experience. Those who have felt their need of Christ, those who have mourned because of sin and have sat with Christ in the school of affliction, will learn meekness from the divine Teacher.

Patience and gentleness under wrong were not characteristics prized by the heathen or by the Jews. The statement made by Moses under the inspiration of the Holy Spirit, that he was the meekest man upon the earth, would not have been regarded by the people of his time as a commendation; it would rather have excited pity or contempt. But Jesus places meekness among the first qualifications for His kingdom. In His own life and character the divine beauty of this precious grace is revealed.

Jesus, the brightness of the Father's glory, thought "it not a thing to be grasped to be on an equality with God, but emptied Himself, taking the form of a servant." Philippians 2:6, 7, R.V., margin. Through all the lowly experiences of life He consented to pass, walking among the children of men, not as a king, to demand homage, but as one whose mission it was to serve others. There was in His manner no taint of bigotry, no cold austerity. The world's Redeemer had a greater than angelic nature, yet united with His divine majesty were meekness and humility that attracted all to Himself.

Jesus emptied Himself, and in all that He did, self did not appear. He subordinated all things to the will of His Father. When His mission on earth was about to close, He could say, "I have glorified Thee on the earth: I have finished the work which Thou gavest Me to do." John 17:4. And He bids us, "Learn of Me; for I am meek and lowly in heart." "If any man will come after Me, let him deny himself" (Matthew 11:29; 16:24); let self be dethroned and no longer hold the supremacy of the soul.

He who beholds Christ in His self-denial, His lowliness of heart, will be constrained to say, as did Daniel, when he beheld One like the sons of men, "My comeliness was turned in me into corruption." Daniel 10:8. The independence and self-supremacy in which we glory are seen in their true vileness as tokens of servitude to Satan. Human nature is ever struggling for expression, ready for contest; but he who learns of Christ is emptied of self, of pride, of love of supremacy, and there is silence in the soul. Self is yielded to the disposal of the Holy Spirit. Then we are not anxious to have the highest place. We have no ambition to crowd and elbow ourselves into notice; but we feel that our highest place is at the feet of our Saviour. We look to Jesus, waiting for His hand to lead, listening for His voice to guide. The apostle Paul had this experience, and he said, "I am crucified with Christ: nevertheless I live; yet not I, but Christ liveth in me: and the life which I now live in the flesh I live by the faith of the Son of God, who loved me, and gave Himself for me." Galatians 2:20.

When we receive Christ as an abiding guest in the soul, the peace of God, which passeth all understanding, will keep our hearts and minds through Christ Jesus. The Saviour's life on earth, though lived in the midst of conflict, was a life of peace. While angry enemies were constantly pursuing Him, He said, "He that sent Me is with Me: the Father hath not left Me alone; for I do always those things that please Him." John 8:29. No storm of human or satanic wrath could disturb the calm of that perfect communion with God. And He says to us, "Peace I leave with you, My peace I give unto you." "Take My yoke upon you, and learn of Me; for I am meek and lowly in heart: and ye shall find rest." John 14:27; Matthew 11:29. Bear with Me the yoke of service for the glory of God and the uplifting of humanity, and you will find the yoke easy and the burden light.

It is the love of self that destroys our peace. While self is all alive, we stand ready continually to guard it from mortification and insult; but when we are dead, and our life is hid with Christ in God, we shall not take neglects or slights to heart. We shall be deaf to reproach and blind to scorn and insult. "Love suffereth long, and is kind; love envieth not; love vaunteth not itself, is not puffed up, doth not behave itself unseemly, seeketh not its own, is not provoked, taketh not account of evil; rejoiceth not in unrighteousness, but rejoiceth with the truth; beareth all things, believeth all things, hopeth all things, endureth all things. Love never faileth." 1 Corinthians 13:4–8, R.V.

Happiness drawn from earthly sources is as changeable as varying circumstances can make it; but the peace of Christ is a constant and abiding peace. It does not depend upon any circumstances in life, on the amount of worldly goods or the number of earthly friends. Christ is the fountain of living water, and happiness drawn from Him can never fail.

The meekness of Christ, manifested in the home, will make the inmates happy; it provokes no quarrel, gives back no angry answer, but soothes the irritated temper and diffuses a gentleness that is felt by all within its charmed circle. Wherever cherished, it makes the families of earth a part of the one great family above.

Far better would it be for us to suffer under false accusation than to inflict upon ourselves the torture of retaliation upon our enemies. The spirit of hatred and revenge originated with Satan, and can bring only evil to him who cherishes it. Lowliness of heart, that meekness which is the fruit of abiding in Christ, is the true secret of blessing. "He will beautify the meek with salvation." Psalm 149:4.

The meek "shall inherit the earth." It was through the desire for self-exaltation that sin entered into the world, and our first parents lost the dominion over this fair earth, their kingdom. It is through self-abnegation that Christ redeems what was lost. And He says we are to overcome as He did. Revelation 3:21. Through humility and self-surrender we may become heirs with Him when "the meek shall inherit the earth." Psalm 37:11.

The earth promised to the meek will not be like this, darkened with the shadow of death and the curse. "We, according to His promise, look for new heavens and a new earth, wherein dwelleth righteousness." "There shall be no more curse: but the throne of God and of the Lamb shall be in it; and His servants shall serve Him." 2 Peter 3:13; Revelation 22:3.

There is no disappointment, no sorrow, no sin, no one who shall say, I am sick; there are no burial trains, no mourning, no death, no partings, no broken hearts; but Jesus is there, peace is there. There "they shall not hunger nor thirst; neither shall the heat nor sun smite them: for He that hath mercy on them shall lead them, even by the springs of water shall He guide them." Isaiah 49:10.

"Blessed are they which do hunger and thirst after righteousness: for they shall be filled." Matthew 5:6.

Righteousness is holiness, likeness to God, and "God is love." 1 John 4:16. It is conformity to the law of God, for "all Thy commandments are righteousness" (Psalm 119:172), and "love is the fulfilling of the law" (Romans 13:10). Righteousness is love, and love is the light and the life of God. The righteousness of God is embodied in Christ. We receive righteousness by receiving Him.

Not by painful struggles or wearisome toil, not by gift or sacrifice, is righteousness obtained; but it is freely given to every soul who hungers and thirsts to receive it. "Ho, every one that thirsteth, come ye to the waters, and he that hath no money; come ye, buy, and eat,...without money and without price." "Their righteousness is of Me, saith the Lord," and, "This is His name whereby He shall be called, The Lord Our Righteousness." Isaiah 55:1; 54: 17; Jeremiah 23:6.

No human agent can supply that which will satisfy the hunger and thirst of the soul. But Jesus says, "Behold, I stand at the door, and knock: if any man hear My voice, and open the door, I will come in to him, and will sup with him, and he with Me." "I am the bread of life: he that cometh to Me shall never hunger; and he that believeth on Me shall never thirst." Revelation 3:20; John 6:35.

As we need food to sustain our physical strength, so do we need Christ, the Bread from heaven, to sustain spiritual life and impart strength to work the works of God. As the body is continually receiving the nourishment that sustains life and vigor, so the soul must be constantly communing with Christ, submitting to Him and depending wholly upon Him.

As the weary traveler seeks the spring in the desert and, finding it, quenches his burning thirst, so will the Christian thirst for and obtain the pure water of life, of which Christ is the fountain.

As we discern the perfection of our Saviour's character we shall desire to become wholly transformed and renewed in the image of His purity. The more we know of God, the higher will be our ideal of character and the more earnest our longing to reflect His likeness. A divine element combines with the human when the soul reaches out after God and the longing heart can say, "My soul, wait thou only upon God; for my expectation is from Him." Psalm 62:5.

If you have a sense of need in your soul, if you hunger and thirst after righteousness, this is an evidence that Christ has wrought upon your heart, in order that He may be sought unto to do for you, through the endowment of the Holy Spirit, those things which it is impossible for you to do for yourself. We need not seek to quench our thirst at shallow streams; for the great fountain is just above us, of whose abundant waters we may freely drink, if we will rise a little higher in the pathway of faith.

The words of God are the wellsprings of life. As you seek unto those living springs you will, through the Holy Spirit, be brought into communion with Christ. Familiar truths will present themselves to your mind in a new aspect, texts of Scripture will burst upon you with a new meaning as a flash of light, you will see the relation of other truths to the work of redemption, and you will know that Christ is leading you, a divine Teacher is at your side.

Jesus said, "The water that I shall give him shall be in him a well of water springing up into everlasting life." John 4:14. As the Holy Spirit opens to you the truth you will treasure up the most precious experiences and will long to speak to others of the comforting things that have been revealed to you. When brought into association with them you will communicate some fresh thought in regard to the character or the work of Christ. You will have some fresh revelation of His pitying love to impart to those who love Him and to those who love Him not.

"Give, and it shall be given unto you" (Luke 6: 38); for the word of God is "a fountain of gardens, a well of living waters, and streams of Lebanon" (Song of Solomon 4:15). The heart that has once tasted the love of Christ, cries out continually for a deeper draft, and as you impart you will receive in richer and more abundant measure. Every revelation of God to the soul increases the capacity to know and to love. The continual cry of the heart is, "More of Thee," and ever the Spirit's answer is, "Much more." Romans 5:9,10. For our God delights to do "exceeding abundantly above all that we ask or think." Ephesians 3:20. To Jesus, who emptied Himself for the salvation of lost humanity, the Holy Spirit was given without measure. So it will be given to every follower of Christ when the whole heart is surrendered for His indwelling. Our Lord Himself has given the command, "Be filled with the Spirit" (Ephesians 5:18), and this command is also a promise of its fulfillment. It was the good pleasure of the Father that in Christ should "all the fullness dwell," and "in Him ye are made full." Colossians 1:19, R.V.; 2:10, R.V.

God has poured out His love unstintedly, as the showers that refresh the earth. He says, "Let the skies pour down righteousness: let the earth open, and let them bring forth salvation, and let righteousness spring up together." "When the poor and needy seek water, and there is none, and their tongue faileth for thirst, I the Lord will hear them, I the God of Israel will not forsake them. I will open rivers in high places, and fountains in the midst of the valleys: I will make the wilderness a pool of water, and the dry land springs of water." Isaiah 45:8; 41:17, 18.

"Of His fullness have all we received, and grace for grace." John 1:16.

"Blessed are the merciful: for they shall obtain mercy." Matthew 5:7.

The heart of man is by nature cold and dark and unloving; whenever one manifests a spirit of mercy and forgiveness, he does it not of himself, but through the influence of the divine Spirit moving upon his heart. "We love, because He first loved us." 1 John 4:19, R.V.

God is Himself the source of all mercy. His name is "merciful and gracious." Exodus 34:6. He does not treat us according to our desert. He does not ask if we are worthy of His love, but He pours upon us the riches of His love, to make us worthy. He is not vindictive. He seeks not to punish, but to redeem. Even the severity which He manifests through His providences is manifested for the salvation of the wayward. He yearns with intense desire to relieve the woes of men and to apply His balsam to their wounds. It is true that God "will by no means clear the guilty" (Exodus 34:7), but He would take away the guilt.

The merciful are "partakers of the divine nature," and in them the compassionate love of God finds expression. All whose hearts are in sympathy with the heart of Infinite Love will seek to reclaim and not to condemn. Christ dwelling in the soul is a spring that never runs dry. Where He abides, there will be an overflowing of beneficence.

To the appeal of the erring, the tempted, the wretched victims of want and sin, the Christian does not ask, Are they worthy? but, How can I benefit them? In the most wretched, the most debased, he sees souls whom Christ died to save and for whom God has given to His children the ministry of reconciliation.

The merciful are those who manifest compassion to the poor, the suffering, and the oppressed. Job declares, "I delivered the poor that cried, and the fatherless, and him that had none to help him. The blessing of him that was ready to perish came upon me: and I caused the widow's heart to sing for joy. I put on righteousness, and it clothed me: my judgment was as a robe and a diadem. I was eyes to the blind, and feet was I to the lame. I was a father to the poor: and the cause which I knew not I searched out." Job 29:12–16.

There are many to whom life is a painful struggle; they feel their deficiencies and are miserable and unbelieving; they think they have nothing for which to be grateful. Kind words, looks of sympathy, expressions of appreciation, would be to many a struggling and lonely one as the cup of cold water to a thirsty soul. A word of sympathy, an act of kindness, would lift burdens that rest heavily upon weary shoulders. And every word or deed of unselfish kindness is an expression of the love of Christ for lost humanity.

The merciful "shall obtain mercy." "The soul of blessing shall be made fat: and he that watereth shall be watered also himself." Proverbs 11:25, margin. There is sweet peace for the compassionate spirit, a blessed satisfaction in the life of self-forgetful service for the good of others. The Holy Spirit that abides in the soul and is manifest in the life will soften hard hearts and awaken sympathy and tenderness. You will reap that which you sow. "Blessed is he that considereth the poor.... The Lord will preserve him, and keep him alive; and he shall be blessed upon the earth: and Thou wilt not deliver him unto the will of his enemies. The Lord will strengthen him upon the bed of languishing: Thou wilt make all his bed in his sickness." Psalm 41:1–3.

He who has given his life to God in ministry to His children is linked with Him who has all the resources of the universe at His command. His life is bound up by the golden chain of the immutable promises with the life of God. The Lord will not fail him in the hour of suffering and need. "My God shall supply all your need according to His riches in glory by Christ Jesus." Philippians 4:19. And in the hour of final need the merciful shall find refuge in the mercy of the compassionate Saviour and shall be received into everlasting habitations.

"Blessed are the pure in heart: for they shall see God." Matthew 5:8.

The Jews were so exacting in regard to ceremonial purity that their regulations were extremely burdensome. Their minds were occupied with rules and restrictions and the fear of outward defilement, and they did not perceive the stain that selfishness and malice impart to the soul.

Jesus does not mention this ceremonial purity as one of the conditions of entering into His kingdom, but points out the need of purity of heart. The wisdom that is from above "is first pure." James 3:17. Into the city of God there will enter nothing that defiles. All who are to be dwellers there will here have become pure in heart. In one who is learning of Jesus, there will be manifest a growing distaste for careless manners, unseemly language, and coarse thought. When Christ abides in the heart, there will be purity and refinement of thought and manner.

But the words of Jesus, "Blessed are the pure in heart," have a deeper meaning—not merely pure in the sense in which the world understands purity, free from that which is sensual, pure from lust, but true in the hidden purposes and motives of the soul, free from pride and self-seeking, humble, unselfish, childlike.

Only like can appreciate like. Unless you accept in your own life the principle of self-sacrificing love, which is the principle of His character, you cannot know God. The heart that is deceived by Satan, looks upon God as a tyrannical, relentless being; the selfish characteristics of humanity, even of Satan himself, are attributed to the loving Creator. "Thou thoughtest," He says, "that I was altogether such an one as thyself." Psalm 50:21. His providences are interpreted as the expression of an arbitrary, vindictive nature. So with the Bible, the treasure house of the riches of His grace. The glory of its truths, that are as high as heaven and compass eternity, is undiscerned. To the great mass of mankind, Christ Himself is "as a root out of a dry ground," and they see in Him "no beauty that" they "should desire Him." Isaiah 53:2. When Jesus was among men, the revelation of God in humanity, the scribes and Pharisees declared to Him, "Thou art a Samaritan, and hast a devil." John 8:48. Even His disciples were so blinded by the selfishness of their hearts that they were slow to understand Him who had come to manifest to them the Father's love. This was why Jesus walked in solitude in the midst of men. He was understood fully in heaven alone.

When Christ shall come in His glory, the wicked cannot endure to behold Him. The light of His presence, which is life to those who love Him, is death to the ungodly. The expectation of His coming is to them a "fearful looking for of judgment and fiery indignation." Hebrews 10:27. When He shall appear, they will pray to be hidden from the face of Him who died to redeem them.

But to hearts that have become purified through the indwelling of the Holy Spirit, all is changed. These can know God. Moses was hid in the cleft of the rock when the glory of the Lord was revealed to him; and it is when we are hid in Christ that we behold the love of God.

"He that loveth pureness of heart, for the grace of his lips the King shall be his friend." Proverbs 22:11. By faith we behold Him here and now. In our daily experience we discern His goodness and compassion in the manifestation of His providence. We recognize Him in the character of His Son. The Holy Spirit takes the truth concerning God and Him whom He hath sent, and opens it to the understanding and to the heart. The pure in heart see God in a new and endearing relation, as their Redeemer; and while they discern the purity and loveliness of His character, they long to reflect His image. They see Him as a Father longing to embrace a repenting son, and their hearts are filled with joy unspeakable and full of glory.

The pure in heart discern the Creator in the works of His mighty hand, in the things of beauty that comprise the universe. In His written word they read in clearer lines the revelation of His mercy, His goodness, and His grace. The truths that are hidden from the wise and prudent are revealed to babes. The beauty and preciousness of truth, which are undiscerned by the worldly-wise, are constantly unfolding to those who have a trusting, child-like desire to know and to do the will of God. We discern the truth by becoming, ourselves, partakers of the divine nature.

The pure in heart live as in the visible presence of God during the time He apportions them in this world. And they will also see Him face to face in the future, immortal state, as did Adam when he walked and talked with God in Eden. "Now we see through a glass, darkly; but then face to face." 1 Corinthians 13:12.

"Blessed are the peacemakers: for they shall be called the children of God." Matthew 5:9.

Christ is "the Prince of Peace" (Isaiah 9:6), and it is His mission to restore to earth and heaven the peace that sin has broken. "Being justified by faith, we have peace with God through our Lord Jesus Christ." Romans 5:1. Whoever consents to renounce sin and open his heart to the love of Christ, becomes a partaker of this heavenly peace.

There is no other ground of peace than this. The grace of Christ received into the heart, subdues enmity; it allays strife and fills the soul with love. He who is at peace with God and his fellow men cannot be made miserable. Envy will not be in his heart; evil surmisings will find no room there; hatred cannot exist. The heart that is in harmony with God is a partaker of the peace of heaven and will diffuse its blessed influence on all around. The spirit of peace will rest like dew upon hearts weary and troubled with worldly strife.

Christ's followers are sent to the world with the message of peace. Whoever, by the quiet, unconscious influence of a holy life, shall reveal the love of Christ; whoever, by word or deed, shall lead another to renounce sin and yield his heart to God, is a peacemaker.

And "blessed are the peacemakers: for they shall be called the children of God." The spirit of peace is evidence of their connection with heaven. The sweet savor of Christ surrounds them. The fragrance of the life, the loveliness of the character, reveal to the world the fact that they are children of God. Men take knowledge of them that they have been with Jesus. "Everyone that loveth is born of God." "If any man have not the Spirit of Christ, he is none of His;" but "as many as are led by the Spirit of God, they are the sons of God." 1 John 4:7; Romans 8:9, 14.

"And the remnant of Jacob shall be in the midst of many people as a dew from the Lord, as the showers upon the grass, that tarrieth not for man, nor waiteth for the sons of men." Micah 5:7.

"Blessed are they which are persecuted for righteousness' sake: for theirs is the kingdom of heaven." Matthew 5:10.

Jesus does not present to His followers the hope of attaining earthly glory and riches, and of having a life free from trial, but He presents to them the privilege of walking with their Master in the paths of self-denial and reproach, because the world knows them not.

He who came to redeem the lost world was opposed by the united forces of the adversaries of God and man. In an unpitying confederacy, evil men and evil angels arrayed themselves against the Prince of Peace. Though His every word and act breathed of divine compassion, His unlikeness to the world provoked the bitterest hostility. Because He would give no license for the exercise of the evil passions of our nature, He aroused the fiercest opposition and enmity. So it is with all who will live godly in Christ Jesus. Between righteousness and sin, love and hatred, truth and falsehood, there is an irrepressible conflict. When one presents the love of Christ and the beauty of holiness, he is drawing away the subjects of Satan's kingdom, and the prince of evil is aroused to resist it. Persecution and reproach await all who are imbued with the Spirit of Christ. The character of the persecution changes with the times, but the principle—the spirit that underlies it—is the same that has slain the chosen of the Lord ever since the days of Abel.

As men seek to come into harmony with God, they will find that the offense of the cross has not ceased. Principalities and powers and wicked spirits in high places are arrayed against all who yield obedience to the law of heaven. Therefore, so far from causing grief, persecution should bring joy to the disciples of Christ, for it is an evidence that they are following in the steps of their Master.

While the Lord has not promised His people exemption from trials, He has promised that which is far better. He has said, "As thy days, so shall thy strength be." "My grace is sufficient for thee: for My strength is made perfect in weakness." Deuteronomy 33:25; 2 Corinthians 12:9. If you are called to go through the fiery furnace for His sake, Jesus will be by your side even as He was with the faithful three in Babylon. Those who love their Redeemer will rejoice at every opportunity of sharing with Him humiliation and reproach. The love they bear their Lord makes suffering for His sake sweet.

In all ages Satan has persecuted the people of God. He has tortured them and put them to death, but in dying they became conquerors. They revealed in their steadfast faith a mightier One than Satan. Satan could torture and kill the body, but he could not touch the life that was hid with Christ in God. He could incarcerate in prison walls, but he could not bind the spirit. They could look beyond the gloom to the glory, saying, "I reckon that the sufferings of this present time are not worthy to be compared with the glory which shall be revealed in us." "Our light affliction, which is but for a moment, worketh for us a far more exceeding and eternal weight of glory." Romans 8:18; 2 Corinthians 4:17.

Through trials and persecution, the glory—character—of God is revealed in His chosen ones. The church of God, hated and persecuted by the world, are educated and disciplined in the school of Christ. They walk in narrow paths on earth; they are purified in the furnace of affliction. They follow Christ through sore conflicts; they endure self-denial and experience bitter disappointments; but their painful experience teaches them the guilt and woe of sin, and they look upon it with abhorrence. Being partakers of Christ's sufferings, they are destined to be partakers of His glory. In holy vision the prophet saw the triumph of the people of God. He says, "I saw as it were a sea of glass mingled with fire: and them that had gotten the victory,...stand on the sea of glass, having the harps of God. And they sing the song of Moses the servant of God, and the song of the Lamb, saying, Great and marvelous are Thy works, Lord God Almighty; just and true are Thy ways, Thou King of saints." "These are they which came out of great tribulation, and have washed their robes, and made them white in the blood of the Lamb. Therefore are they before the throne of God, and serve Him day and night in His temple: and He that sitteth on the throne shall dwell among them." Revelation 15:2, 3; 7:14, 15.

"Blessed are ye, when men shall revile you." Matthew 5:11.

Ever since his fall, Satan has worked by means of deception. As he has misrepresented God, so, through his agents, he misrepresents the children of God. The Saviour says, "The reproaches of them that reproached Thee are fallen upon Me." Psalm 69:9. In like manner they fall upon His disciples.

There was never one who walked among men more cruelly slandered than the Son of man. He was derided and mocked because of His unswerving obedience to the principles of God's holy law. They hated Him without a cause. Yet He stood calmly before His enemies, declaring that reproach is a part of the Christian's legacy, counseling His followers how to meet the arrows of malice, bidding them not to faint under persecution.

While slander may blacken the reputation, it cannot stain the character. That is in God's keeping. So long as we do not consent to sin, there is no power, whether human or satanic, that can bring a stain upon the soul. A man whose heart is stayed upon God is just the same in the hour of his most afflicting trials and most discouraging surroundings as when he was in prosperity, when the light and favor of God seemed to be upon him. His words, his motives, his actions, may be misrepresented and falsified, but he does not mind it, because he has greater interests at stake. Like Moses, he endures as "seeing Him who is invisible" (Hebrews 11:27); looking "not at the things which are seen, but at the things which are not seen" (2 Corinthians 4:18).

Christ is acquainted with all that is misunderstood and misrepresented by men. His children can afford to wait in calm patience and trust, no matter how much maligned and despised; for nothing is secret that shall not be made manifest, and those who honor God shall be honored by Him in the presence of men and angels.

"When men shall revile you, and persecute you," said Jesus, "rejoice, and be exceeding glad." And He pointed His hearers to the prophets who had spoken in the name of the Lord, as "an example of suffering affliction, and of patience." James 5:10. Abel, the very first Christian of Adam's children, died a martyr. Enoch walked with God, and the world knew him not. Noah was mocked as a fanatic and an alarmist. "Others had trial of cruel mockings and scourgings, yea, moreover of bonds and imprisonment." "Others were tortured, not accepting deliverance; that they might obtain a better resurrection." Hebrews 11:36, 35.

In every age God's chosen messengers have been reviled and persecuted, yet through their affliction the knowledge of God has been spread abroad. Every disciple of Christ is to step into the ranks and carry forward the same work, knowing that its foes can do nothing against the truth, but for the truth. God means that truth shall be brought to the front and become the subject of examination and discussion, even through the contempt placed upon it. The minds of the people must be agitated; every controversy, every reproach, every effort to restrict liberty of conscience, is God's means of awakening minds that otherwise might slumber.

How often this result has been seen in the history of God's messengers! When the noble and eloquent Stephen was stoned to death at the instigation of the Sanhedrin council, there was no loss to the cause of the gospel. The light of heaven that glorified his face, the divine compassion breathed in his dying prayer, were as a sharp arrow of conviction to the bigoted Sanhedrist who stood by, and Saul, the persecuting Pharisee, became a chosen vessel to bear the name of Christ before Gentiles and kings and the children of Israel. And long afterward Paul the aged wrote from his prison house at Rome: "Some indeed preach Christ even of envy and strife:... not sincerely, supposing to add affliction to my bonds.... Notwithstanding, every way, whether in pretense, or in truth, Christ is preached." Philippians 1:15–18. Through Paul's imprisonment the gospel was spread abroad, and souls were won for Christ in the very palace of the Caesars. By the efforts of Satan to destroy it, the "incorruptible" seed of the word of God, "which liveth and abideth forever" (1 Peter 1:23), is sown in the hearts of men; through the reproach and persecution of His children the name of Christ is magnified and souls are saved.

Great is the reward in heaven of those who are witnesses for Christ through persecution and reproach. While the people are looking for earthly good, Jesus points them to a heavenly reward. But He does not place it all in the future life; it begins here. The Lord appeared of old time to Abraham and said, "*I* am thy shield, and thy exceeding great reward." Genesis 15:1. This is the reward of all who follow Christ. Jehovah Immanuel—He "in whom are hid all the treasures of wisdom and knowledge," in whom dwells "all the fullness of the Godhead bodily" (Colossians 2:3, 9)—to be brought into sympathy with Him, to know Him, to possess Him, as the heart opens more and more to receive His attributes; to know His love and power, to possess the unsearchable riches of Christ, to comprehend more and more "what is the breadth, and length, and depth, and height; and to know the love of Christ, which passeth knowledge, that ye might be filled with all the fullness of God" (Ephesians 3:18, 19)—"this is the heritage of the servants of the Lord, and their righteousness is of Me, saith the Lord." Isaiah 54:17.

It was this joy that filled the hearts of Paul and Silas when they prayed and sang praises to God at midnight in the Philippian dungeon. Christ was beside them there, and the light of His presence irradiated the gloom with the glory of the courts above. From Rome, Paul wrote, unmindful of his fetters as he saw the spread of the gospel, "I therein do rejoice, yea, and will rejoice." Philippians 1:18. And the very words of Christ upon the mount are re-echoed in Paul's message to the Philippian church, in the midst of their persecutions, "Rejoice in the Lord alway: and again I say, Rejoice." Philippians 4:4.

"Ye are the salt of the earth." Matthew 5:13.

Salt is valued for its preservative properties; and when God calls His children salt, He would teach them that His purpose in making them the subjects of His grace is that they may become agents in saving others. The object of God in choosing a people before all the world was not only that He might adopt them as His sons and daughters, but that through them the world might receive the grace that bringeth salvation. Titus 2:11. When the Lord chose Abraham, it was not simply to be the special friend of God, but to be a medium of the peculiar privileges the Lord desired to bestow upon the nations. Jesus, in that last prayer with His disciples before His crucifixion, said, "For their sakes I sanctify Myself, that they also might be sanctified through the truth." John 17:19. In like manner Christians who are purified through the truth will possess saving qualities that preserve the world from utter moral corruption.

Salt must be mingled with the substance to which it is added; it must penetrate and infuse in order to preserve. So it is through personal contact and association that men are reached by the saving power of the gospel. They are not saved in masses, but as individuals. Personal influence is a power. We must come close to those whom we desire to benefit.

The savor of the salt represents the vital power of the Christian—the love of Jesus in the heart, the righteousness of Christ pervading the life. The love of Christ is diffusive and aggressive. If it is dwelling in us, it will flow out to others. We shall come close to them till their hearts are warmed by our unselfish interest and love. The sincere believers diffuse vital energy, which is penetrating and imparts new moral power to the souls for whom they labor. It is not the power of the man himself, but the power of the Holy Spirit that does the transforming work.

Jesus added the solemn warning: "If the salt have lost his savor, wherewith shall it be salted? It is thenceforth good for nothing, but to be cast out, and to be trodden underfoot of men."

As they listened to the words of Christ, the people could see the white salt glistening in the pathways where it had been cast out because it had lost its savor and was therefore useless. It well represented the condition of the Pharisees and the effect of their religion upon society. It represents the life of every soul from whom the power of the grace of God has departed and who has become cold and Christless. Whatever may be his profession, such a one is looked upon by men and angels as insipid and disagreeable. It is to such that Christ says: "I would thou wert cold or hot. So then because thou art lukewarm, and neither cold nor hot, I will spue thee out of My mouth." Revelation 3:15, 16.

Without a living faith in Christ as a personal Saviour it is impossible to make our influence felt in a skeptical world. We cannot give to others that which we do not ourselves possess. It is in proportion to our own devotion and consecration to Christ that we exert an influence for the blessing and uplifting of mankind. If there is no actual service, no genuine love, no reality of experience, there is no power to help, no connection with heaven, no savor of Christ in the life. Unless the Holy Spirit can use us as agents through whom to communicate to the world the truth as it is in Jesus, we are as salt that has lost its savor and is entirely worthless. By our lack of the grace of Christ we testify to the world that the truth which we claim to believe has no sanctifying power; and thus, so far as our influence goes, we make of no effect the word of God. "If I speak with the tongues of men and of angels, but have not love, I am become sounding brass, or a clanging cymbal. And if I have the gift of prophecy, and know all mysteries and all knowledge; and if I have all faith, so as to remove mountains, but have not love, I am nothing. And if I bestow all my goods to feed the poor, and if I give my body to be burned, but have not love, it profiteth me nothing." 1 Corinthians 13:1–3, A.R.V.

When love fills the heart, it will flow out to others, not because of favors received from them, but because love is the principle of action. Love modifies the character, governs the impulses, subdues enmity, and ennobles the affections. This love is as broad as the universe, and is in harmony with that of the angel workers. Cherished in the heart, it sweetens the entire life and sheds its blessing upon all around. It is this, and this only, that can make us the salt of the earth.

"Ye are the light of the world." Matthew 5:14.

As Jesus taught the people, He made His lessons interesting and held the attention of His hearers by frequent illustrations from the scenes of nature about them. The people had come together while it was yet morning. The glorious sun, climbing higher and higher in the blue sky, was chasing away the shadows that lurked in the valleys and among the narrow defiles of the mountains. The glory of the eastern heavens had not yet faded out. The sunlight flooded the land with its splendor; the placid surface of the lake reflected the golden light and mirrored the rosy clouds of morning. Every bud and flower and leafy spray glistened with dewdrops. Nature smiled under the benediction of a new day, and the birds sang sweetly among the trees. The Saviour looked upon the company before Him, and then to the rising sun, and said to His disciples, "Ye are the light of the world." As the sun goes forth on its errand of love, dispelling the shades of night and awakening the world to life, so the followers of Christ are to go forth on their mission, diffusing the light of heaven upon those who are in the darkness of error and sin.

In the brilliant light of the morning, the towns and villages upon the surrounding hills stood forth clearly, making an attractive feature of the scene. Pointing to them, Jesus said, "A city set on a hill cannot be hid." And he added, "Neither do men light a lamp, and put it under the bushel, but on the stand; and it shineth unto all that are in the house." R.V. Most of those who listened to the words of Jesus were peasants and fishermen whose lowly dwellings contained but one room, in which the single lamp on its stand shone to all in the house. Even so, said Jesus, "Let your light so shine before men, that they may see your good works, and glorify your Father which is in heaven."

No other light ever has shone or ever will shine upon fallen man save that which emanates from Christ. Jesus, the Saviour, is the only light that can illuminate the darkness of a world lying in sin. Of Christ it is written, "In Him was life; and the life was the light of men." John 1:4. It was by receiving of His life that His disciples could become light bearers. The life of Christ in the soul, His love revealed in the character, would make them the light of the world.

Humanity has in itself no light. Apart from Christ we are like an unkindled taper, like the moon when her face is turned away from the sun; we have not a single ray of brightness to shed into the darkness of the world. But when we turn toward the Sun of Righteousness, when we come in touch with Christ, the whole soul is aglow with the brightness of the divine presence.

Christ's followers are to be more than a light in the midst of men. They are *the* light of the world. Jesus says to all who have named His name, You have given yourselves to Me, and I have given you to the world as My representatives. As the Father had sent Him into the world, so, He declares, "have I also sent them into the world." John 17:18. As Christ is the channel for the revelation of the Father, so we are to be the channel for the revelation of Christ. While our Saviour is the great source of illumination, forget not, O Christian, that He is revealed through humanity. God's blessings are bestowed through human instrumentality. Christ Himself came to the world as the Son of man. Humanity, united to the divine nature, must touch humanity. The church of Christ, every individual disciple of the Master, is heaven's appointed channel for the revelation of God to men. Angels of glory wait to communicate through you heaven's light and power to souls that are ready to perish. Shall the human agent fail of accomplishing his appointed work? Oh, then to that degree is the world robbed of the promised influence of the Holy Spirit!

But Jesus did not bid the disciples, "Strive to *make* your light shine;" He said, "*Let* it shine." If Christ is dwelling in the heart, it is impossible to conceal the light of His presence. If those who profess to be followers of Christ are not the light of the world, it is because the vital power has left them; if they have no light to give, it is because they have no connection with the Source of light.

In all ages the "Spirit of Christ which was in them" (1 Peter 1:11) has made God's true children the light of the people of their generation. Joseph was a light bearer in Egypt. In his purity and benevolence and filial love he represented Christ in the midst of a nation of idolaters. While the Israelites were on their way from Egypt to the Promised Land, the true-hearted among them were a light to the surrounding nations. Through them God was revealed to the world. From Daniel and his companions in Babylon, and from Mordecai in Persia, bright beams of light shone out amid the darkness of the kingly courts. In like manner the disciples of Christ are set as light bearers on the way to heaven; through them the Father's mercy and goodness are made manifest to a world enshrouded in the darkness of misapprehension of God. By seeing their good works, others are led to glorify the Father who is above; for it is made manifest that there is a God on the throne of the universe whose character is worthy of praise and imitation. The divine love glowing in the heart, the Christlike harmony manifested in the life, are as a glimpse of heaven granted to men of the world, that they may appreciate its excellence.

It is thus that men are led to believe "the love that God hath to us." 1 John 4:16. Thus hearts once sinful and corrupt are purified and transformed, to be presented "faultless before the presence of His glory with exceeding joy." Jude 24.

The Saviour's words, "Ye are the light of the world," point to the fact that He has committed to His followers a world-wide mission. In the days of Christ, selfishness and pride and prejudice had built strong and high the wall of partition between the appointed guardians of the sacred oracles and every other nation on the globe. But the Saviour had come to change all this. The words which the people were hearing from His lips were unlike anything to which they had ever listened from priest or rabbi. Christ tears away the wall of partition, the self-love, the dividing prejudice of nationality, and teaches a love for all the human family. He lifts men from the narrow circle that their selfishness prescribes; He abolishes all territorial lines and artificial distinctions of society. He makes no difference between neighbors and strangers, friends and enemies. He teaches us to look upon every needy soul as our neighbor and the world as our field.

As the rays of the sun penetrate to the remotest corners of the globe, so God designs that the light of the gospel shall extend to every soul upon the earth. If the church of Christ were fulfilling the purpose of our Lord, light would be shed upon all that sit in darkness and in the region and shadow of death. Instead of congregating together and shunning responsibility and cross bearing, the members of the church would scatter into all lands, letting the light of Christ shine out from them, working as He did for the salvation of souls, and this "gospel of the kingdom" would speedily be carried to all the world.

It is thus that God's purpose in calling His people, from Abraham on the plains of Mesopotamia to us in this age, is to reach its fulfillment. He says, "I will bless thee,...and thou shalt be a blessing." Genesis 12:2. The words of Christ through the gospel prophet, which are but re-echoed in the Sermon on the Mount, are for us in this last generation: "Arise, shine; for thy light is come, and the glory of the Lord is risen upon thee." Isaiah 60:1. If upon your spirit the glory of the Lord is risen, if you have beheld His beauty who is "the chiefest among ten thousand" and the One "altogether lovely," if your soul has become radiant in the presence of His glory, to you is this word from the Master sent. Have you stood with Christ on the mount of transfiguration? Down in the plain there are souls enslaved by Satan; they are waiting for the word of faith and prayer to set them free.

We are not only to contemplate the glory of Christ, but also to speak of His excellences. Isaiah not only beheld the glory of Christ, but he also spoke of Him. While David mused, the fire burned; then spoke he with his tongue. While he mused upon the wondrous love of God he could not but speak of that which he saw and felt. Who can by faith behold the wonderful plan of redemption, the glory of the only-begotten Son of God, and not speak of it? Who can contemplate the unfathomable love that was manifested upon the cross of Calvary in the death of Christ, that we might not perish, but have everlasting life—who can behold this and have no words with which to extol the Saviour's glory?

"In His temple doth everyone speak of His glory." Psalm 29:9. The sweet singer of Israel praised Him upon the harp, saying, "I will speak of the glorious honor of Thy majesty, and of Thy wondrous works. And men shall speak of the might of Thy terrible acts: and I will declare Thy greatness." Psalm 145:5, 6.

The cross of Calvary is to be lifted high above the people, absorbing their minds and concentrating their thoughts. Then all the spiritual faculties will be charged with divine power direct from God. Then there will be a concentration of the energies in genuine work for the Master. The workers will send forth to the world beams of light, as living agencies to enlighten the earth.

Christ accepts, oh, so gladly, every human agency that is surrendered to Him. He brings the human into union with the divine, that He may communicate to the world the mysteries of incarnate love. Talk it, pray it, sing it; proclaim abroad the message of His glory, and keep pressing onward to the regions beyond.

Trials patiently borne, blessings gratefully received, temptations manfully resisted, meekness, kindness, mercy, and love habitually revealed, are the lights that shine forth in the character in contrast with the darkness of the selfish heart, into which the light of life has never shone.

3
The Spirituality of the Law

I am not come to destroy, but to fulfill." Matthew 5:17.

It was Christ who, amid thunder and flame, had proclaimed the law upon Mount Sinai. The glory of God, like devouring fire, rested upon its summit, and the mountain quaked at the presence of the Lord. The hosts of Israel, lying prostrate upon the earth, had listened in awe to the sacred precepts of the law. What a contrast to the scene upon the mount of the Beatitudes! Under the summer sky, with no sound to break the stillness but the song of birds, Jesus unfolded the principles of His kingdom. Yet He who spoke to the people that day in accents of love, was opening to them the principles of the law proclaimed upon Sinai.

When the law was given, Israel, degraded by the long bondage in Egypt, had need to be impressed with the power and majesty of God; yet He revealed Himself to them no less as a God of love.

> "The Lord came from Sinai,
> And rose from Seir unto them;
> He shined forth from Mount Paran,
> And He came from the ten thousands of holy ones:
> At His right hand was a fiery law unto them.
> Yea, He loveth the tribes;
> All their holy ones are in Thy hand:
> And they sat down at Thy feet;
> Everyone received of Thy words."
> Deuteronomy 33:2, 3, R.V., margin.

It was to Moses that God revealed His glory in those wonderful words that have been the treasured heritage of the ages: "The Lord, The Lord God, merciful and gracious, long-suffering, and abundant in goodness and truth, keeping mercy for thousands, forgiving iniquity and transgression and sin." Exodus 34:6, 7.

The law given upon Sinai was the enunciation of the principle of love, a revelation to earth of the law of heaven. It was ordained in the hand of a Mediator—spoken by Him through whose power the hearts of men could be brought into harmony with its principles. God had revealed the purpose of the law when He declared to Israel, "Ye shall be holy men unto Me." Exodus 22:31

But Israel had not perceived the spiritual nature of the law, and too often their professed obedience was but an observance of forms and ceremonies, rather than a surrender of the heart to the sovereignty of love. As Jesus in His character and work represented to men the holy, benevolent, and paternal attributes of God, and presented the worthlessness of mere ceremonial obedience, the Jewish leaders did not receive or understand His words. They thought that He dwelt too lightly upon the requirements of the law; and when He set before them the very truths that were the soul of their divinely appointed service, they, looking only at the external, accused Him of seeking to overthrow it.

The words of Christ, though calmly spoken, were uttered with an earnestness and power that stirred the hearts of the people. They listened for a repetition of the lifeless traditions and exactions of the rabbis, but in vain. They "were astonished at His teaching: for He taught them as one having authority, and not as their scribes." Matthew 7:29, R.V. The Pharisees noted the vast difference between their manner of instruction and that of Christ. They saw that the majesty and purity and beauty of the truth, with its deep and gentle influence, was taking firm hold upon many minds. The Saviour's divine love and tenderness drew the hearts of men to Him. The rabbis saw that by His teaching the whole tenor of the instruction they had given to the people was set at nought. He was tearing down the partition wall that had been so flattering to their pride and exclusiveness; and they feared that, if permitted, He would draw the people entirely away from them. Therefore they followed Him with determined hostility, hoping to find some occasion for bringing Him into disfavor with the multitudes and thus enabling the Sanhedrin to secure His condemnation and death.

On the mount, Jesus was closely watched by spies; and as He unfolded the principles of righteousness, the Pharisees caused it to be whispered about that His teaching was in opposition to the precepts that God had given from Sinai. The Saviour said nothing to unsettle faith in the religion and institutions that had been given through Moses; for every ray of divine light that Israel's great leader communicated to his people was received from Christ. While many are saying in their hearts that He has come to do away with the law, Jesus in unmistakable language reveals His attitude toward the divine statutes. "Think not," He said, "that I am come to destroy the law, or the prophets."

It is the Creator of men, the Giver of the law, who declares that it is not His purpose to set aside its precepts. Everything in nature, from the mote in the sunbeam to the worlds on high, is under law. And upon obedience to these laws the order and harmony of the natural world depend. So there are great principles of righteousness to control the life of all intelligent beings, and upon conformity to these principles the well-being of the universe depends. Before this earth was called into being, God's law existed. Angels are governed by its principles, and in order for earth to be in harmony with heaven, man also must obey the divine statutes. To man in Eden Christ made known the precepts of the law "when the morning stars sang together, and all the sons of God shouted for joy." Job 38:7. The mission of Christ on earth was not to destroy the law, but by His grace to bring man back to obedience to its precepts.

The beloved disciple, who listened to the words of Jesus on the mount, writing long afterward under the inspiration of the Holy Spirit, speaks of the law as of perpetual obligation. He says that "sin is the transgression of the law" and that "whosoever committeth sin transgresseth also the law." 1 John 3:4. He makes it plain that the law to which he refers is "an old commandment which ye had from the beginning." 1 John 2:7. He is speaking of the law that existed at the creation and was reiterated upon Mount Sinai.

Speaking of the law, Jesus said, "I am not come to destroy, but to fulfill." He here used the word "fulfill" in the same sense as when He declared to John the Baptist His purpose to "fulfill all righteousness" (Matthew 3:15); that is, to fill up the measure of the law's requirement, to give an example of perfect conformity to the will of God.

His mission was to "magnify the law, and make it honorable." Isaiah 42:21. He was to show the spiritual nature of the law, to present its far-reaching principles, and to make plain its eternal obligation.

The divine beauty of the character of Christ, of whom the noblest and most gentle among men are but a faint reflection; of whom Solomon by the Spirit of inspiration wrote, He is "the chiefest among ten thousand,...yea, He is altogether lovely" (Song of Solomon 5:10–16); of whom David, seeing Him in prophetic vision, said, "Thou art fairer than the children of men" (Psalm 45:2); Jesus, the express image of the Father's person, the effulgence of His glory; the self-denying Redeemer, throughout His pilgrimage of love on earth, was a living representation of the character of the law of God. In His life it is made manifest that heaven-born love, Christlike principles, underlie the laws of eternal rectitude.

"Till heaven and earth pass," said Jesus, "one jot or one tittle shall in nowise pass from the law, till all be fulfilled." By His own obedience to the law, Christ testified to its immutable character and proved that through His grace it could be perfectly obeyed by every son and daughter of Adam. On the mount He declared that not the smallest iota should pass from the law till all things should be accomplished-all things that concern the human race, all that relates to the plan of redemption. He does not teach that the law is ever to be abrogated, but He fixes the eye upon the utmost verge of man's horizon and assures us that until this point is reached the law will retain its authority so that none may suppose it was His mission to abolish the precepts of the law. So long as heaven and earth continue, the holy principles of God's law will remain. His righteousness, "like the great mountains" (Psalm 36:6), will continue, a source of blessing, sending forth streams to refresh the earth.

Because the law of the Lord is perfect, and therefore changeless, it is impossible for sinful men, in themselves, to meet the standard of its requirement. This was why Jesus came as our Redeemer. It was His mission, by making men partakers of the divine nature, to bring them into harmony with the principles of the law of heaven. When we forsake our sins and receive Christ as our Saviour, the law is exalted. The apostle Paul asks, "Do we then make void the law through faith? God forbid: yea, we establish the law." Romans 3:31.

The new-covenant promise is, "I will put My laws into their hearts, and in their minds will I write them." Hebrews 10:16. While the system of types which pointed to Christ as the Lamb of God that should take away the sin of the world was to pass away at His death, the principles of righteousness embodied in the Decalogue are as immutable as the eternal throne. Not one command has been annulled, not a jot or tittle has been changed. Those principles that were made known to man in Paradise as the great law of life will exist unchanged in Paradise restored. When Eden shall bloom on earth again, God's law of love will be obeyed by all beneath the sun.

"Forever, O Lord, Thy word is settled in heaven." "All His commandments are sure. They stand fast for ever and ever, and are done in truth and uprightness." "Concerning Thy testimonies, I have known of old that Thou hast founded them forever." Psalms 119:89; 111:7, 8; 119:152.

"Whosoever...shall break one of these least commandments, and shall teach men so, he shall be called the least in the kingdom of heaven." Matthew 5:19.

That is, he shall have no place therein. For he who willfully breaks one commandment, does not, in spirit and truth, keep any of them. "Whosoever shall keep the whole law, and yet offend in one point, he is guilty of all." James 2:10.

It is not the greatness of the act of disobedience that constitutes sin, but the fact of variance from God's expressed will in the least particular; for this shows that there is yet communion between the soul and sin. The heart is divided in its service. There is a virtual denial of God, a rebellion against the laws of His government.

Were men free to depart from the Lord's requirements and to set up a standard of duty for themselves, there would be a variety of standards to suit different minds and the government would be taken out of the Lord's hands. The will of man would be made supreme, and the high and holy will of God-His purpose of love toward His creatures—would be dishonored, disrespected.

Whenever men choose their own way, they place themselves in controversy with God. They will have no place in the kingdom of heaven, for they are at war with the very principles of heaven. In disregarding the will of God, they are placing themselves on the side of Satan, the enemy of God and man. Not by one word, not by many words, but by every word that God has spoken, shall man live. We cannot disregard one word, however trifling it may seem to us, and be safe. There is not a commandment of the law that is not for the good and happiness of man, both in this life and in the life to come. In obedience to God's law, man is surrounded as with a hedge and kept from the evil. He who breaks down this divinely erected barrier at one point has destroyed its power to protect him; for he has opened a way by which the enemy can enter to waste and ruin.

By venturing to disregard the will of God upon one point, our first parents opened the floodgates of woe upon the world. And every individual who follows their example will reap a similar result. The love of God underlies every precept of His law, and he who departs from the commandment is working his own unhappiness and ruin.

"Except your righteousness shall exceed the righteousness of the scribes and Pharisees, ye shall in no case enter into the kingdom of heaven." Matthew 5:20.

The scribes and Pharisees had accused not only Christ but His disciples as sinners because of their disregard of the rabbinical rites and observances. Often the disciples had been perplexed and troubled by censure and accusation from those whom they had been accustomed to revere as religious teachers. Jesus unveiled the deception. He declared that the righteousness upon which the Pharisees set so great value was worthless. The Jewish nation had claimed to be the special, loyal people who were favored of God; but Christ represented their religion as devoid of saving faith. All their pretensions of piety, their human inventions and ceremonies, and even their boasted performance of the outward requirements of the law, could not avail to make them holy. They were not pure in heart or noble and Christlike in character.

A legal religion is insufficient to bring the soul into harmony with God. The hard, rigid orthodoxy of the Pharisees, destitute of contrition, tenderness, or love, was only a stumbling block to sinners. They were like the salt that had lost its savor; for their influence had no power to preserve the world from corruption. The only true faith is that which "worketh by love" (Galatians 5:6) to purify the soul. It is as leaven that transforms the character.

All this the Jews should have learned from the teachings of the prophets. Centuries before, the cry of the soul for justification with God had found voice and answer in the words of the prophet Micah: "Wherewith shall I come before the Lord, and bow myself before the high God? shall I come before Him with burnt offerings, with calves of a year old? Will the Lord be pleased with thousands of rams, or with ten thousands of rivers of oil?... He hath showed thee, O man, what is good; and what doth the Lord require of thee, but to do justly, and to love mercy, and to walk humbly with thy God?" Micah 6:6–8.

The prophet Hosea had pointed out what constitutes the very essence of Pharisaism, in the words, "Israel is an empty vine, he bringeth forth fruit unto himself." Hosea 10:1. In their professed service to God, the Jews were really working for self. Their righteousness was the fruit of their own efforts to keep the law according to their own ideas and for their own selfish benefit. Hence it could be no better than they were. In their endeavor to make themselves holy, they were trying to bring a clean thing out of an unclean. The law of God is as holy as He is holy, as perfect as He is perfect. It presents to men the righteousness of God. It is impossible for man, of himself, to keep this law; for the nature of man is depraved, deformed, and wholly unlike the character of God. The works of the selfish heart are "as an unclean thing;" and "all our righteousnesses are as filthy rags." Isaiah 64:6.

While the law is holy, the Jews could not attain righteousness by their own efforts to keep the law. The disciples of Christ must obtain righteousness of a different character from that of the Pharisees, if they would enter the kingdom of heaven. God offered them, in His Son, the perfect righteousness of the law. If they would open their hearts fully to receive Christ, then the very life of God, His love, would dwell in them, transforming them into His own likeness; and thus through God's free gift they would possess the righteousness which the law requires. But the Pharisees rejected Christ; "being ignorant of God's righteousness, and going about to establish their own righteousness" (Romans 10:3), they would not submit themselves unto the righteousness of God.

Jesus proceeded to show His hearers what it means to keep the commandments of God—that it is a reproduction in themselves of the character of Christ. For in Him, God was daily made manifest before them.

"Everyone who is angry with his brother shall be in danger of the judgment." Matthew 5:22, R.V.

Through Moses the Lord had said, "Thou shalt not hate thy brother in thine heart.... Thou shalt not avenge, nor bear any grudge against the children of thy people, but thou shalt love thy neighbor as thyself." Leviticus 19:17, 18. The truths which Christ presented were the same that had been taught by the prophets, but they had become obscured through hardness of heart and love of sin.

The Saviour's words revealed to His hearers the fact that, while they were condemning others as transgressors, they were themselves equally guilty; for they were cherishing malice and hatred.

Across the sea from the place where they were assembled was the country of Bashan, a lonely region, whose wild gorges and wooded hills had long been a favorite lurking ground for criminals of all descriptions. Reports of robbery and murder committed there were fresh in the minds of the people, and many were zealous in denouncing these evildoers. At the same time they were themselves passionate and contentious; they cherished the most bitter hatred of their Roman oppressors and felt themselves at liberty to hate and despise all other peoples, and even their own countrymen who did not in all things conform to their ideas. In all this they were violating the law which declares, "Thou shalt not kill."

The spirit of hatred and revenge originated with Satan, and it led him to put to death the Son of God. Whoever cherishes malice or unkindness is cherishing the same spirit, and its fruit will be unto death. In the revengeful thought the evil deed lies enfolded, as the plant in the seed. "Whosoever hateth his brother is a murderer: and ye know that no murderer hath eternal life abiding in him." 1 John 3:15.

"Whosoever shall say to his brother, Raca [vain fellow], shall be in danger of the council." In the gift of His Son for our redemption, God has shown how high a value He places upon every human soul, and He gives to no man liberty to speak contemptuously of another. We shall see faults and weaknesses in those about us, but God claims every soul as His property—His by creation, and doubly His as purchased by the precious blood of Christ. All were created in His image, and even the most degraded are to be treated with respect and tenderness. God will hold us accountable for even a word spoken in contempt of one soul for whom Christ laid down His life.

"Who maketh thee to differ from another? and what hast thou that thou didst not receive? now if thou didst receive it, why dost thou glory, as if thou hadst not received it?" "Who art thou that judgest another man's servant? to his own master he standeth or falleth." 1 Corinthians 4:7; Romans 14:4.

"Whosoever shall say, Thou fool, shall be in danger of the hell of fire." R.V. In the Old Testament the word "fool" is used to designate an apostate, or one who has abandoned himself to wickedness. Jesus says that whoever shall condemn his brother as an apostate or a despiser of God shows that he himself is worthy of the same condemnation.

Christ Himself, when contending with Satan about the body of Moses, "durst not bring against him a railing accusation." Jude 9. Had He done this, He would have placed Himself on Satan's ground, for accusation is the weapon of the evil one. He is called in Scripture, "the accuser of our brethren." Revelation 12:10. Jesus would employ none of Satan's weapons. He met him with the words, "The Lord rebuke thee." Jude 9.

His example is for us. When we are brought in conflict with the enemies of Christ, we should say nothing in a spirit of retaliation or that would bear even the appearance of a railing accusation. He who stands as a mouthpiece for God should not utter words which even the Majesty of heaven would not use when contending with Satan. We are to leave with God the work of judging and condemning.

"Be reconciled to thy brother." Matthew 5:24.

The love of God is something more than a mere negation; it is a positive and active principle, a living spring, ever flowing to bless others. If the love of Christ dwells in us, we shall not only cherish no hatred toward our fellows, but we shall seek in every way to manifest love toward them.

Jesus said, "If thou bring thy gift to the altar, and there rememberest that thy brother hath aught against thee; leave there thy gift before the altar, and go thy way; first be reconciled to thy brother, and then come and offer thy gift." The sacrificial offerings expressed faith that through Christ the offerer had become a partaker of the mercy and love of God. But for one to express faith in God's pardoning love, while he himself indulged an unloving spirit, would be a mere farce.

When one who professes to serve God wrongs or injures a brother, he misrepresents the character of God to that brother, and the wrong must be confessed, he must acknowledge it to be sin, in order to be in harmony with God. Our brother may have done us a greater wrong than we have done him, but this does not lessen our responsibility. If when we come before God we remember that another has aught against us, we are to leave our gift of prayer, of thanksgiving, of freewill offering, and go to the brother with whom we are at variance, and in humility confess our own sin and ask to be forgiven.

If we have in any manner defrauded or injured our brother, we should make restitution. If we have unwittingly borne false witness, if we have misstated his words, if we have injured his influence in any way, we should go to the ones with whom we have conversed about him, and take back all our injurious misstatements.

If matters of difficulty between brethren were not laid open before others, but frankly spoken of between themselves in the spirit of Christian love, how much evil might be prevented! How many roots of bitterness whereby many are defiled would be destroyed, and how closely and tenderly might the followers of Christ be united in His love!

"Whosoever looketh on a woman to lust after her hath committed adultery with her already in his heart." Matthew 5:28.

The Jews prided themselves on their morality and looked with horror upon the sensual practices of the heathen. The presence of the Roman officers whom the imperial rule had brought into Palestine was a continual offense to the people, for with these foreigners had come in a flood of heathen customs, lust, and dissipation. In Capernaum, Roman officials with their gay paramours haunted the parades and promenades, and often the sound of revelry broke upon the stillness of the lake as their pleasure boats glided over the quiet waters. The people expected to hear from Jesus a stern denunciation of this class, but what was their astonishment as they listened to words that laid bare the evil of their own hearts!

When the thought of evil is loved and cherished, however secretly, said Jesus, it shows that sin still reigns in the heart. The soul is still in the gall of bitterness and in the bond of iniquity. He who finds pleasure in dwelling upon scenes of impurity, who indulges the evil thought, the lustful look, may behold in the open sin, with its burden of shame and heart-breaking grief, the true nature of the evil which he has hidden in the chambers of the soul. The season of temptation, under which, it may be, one falls into grievous sin, does not create the evil that is revealed, but only develops or makes manifest that which was hidden and latent in the heart. As a man "thinketh in his heart, so is he;" for out of the heart "are the issues of life." Proverbs 23:7; 4:23.

"If thy right hand causeth thee to stumble, cut it off, and cast it from thee." Matthew 5:30, R.V.

To prevent disease from spreading to the body and destroying life, a man would submit to part even with his right hand. Much more should he be willing to surrender that which imperils the life of the soul.

Through the gospel, souls that are degraded and enslaved by Satan are to be redeemed to share the glorious liberty of the sons of God. God's purpose is not merely to deliver from the suffering that is the inevitable result of sin, but to save from sin itself. The soul, corrupted and deformed, is to be purified, transformed, that it may be clothed in "the beauty of the Lord our God," "conformed to the image of His Son." "Eye hath not seen, nor ear heard, neither have entered into the heart of man, the things which God hath prepared for them that love Him." Psalm 90:17; Romans 8:29; 1 Corinthians 2:9. Eternity alone can reveal the glorious destiny to which man, restored to God's image, may attain.

In order for us to reach this high ideal, that which causes the soul to stumble must be sacrificed. It is through the will that sin retains its hold upon us. The surrender of the will is represented as plucking out the eye or cutting off the hand. Often it seems to us that to surrender the will to God is to consent to go through life maimed or crippled. But it is better, says Christ, for self to be maimed, wounded, crippled, if thus you may enter into life. That which you look upon as disaster is the door to highest benefit.

God is the fountain of life, and we can have life only as we are in communion with Him. Separated from God, existence may be ours for a little time, but we do not possess life. "She that liveth in pleasure is dead while she liveth." 1 Timothy 5:6. Only through the surrender of our will to God is it possible for Him to impart life to us. Only by receiving His life through self-surrender is it possible, said Jesus, for these hidden sins, which I have pointed out, to be overcome. It is possible that you may bury them in your hearts and conceal them from human eyes, but how will you stand in God's presence?

If you cling to self, refusing to yield your will to God, you are choosing death. To sin, wherever found, God is a consuming fire. If you choose sin, and refuse to separate from it, the presence of God, which consumes sin, must consume you.

It will require a sacrifice to give yourself to God; but it is a sacrifice of the lower for the higher, the earthly for the spiritual, the perishable for the eternal. God does not design that our will should be destroyed, for it is only through its exercise that we can accomplish what He would have us do. Our will is to be yielded to Him, that we may receive it again, purified and refined, and so linked in sympathy with the Divine that He can pour through us the tides of His love and power. However bitter and painful this surrender may appear to the willful, wayward heart, yet "it is profitable for thee."

Not until he fell crippled and helpless upon the breast of the covenant angel did Jacob know the victory of conquering faith and receive the title of a prince with God. It was when he "halted upon his thigh" (Genesis 32:31) that the armed bands of Esau were stilled before him, and the Pharaoh, proud heir of a kingly line, stooped to crave his blessing. So the Captain of our salvation was made "perfect through sufferings" (Hebrews 2:10), and the children of faith "out of weakness were made strong," and "turned to flight the armies of the aliens" (Hebrews 11:34). So do "the lame take the prey" (Isaiah 33:23), and the weak become "as David," and "the house of David...as the angel of the Lord" (Zechariah 12:8).

Is it lawful for a man to put away his wife?" Matthew 19:3.

Among the Jews a man was permitted to put away his wife for the most trivial offenses, and the woman was then at liberty to marry again. This practice led to great wretchedness and sin. In the Sermon on the Mount Jesus declared plainly that there could be no dissolution of the marriage tie, except for unfaithfulness to the marriage vow. "Everyone," He said, "that putteth away his wife, saving for the cause of fornication, maketh her an adulteress: and whosoever shall marry her when she is put away committeth adultery." R.V.

When the Pharisees afterward questioned Him concerning the lawfulness of divorce, Jesus pointed His hearers back to the marriage institution as ordained at creation. "Because of the hardness of your hearts," He said,

Moses "suffered you to put away your wives: but from the beginning it was not so." Matthew 19:8. He referred them to the blessed days of Eden, when God pronounced all things "very good." Then marriage and the Sabbath had their origin, twin institutions for the glory of God in the benefit of humanity. Then, as the Creator joined the hands of the holy pair in wedlock, saying, A man shall "leave his father and his mother, and shall cleave unto his wife: and they shall be one" (Genesis 2:24), He enunciated the law of marriage for all the children of Adam to the close of time. That which the Eternal Father Himself had pronounced good was the law of highest blessing and development for man.

Like every other one of God's good gifts entrusted to the keeping of humanity, marriage has been perverted by sin; but it is the purpose of the gospel to restore its purity and beauty. In both the Old and the New Testament the marriage relation is employed to represent the tender and sacred union that exists between Christ and His people, the redeemed ones whom He has purchased at the cost of Calvary. "Fear not," He says; "thy Maker is thine husband; the Lord of hosts is His name; and thy Redeemer, the Holy One of Israel." "Turn, O backsliding children, saith the Lord; for I am married unto you." Isaiah 54:4, 5; Jeremiah 3:14. In the "Song of Songs" we hear the bride's voice saying, "My Beloved is mine, and I am His." And He who is to her "the chiefest among ten thousand," speaks to His chosen one, "Thou art all fair, My love; there is no spot in thee." Song of Solomon 2:16; 5:10; 4:7.

In later times Paul the apostle, writing to the Ephesian Christians, declares that the Lord has constituted the husband the head of the wife, to be her protector, the house-band, binding the members of the family together, even as Christ is the head of the church and the Saviour of the mystical body. Therefore he says, "As the church is subject unto Christ, so let the wives be to their own husbands in everything. Husbands, love your wives, even as Christ also loved the church, and gave Himself for it; that He might sanctify and cleanse it with the washing of water by the word, that He might present it to Himself a glorious church, not having spot, or wrinkle, or any such thing; but that it should be holy and without blemish. So ought men to love their wives." Ephesians 5:24–28.

The grace of Christ, and this alone, can make this institution what God designed it should be—an agent for the blessing and uplifting of humanity. And thus the families of earth, in their unity and peace and love, may represent the family of heaven.

Now, as in Christ's day, the condition of society presents a sad comment upon heaven's ideal of this sacred relation. Yet even for those who have found bitterness and disappointment where they had hoped for companionship and joy, the gospel of Christ offers a solace. The patience and gentleness which His Spirit can impart will sweeten the bitter lot. The heart in which Christ dwells will be so filled, so satisfied, with His love that it will not be consumed with longing to attract sympathy and attention to itself. And through the surrender of the soul to God, His wisdom can accomplish what human wisdom fails to do. Through the revelation of His grace, hearts that were once indifferent or estranged may be united in bonds that are firmer and more enduring than those of earth—the golden bonds of a love that will bear the test of trial.

"Swear not at all." Matthew 5:34.

The reason for this command is given: We are not to swear "by the heaven, for it is the throne of God; nor by the earth, for it is the footstool of His feet; nor by Jerusalem, for it is the city of the great King. Neither shalt thou swear by thy head, for thou canst not make one hair white or black." R.V.

All things come of God. We have nothing that we have not received; and, more than this, we have nothing that has not been purchased for us by the blood of Christ. Everything we possess comes to us stamped with the cross, bought with the blood that is precious above all estimate, because it is the life of God. Hence there is nothing that we have a right to pledge, as if it were our own, for the fulfillment of our word.

The Jews understood the third commandment as prohibiting the profane use of the name of God; but they thought themselves at liberty to employ other oaths. Oath taking was common among them. Through Moses they had been forbidden to swear falsely, but they had many devices for freeing themselves from the obligation imposed by an oath. They did not fear to indulge in what was really profanity, nor did they shrink from perjury so long as it was veiled by some technical evasion of the law.

Jesus condemned their practices, declaring that their custom in oath taking was a transgression of the commandment of God. Our Saviour did not, however, forbid the use of the judicial oath, in which God is solemnly called to witness that what is said is truth and nothing but the truth. Jesus Himself, at His trial before the Sanhedrin, did not refuse to testify under oath. The high priest said unto Him, "I adjure Thee by the living God, that Thou tell us whether Thou be the Christ, the Son of God." Jesus answered, "Thou hast said." Matthew 26:63, 64. Had Christ in the Sermon on the Mount condemned the judicial oath, He would at His trial have reproved the high priest and thus, for the benefit of His followers, have enforced His own teaching.

There are very many who do not fear to deceive their fellow men, but they have been taught, and have been impressed by the Spirit of God, that it is a fearful thing to lie to their Maker. When put under oath they are made to feel that they are not testifying merely before men, but before God; that if they bear false witness, it is to Him who reads the heart and who knows the exact truth. The knowledge of the fearful judgments that have followed this sin has a restraining influence upon them.

But if there is anyone who can consistently testify under oath, it is the Christian. He lives constantly as in the presence of God, knowing that every thought is open to the eyes of Him with whom we have to do; and when required to do so in a lawful manner, it is right for him to appeal to God as a witness that what he says is the truth, and nothing but the truth.

Jesus proceeded to lay down a principle that would make oath taking needless. He teaches that the exact truth should be the law of speech. "Let your speech be, Yea, yea; Nay, nay: and whatsoever is more than these is of the evil one." R.V.

These words condemn all those meaningless phrases and expletives that border on profanity. They condemn the deceptive compliments, the evasion of truth, the flattering phrases, the exaggerations, the misrepresentations in trade, that are current in society and in the business world. They teach that no one who tries to appear what he is not, or whose words do not convey the real sentiment of his heart, can be called truthful.

If these words of Christ were heeded, they would check the utterance of evil surmising and unkind criticism; for in commenting upon the actions and motives of another, who can be certain of speaking the exact truth? How often pride, passion, personal resentment, color the impression given! A glance, a word, even an intonation of the voice, may be vital with falsehood. Even facts may be so stated as to convey a false impression. And "whatsoever is more than" truth, "is of the evil one."

Everything that Christians do should be as transparent as the sunlight. Truth is of God; deception, in every one of its myriad forms, is of Satan; and whoever in any way departs from the straight line of truth is betraying himself into the power of the wicked one. Yet it is not a light or an easy thing to speak the exact truth. We cannot speak the truth unless we know the truth; and how often preconceived opinions, mental bias, imperfect knowledge, errors of judgment, prevent a right understanding of matters with which we have to do! We cannot speak the truth unless our minds are continually guided by Him who is truth.

Through the apostle Paul, Christ bids us, "Let your speech be alway with grace." "Let no corrupt communication proceed out of your mouth, but that which is good to the use of edifying, that it may minister grace unto the hearers." Colossians 4:6; Ephesians 4:29. In the light of these scriptures the words of Christ upon the mount are seen to condemn jesting, trifling, and unchaste conversation. They require that our words should be not only truthful, but pure.

Those who have learned of Christ will "have no fellowship with the unfruitful works of darkness." Ephesians 5:11. In speech, as in life, they will be simple, straightforward, and true; for they are preparing for the fellowship of those holy ones in whose mouth "was found no guile." Revelation 14:5.

"Resist not him that is evil: but whosoever smiteth thee on thy right cheek, turn to him the other also." Matthew 5:39, R.V.

Occasions of irritation to the Jews were constantly arising from their contact with the Roman soldiery. Detachments of troops were stationed at different points throughout Judea and Galilee, and their presence reminded the people of their own degradation as a nation. With bitterness of soul they heard the loud blast of the trumpet and saw the troops forming around the standard of Rome and bowing in homage to this symbol of her power. Collisions between the people and the soldiers were frequent, and these inflamed the popular hatred. Often as some Roman official with his guard of soldiers hastened from point to point, he would seize upon the Jewish peasants who were laboring in the field and compel them to carry burdens up the mountainside or render any other service that might be needed. This was in accordance with the Roman law and custom, and resistance to such demands only called forth taunts and cruelty. Every day deepened in the hearts of the people the longing to cast off the Roman yoke. Especially among the bold, rough-handed Galileans the spirit of insurrection was rife. Capernaum, being a border town, was the seat of a Roman garrison, and even while Jesus was teaching, the sight of a company of soldiers recalled to His hearers the bitter thought of Israel's humiliation. The people looked eagerly to Christ, hoping that He was the One who was to humble the pride of Rome.

With sadness Jesus looks into the upturned faces before Him. He notes the spirit of revenge that has stamped its evil imprint upon them, and knows how bitterly the people long for power to crush their oppressors. Mournfully He bids them, "Resist not him that is evil: but whosoever smiteth thee on thy right cheek, turn to him the other also."

These words were but a reiteration of the teaching of the Old Testament. It is true that the rule, "Eye for eye, tooth for tooth" (Leviticus 24:20), was a provision in the laws given through Moses; but it was a civil statute. None were justified in avenging themselves, for they had the words of the Lord: "Say not thou, I will recompense evil." "Say not, I will do so to him as he hath done to me." "Rejoice not when thine enemy falleth." "If he that hateth thee be hungry, give him bread to eat; and if he be thirsty, give him water to drink." Proverbs 20:22; 24:29, 17; 25:21, 22, R.V., margin.

The whole earthly life of Jesus was a manifestation of this principle. It was to bring the bread of life to His enemies that our Saviour left His home in heaven. Though calumny and persecution were heaped upon Him from the cradle to the grave, they called forth from Him only the expression of forgiving love. Through the prophet Isaiah He says," I gave My back to the smiters, and My cheeks to them that plucked off the hair: I hid not My face from shame and spitting." "He was oppressed, and He was afflicted, yet He opened not His mouth: He is brought as a lamb to the slaughter, and as a sheep before her shearers is dumb, so He openeth not His mouth." Isaiah 50:6; 53:7. And from the cross of Calvary there come down through the ages His prayer for His murderers and the message of hope to the dying thief.

The Father's presence encircled Christ, and nothing befell Him but that which infinite love permitted for the blessing of the world. Here was His source of comfort, and it is for us. He who is imbued with the Spirit of Christ abides in Christ. The blow that is aimed at him falls upon the Saviour, who surrounds him with His presence. Whatever comes to him comes from Christ. He has no need to resist evil, for Christ is his defense. Nothing can touch him except by our Lord's permission, and "all things" that are permitted "work together for good to them that love God." Romans 8:28.

"If any man would go to law with thee, and take away thy coat [tunic], let him have thy cloak [mantle] also. And whosoever shall impress thee to go one mile, go with him twain." R.V., margin.

Jesus bade His disciples, instead of resisting the demands of those in authority, to do even more than was required of them. And, so far as possible, they should discharge every obligation, even if it were beyond what the law of the land required. The law, as given through Moses, enjoined a very tender regard for the poor. When a poor man gave his garment as a pledge, or as security for a debt, the creditor was not permitted to enter the dwelling to obtain it; he must wait in the street for the pledge to be brought to him. And whatever the circumstances the pledge must be returned to its owner at nightfall. Deuteronomy 24:10–13. In the days of Christ these merciful provisions were little regarded; but Jesus taught His disciples to submit to the decision of the court, even though this should demand more than the law of Moses authorized. Though it should demand a part of their raiment, they were to yield. More than this, they were to give to the creditor his due, if necessary surrendering even more than the court gave him authority to seize. "If any man would go to law with thee," He said, "and take away thy coat, let him have thy cloak also." R.V. And if the couriers require you to go a mile with them, go two miles.

Jesus added, "Give to him that asketh thee, and from him that would borrow of thee turn not thou away." The same lesson had been taught through Moses: "Thou shalt not harden thine heart, nor shut thine hand from thy poor brother: but thou shalt open thine hand wide unto him, and shalt surely lend him sufficient for his need, in that which he wanteth." Deuteronomy 15:7, 8.

This scripture makes plain the meaning of the Saviour's words. Christ does not teach us to give indiscriminately to all who ask for charity; but He says, "Thou shalt surely lend him sufficient for his need;" and this is to be a gift, rather than a loan; for we are to "lend, hoping for nothing again." Luke 6:35.

> "Who gives himself with his alms feeds three,
> Himself, his hungering neighbor, and Me."

"Love your enemies." Matthew 5:44.

The Saviour's lesson, "Resist not him that is evil," was a hard saying for the revengeful Jews, and they murmured against it among themselves. But Jesus now made a still stronger declaration:

"Ye have heard that it hath been said, Thou shalt love thy neighbor, and hate thine enemy. But I say unto you, Love your enemies, bless them that curse you, do good to them that hate you, and pray for them which despitefully use you and persecute you; that ye may be the children of your Father which is in heaven."

Such was the spirit of the law which the rabbis had misinterpreted as a cold and rigid code of exactions. They regarded themselves as better than other men, and as entitled to the special favor of God by virtue of their birth as Israelites; but Jesus pointed to the spirit of forgiving love as that which would give evidence that they were actuated by any higher motives than even the publicans and sinners, whom they despised.

He pointed His hearers to the Ruler of the universe, under the new name, "Our Father." He would have them understand how tenderly the heart of God yearned over them. He teaches that God cares for every lost soul; that "like as a father pitieth his children, so the Lord pitieth them that fear Him." Psalm 103:13. Such a conception of God was never given to the world by any religion but that of the Bible. Heathenism teaches men to look upon the Supreme Being as an object of fear rather than of love—a malign deity to be appeased by sacrifices, rather than a Father pouring upon His children the gift of His love. Even the people of Israel had become so blinded to the precious teaching of the prophets concerning God that this revelation of His paternal love was as an original subject, a new gift to the world.

The Jews held that God loved those who served Him—according to their view, those who fulfilled the requirements of the rabbis—and that all the rest of the world lay under His frown and curse. Not so, said Jesus; the whole world, the evil and the good, lies in the sunshine of His love. This truth you should have learned from nature itself; for God "maketh His sun to rise on the evil and on the good, and sendeth rain on the just and on the unjust."

It is not because of inherent power that year by year the earth produces her bounties and continues her motion round the sun. The hand of God guides the planets and keeps them in position in their orderly march through the heavens. It is through His power that summer and winter, seedtime and harvest, day and night follow each other in their regular succession. It is by His word that vegetation flourishes, that the leaves appear and the flowers bloom. Every good thing we have, each ray of sunshine and shower of rain, every morsel of food, every moment of life, is a gift of love.

While we were yet unloving and unlovely in character, "hateful, and hating one another," our heavenly Father had mercy on us. "After that the kindness and love of God our Saviour toward man appeared, not by works of righteousness which we have done, but according to His mercy He saved us." Titus 3:3–5. His love received, will make us, in like manner, kind and tender, not merely toward those who please us, but to the most faulty and erring and sinful.

The children of God are those who are partakers of His nature. It is not earthly rank, nor birth, nor nationality, nor religious privilege, which proves that we are members of the family of God; it is love, a love that embraces all humanity. Even sinners whose hearts are not utterly closed to God's Spirit, will respond to kindness; while they may give hate for hate, they will also give love for love. But it is only the Spirit of God that gives love for hatred. To be kind to the unthankful and to the evil, to do good hoping for nothing again, is the insignia of the royalty of heaven, the sure token by which the children of the Highest reveal their high estate.

"Be ye therefore perfect, even as your Father which is in heaven is perfect." Matthew 5:48.

The word "therefore" implies a conclusion, an inference from what has gone before. Jesus has been describing to His hearers the unfailing mercy and love of God, and He bids them therefore to be perfect. Because your heavenly Father "is kind unto the unthankful and to the evil" (Luke 6:35), because He has stooped to lift you up, therefore, said Jesus, you may become like Him in character, and stand without fault in the presence of men and angels.

The conditions of eternal life, under grace, are just what they were in Eden—perfect righteousness, harmony with God, perfect conformity to the principles of His law. The standard of character presented in the Old Testament is the same that is presented in the New Testament. This standard is not one to which we cannot attain. In every command or injunction that God gives there is a promise, the most positive, underlying the command. God has made provision that we may become like unto Him, and He will accomplish this for all who do not interpose a perverse will and thus frustrate His grace.

With untold love our God has loved us, and our love awakens toward Him as we comprehend something of the length and breadth and depth and height of this love that passeth knowledge. By the revelation of the attractive loveliness of Christ, by the knowledge of His love expressed to us while we were yet sinners, the stubborn heart is melted and subdued, and the sinner is transformed and becomes a child of heaven. God does not employ compulsory measures; love is the agent which He uses to expel sin from the heart. By it He changes pride into humility, and enmity and unbelief into love and faith.

The Jews had been wearily toiling to reach perfection by their own efforts, and they had failed. Christ had already told them that their righteousness could never enter the kingdom of heaven. Now He points out to them the character of the righteousness that all who enter heaven will possess. Throughout the Sermon on the Mount He describes its fruits, and now in one sentence He points out its source and its nature: Be perfect as God is perfect. The law is but a transcript of the character of God. Behold in your heavenly Father a perfect manifestation of the principles which are the foundation of His government.

God is love. Like rays of light from the sun, love and light and joy flow out from Him to all His creatures. It is His nature to give. His very life is the outflow of unselfish love.

> "His glory is His children's good;
> His joy, His tender Fatherhood."

He tells us to be perfect as He is, in the same manner. We are to be centers of light and blessing to our little circle, even as He is to the universe. We have nothing of ourselves, but the light of His love shines upon us, and we are to reflect its brightness. "In His borrowed goodness good," we may be perfect in our sphere, even as God is perfect in His.

Jesus said, Be perfect as *your Father* is perfect. If you are the children of God you are partakers of His nature, and you cannot but be like Him. Every child lives by the life of his father. If you are God's children, begotten by His Spirit, you live by the life of God. In Christ dwells "all the fullness of the Godhead bodily" (Colossians 2:9); and the life of Jesus is made manifest "in our mortal flesh" (2 Corinthians 4:11). That life in you will produce the same character and manifest the same works as it did in Him. Thus you will be in harmony with every precept of His law; for "the law of the Lord is perfect, restoring the soul." Psalm 19:7, margin. Through love "the righteousness of the law" will be "fulfilled in us, who walk not after the flesh, but after the Spirit." Romans 8:4.

4
The True Motive in Service

"Take heed that ye do not your righteousness before men, to be seen of them." Matthew 6:1, margin.

The words of Christ on the mount were an expression of that which had been the unspoken teaching of His life, but which the people had failed to comprehend. They could not understand how, having such great power, He neglected to use it in securing what they regarded as the chief good. Their spirit and motives and methods were the opposite of His. While they claimed to be very jealous for the honor of the law, self-glory was the real object which they sought; and Christ would make it manifest to them that the lover of self is a transgressor of the law.

But the principles cherished by the Pharisees are such as are characteristic of humanity in all ages. The spirit of Pharisaism is the spirit of human nature; and as the Saviour showed the contrast between His own spirit and methods and those of the rabbis, His teaching is equally applicable to the people of all time.

In the days of Christ the Pharisees were continually trying to earn the favor of Heaven in order to secure the worldly honor and prosperity which they regarded as the reward of virtue. At the same time they paraded their acts of charity before the people in order to attract their attention and gain a reputation for sanctity.

Jesus rebuked their ostentation, declaring that God does not recognize such service and that the flattery and admiration of the people, which they so eagerly sought, was the only reward they would ever receive.

"When thou doest alms," He said, "let not thy left hand know what thy right hand doeth: that thine alms may be in secret: and thy Father which seeth in secret Himself shall reward thee openly."

In these words Jesus did not teach that acts of kindness should always be kept secret. Paul the apostle, writing by the Holy Spirit, did not conceal the generous self-sacrifice of the Macedonian Christians, but told of the grace that Christ had wrought in them, and thus others were imbued with the same spirit. He also wrote to the church at Corinth and said, "Your zeal hath stirred up very many." 2 Corinthians 9:2, R.V.

Christ's own words make His meaning plain, that in acts of charity the aim should not be to secure praise and honor from men. Real godliness never prompts an effort at display. Those who desire words of praise and flattery, and feed upon them as a sweet morsel, are Christians in name only.

By their good works, Christ's followers are to bring glory, not to themselves, but to Him through whose grace and power they have wrought. It is through the Holy Spirit that every good work is accomplished, and the Spirit is given to glorify, not the receiver, but the Giver. When the light of Christ is shining in the soul, the lips will be filled with praise and thanksgiving to God. Your prayers, your performance of duty, your benevolence, your self-denial, will not be the theme of your thought or conversation. Jesus will be magnified, self will be hidden, and Christ will appear as all in all.

We are to give in sincerity, not to make a show of our good deeds, but from pity and love to the suffering ones. Sincerity of purpose, real kindness of heart, is the motive that Heaven values. The soul that is sincere in its love, wholehearted in its devotion, God regards as more precious than the golden wedge of Ophir.

We are not to think of reward, but of service; yet kindness shown in this spirit will not fail of its recompense. "Thy Father which seeth in secret Himself shall reward thee openly." While it is true that God Himself is the great Reward, that embraces every other, the soul receives and enjoys Him only as it becomes assimilated to Him in character. Only like can appreciate like. It is as we give ourselves to God for the service of humanity that He gives Himself to us.

No one can give place in his own heart and life for the stream of God's blessing to flow to others, without receiving in himself a rich reward. The hillsides and plains that furnish a channel for the mountain streams to reach the sea suffer no loss thereby. That which they give is repaid a hundredfold. For the stream that goes singing on its way leaves behind its gift of verdure and fruitfulness. The grass on its banks is a fresher green, the trees have a richer verdure, the flowers are more abundant. When the earth lies bare and brown under the summer's parching heat, a line of verdure marks the river's course; and the plain that opened her bosom to bear the mountain's treasure to the sea is clothed with freshness and beauty, a witness to the recompense that God's grace imparts to all who give themselves as a channel for its outflow to the world.

This is the blessing of those who show mercy to the poor. The prophet Isaiah says, "Is it not to deal thy bread to the hungry, and that thou bring the poor that are cast out to thy house? when thou seest the naked, that thou cover him; and that thou hide not thyself from thine own flesh? Then shall thy light break forth as the morning, and thine health shall spring forth speedily.... And the Lord shall guide thee continually, and satisfy thy soul in drought:... and thou shalt be like a watered garden, and like a spring of water, whose waters fail not." Isaiah 58:7–11.

The work of beneficence is twice blessed. While he that gives to the needy blesses others, he himself is blessed in a still greater degree. The grace of Christ in the soul is developing traits of character that are the opposite of selfishness—traits that will refine, ennoble, and enrich the life. Acts of kindness performed in secret will bind hearts together, and will draw them closer to the heart of Him from whom every generous impulse springs. The little attentions, the small acts of love and self-sacrifice, that flow out from the life as quietly as the fragrance from a flower—these constitute no small share of the blessings and happiness of life. And it will be found at last that the denial of self for the good and happiness of others, however humble and uncommended here, is recognized in heaven as the token of our union with Him, the King of glory, who was rich, yet for our sake became poor.

The deeds of kindness may have been done in secret, but the result upon the character of the doer cannot be hidden. If we work with wholehearted interest as a follower of Christ, the heart will be in close sympathy with God, and the Spirit of God, moving upon our spirit, will call forth the sacred harmonies of the soul in answer to the divine touch.

He who gives increased talents to those who have made a wise improvement of the gifts entrusted to them is pleased to acknowledge the service of His believing people in the Beloved, through whose grace and strength they have wrought. Those who have sought for the development and perfection of Christian character by exercising their faculties in good works, will, in the world to come, reap that which they have sown. The work begun upon earth will reach its consummation in that higher and holier life to endure throughout eternity.

"When thou prayest, thou shalt not be as the hypocrites are." Matthew 6:5.

The Pharisees had stated hours for prayer; and when, as often came to pass, they were abroad at the appointed time, they would pause wherever they might be—perhaps in the street or the market place, amid the hurrying throngs of men—and there in a loud voice rehearse their formal prayers. Such worship, offered merely for self-glorification, called forth unsparing rebuke from Jesus. He did not, however, discountenance public prayer, for He Himself prayed with His disciples and in the presence of the multitude. But He teaches that private prayer is not to be made public. In secret devotion our prayers are to reach the ears of none but the prayer-hearing God. No curious ear is to receive the burden of such petitions.

"When thou prayest, enter into thy closet." Have a place for secret prayer. Jesus had select places for communion with God, and so should we. We need often to retire to some spot, however humble, where we can be alone with God.

"Pray to thy Father which is in secret." In the name of Jesus we may come into God's presence with the confidence of a child. No man is needed to act as a mediator. Through Jesus we may open our hearts to God as to one who knows and loves us.

In the secret place of prayer, where no eye but God's can see, no ear but His can hear, we may pour out our most hidden desires and longings to the Father of infinite pity, and in the hush and silence of the soul that voice which never fails to answer the cry of human need will speak to our hearts.

"The Lord is very pitiful, and of tender mercy." James 5:11. He waits with unwearied love to hear the confessions of the wayward and to accept their penitence. He watches for some return of gratitude from us, as the mother watches for the smile of recognition from her beloved child. He would have us understand how earnestly and tenderly His heart yearns over us. He invites us to take our trials to His sympathy, our sorrows to His love, our wounds to His healing, our weakness to His strength, our emptiness to His fullness. Never has one been disappointed who came unto Him. "They looked unto Him, and were lightened: and their faces were not ashamed." Psalm 34:5.

Those who seek God in secret telling the Lord their needs and pleading for help, will not plead in vain. "Thy Father which seeth in secret Himself shall reward thee openly." As we make Christ our daily companion we shall feel that the powers of an unseen world are all around us; and by looking unto Jesus we shall become assimilated to His image. By beholding we become changed. The character is softened, refined, and ennobled for the heavenly kingdom. The sure result of our intercourse and fellowship with our Lord will be to increase piety, purity, and fervor. There will be a growing intelligence in prayer. We are receiving a divine education, and this is illustrated in a life of diligence and zeal.

The soul that turns to God for its help, its support, its power, by daily, earnest prayer, will have noble aspirations, clear perceptions of truth and duty, lofty purposes of action, and a continual hungering and thirsting after righteousness. By maintaining a connection with God, we shall be enabled to diffuse to others, through our association with them, the light, the peace, the serenity, that rule in our hearts. The strength acquired in prayer to God, united with persevering effort in training the mind in thoughtfulness and care-taking, prepares one for daily duties and keeps the spirit in peace under all circumstances.

If we draw near to God, He will put a word in our mouth to speak for Him, even praise unto His name. He will teach us a strain from the song of the angels, even thanksgiving to our heavenly Father. In every act of life, the light and love of an indwelling Saviour will be revealed. Outward troubles cannot reach the life that is lived by faith in the Son of God.

"When ye pray, use not vain repetitions, as the heathen do." Matthew 6:7.

The heathen looked upon their prayers as having in themselves merit to atone for sin. Hence the longer the prayer the greater the merit. If they could become holy by their own efforts they would have something in themselves in which to rejoice, some ground for boasting. This idea of prayer is an outworking of the principle of self-expiation which lies at the foundation of all systems of false religion. The Pharisees had adopted this pagan idea of prayer, and it is by no means extinct in our day, even among those who profess to be Christians. The repetition of set, customary phrases, when the heart feels no need of God, is of the same character as the "vain repetitions" of the heathen.

Prayer is not an expiation for sin; it has no virtue or merit of itself. All the flowery words at our command are not equivalent to one holy desire. The most eloquent prayers are but idle words if they do not express the true sentiments of the heart. But the prayer that comes from an earnest heart, when the simple wants of the soul are expressed, as we would ask an earthly friend for a favor, expecting it to be granted—this is the prayer of faith. God does not desire our ceremonial compliments, but the unspoken cry of the heart broken and subdued with a sense of its sin and utter weakness finds its way to the Father of all mercy.

"When ye fast, be not, as the hypocrites." Matthew 6:16.

The fasting which the word of God enjoins is something more than a form. It does not consist merely in refusing food, in wearing sackcloth, in sprinkling ashes upon the head. He who fasts in real sorrow for sin will never court display.

The object of the fast which God calls upon us to keep is not to afflict the body for the sin of the soul, but to aid us in perceiving the grievous character of sin, in humbling the heart before God and receiving His pardoning grace. His command to Israel was, "Rend your heart, and not your garments, and turn unto the Lord your God." Joel 2:13.

It will avail nothing for us to do penance or to flatter ourselves that by our own works we shall merit or purchase an inheritance among the saints. When the question was asked Christ, "What shall we do, that we might work the works of God?" He answered, "This is the work of God, that ye believe on Him whom He hath sent." John 6:28, 29. Repentance is turning from self to Christ; and when we receive Christ so that through faith He can live His life in us, good works will be manifest.

Jesus said, "When thou fastest, anoint thine head, and wash thy face; that thou appear not unto men to fast, but unto thy Father which is in secret." Matthew 6:17, 18. Whatever is done to the glory of God is to be done with cheerfulness, not with sadness and gloom. There is nothing gloomy in the religion of Jesus. If Christians give the impression by a mournful attitude that they have been disappointed in their Lord, they misrepresent His character and put arguments into the mouth of His enemies. Though in words they may claim God as their Father, yet in gloom and sorrow they present to the world the aspect of orphans.

Christ desires us to make His service appear attractive, as it really is. Let the self-denials and the secret heart trials be revealed to the compassionate Saviour. Let the burdens be left at the foot of the cross, and go on your way rejoicing in His love who first loved you. Men may never know of the work going on secretly between the soul and God, but the result of the Spirit's work upon the heart will be manifest to all, for He "which seeth in secret, shall reward thee openly."

"Lay not up for yourselves treasures upon earth." Matthew 6:19.

Treasure laid up on earth will not endure; thieves break through and steal; moth and rust corrupt; fire and storm sweep away your possessions. And "where your treasure is, there will your heart be also." Treasure laid up on the earth will engross the mind to the exclusion of heavenly things.

The love of money was the ruling passion in the Jewish age. Worldliness usurped the place of God and religion in the soul. So it is now. Avaricious greed for wealth exerts such a fascinating, bewitching influence over the life that it results in perverting the nobility and corrupting the humanity of men until they are drowned in perdition. The service of Satan is full of care, perplexity, and wearing labor, and the treasure men toil to accumulate on earth is only for a season.

Jesus said, "Lay up for yourselves treasures in heaven, where neither moth nor rust doth corrupt, and where thieves do not break through nor steal: for where your treasure is, there will your heart be also."

The instruction is to "lay up for *yourselves* treasures in heaven." It is for your own interest to secure heavenly riches. These alone, of all that you possess, are really yours. The treasure laid up in heaven is imperishable. No fire or flood can destroy it, no thief despoil it, no moth or rust corrupt it; for it is in the keeping of God.

This treasure, which Christ esteems as precious above all estimate, is "the riches of the glory of His inheritance in the saints." Ephesians 1:18. The disciples of Christ are called His jewels, His precious and peculiar treasure. He says, "They shall be as the stones of a crown." "I will make a man more precious than fine gold; even a man than the golden wedge of Ophir." Zechariah 9:16; Isaiah 13:12. Christ looks upon His people in their purity and perfection as the reward of all His sufferings, His humiliation, and His love, and the supplement of His glory—Christ, the great Center, from whom radiates all glory.

And we are permitted to unite with Him in the great work of redemption and to be sharers with Him in the riches which His death and suffering have won. The apostle Paul wrote to the Thessalonian Christians: "What is our hope, or joy, or crown of rejoicing? Are not even ye in the presence of our Lord Jesus Christ at His coming? for ye are our glory and joy." 1 Thessalonians 2:19, 20. This is the treasure for which Christ bids us labor. Character is the great harvest of life. And every word or deed that through the grace of Christ shall kindle in one soul an impulse that reaches heavenward, every effort that tends to the formation of a Christlike character, is laying up treasure in heaven.

Where the treasure is, there the heart will be. In every effort to benefit others, we benefit ourselves. He who gives money or time for spreading the gospel enlists his own interest and prayers for the work, and for the souls to be reached through it; his affections go out to others, and he is stimulated to greater devotion to God, that he may be enabled to do them the greatest good.

And at the final day, when the wealth of earth shall perish, he who has laid up treasure in heaven will behold that which his life has gained. If we have given heed to the words of Christ, then, as we gather around the great white throne, we shall see souls who have been saved through our agency, and shall know that one has saved others, and these still others—a large company brought into the haven of rest as the result of our labors, there to lay their crowns at Jesus' feet, and praise Him through the ceaseless ages of eternity. With what joy will the worker for Christ behold these redeemed ones, who share the glory of the Redeemer! How precious will heaven be to those who have been faithful in the work of saving souls!

"If ye then be risen with Christ, seek those things which are above, where Christ sitteth on the right hand of God." Colossians 3:1.

"If...thine eye be single, thy whole body shall be full of light." Matthew 6:22.

Singleness of purpose, wholehearted devotion to God, is the condition pointed out by the Saviour's words. Let the purpose be sincere and unwavering to discern the truth and to obey it at whatever cost, and you will receive divine enlightenment. Real piety begins when all compromise with sin is at an end. Then the language of the heart will be that of the apostle Paul: "This one thing I do, forgetting those things which are behind, and reaching forth unto those things which are before, I press toward the mark for the prize of the high calling of God in Christ Jesus." "I count all things but loss for the excellency of the knowledge of Christ Jesus my Lord: for whom I have suffered the loss of all things, and do count them but dung, that I may win Christ." Philippians 3:13, 14, 8.

But when the eye is blinded by the love of self, there is only darkness. "If thine eye be evil, thy whole body shall be full of darkness." It was this fearful darkness that wrapped the Jews in stubborn unbelief, making it impossible for them to appreciate the character and mission of Him who came to save them from their sins.

Yielding to temptation begins in permitting the mind to waver, to be inconstant in your trust in God. If we do not choose to give ourselves fully to God then we are in darkness. When we make any reserve we are leaving open a door through which Satan can enter to lead us astray by his temptations. He knows that if he can obscure our vision, so that the eye of faith cannot see God, there will be no barrier against sin.

The prevalence of a sinful desire shows the delusion of the soul. Every indulgence of that desire strengthens the soul's aversion to God. In following the path of Satan's choosing, we are encompassed by the shadows of evil, and every step leads into deeper darkness and increases the blindness of the heart.

The same law obtains in the spiritual as in the natural world. He who abides in darkness will at last lose the power of vision. He is shut in by a deeper than midnight blackness; and to him the brightest noontide can bring no light. He "walketh in darkness, and knoweth not whither he goeth, because that darkness hath blinded his eyes." 1 John 2:11. Through persistently cherishing evil, willfully disregarding the pleadings of divine love, the sinner loses the love for good, the desire for God, the very capacity to receive the light of heaven. The invitation of mercy is still full of love, the light is shining as brightly as when it first dawned upon his soul; but the voice falls on deaf ears, the light on blinded eyes.

No soul is ever finally deserted of God, given up to his own ways, so long as there is any hope of his salvation. "Man turns from God, not God from him." Our heavenly Father follows us with appeals and warnings and assurances of compassion, until further opportunities and privileges would be wholly in vain. The responsibility rests with the sinner. By resisting the Spirit of God today, he prepares the way for a second resistance of light when it comes with mightier power. Thus he passes on from one stage of resistance to another, until at last the light will fail to impress, and he will cease to respond in any measure to the Spirit of God. Then even "the light that is in thee" has become darkness. The very truth we do know has become so perverted as to increase the blindness of the soul.

"No man can serve two masters." Matthew 6:24.

Christ does not say that man will not or shall not serve two masters, but that he *cannot*. The interests of God and the interests of mammon have no union or sympathy. Just where the conscience of the Christian warns him to forbear, to deny himself, to stop, just there the worldling steps over the line, to indulge his selfish propensities. On one side of the line is the self-denying follower of Christ; on the other side is the self-indulgent world lover, pandering to fashion, engaging in frivolity, and pampering himself in forbidden pleasure. On that side of the line the Christian cannot go.

No one can occupy a neutral position; there is no middle class, who neither love God nor serve the enemy of righteousness. Christ is to live in His human agents and work through their faculties and act through their capabilities. Their will must be submitted to His will; they must act with His Spirit. Then it is no more they that live, but Christ that lives in them. He who does not give himself wholly to God is under the control of another power, listening to another voice, whose suggestions are of an entirely different character. Half-and-half service places the human agent on the side of the enemy as a successful ally of the hosts of darkness. When men who claim to be soldiers of Christ engage with the confederacy of Satan, and help along his side, they prove themselves enemies of Christ. They betray sacred trusts. They form a link between Satan and the true soldiers, so that through these agencies the enemy is constantly working to steal away the hearts of Christ's soldiers.

The strongest bulwark of vice in our world is not the iniquitous life of the abandoned sinner or the degraded outcast; it is that life which otherwise appears virtuous, honorable, and noble, but in which one sin is fostered, one vice indulged. To the soul that is struggling in secret against some giant temptation, trembling upon the very verge of the precipice, such an example is one of the most powerful enticements to sin. He who, endowed with high conceptions of life and truth and honor, does yet willfully transgress one precept of God's holy law, has perverted His noble gifts into a lure to sin. Genius, talent, sympathy, even generous and kindly deeds, may become decoys of Satan to entice other souls over the precipice of ruin for this life and the life to come.

"Love not the world, neither the things that are in the world. If any man love the world, the love of the Father is not in him. For all that is in the world, the lust of the flesh, and the lust of the eyes, and the pride of life, is not of the Father, but is of the world." 1 John 2:15, 16.

"Be not anxious." Matthew 6:25, R.V.

He who has given you life knows your need of food to sustain it. He who created the body is not unmindful of your need of raiment. Will not He who has bestowed the greater gift bestow also what is needed to make it complete?

Jesus pointed His hearers to the birds as they warbled their carols of praise, unencumbered with thoughts of care, for "they sow not, neither do they reap;" and yet the great Father provides for their needs. And He asks, "Are not ye of much more value than they?" R.V.

"No sparrow falls without His care,
No soul bows low but Jesus knows;
For He is with us everywhere,
And marks each bitter tear that flows.
And He will never, never, never
Forsake the soul that trusts Him ever."

The hillsides and the fields were bright with flowers, and, pointing to them in the dewy freshness of the morning, Jesus said, "Consider the lilies of the field, how they grow." The graceful forms and delicate hues of the plants and flowers may be copied by human skill, but what touch can impart life to even one flower or blade of grass? Every wayside blossom owes its being to the same power that set the starry worlds on high. Through all created things thrills one pulse of life from the great heart of God. The flowers of the field are clothed by His hand in richer robes than have ever graced the forms of earthly kings. And "if God so clothe the grass of the field, which today is, and tomorrow is cast into the oven, shall He not much more clothe you, O ye of little faith?"

It is He who made the flowers and who gave to the sparrow its song who says, "Consider the lilies," "Behold the birds." R.V. In the loveliness of the things of nature you may learn more of the wisdom of God than the schoolmen know. On the lily's petals, God has written a message for you, written in language that your heart can read only as it unlearns the lessons of distrust and selfishness and corroding care. Why has He given you the singing birds and the gentle blossoms, but from the overflowing love of a Father's heart, that would brighten and gladden your path of life? All that was needed for existence would have been yours without the flowers and birds, but God was not content to provide what would suffice for mere existence. He has filled earth and air and sky with glimpses of beauty to tell you of His loving thought for you. The beauty of all created things is but a gleam from the shining of His glory. If He has lavished such infinite skill upon the things of nature, for your happiness and joy, can you doubt that He will give you every needed blessing?

"Consider the lilies." Every flower that opens its petals to the sunshine obeys the same great laws that guide the stars, and how simple and beautiful and how sweet its life! Through the flowers, God would call our attention to the loveliness of Christlike character. He who has given such beauty to the blossoms desires far more that the soul should be clothed with the beauty of the character of Christ.

Consider, says Jesus, how the lilies grow; how, springing from the cold, dark earth, or from the mud of the river bed, the plants unfold in loveliness and fragrance. Who would dream of the possibilities of beauty in the rough brown bulb of the lily? But when the life of God, hidden therein, unfolds at His call in the rain and the sunshine, men marvel at the vision of grace and loveliness. Even so will the life of God unfold in every human soul that will yield itself to the ministry of His grace, which, free as the rain and the sunshine, comes with its benediction to all. It is the word of God that creates the flowers, and the same word will produce in you the graces of His Spirit.

God's law is the law of love. He has surrounded you with beauty to teach you that you are not placed on earth merely to delve for self, to dig and build, to toil and spin, but to make life bright and joyous and beautiful with the love of Christ—like the flowers, to gladden other lives by the ministry of love.

Fathers and mothers, let your children learn from the flowers. Take them with you into garden and field and under the leafy trees, and teach them to read in nature the message of God's love. Let the thoughts of Him be linked with bird and flower and tree. Lead the children to see in every pleasant and beautiful thing an expression of God's love for them. Recommend your religion to them by its pleasantness. Let the law of kindness be in your lips.

Teach the children that because of God's great love their natures may be changed and brought into harmony with His. Teach them that He would have their lives beautiful with the graces of the flowers. Teach them, as they gather the sweet blossoms, that He who made the flowers is more beautiful than they. Thus the tendrils of their hearts will be entwined about Him. He who is "altogether lovely" will become to them as a daily companion and familiar friend, and their lives will be transformed into the image of His purity.

"Seek ye first the kingdom of God." Matthew 6:33.

The people who listened to the words of Christ were still anxiously watching for some announcement of the earthly kingdom. While Jesus was opening to them the treasures of heaven, the question uppermost in many minds was, How will a connection with Him advance our prospects in the world? Jesus shows that in making the things of the world their supreme anxiety they were like the heathen nations about them, living as if there were no God, whose tender care is over His creatures.

"All these things," said Jesus, "do the nations of the world seek after." "Your heavenly Father knoweth that ye have need of all these things. But seek ye first the kingdom of God, and His righteousness; and all these things shall be added unto you." Luke 12: 30; Matthew. 6:32, 33. I have come to open to you the kingdom of love and righteousness and peace. Open your hearts to receive this kingdom, and make its service your highest interest. Though it is a spiritual kingdom, fear not that your needs for this life will be uncared-for. If you give yourself to God's service, He who has all power in heaven and earth will provide for your needs.

Jesus does not release us from the necessity of effort, but He teaches that we are to make Him first and last and best in everything. We are to engage in no business, follow no pursuit, seek no pleasure, that would hinder the outworking of His righteousness in our character and life. Whatever we do is to be done heartily, as unto the Lord.

Jesus, while He dwelt on earth, dignified life in all its details by keeping before men the glory of God, and by subordinating everything to the will of His Father. If we follow His example, His assurance to us is that all things needful in this life "shall be added." Poverty or wealth, sickness or health, simplicity or wisdom—all are provided for in the promise of His grace.

God's everlasting arm encircles the soul that turns to Him for aid, however feeble that soul may be. The precious things of the hills shall perish, but the soul that lives for God shall abide with Him. "The world passeth away, and the lust thereof; but he that doeth the will of God abideth forever." 1 John 2:17. The city of God will open its golden gates to receive him who learned while on earth to lean on God for guidance and wisdom, for comfort and hope, amid loss and affliction. The songs of the angels will welcome him there, and for him the tree of life shall yield its fruit. "The mountains shall depart, and the hills be removed; but My kindness shall not depart from thee, neither shall the covenant of My peace be removed, saith the Lord that hath mercy on thee." Isaiah 54:10.

Be not therefore anxious for the morrow.... Sufficient unto the day is the evil thereof." Matthew 6:34, R.V.

If you have given yourself to God, to do His work, you have no need to be anxious for tomorrow. He whose servant you are, knows the end from the beginning. The events of tomorrow, which are hidden from your view, are open to the eyes of Him who is omnipotent.

When we take into our hands the management of things with which we have to do, and depend upon our own wisdom for success, we are taking a burden which God has not given us, and are trying to bear it without His aid. We are taking upon ourselves the responsibility that belongs to God, and thus are really putting ourselves in His place. We may well have anxiety and anticipate danger and loss, for it is certain to befall us. But when we really believe that God loves us and means to do us good we shall cease to worry about the future. We shall trust God as a child trusts a loving parent. Then our troubles and torments will disappear, for our will is swallowed up in the will of God.

Christ has given us no promise of help in bearing today the burdens of tomorrow. He has said, "My grace is sufficient for thee" (2 Corinthians 12:9); but, like the manna given in the wilderness, His grace is bestowed daily, for the day's need. Like the hosts of Israel in their pilgrim life, we may find morning by morning the bread of heaven for the day's supply.

One day alone is ours, and during this day we are to live for God. For this one day we are to place in the hand of Christ, in solemn service, all our purposes and plans, casting all our care upon Him, for He careth for us. "I know the thoughts that I think toward you, saith the Lord, thoughts of peace, and not of evil, to give you an expected end." "In returning and rest shall ye be saved; in quietness and in confidence shall be your strength." Jeremiah 29:11; Isaiah 30:15.

If you will seek the Lord and be converted every day; if you will of your own spiritual choice be free and joyous in God; if with gladsome consent of heart to His gracious call you come wearing the yoke of Christ—the yoke of obedience and service—all your murmurings will be stilled, all your difficulties will be removed, all the perplexing problems that now confront you will be solved.

5
The Lord's Prayer

"After this manner therefore pray ye." Matthew 6:9.

The Lord's Prayer was twice given by our Saviour, first to the multitude in the Sermon on the Mount, and again, some months later, to the disciples alone. The disciples had been for a short time absent from their Lord, when on their return they found Him absorbed in communion with God. Seeming unconscious of their presence, He continued praying aloud. The Saviour's face was irradiated with a celestial brightness. He seemed to be in the very presence of the Unseen, and there was a living power in His words as of one who spoke with God.

The hearts of the listening disciples were deeply moved. They had marked how often He spent long hours in solitude in communion with His Father. His days were passed in ministry to the crowds that pressed upon Him, and in unveiling the treacherous sophistry of the rabbis, and this incessant labor often left Him so utterly wearied that His mother and brothers, and even His disciples, had feared that His life would be sacrificed. But as He returned from the hours of prayer that closed the toilsome day, they marked the look of peace upon His face, the sense of refreshment that seemed to pervade His presence. It was from hours spent with God that He came forth, morning by morning, to bring the light of heaven to men. The disciples had come to connect His hours of prayer with the power of His words and works. Now, as they listened to His supplication, their hearts were awed and humbled. As He ceased praying, it was with a conviction of their own deep need that they exclaimed, "Lord, teach us to pray." Luke 11:1.

Jesus gives them no new form of prayer. That which He has before taught them He repeats, as if He would say, You need to understand what I have already given. It has a depth of meaning you have not yet fathomed.

The Saviour does not, however, restrict us to the use of these exact words. As one with humanity, He presents His own ideal of prayer, words so simple that they may be adopted by the little child, yet so comprehensive that their significance can never be fully grasped by the greatest minds. We are taught to come to God with our tribute of thanksgiving, to make known our wants, to confess our sins, and to claim His mercy in accordance with His promise.

"When ye pray, say Our Father." Luke 11:2.

Jesus teaches us to call His Father our Father. He is not ashamed to call us brethren. Hebrews 2:11. So ready, so eager, is the Saviour's heart to welcome us as members of the family of God, that in the very first words we are to use in approaching God He places the assurance of our divine relationship, "Our Father."

Here is the announcement of that wonderful truth, so full of encouragement and comfort, that God loves us as He loves His Son. This is what Jesus said in His last prayer for His disciples, Thou "hast loved them, as Thou hast loved Me." John 17:23.

The world that Satan has claimed and has ruled over with cruel tyranny, the Son of God has, by one vast achievement, encircled in His love and connected again with the throne of Jehovah. Cherubim and seraphim, and the unnumbered hosts of all the unfallen worlds, sang anthems of praise to God and the Lamb when this triumph was assured. They rejoiced that the way of salvation had been opened to the fallen race and that the earth would be redeemed from the curse of sin. How much more should those rejoice who are the objects of such amazing love!

How can we ever be in doubt and uncertainty, and feel that we are orphans? It was in behalf of those who had transgressed the law that Jesus took upon Him human nature; He became like unto us, that we might have everlasting peace and assurance. We have an Advocate in the heavens, and whoever accepts Him as a personal Saviour is not left an orphan to bear the burden of his own sins.

"Beloved, now are we the sons of God." "And if children, then heirs; heirs of God, and joint heirs with Christ; if so be that we suffer with Him, that we may be also glorified together." "It doth not yet appear what we shall be: but we know that, when He shall appear, we shall be like Him; for we shall see Him as He is." 1 John 3:2; Romans 8:17.

The very first step in approaching God is to know and believe the love that He has to us (1 John 4:16); for it is through the drawing of His love that we are led to come to Him.

The perception of God's love works the renunciation of selfishness. In calling God our Father, we recognize all His children as our brethren. We are all a part of the great web of humanity, all members of one family. In our petitions we are to include our neighbors as well as ourselves. No one prays aright who seeks a blessing for himself alone.

The infinite God, said Jesus, makes it your privilege to approach Him by the name of Father. Understand all that this implies. No earthly parent ever pleaded so earnestly with an erring child as He who made you pleads with the transgressor. No human, loving interest ever followed the impenitent with such tender invitations. God dwells in every abode; He hears every word that is spoken, listens to every prayer that is offered, tastes the sorrows and disappointments of every soul, regards the treatment that is given to father, mother, sister, friend, and neighbor. He cares for our necessities, and His love and mercy and grace are continually flowing to satisfy our need.

But if you call God your Father you acknowledge yourselves His children, to be guided by His wisdom and to be obedient in all things, knowing that His love is changeless. You will accept His plan for your life. As children of God, you will hold His honor, His character, His family, His work, as the objects of your highest interest. It will be your joy to recognize and honor your relation to your Father and to every member of His family. You will rejoice to do any act, however humble, that will tend to His glory or to the well-being of your kindred.

"Which art in heaven." He to whom Christ bids us look as "our Father" "is in the heavens: He hath done whatsoever He hath pleased." In His care we may safely rest, saying, "What time I am afraid, I will trust in Thee." Psalms 115:3; 56:3.

"Hallowed be Thy name." Matthew 6:9.

To hallow the name of the Lord requires that the words in which we speak of the Supreme Being be uttered with reverence. "Holy and reverend is His name." Psalm 111:9. We are never in any manner to treat lightly the titles or appellations of the Deity. In prayer we enter the audience chamber of the Most High; and we should come before Him with holy awe. The angels veil their faces in His presence. The cherubim and the bright and holy seraphim approach His throne with solemn reverence. How much more should we, finite, sinful beings, come in a reverent manner before the Lord, our Maker!

But to hallow the name of the Lord means much more than this. We may, like the Jews in Christ's day, manifest the greatest outward reverence for God, and yet profane His name continually. "The name of the Lord" is "merciful and gracious, long-suffering, and abundant in goodness and truth,… forgiving iniquity and transgression and sin." Exodus 34:5–7. Of the church of Christ it is written, "This is the name wherewith she shall be called, The Lord our Righteousness." Jeremiah 33:16. This name is put upon every follower of Christ. It is the heritage of the child of God. The family are called after the Father. The prophet Jeremiah, in the time of Israel's sore distress and tribulation, prayed, "We are called by Thy name; leave us not." Jeremiah 14:9.

This name is hallowed by the angels of heaven, by the inhabitants of unfallen worlds. When you pray, "Hallowed be Thy name," you ask that it may be hallowed in this world, hallowed in you. God has acknowledged you before men and angels as His child; pray that you may do no dishonor to the "worthy name by which ye are called." James 2:7. God sends you into the world as His representative. In every act of life you are to make manifest the name of God. This petition calls upon you to possess His character. You cannot hallow His name, you cannot represent Him to the world, unless in life and character you represent the very life and character of God. This you can do only through the acceptance of the grace and righteousness of Christ.

"Thy kingdom come." Matthew 6:10.

God is our Father, who loves and cares for us as His children; He is also the great King of the universe. The interests of His kingdom are our interests, and we are to work for its upbuilding.

The disciples of Christ were looking for the immediate coming of the kingdom of His glory, but in giving them this prayer Jesus taught that the kingdom was not then to be established. They were to pray for its coming as an event yet future. But this petition was also an assurance to them. While they were not to behold the coming of the kingdom in their day, the fact that Jesus bade them pray for it is evidence that in God's own time it will surely come.

The kingdom of God's grace is now being established, as day by day hearts that have been full of sin and rebellion yield to the sovereignty of His love. But the full establishment of the kingdom of His glory will not take place until the second coming of Christ to this world. "The kingdom and dominion, and the greatness of the kingdom under the whole heaven," is to be given to "the people of the saints of the Most High." Daniel 7:27. They shall inherit the kingdom prepared for them "from the foundation of the world." Matthew 25:34. And Christ will take to Himself His great power and will reign.

The heavenly gates are again to be lifted up, and with ten thousand times ten thousand and thousands of thousands of holy ones, our Saviour will come forth as King of kings and Lord of lords. Jehovah Immanuel "shall be king over all the earth: in that day shall there be one Lord, and His name one." "The tabernacle of God" shall be with men, "and He will dwell with them, and they shall be His people, and God Himself shall be with them, and be their God." Zechariah 14:9; Revelation 21:3.

But before that coming, Jesus said, "This gospel of the kingdom shall be preached in all the world for a witness unto all nations." Matthew 24:14. His kingdom will not come until the good tidings of His grace have been carried to all the earth. Hence, as we give ourselves to God, and win other souls to Him, we hasten the coming of His kingdom. Only those who devote themselves to His service, saying, "Here am I; send me" (Isaiah 6:8), to open blind eyes, to turn men "from darkness to light and from the power of Satan unto God, that they may receive forgiveness of sins and inheritance among them which are sanctified" (Acts 26:18)—they alone pray in sincerity, "Thy kingdom come."

"Thy will be done in earth, as it is in heaven." Matthew 6:10.

The will of God is expressed in the precepts of His holy law, and the principles of this law are the principles of heaven. The angels of heaven attain unto no higher knowledge than to know the will of God, and to do His will is the highest service that can engage their powers.

But in heaven, service is not rendered in the spirit of legality. When Satan rebelled against the law of Jehovah, the thought that there was a law came to the angels almost as an awakening to something unthought of. In their ministry the angels are not as servants, but as sons. There is perfect unity between them and their Creator. Obedience is to them no drudgery. Love for God makes their service a joy. So in every soul wherein Christ, the hope of glory, dwells, His words are re-echoed, "I delight to do Thy will, O My God: yea, Thy law is within My heart." Psalm 40:8.

The petition, "Thy will be done in earth, as it is in heaven," is a prayer that the reign of evil on this earth may be ended, that sin may be forever destroyed, and the kingdom of righteousness be established. Then in earth as in heaven will be fulfilled "all the good pleasure of His goodness." 2 Thessalonians 1:11.

"Give us this day our daily bread." Matthew 6:11.

The first half of the prayer Jesus has taught us is in regard to the name and kingdom and will of God-that His name may be honored, His kingdom established, His will performed. When you have thus made God's service your first interest, you may ask with confidence that your own needs may be supplied. If you have renounced self and given yourself to Christ you are a member of the family of God, and everything in the Father's house is for you. All the treasures of God are opened to you, both the world that now is and that which is to come. The ministry of angels, the gift of His Spirit, the labors of His servants—all are for you. The world, with everything in it, is yours so far as it can do you good. Even the enmity of the wicked will prove a blessing by disciplining you for heaven. If "ye are Christ's," "all things are yours." 1 Corinthians 3:23, 21.

But you are as a child who is not yet placed in control of his inheritance. God does not entrust to you your precious possession, lest Satan by his wily arts should beguile you, as he did the first pair in Eden. Christ holds it for you, safe beyond the spoiler's reach. Like the child, you shall receive day by day what is required for the day's need. Every day you are to pray, "Give us this day our daily bread." Be not dismayed if you have not sufficient for tomorrow. You have the assurance of His promise, "So shalt thou dwell in the land, and verily thou shalt be fed." David says, "I have been young, and now am old; yet have I not seen the righteous forsaken, nor his seed begging bread." Psalm 37:3, 25. That God who sent the ravens to feed Elijah by the brook Cherith will not pass by one of His faithful, self-sacrificing children. Of him that walketh righteously it is written: "Bread shall be given him; his waters shall be sure." "They shall not be ashamed in the evil time: and in the days of famine they shall be satisfied." "He that spared not His own Son, but delivered Him up for us all, how shall He not with Him also freely give us all things?" Isaiah 33:16; Psalm 37:19; Romans 8:32. He who lightened the cares and anxieties of His widowed mother and helped her to provide for the household at Nazareth, sympathizes with every mother in her struggle to provide her children food. He who had compassion on the multitude because they "fainted, and were scattered abroad" (Matthew 9:36), still has compassion on the suffering poor. His hand is stretched out toward them in blessing; and in the very prayer which He gave His disciples, He teaches us to remember the poor.

When we pray, "Give us this day our daily bread," we ask for others as well as ourselves. And we acknowledge that what God gives us is not for ourselves alone. God gives to us in trust, that we may feed the hungry. Of His goodness He has prepared for the poor. Psalm 68:10. And He says, "When thou makest a dinner or a supper, call not thy friends, nor thy brethren, neither thy kinsmen, nor thy rich neighbors.... But when thou makest a feast, call the poor, the maimed, the lame, the blind: and thou shalt be blessed; for they cannot recompense thee: for thou shalt be recompensed at the resurrection of the just." Luke 14:12–14.

"God is able to make all grace abound toward you; that ye, always having all sufficiency in all things, may abound to every good work." "He which soweth sparingly shall reap also sparingly; and he which soweth bountifully shall reap also bountifully." 2 Corinthians 9:8, 6.

The prayer for daily bread includes not only food to sustain the body, but that spiritual bread which will nourish the soul unto life everlasting. Jesus bids us, "Labor not for the meat which perisheth, but for that meat which endureth unto everlasting life." John 6:27. He says, "I am the living bread which came down from heaven: if any man eat of this bread, he shall live forever." Verse 51. Our Saviour is the bread of life, and it is by beholding His love, by receiving it into the soul, that we feed upon the bread which came down from heaven.

We receive Christ through His word, and the Holy Spirit is given to open the word of God to our understanding, and bring home its truths to our hearts. We are to pray day by day that as we read His word, God will send His Spirit to reveal to us the truth that will strengthen our souls for the day's need.

In teaching us to ask every day for what we need-both temporal and spiritual blessings—God has a purpose to accomplish for our good. He would have us realize our dependence upon His constant care, for He is seeking to draw us into communion with Himself. In this communion with Christ, through prayer and the study of the great and precious truths of His word, we shall as hungry souls be fed; as those that thirst, we shall be refreshed at the fountain of life.

"Forgive us our sins; for we also forgive everyone that is indebted to us." Luke 11:4.

Jesus teaches that we can receive forgiveness from God only as we forgive others. It is the love of God that draws us unto Him, and that love cannot touch our hearts without creating love for our brethren.

After completing the Lord's Prayer, Jesus added: "If ye forgive men their trespasses, your heavenly Father will also forgive you: but if ye forgive not men their trespasses, neither will your Father forgive your trespasses." He who is unforgiving cuts off the very channel through which alone he can receive mercy from God. We should not think that unless those who have injured us confess the wrong we are justified in withholding from them our forgiveness. It is their part, no doubt, to humble their hearts by repentance and confession; but we are to have a spirit of compassion toward those who have trespassed against us, whether or not they confess their faults. However sorely they may have wounded us, we are not to cherish our grievances and sympathize with ourselves over our injuries; but as we hope to be pardoned for our offenses against God we are to pardon all who have done evil to us.

But forgiveness has a broader meaning than many suppose. When God gives the promise that He "will abundantly pardon," He adds, as if the meaning of that promise exceeded all that we could comprehend: "My thoughts are not your thoughts, neither are your ways My ways, saith the Lord. For as the heavens are higher than the earth, so are My ways higher than your ways, and My thoughts than your thoughts." Isaiah 55:7–9. God's forgiveness is not merely a judicial act by which He sets us free from condemnation. It is not only forgiveness *for* sin, but reclaiming *from* sin. It is the outflow of redeeming love that transforms the heart. David had the true conception of forgiveness when he prayed, "Create in me a clean heart, O God; and renew a right spirit within me." Psalm 51:10. And again he says, "As far as the east is from the west, so far hath He removed our transgressions from us." Psalm 103:12.

God in Christ gave Himself for our sins. He suffered the cruel death of the cross, bore for us the burden of guilt, "the just for the unjust," that He might reveal to us His love and draw us to Himself. And He says, "Be ye kind one to another, tenderhearted, forgiving each other, even as God also in Christ forgave you." Ephesians 4:32, R.V. Let Christ, the divine Life, dwell in you and through you reveal the heaven-born love that will inspire hope in the hopeless and bring heaven's peace to the sin-stricken heart. As we come to God, this is the condition which meets us at the threshold, that, receiving mercy from Him, we yield ourselves to reveal His grace to others.

The one thing essential for us in order that we may receive and impart the forgiving love of God is to know and believe the love that He has to us. 1 John 4:16. Satan is working by every deception he can command, in order that we may not discern that love. He will lead us to think that our mistakes and transgressions have been so grievous that the Lord will not have respect unto our prayers and will not bless and save us. In ourselves we can see nothing but weakness, nothing to recommend us to God, and Satan tells us that it is of no use; we cannot remedy our defects of character. When we try to come to God, the enemy will whisper, It is of no use for you to pray; did not you do that evil thing? Have you not sinned against God and violated your own conscience? But we may tell the enemy that "the blood of Jesus Christ His Son cleanseth us from all sin." 1 John 1:7. When we feel that we have sinned and cannot pray, it is then the time to pray. Ashamed we may be and deeply humbled, but we must pray and believe. "This is a faithful saying, and worthy of all acceptation, that Christ Jesus came into the world to save sinners; of whom I am chief." 1 Timothy 1:15. Forgiveness, reconciliation with God, comes to us, not as a reward for our works, it is not bestowed because of the merit of sinful men, but it is a gift unto us, having in the spotless righteousness of Christ its foundation for bestowal.

We should not try to lessen our guilt by excusing sin. We must accept God's estimate of sin, and that is heavy indeed. Calvary alone can reveal the terrible enormity of sin. If we had to bear our own guilt, it would crush us. But the sinless One has taken our place; though undeserving, He has borne our iniquity. "If we confess our sins," God "is faithful and just to forgive us our sins, and to cleanse us from all unrighteousness." 1 John 1:9. Glorious truth!—just to His own law, and yet the Justifier of all that believe in Jesus. "Who is a God like unto Thee, that pardoneth iniquity, and passeth by the transgression of the remnant of His heritage? He retaineth not His anger forever, because He delighteth in mercy." Micah 7:18.

"Bring us not into temptation, but deliver us from the evil one." Matthew 6:13, R.V.

Temptation is enticement to sin, and this does not proceed from God, but from Satan and from the evil of our own hearts. "God cannot be tempted with evil, and He Himself tempteth no man." James 1:13, R.V.

Satan seeks to bring us into temptation, that the evil of our characters may be revealed before men and angels, that he may claim us as his own. In the symbolic prophecy of Zechariah, Satan is seen standing at the right hand of the Angel of the Lord, accusing Joshua, the high priest, who is clothed in filthy garments, and resisting the work that the Angel desires to do for him.

This represents the attitude of Satan toward every soul whom Christ is seeking to draw unto Himself. The enemy leads us into sin, and then he accuses us before the heavenly universe as unworthy of the love of God. But "the Lord said unto Satan, The Lord rebuke thee, O Satan; even the Lord that hath chosen Jerusalem rebuke thee: is not this a brand plucked out of the fire?" And unto Joshua He said, "Behold, I have caused thine iniquity to pass from thee, and I will clothe thee with change of raiment." Zechariah 3:1–4.

God in His great love is seeking to develop in us the precious graces of His Spirit. He permits us to encounter obstacles, persecution, and hardships, not as a curse, but as the greatest blessing of our lives. Every temptation resisted, every trial bravely borne, gives us a new experience and advances us in the work of character building. The soul that through divine power resists temptation reveals to the world and to the heavenly universe the efficiency of the grace of Christ.

But while we are not to be dismayed by trial, bitter though it be, we should pray that God will not permit us to be brought where we shall be drawn away by the desires of our own evil hearts. In offering the prayer that Christ has given, we surrender ourselves to the guidance of God, asking Him to lead us in safe paths. We cannot offer this prayer in sincerity, and yet decide to walk in any way of our own choosing. We shall wait for His hand to lead us; we shall listen to His voice, saying, "This is the way, walk ye in it." Isaiah 30:21.

It is not safe for us to linger to contemplate the advantages to be reaped through yielding to Satan's suggestions. Sin means dishonor and disaster to every soul that indulges in it; but it is blinding and deceiving in its nature, and it will entice us with flattering presentations. If we venture on Satan's ground we have no assurance of protection from his power. So far as in us lies, we should close every avenue by which the tempter may find access to us.

The prayer, "Bring us not into temptation," is itself a promise. If we commit ourselves to God we have the assurance, He "will not suffer you to be tempted above that ye are able; but will with the temptation also make a way to escape, that ye may be able to bear it." 1 Corinthians 10:13.

The only safeguard against evil is the indwelling of Christ in the heart through faith in His righteousness. It is because selfishness exists in our hearts that temptation has power over us. But when we behold the great love of God, selfishness appears to us in its hideous and repulsive character, and we desire to have it expelled from the soul. As the Holy Spirit glorifies Christ, our hearts are softened and subdued, the temptation loses its power, and the grace of Christ transforms the character.

Christ will never abandon the soul for whom He has died. The soul may leave Him and be overwhelmed with temptation, but Christ can never turn from one for whom He has paid the ransom of His own life. Could our spiritual vision be quickened, we should see souls bowed under oppression and burdened with grief, pressed as a cart beneath sheaves and ready to die in discouragement. We should see angels flying swiftly to aid these tempted ones, who are standing as on the brink of a precipice. The angels from heaven force back the hosts of evil that encompass these souls, and guide them to plant their feet on the sure foundation. The battles waging between the two armies are as real as those fought by the armies of this world, and on the issue of the spiritual conflict eternal destinies depend.

To us, as to Peter, the word is spoken, "Satan hath desired to have you, that he may sift you as wheat: but I have prayed for thee, that thy faith fail not." Luke 22:31, 32. Thank God, we are not left alone. He who "so loved the world, that He gave His only-begotten Son, that whosoever believeth in Him should not perish, but have everlasting life" (John 3:16), will not desert us in the battle with the adversary of God and man. "Behold," He says, "I give unto you power to tread on serpents and scorpions, and over all the power of the enemy: and nothing shall by any means hurt you." Luke 10:19.

Live in contact with the living Christ, and He will hold you firmly by a hand that will never let go. Know and believe the love that God has to us, and you are secure; that love is a fortress impregnable to all the delusions and assaults of Satan. "The name of the Lord is a strong tower: the righteous runneth into it, and is safe." Proverbs 18:10.

"Thine is the kingdom, and the power, and the glory." Matthew 6:13.

The last like the first sentence of the Lord's Prayer, points to our Father as above all power and authority and every name that is named. The Saviour beheld the years that stretched out before His disciples, not, as they had dreamed, lying in the sunshine of worldly prosperity and honor, but dark with the tempests of human hatred and satanic wrath. Amid national strife and ruin, the steps of the disciples would be beset with perils, and often their hearts would be oppressed by fear. They were to see Jerusalem a desolation, the temple swept away, its worship forever ended, and Israel scattered to all lands, like wrecks on a desert shore. Jesus said, "Ye shall hear of wars and rumors of wars." "Nation shall rise against nation, and kingdom against kingdom: and there shall be famines, and pestilences, and earthquakes, in divers places. All these are the beginning of sorrows." Matthew 24:6–8. Yet Christ's followers were not to fear that their hope was lost or that God had forsaken the earth. The power and the glory belong unto Him whose great purposes would still move on unthwarted toward their consummation. In the prayer that breathes their daily wants, the disciples of Christ were directed to look above all the power and dominion of evil, unto the Lord their God, whose kingdom ruleth over all and who is their Father and everlasting Friend.

The ruin of Jerusalem was a symbol of the final ruin that shall overwhelm the world. The prophecies that received a partial fulfillment in the overthrow of Jerusalem have a more direct application to the last days. We are now standing on the threshold of great and solemn events. A crisis is before us, such as the world has never witnessed. And sweetly to us, as to the first disciples, comes the assurance that God's kingdom ruleth over all. The program of coming events is in the hands of our Maker. The Majesty of heaven has the destiny of nations, as well as the concerns of His church, in His own charge. The divine Instructor is saying to every agent in the accomplishment of His plans, as He said to Cyrus, "I girded thee, though thou hast not known Me." Isaiah 45:5.

In the vision of the prophet Ezekiel there was the appearance of a hand beneath the wings of the cherubim. This is to teach His servants that it is divine power which gives them success. Those whom God employs as His messengers are not to feel that His work is dependent upon them. Finite beings are not left to carry this burden of responsibility. He who slumbers not, who is continually at work for the accomplishment of His designs, will carry forward His own work. He will thwart the purposes of wicked men, and will bring to confusion the counsels of those who plot mischief against His people. He who is the King, the Lord of hosts, sitteth between the cherubim, and amid the strife and tumult of nations He guards His children still. He who ruleth in the heavens is our Saviour. He measures every trial, He watches the furnace fire that must test every soul. When the strongholds of kings shall be overthrown, when the arrows of wrath shall strike through the hearts of His enemies, His people will be safe in His hands.

"Thine, O Lord, is the greatness, and the power, and the glory, and the victory, and the majesty: for all that is in the heaven and in the earth is Thine.... In Thine hand is power and might; and in Thine hand it is to make great, and to give strength unto all." 1 Chronicles 29:11, 12.

6
Not Judging, but Doing

"Judge not, that ye be not judged." Matthew 7:1.

The effort to earn salvation by one's own works inevitably leads men to pile up human exactions as a barrier against sin. For, seeing that they fail to keep the law, they will devise rules and regulations of their own to force themselves to obey. All this turns the mind away from God to self. His love dies out of the heart, and with it perishes love for his fellow men. A system of human invention, with its multitudinous exactions, will lead its advocates to judge all who come short of the prescribed human standard. The atmosphere of selfish and narrow criticism stifles the noble and generous emotions, and causes men to become self-centered judges and petty spies.

The Pharisees were of this class. They came forth from their religious services, not humbled with a sense of their own weakness, not grateful for the great privileges that God had given them. They came forth filled with spiritual pride, and their theme was, "Myself, my feelings, my knowledge, my ways." Their own attainments became the standard by which they judged others. Putting on the robes of self-dignity, they mounted the judgment seat to criticize and condemn.

The people partook largely of the same spirit, intruding upon the province of conscience and judging one another in matters that lay between the soul and God. It was in reference to this spirit and practice that Jesus said, "Judge not, that ye be not judged." That is, do not set yourself up as a standard. Do not make your opinions, your views of duty, your interpretations of Scripture, a criterion for others and in your heart condemn them if they do not come up to your ideal. Do not criticize others, conjecturing as to their motives and passing judgment upon them.

"Judge nothing before the time, until the Lord come, who both will bring to light the hidden things of darkness, and will make manifest the counsels of the hearts." 1 Corinthians 4:5. We cannot read the heart. Ourselves faulty, we are not qualified to sit in judgment upon others. Finite men can judge only from outward appearance. To Him alone who knows the secret springs of action, and who deals tenderly and compassionately, is it given to decide the case of every soul.

"Thou art inexcusable, O man, whosoever thou art that judgest: for wherein thou judgest another, thou condemnest thyself; for thou that judgest doest the same things." Romans 2:1. Thus those who condemn or criticize others, proclaim themselves guilty, for they do the same things. In condemning others, they are passing sentence upon themselves, and God declares that this sentence is just. He accepts their own verdict against themselves.

"These clumsy feet, still in the mire,
Go crushing blossoms without end;
These hard, well-meaning hands we thrust
Among the heartstrings of a friend."

"Why beholdest thou the mote that is in thy brother's eye?" Matthew 7:3.

Even the sentence, "Thou that judgest doest the same things," does not reach the magnitude of his sin who presumes to criticize and condemn his brother. Jesus said, "Why beholdest thou the mote that is in thy brother's eye, but considerest not the beam that is in thine own eye?"

His words describe one who is swift to discern a defect in others. When he thinks he has detected a flaw in the character or the life he is exceedingly zealous in trying to point it out; but Jesus declares that the very trait of character developed in doing this un-Christlike work, is, in comparison with the fault criticized, as a beam in proportion to a mote. It is one's own lack of the spirit of forbearance and love that leads him to make a world of an atom. Those who have never experienced the contrition of an entire surrender to Christ do not in their life make manifest the softening influence of the Saviour's love. They misrepresent the gentle, courteous spirit of the gospel and wound precious souls, for whom Christ died. According to the figure that our Saviour uses, he who indulges a censorious spirit is guilty of greater sin than is the one he accuses, for he not only commits the same sin, but adds to it conceit and censoriousness.

Christ is the only true standard of character, and he who sets himself up as a standard for others is putting himself in the place of Christ. And since the Father "hath committed all judgment unto the Son" (John 5:22), whoever presumes to judge the motives of others is again usurping the prerogative of the Son of God. These would-be judges and critics are placing themselves on the side of antichrist, "who opposeth and exalteth himself above all that is called God, or that is worshiped; so that he as God sitteth in the temple of God, showing himself that he is God." 2 Thessalonians 2:4.

The sin that leads to the most unhappy results is the cold, critical, unforgiving spirit that characterizes Pharisaism. When the religious experience is devoid of love, Jesus is not there; the sunshine of His presence is not there. No busy activity or Christless zeal can supply the lack. There may be a wonderful keenness of perception to discover the defects of others; but to everyone who indulges this spirit, Jesus says, "Thou hypocrite, first cast out the beam out of thine own eye; and then shalt thou see clearly to cast out the mote out of thy brother's eye." He who is guilty of wrong is the first to suspect wrong. By condemning another he is trying to conceal or excuse the evil of his own heart. It was through sin that men gained the knowledge of evil; no sooner had the first pair sinned than they began to accuse each other; and this is what human nature will inevitably do when uncontrolled by the grace of Christ.

When men indulge this accusing spirit, they are not satisfied with pointing out what they suppose to be a defect in their brother. If milder means fail of making him do what they think ought to be done, they will resort to compulsion. Just as far as lies in their power they will force men to comply with their ideas of what is right. This is what the Jews did in the days of Christ and what the church has done ever since whenever she has lost the grace of Christ. Finding herself destitute of the power of love, she has reached out for the strong arm of the state to enforce her dogmas and execute her decrees. Here is the secret of all religious laws that have ever been enacted, and the secret of all persecution from the days of Abel to our own time.

Christ does not drive but draws men unto Him. The only compulsion which He employs is the constraint of love. When the church begins to seek for the support of secular power, it is evident that she is devoid of the power of Christ—the constraint of divine love.

But the difficulty lies with the individual members of the church, and it is here that the cure must be wrought. Jesus bids the accuser first cast the beam out of his own eye, renounce his censorious spirit, confess and forsake his own sin, before trying to correct others. For "a good tree bringeth not forth corrupt fruit; neither doth a corrupt tree bring forth good fruit." Luke 6:43. This accusing spirit which you indulge is evil fruit, and shows that the tree is evil. It is useless for you to build yourselves up in self-righteousness. What you need is a change of heart. You must have this experience before you are fitted to correct others; for "out of the abundance of the heart the mouth speaketh." Matthew 12:34.

When a crisis comes in the life of any soul, and you attempt to give counsel or admonition, your words will have only the weight of influence for good that your own example and spirit have gained for you. You must *be* good before you can *do* good. You cannot exert an influence that will transform others until your own heart has been humbled and refined and made tender by the grace of Christ. When this change has been wrought in you, it will be as natural for you to live to bless others as it is for the rosebush to yield its fragrant bloom or the vine its purple clusters.

If Christ is in you "the hope of glory," you will have no disposition to watch others, to expose their errors. Instead of seeking to accuse and condemn, it will be your object to help, to bless, and to save. In dealing with those who are in error, you will heed the injunction, Consider "thyself, lest thou also be tempted." Galatians 6:1. You will call to mind the many times you have erred and how hard it was to find the right way when you had once left it. You will not push your brother into greater darkness, but with a heart full of pity will tell him of his danger.

He who looks often upon the cross of Calvary, remembering that his sins placed the Saviour there, will never try to estimate the degree of his guilt in comparison with that of others. He will not climb upon the judgment seat to bring accusation against another. There can be no spirit of criticism or self-exaltation on the part of those who walk in the shadow of Calvary's cross.

Not until you feel that you could sacrifice your own self-dignity, and even lay down your life in order to save an erring brother, have you cast the beam out of your own eye so that you are prepared to help your brother. Then you can approach him and touch his heart. No one has ever been reclaimed from a wrong position by censure and reproach; but many have thus been driven from Christ and led to seal their hearts against conviction. A tender spirit, a gentle, winning deportment, may save the erring and hide a multitude of sins. The revelation of Christ in your own character will have a transforming power upon all with whom you come in contact. Let Christ be daily made manifest in you, and He will reveal through you the creative energy of His word—a gentle, persuasive, yet mighty influence to re-create other souls in the beauty of the Lord our God.

"Give not that which is holy unto the dogs," Matthew 7:6 .

Jesus here refers to a class who have no desire to escape from the slavery of sin. By indulgence in the corrupt and vile their natures have become so degraded that they cling to the evil and will not be separated from it. The servants of Christ should not allow themselves to be hindered by those who would make the gospel only a matter of contention and ridicule.

But the Saviour never passed by one soul, however sunken in sin, who was willing to receive the precious truths of heaven. To publicans and harlots His words were the beginning of a new life. Mary Magdalene, out of whom He cast seven devils, was the last at the Saviour's tomb and the first whom He greeted in the morning of His resurrection. It was Saul of Tarsus, one of the most determined enemies of the gospel, who became Paul the devoted minister of Christ. Beneath an appearance of hatred and contempt, even beneath crime and degradation, may be hidden a soul that the grace of Christ will rescue to shine as a jewel in the Redeemer's crown.

"Ask, and it shall be given you; seek, and ye shall find; knock, and it shall be opened unto you." Matthew 7:7.

To leave no chance for unbelief, misunderstanding, or misinterpretation of His words, the Lord repeats the thrice-given promise. He longs to have those who would seek after God believe in Him who is able to do all things. Therefore He adds, "For everyone that asketh receiveth; and he that seeketh findeth; and to him that knocketh it shall be opened."

The Lord specifies no conditions except that you hunger for His mercy, desire His counsel, and long for His love. "Ask." The asking, makes it manifest that you realize your necessity; and if you ask in faith you will receive. The Lord has pledged His word, and it cannot fail. If you come with true contrition you need not feel that you are presumptuous in asking for what the Lord has promised. When you ask for the blessings you need, that you may perfect a character after Christ's likeness, the Lord assures you that you are asking according to a promise that will be verified. That you feel and know you are a sinner is sufficient ground for asking for His mercy and compassion. The condition upon which you may come to God is not that you shall be holy, but that you desire Him to cleanse you from all sin and purify you from all iniquity. The argument that we may plead now and ever is our great need, our utterly helpless state, that makes Him and His redeeming power a necessity.

"Seek." Desire not merely His blessing, but Himself. "Acquaint now thyself with Him, and be at peace." Job 22:21. Seek, and you shall find. God is seeking you, and the very desire you feel to come to Him is but the drawing of His Spirit. Yield to that drawing. Christ is pleading the cause of the tempted, the erring, and the faithless. He is seeking to lift them into companionship with Himself. "If thou seek Him, He will be found of thee." 1 Chronicles 28:9.

"Knock." We come to God by special invitation, and He waits to welcome us to His audience chamber. The first disciples who followed Jesus were not satisfied with a hurried conversation with Him by the way; they said, "Rabbi,...where dwellest Thou?... They came and saw where He dwelt, and abode with Him that day." John 1:38, 39. So we may be admitted into closest intimacy and communion with God. "He that dwelleth in the secret place of the Most High shall abide under the shadow of the Almighty." Psalm 91:1. Let those who desire the blessing of God knock and wait at the door of mercy with firm assurance, saying, For Thou, O Lord, hast said, "Everyone that asketh receiveth; and he that seeketh findeth; and to him that knocketh it shall be opened."

Jesus looked upon those who were assembled to hear His words, and earnestly desired that the great multitude might appreciate the mercy and loving-kindness of God. As an illustration of their need, and of God's willingness to give, He presents before them a hungry child asking his earthly parent for bread. "What man is there of *you*," He said, "whom if his son ask bread, will he give him a stone?" He appeals to the tender, natural affection of a parent for his child and then says, "If ye then, being evil, know how to give good gifts unto your children, how much more shall your Father which is in heaven give good things to them that ask Him?" No man with a father's heart would turn from his son who is hungry and is asking for bread. Would they think him capable of trifling with his child, of tantalizing him by raising his expectations only to disappoint him? Would he promise to give him good and nourishing food, and then give him a stone? And should anyone dishonor God by imagining that He would not respond to the appeals of His children?

If ye, then, being human and evil, "know how to give good gifts unto your children: how much more shall your heavenly Father give the Holy Spirit to them that ask Him?" Luke 11:13. The Holy Spirit, the representative of Himself, is the greatest of all gifts. All "good things" are comprised in this. The Creator Himself can give us nothing greater, nothing better. When we beseech the Lord to pity us in our distress, and to guide us by His Holy Spirit, He will never turn away our prayer. It is possible even for a parent to turn away from his hungry child, but God can never reject the cry of the needy and longing heart. With what wonderful tenderness He has described His love! To those who in days of darkness feel that God is unmindful of them, this is the message from the Father's heart: "Zion said, The Lord hath forsaken me, and my Lord hath forgotten me. Can a woman forget her sucking child, that she should not have compassion on the son of her womb? Yea, they may forget, yet will I not forget thee. Behold, I have graven thee upon the palms of My hands." Isaiah 49:14–16.

Every promise in the word of God furnishes us with subject matter for prayer, presenting the pledged word of Jehovah as our assurance. Whatever spiritual blessing we need, it is our privilege to claim through Jesus. We may tell the Lord, with the simplicity of a child, exactly what we need. We may state to Him our temporal matters, asking Him for bread and raiment as well as for the bread of life and the robe of Christ's righteousness. Your heavenly Father knows that you have need of all these things, and you are invited to ask Him concerning them. It is through the name of Jesus that every favor is received. God will honor that name, and will supply your necessities from the riches of His liberality.

But do not forget that in coming to God as a father you acknowledge your relation to Him as a child. You not only trust His goodness, but in all things yield to His will, knowing that His love is changeless. You give yourself to do His work. It was to those whom He had bidden to seek first the kingdom of God and His righteousness that Jesus gave the promise, "Ask, and ye shall receive." John 16:24.

The gifts of Him who has all power in heaven and earth are in store for the children of God. Gifts so precious that they come to us through the costly sacrifice of the Redeemer's blood; gifts that will satisfy the deepest craving of the heart, gifts lasting as eternity, will be received and enjoyed by all who will come to God as little children. Take God's promises as your own, plead them before Him as His own words, and you will receive fullness of joy.

"Therefore all things whatsoever ye would that men should do to you, do ye even so to them." Matthew 7:12.

On the assurance of the love of God toward us, Jesus enjoins love to one another, in one comprehensive principle covering all the relations of human fellowship.

The Jews had been concerned about what they should receive; the burden of their anxiety was to secure what they thought their due of power and respect and service. But Christ teaches that our anxiety should not be, How much are we to receive? but, How much can we give? The standard of our obligation to others is found in what we ourselves would regard as their obligation to us.

In your association with others, put yourself in their place. Enter into their feelings, their difficulties, their disappointments, their joys, and their sorrows. Identify yourself with them, and then do to them as, were you to exchange places with them, you would wish them to deal with you. This is the true rule of honesty. It is another expression of the law. "Thou shalt love thy neighbor as thyself." Matthew 22:39. And it is the substance of the teaching of the prophets. It is a principle of heaven, and will be developed in all who are fitted for its holy companionship.

The golden rule is the principle of true courtesy, and its truest illustration is seen in the life and character of Jesus. Oh, what rays of softness and beauty shone forth in the daily life of our Saviour! What sweetness flowed from His very presence! The same spirit will be revealed in His children. Those with whom Christ dwells will be surrounded with a divine atmosphere. Their white robes of purity will be fragrant with perfume from the garden of the Lord. Their faces will reflect light from His, brightening the path for stumbling and weary feet.

No man who has the true ideal of what constitutes a perfect character will fail to manifest the sympathy and tenderness of Christ. The influence of grace is to soften the heart, to refine and purify the feelings, giving a heaven-born delicacy and sense of propriety.

But there is a yet deeper significance to the golden rule. Everyone who has been made a steward of the manifold grace of God is called upon to impart to souls in ignorance and darkness, even as, were he in their place, he would desire them to impart to him. The apostle Paul said, "I am debtor both to the Greeks, and to the barbarians; both to the wise, and to the unwise." Romans 1:14. By all that you have known of the love of God, by all that you have received of the rich gifts of His grace above the most benighted and degraded soul upon the earth are you in debt to that soul to impart these gifts unto him.

So also with the gifts and blessings of this life: whatever you may possess above your fellows places you in debt, to that degree, to all who are less favored. Have we wealth, or even the comforts of life, then we are under the most solemn obligation to care for the suffering sick, the widow, and the fatherless exactly as we would desire them to care for us were our condition and theirs to be reversed.

The golden rule teaches, by implication, the same truth which is taught elsewhere in the Sermon on the Mount, that "with what measure ye mete, it shall be measured to you again." That which we do to others, whether it be good or evil, will surely react upon ourselves, in blessing or in cursing. Whatever we give, we shall receive again. The earthly blessings which we impart to others may be, and often are, repaid in kind. What we give does, in time of need, often come back to us in fourfold measure in the coin of the realm. But, besides this, all gifts are repaid, even in this life, in the fuller inflowing of His love, which is the sum of all heaven's glory and its treasure. And evil imparted also returns again. Everyone who has been free to condemn or discourage, will in his own experience be brought over the ground where he has caused others to pass; he will feel what they have suffered because of his want of sympathy and tenderness.

It is the love of God toward us that has decreed this. He would lead us to abhor our own hardness of heart and to open our hearts to let Jesus abide in them. And thus, out of evil, good is brought, and what appeared a curse becomes a blessing.

The standard of the golden rule is the true standard of Christianity; anything short of it is a deception. A religion that leads men to place a low estimate upon human beings, whom Christ has esteemed of such value as to give Himself for them; a religion that would lead us to be careless of human needs, sufferings, or rights, is a spurious religion. In slighting the claims of the poor, the suffering, and the sinful, we are proving ourselves traitors to Christ. It is because men take upon themselves the name of Christ, while in life they deny His character, that Christianity has so little power in the world. The name of the Lord is blasphemed because of these things.

Of the apostolic church, in those bright days when the glory of the risen Christ shone upon them, it is written that no man said "that aught of the things which he possessed was his own." "Neither was there any among them that lacked." "And with great power gave the apostles witness of the resurrection of the Lord Jesus: and great grace was upon them all." "And they, continuing daily with one accord in the temple, and breaking bread from house to house, did eat their meat with gladness and singleness of heart, praising God, and having favor with all the people. And the Lord added to the church daily such as should be saved." Acts 4:32, 34, 33; 2:46, 47.

Search heaven and earth, and there is no truth revealed more powerful than that which is made manifest in works of mercy to those who need our sympathy and aid. This is the truth as it is in Jesus. When those who profess the name of Christ shall practice the principles of the golden rule, the same power will attend the gospel as in apostolic times.

"Strait is the gate, and narrow is the way, which leadeth unto life." Matthew 7:14.

In the time of Christ the people of Palestine lived in walled towns, which were mostly situated upon hills or mountains. The gates, which were closed at sunset, were approached by steep, rocky roads, and the traveler journeying homeward at the close of the day often had to press his way in eager haste up the difficult ascent in order to reach the gate before nightfall. The loiterer was left without.

The narrow, upward road leading to home and rest furnished Jesus with an impressive figure of the Christian way. The path which I have set before you, He said, is narrow; the gate is difficult of entrance; for the golden rule excludes all pride and self-seeking. There is, indeed, a wider road; but its end is destruction. If you would climb the path of spiritual life, you must constantly ascend; for it is an upward way. You must go with the few; for the multitude will choose the downward path.

In the road to death the whole race may go, with all their worldliness, all their selfishness, all their pride, dishonesty, and moral debasement. There is room for every man's opinions and doctrines, space to follow his inclinations, to do whatever his self-love may dictate. In order to go in the path that leads to destruction, there is no need of searching for the way; for the gate is wide, and the way is broad, and the feet naturally turn into the path that ends in death.

But the way to life is narrow and the entrance strait. If you cling to any besetting sin you will find the way too narrow for you to enter. Your own ways, your own will, your evil habits and practices, must be given up if you would keep the way of the Lord. He who would serve Christ cannot follow the world's opinions or meet the world's standard. Heaven's path is too narrow for rank and riches to ride in state, too narrow for the play of self-centered ambition, too steep and rugged for lovers of ease to climb. Toil, patience, self-sacrifice, reproach, poverty, the contradiction of sinners against Himself, was the portion of Christ, and it must be our portion, if we ever enter the Paradise of God.

Yet do not therefore conclude that the upward path is the hard and the downward road the easy way. All along the road that leads to death there are pains and penalties, there are sorrows and disappointments, there are warnings not to go on. God's love has made it hard for the heedless and headstrong to destroy themselves. It is true that Satan's path is made to appear attractive, but it is all a deception; in the way of evil there are bitter remorse and cankering care. We may think it pleasant to follow pride and worldly ambition, but the end is pain and sorrow. Selfish plans may present flattering promises and hold out the hope of enjoyment, but we shall find that our happiness is poisoned and our life embittered by hopes that center in self. In the downward road the gateway may be bright with flowers, but thorns are in the path. The light of hope which shines from its entrance fades into the darkness of despair, and the soul who follows that path descends into the shadows of unending night.

"The way of transgressors is hard," but wisdom's "ways are ways of pleasantness and all her paths are peace." Proverbs 13:15; 3:17. Every act of obedience to Christ, every act of self-denial for His sake, every trial well endured, every victory gained over temptation, is a step in the march to the glory of final victory. If we take Christ for our guide, He will lead us safely. The veriest sinner need not miss his way. Not one trembling seeker need fail of walking in pure and holy light. Though the path is so narrow, so holy that sin cannot be tolerated therein, yet access has been secured for all, and not one doubting, trembling soul need say, "God cares nought for me."

The road may be rough and the ascent steep; there may be pitfalls upon the right hand and upon the left; we may have to endure toil in our journey; when weary, when longing for rest, we may have to toil on; when faint, we may have to fight; when discouraged, we must still hope; but with Christ as our guide we shall not fail of reaching the desired haven at last. Christ Himself has trodden the rough way before us and has smoothed the path for our feet.

And all the way up the steep road leading to eternal life are well-springs of joy to refresh the weary. Those who walk in wisdom's ways are, even in tribulation, exceeding joyful; for He whom their soul loveth, walks, invisible, beside them. At each upward step they discern more distinctly the touch of His hand; at every step brighter gleamings of glory from the Unseen fall upon their path; and their songs of praise, reaching ever a higher note, ascend to join the songs of angels before the throne. "The path of the righteous is as the light of dawn, that shineth more and more unto the perfect day." Proverbs 4:18, R.V., margin.

"Strive to enter in at the strait gate." Luke 13:24.

The belated traveler, hurrying to reach the city gate by the going down of the sun, could not turn aside for any attractions by the way. His whole mind was bent on the one purpose of entering the gate. The same intensity of purpose, said Jesus, is required in the Christian life. I have opened to you the glory of character, which is the true glory of My kingdom. It offers you no promise of earthly dominion; yet it is worthy of your supreme desire and effort. I do not call you to battle for the supremacy of the world's great empire, but do not therefore conclude that there is no battle to be fought nor victories to be won. I bid you strive, agonize, to enter into My spiritual kingdom.

The Christian life is a battle and a march. But the victory to be gained is not won by human power. The field of conflict is the domain of the heart. The battle which we have to fight—the greatest battle that was ever fought by man—is the surrender of self to the will of God, the yielding of the heart to the sovereignty of love. The old nature, born of blood and of the will of the flesh, cannot inherit the kingdom of God. The hereditary tendencies, the former habits, must be given up.

He who determines to enter the spiritual kingdom will find that all the powers and passions of an unregenerate nature, backed by the forces of the kingdom of darkness, are arrayed against him. Selfishness and pride will make a stand against anything that would show them to be sinful. We cannot, of ourselves, conquer the evil desires and habits that strive for the mastery. We cannot overcome the mighty foe who holds us in his thrall. God alone can give us the victory. He desires us to have the mastery over ourselves, our own will and ways. But He cannot work in us without our consent and co-operation. The divine Spirit works through the faculties and powers given to man. Our energies are required to co-operate with God.

The victory is not won without much earnest prayer, without the humbling of self at every step. Our will is not to be forced into co-operation with divine agencies, but it must be voluntarily submitted. Were it possible to force upon you with a hundredfold greater intensity the influence of the Spirit of God, it would not make you a Christian, a fit subject for heaven. The stronghold of Satan would not be broken. The will must be placed on the side of God's will. You are not able, of yourself, to bring your purposes and desires and inclinations into submission to the will of God; but if you are "willing to be made willing," God will accomplish the work for you, even "casting down imaginations, and every high thing that exalteth itself against the knowledge of God, and bringing into captivity every thought to the obedience of Christ." 2 Corinthians 10:5. Then you will "work out your own salvation with fear and trembling. For it is God which worketh in you both to will and to do of His good pleasure." Philippians 2:12, 13.

But many are attracted by the beauty of Christ and the glory of heaven, who yet shrink from the conditions by which alone these can become their own. There are many in the broad way who are not fully satisfied with the path in which they walk. They long to break from the slavery of sin, and in their own strength they seek to make a stand against their sinful practices. They look toward the narrow way and the strait gate; but selfish pleasure, love of the world, pride, unsanctified ambition, place a barrier between them and the Saviour. To renounce their own will, their chosen objects of affection or pursuit, requires a sacrifice at which they hesitate and falter and turn back. Many "will seek to enter in, and shall not be able." Luke 13:24. They desire the good, they make some effort to obtain it; but they do not choose it; they have not a settled purpose to secure it at the cost of all things.

The only hope for us if we would overcome is to unite our will to God's will and work in co-operation with Him, hour by hour and day by day. We cannot retain self and yet enter the kingdom of God. If we ever attain unto holiness, it will be through the renunciation of self and the reception of the mind of Christ. Pride and self-sufficiency must be crucified. Are we willing to pay the price required of us? Are we willing to have our will brought into perfect conformity to the will of God? Until we are willing, the transforming grace of God cannot be manifest upon us.

The warfare which we are to wage is the "good fight of faith." "I also labor," said the apostle Paul, "striving according to His working, which worketh in me mightily." Colossians 1:29.

Jacob, in the great crisis of his life, turned aside to pray. He was filled with one overmastering purpose—to seek for transformation of character. But while he was pleading with God, an enemy, as he supposed, placed his hand upon him, and all night he wrestled for his life. But the purpose of his soul was not changed by peril of life itself. When his strength was nearly spent, the Angel put forth His divine power, and at His touch Jacob knew Him with whom he had been contending. Wounded and helpless, he fell upon the Saviour's breast, pleading for a blessing. He would not be turned aside nor cease his intercession, and Christ granted the petition of this helpless, penitent soul, according to His promise, "Let him take hold of My strength, that he may make peace with Me; and he shall make peace with Me." Isaiah 27:5. Jacob pleaded with determined spirit, "I will not let Thee go, except Thou bless me." Genesis 32:26. This spirit of persistence was inspired by Him who wrestled with the patriarch. It was He who gave him the victory, and He changed his name from Jacob to Israel, saying, "As a prince hast thou power with God and with men, and hast prevailed." Genesis 32:28. That for which Jacob had vainly wrestled in his own strength was won through self-surrender and steadfast faith. "This is the victory that overcometh the world, even our faith." 1 John 5:4.

"Beware of false prophets." Matthew 7:15.

Teachers of falsehood will arise to draw you away from the narrow path and the strait gate. Beware of them; though concealed in sheep's clothing, inwardly they are ravening wolves. Jesus gives a test by which false teachers may be distinguished from the true. "Ye shall know them by their fruits," He says. "Do men gather grapes of thorns, or figs of thistles?"

We are not bidden to prove them by their fair speeches and exalted professions. They are to be judged by the word of God. "To the law and to the testimony: if they speak not according to this word it is because there is no light in them." "Cease, my son, to hear the instruction that causeth to err from the words of knowledge." Isaiah 8:20; Proverbs 19:27. What message do these teachers bring? Does it lead you to reverence and fear God? Does it lead you to manifest your love for Him by loyalty to His commandments? If men do not feel the weight of the moral law; if they make light of God's precepts; if they break one of the least of His commandments, and teach men so, they shall be of no esteem in the sight of heaven. We may know that their claims are without foundation. They are doing the very work that originated with the prince of darkness, the enemy of God.

Not all who profess His name and wear His badge are Christ's. Many who have taught in My name, said Jesus, will be found wanting at last. "Many will say to Me in that day, Lord, Lord, have we not prophesied in Thy name? and in Thy name have cast out devils? and in Thy name done many wonderful works? And then will I profess unto them, I never knew you: depart from Me, ye that work iniquity."

There are persons who believe that they are right, when they are wrong. While claiming Christ as their Lord, and professedly doing great works in His name, they are workers of iniquity. "With their mouth they show much love, but their heart goeth after their covetousness." He who declares God's word is to them "as a very lovely song of one that hath a pleasant voice, and can play well on an instrument: for they hear Thy words, but they do them not." Ezekiel 33:31, 32.

A mere profession of discipleship is of no value. The faith in Christ which saves the soul is not what it is represented to be by many. "Believe, believe," they say, "and you need not keep the law." But a belief that does not lead to obedience is presumption. The apostle John says, "He that saith, I know Him, and keepeth not His commandments, is a liar, and the truth is not in him." 1 John 2:4. Let none cherish the idea that special providences or miraculous manifestations are to be the proof of the genuineness of their work or of the ideas they advocate. When persons will speak lightly of the word of God, and set their impressions, feelings, and exercises above the divine standard, we may know that they have no light in them.

Obedience is the test of discipleship. It is the keeping of the commandments that proves the sincerity of our professions of love. When the doctrine we accept kills sin in the heart, purifies the soul from defilement, bears fruit unto holiness, we may know that it is the truth of God. When benevolence, kindness, tenderheartedness, sympathy, are manifest in our lives; when the joy of right doing is in our hearts; when we exalt Christ, and not self, we may know that our faith is of the right order. "Hereby we do know that we know Him, if we keep His commandments." 1 John 2:3.

"It fell not; for it was founded upon the rock." Matthew 7:25, R.V.

The people had been deeply moved by the words of Christ. The divine beauty of the principles of truth attracted them; and Christ's solemn warnings had come to them as the voice of the heart-searching God. His words had struck at the very root of their former ideas and opinions; to obey His teaching would require a change in all their habits of thought and action. It would bring them into collision with their religious teachers; for it would involve the overthrow of the whole structure which for generations the rabbis had been rearing. Therefore, while the hearts of the people responded to His words, few were ready to accept them as the guide of life.

Jesus ended His teaching on the mount with an illustration that presented with startling vividness the importance of putting in practice the words He had spoken. Among the crowds that thronged about the Saviour were many who had spent their lives about the Sea of Galilee. As they sat upon the hillside, listening to the words of Christ, they could see valleys and ravines through which the mountain streams found their way to the sea. In summer these streams often wholly disappeared, leaving only a dry and dusty channel. But when the wintry storms burst upon the hills, the rivers became fierce, raging torrents, at times overspreading the valleys and bearing everything away on their resistless flood. Often, then, the hovels reared by the peasants on the grassy plain, apparently beyond the reach of danger, were swept away. But high upon the hills were houses built upon the rock. In some parts of the land were dwellings built wholly of rock, and many of them had withstood the tempests of a thousand years. These houses were reared with toil and difficulty. They were not easy of access, and their location appeared less inviting than the grassy plain. But they were founded upon the rock, and wind and flood and tempest beat upon them in vain.

Like the builders of these houses on the rock, said Jesus, is he who shall receive the words that I have spoken to you, and make them the foundation of his character and life. Centuries before, the prophet Isaiah had written, "The word of our God shall stand forever" (Isaiah 40:8); and Peter, long after the Sermon on the Mount was given, quoting these words of Isaiah added, "This is the word which by the gospel is preached unto you" (1 Peter 1:25). The word of God is the only steadfast thing our world knows. It is the sure foundation. "Heaven and earth shall pass away," said Jesus, "but My words shall not pass away." Matthew 24:35.

The great principles of the law, of the very nature of God, are embodied in the words of Christ on the mount. Whoever builds upon them is building upon Christ, the Rock of Ages. In receiving the word, we receive Christ. And only those who thus receive His words are building upon Him. "Other foundation can no man lay than that is laid, which is Jesus Christ." 1 Corinthians 3:11. "There is none other name under heaven, given among men, whereby we must be saved." Acts 4:12. Christ, the Word, the revelation of God—the manifestation of His character, His law, His love, His life—is the only foundation upon which we can build a character that will endure.

We build on Christ by obeying His word. It is not he who merely enjoys righteousness, that is righteous, but he who does righteousness. Holiness is not rapture; it is the result of surrendering all to God; it is doing the will of our heavenly Father. When the children of Israel were encamped on the borders of the Promised Land, it was not enough for them to have a knowledge of Canaan, or to sing the songs of Canaan. This alone would not bring them into possession of the vineyards and olive groves of the goodly land. They could make it theirs in truth only by occupation, by complying with the conditions, by exercising living faith in God, by appropriating His promises to themselves, while they obeyed His instruction.

Religion consists in doing the words of Christ; not doing to earn God's favor, but because, all undeserving, we have received the gift of His love. Christ places the salvation of man, not upon profession merely, but upon faith that is made manifest in works of righteousness. Doing, not saying merely, is expected of the followers of Christ. It is through action that character is built. "As many as are *led* by the Spirit of God, they are the sons of God." Romans 8:14. Not those whose hearts are touched by the Spirit, not those who now and then yield to its power, but they that are led by the Spirit, are the sons of God.

Do you desire to become a follower of Christ, yet know not how to begin? Are you in darkness and know not how to find the light? Follow the light you have. Set your heart to obey what you do know of the word of God. His power, His very life, dwells in His word. As you receive the word in faith, it will give you power to obey. As you give heed to the light you have, greater light will come. You are building on God's word, and your character will be builded after the similitude of the character of Christ.

Christ, the true foundation, is a living stone; His life is imparted to all that are built upon Him. "Ye also, as living stones, are built up a spiritual house." "Each several building, fitly framed together, groweth into a holy temple in the Lord." 1 Peter 2:5, R.V.; Ephesians 2:21, R.V. The stones became one with the foundation; for a common life dwells in all. That building no tempest can overthrow; for—

"That which shares the life of God,
With Him surviveth all."

But every building erected on other foundation than God's word will fall. He who, like the Jews in Christ's day, builds on the foundation of human ideas and opinions, of forms and ceremonies of man's invention, or on any works that he can do independently of the grace of Christ, is erecting his structure of character upon the shifting sand. The fierce tempests of temptation will sweep away the sandy foundation and leave his house a wreck on the shores of time.

"Therefore thus saith the Lord God,…Judgment also will I lay to the line, and righteousness to the plummet: and the hail shall sweep away the refuge of lies, and the waters shall overflow the hiding place." Isaiah 28:16, 17.

But today mercy pleads with the sinner. "As I live, saith the Lord God, I have no pleasure in the death of the wicked; but that the wicked turn from his way and live: turn ye, turn ye from your evil ways; for why will ye die?" Ezekiel 33:11. The voice that speaks to the impenitent today is the voice of Him who in heart anguish exclaimed as He beheld the city of His love: "O Jerusalem, Jerusalem, which killeth the prophets, and stoneth them that are sent unto her! how often would I have gathered thy children together, even as a hen gathereth her own brood under her wings, and ye would not! Behold, your house is left unto you desolate." Luke 13:34, 35, R.V. In Jerusalem, Jesus beheld a symbol of the world that had rejected and despised His grace. He was weeping, O stubborn heart, for you! Even when Jesus' tears were shed upon the mount, Jerusalem might yet have repented, and escaped her doom. For a little space the Gift of heaven still waited her acceptance. So, O heart, to you Christ is still speaking in accents of love: "Behold, I stand at the door, and knock: if any man hear My voice, and open the door, I will come in to him, and will sup with him, and he with Me." "Now is the accepted time; behold, now is the day of salvation." Revelation 3:20; 2 Corinthians 6:2.

You who are resting your hope on self are building on the sand. But it is not yet too late to escape the impending ruin. Before the tempest breaks, flee to the sure foundation. "Thus saith the Lord God, Behold, I lay in Zion for a foundation a stone, a tried stone, a precious cornerstone, of sure foundation: he that believeth shall not make haste." "Look unto Me, and be ye saved, all the ends of the earth: for I am God, and there is none else." "Fear thou not; for I am with thee: be not dismayed; for I am thy God: I will strengthen thee; yea, I will help thee; yea, I will uphold thee with the right hand of My righteousness." "Ye shall not be ashamed nor confounded world without end." Isaiah 28:16, R.V.; 45:22; 41:10; 45:17.

Index to Scripture References

Page numbers in this index refer to bracketed numbers at the bottom of each page.

Jeremiah

Lamentations

Ezekiel

Daniel

Hosea

Joel

Micah

Zechariah

Malachi

Matthew

Page numbers in this index refer to bracketed numbers at the bottom of each page.

Mark

Luke

John

Acts

Romans

I Corinthians

II Corinthians

Galatians

Ephesians

Philippians

Colossians

I Thessalonians

II Thessalonians

I Timothy

Titus

Hebrews

James

I Peter

II Peter

I John

Jude

Revelation

Page numbers in this index refer to bracketed numbers at the bottom of each page.

Christ's Object Lessons

1
Teaching in Parables

In Christ's parable teaching the same principle is seen as in His own mission to the world. That we might become acquainted with His divine character and life, Christ took our nature and dwelt among us. Divinity was revealed in humanity; the invisible glory in the visible human form. Men could learn of the unknown through the known; heavenly things were revealed through the earthly; God was made manifest in the likeness of men. So it was in Christ's teaching: the unknown was illustrated by the known; divine truths by earthly things with which the people were most familiar.

The Scripture says, "All these things spake Jesus unto the multitude in parables;...that it might be fulfilled which was spoken by the prophet, saying, I will open My mouth in parables; I will utter things which have been kept secret from the foundation of the world." Matthew 13:34, 35. Natural things were the medium for the spiritual; the things of nature and the life-experience of His hearers were connected with the truths of the written word. Leading thus from the natural to the spiritual kingdom, Christ's parables are links in the chain of truth that unites man with God, and earth with heaven.

In His teaching from nature, Christ was speaking of the things which His own hands had made, and which had qualities and powers that He Himself had imparted. In their original perfection all created things were an expression of the thought of God. To Adam and Eve in their Eden home nature was full of the knowledge of God, teeming with divine instruction. Wisdom spoke to the eye and was received into the heart; for they communed with God in His created works. As soon as the holy pair transgressed the law of the Most High, the brightness from the face of God departed from the face of nature. The earth is now marred and defiled by sin. Yet even in its blighted state much that is beautiful remains. God's object lessons are not obliterated; rightly understood, nature speaks of her Creator.

In the days of Christ these lessons had been lost sight of. Men had well-nigh ceased to discern God in His works. The sinfulness of humanity had cast a pall over the fair face of creation; and instead of manifesting God, His works became a barrier that concealed Him. Men "worshiped and served the creature more than the Creator." Thus the heathen "became vain in their imaginations, and their foolish heart was darkened." Romans 1:25, 21. So in Israel, man's teaching had been put in the place of God's. Not only the things of nature, but the sacrificial service and the Scriptures themselves—all given to reveal God—were so perverted that they became the means of concealing Him.

Christ sought to remove that which obscured the truth. The veil that sin has cast over the face of nature, He came to draw aside, bringing to view the spiritual glory that all things were created to reflect. His words placed the teachings of nature as well as of the Bible in a new aspect, and made them a new revelation.

Jesus plucked the beautiful lily, and placed it in the hands of children and youth; and as they looked into His own youthful face, fresh with the sunlight of His Father's countenance, He gave the lesson, "Consider the lilies of the field, how they grow [in the simplicity of natural beauty]; they toil not, neither do they spin; and yet I say unto you, that even Solomon in all his glory was not arrayed like one of these." Then followed the sweet assurance and the important lesson, "Wherefore, if God so clothe the grass of the field, which today is, and tomorrow is cast into the oven, shall He not much more clothe you, O ye of little faith?"

In the sermon on the mount these words were spoken to others besides children and youth. They were spoken to the multitude, among whom were men and women full of worries and perplexities, and sore with disappointment and sorrow. Jesus continued: "Therefore take no thought, saying, What shall we eat? or, What shall we drink? or, Wherewithal shall we be clothed? (for after all these things do the Gentiles seek:) for your Heavenly Father knoweth that ye have need of all these things." Then spreading out His hands to the surrounding multitude, He said, "But seek ye first the kingdom of God, and His righteousness; and all these things shall be added unto you." Matthew 6:28–33.

Thus Christ interpreted the message which He Himself had given to the lilies and the grass of the field. He desires us to read it in every lily and every spire of grass. His words are full of assurance, and tend to confirm trust in God.

So wide was Christ's view of truth, so extended His teaching, that every phase of nature was employed in illustrating truth. The scenes upon which the eye daily rests were all connected with some spiritual truth, so that nature is clothed with the parables of the Master.

In the earlier part of His ministry, Christ had spoken to the people in words so plain that all His hearers might have grasped truths which would make them wise unto salvation. But in many hearts the truth had taken no root, and it had been quickly caught away. "Therefore speak I to them in parables." He said; "because they seeing see not; and hearing they hear not, neither do they understand.... For this people's heart is waxed gross, and their ears are dull of hearing, and their eyes they have closed." Matthew 13:13–15.

Jesus desired to awaken inquiry. He sought to arouse the careless, and impress truth upon the heart. Parable teaching was popular, and commanded the respect and attention, not only of the Jews, but of the people of other nations. No more effective method of instruction could He have employed. If His hearers had desired a knowledge of divine things, they might have understood His words; for He was always willing to explain them to the honest inquirer.

Again, Christ had truths to present which the people were unprepared to accept or even to understand. For this reason also He taught them in parables. By connecting His teaching with the scenes of life, experience, or nature, He secured their attention and impressed their hearts. Afterward, as they looked upon the objects that illustrated His lessons, they recalled the words of the divine Teacher. To minds that were open to the Holy Spirit, the significance of the Saviour's teaching unfolded more and more. Mysteries grew clear, and that which had been hard to grasp became evident.

Jesus sought an avenue to every heart. By using a variety of illustrations, He not only presented truth in its different phases, but appealed to the different hearers. Their interest was aroused by figures drawn from the surroundings of their daily life. None who listened to the Saviour could feel that they were neglected or forgotten. The humblest, the most sinful, heard in His teaching a voice that spoke to them in sympathy and tenderness.

And He had another reason for teaching in parables. Among the multitudes that gathered about Him, there were priests and rabbis, scribes and elders, Herodians and rulers, world-loving, bigoted, ambitious men, who desired above all things to find some accusation against Him. Their spies followed His steps day after day, to catch from His lips something that would cause His condemnation, and forever silence the One who seemed to draw the world after Him. The Saviour understood the character of these men, and He presented truth in such a way that they could find nothing by which to bring His case before the Sanhedrim. In parables He rebuked the hypocrisy and wicked works of those who occupied high positions, and in figurative language clothed truth of so cutting a character that had it been spoken in direct denunciation, they would not have listened to His words, and would speedily have put an end to His ministry. But while He evaded the spies, He made truth so clear that error was manifested, and the honest in heart were profited by His lessons. Divine wisdom, infinite grace, were made plain by the things of God's creation. Through nature and the experiences of life, men were taught of God. "The invisible things of Him since the creation of the world," were "perceived through the things that are made, even His everlasting power and divinity." Romans 1:20, R.V.

In the Saviour's parable teaching is an indication of what constitutes the true "higher education." Christ might have opened to men the deepest truths of science. He might have unlocked mysteries which have required many centuries of toil and study to penetrate. He might have made suggestions in scientific lines that would have afforded food for thought and stimulus for invention to the close of time. But He did not do this. He said nothing to gratify curiosity, or to satisfy man's ambition by opening doors to worldly greatness. In all His teaching, Christ brought the mind of man in contact with the Infinite Mind. He did not direct the people to study men's theories about God, His word, or His works. He taught them to behold Him as manifested in His works, in His word, and by His providences.

Christ did not deal in abstract theories, but in that which is essential to the development of character, that which will enlarge man's capacity for knowing God, and increase his efficiency to do good. He spoke to men of those truths that relate to the conduct of life, and that take hold upon eternity.

It was Christ who directed the education of Israel. Concerning the commandments and ordinances of the Lord He said, "Thou shalt teach them diligently unto thy children, and shalt talk of them when thou sittest in thine house, and when thou walkest by the way, and when thou liest down, and when thou risest up. And thou shalt bind them for a sign upon thine hand, and they shall be as frontlets between thine eyes. And thou shalt write them upon the posts of thy house, and on thy gates." Deuteronomy 6:7–9. In His own teaching, Jesus showed how this command is to be fulfilled—how the laws and principles of God's kingdom can be so presented as to reveal their beauty and preciousness. When the Lord was training Israel to be the special representatives of Himself, He gave them homes among the hills and valleys. In their home life and their religious service they were brought in constant contact with nature and with the word of God. So Christ taught His disciples by the lake, on the mountainside, in the fields and groves, where they could look upon the things of nature by which He illustrated His teachings. And as they learned of Christ, they put their knowledge to use by co-operating with Him in His work.

So through the creation we are to become acquainted with the Creator. The book of nature is a great lesson book, which in connection with the Scriptures we are to use in teaching others of His character, and guiding lost sheep back to the fold of God. As the works of God are studied, the Holy Spirit flashes conviction into the mind. It is not the conviction that logical reasoning produces; but unless the mind has become too dark to know God, the eye too dim to see Him, the ear too dull to hear His voice, a deeper meaning is grasped, and the sublime, spiritual truths of the written word are impressed on the heart.

In these lessons direct from nature, there is a simplicity and purity that makes them of the highest value. All need the teaching to be derived from this source. In itself the beauty of nature leads the soul away from sin and worldly attractions, and toward purity, peace, and God. Too often the minds of students are occupied with men's theories and speculations, falsely called science and philosophy. They need to be brought into close contact with nature. Let them learn that creation and Christianity have one God. Let them be taught to see the harmony of the natural with the spiritual. Let everything which their eyes see or their hands handle be made a lesson in character building. Thus the mental powers will be strengthened, the character developed, the whole life ennobled.

Christ's purpose in parable teaching was in direct line with the purpose of the Sabbath. God gave to men the memorial of His creative power, that they might discern Him in the works of His hand. The Sabbath bids us behold in His created works the glory of the Creator. And it was because He desired us to do this that Jesus bound up His precious lessons with the beauty of natural things. On the holy rest day, above all other days, we should study the messages that God has written for us in nature. We should study the Saviour's parables where He spoke them, in the fields and groves, under the open sky, among the grass and flowers. As we come close to the heart of nature, Christ makes His presence real to us, and speaks to our hearts of His peace and love.

And Christ has linked His teaching, not only with the day of rest, but with the week of toil. He has wisdom for him who drives the plow and sows the seed. In the plowing and sowing, the tilling and reaping, He teaches us to see an illustration of His work of grace in the heart. So in every line of useful labor and every association of life, He desires us to find a lesson of divine truth. Then our daily toil will no longer absorb our attention and lead us to forget God; it will continually remind us of our Creator and Redeemer. The thought of God will run like a thread of gold through all our homely cares and occupations. For us the glory of His face will again rest upon the face of nature. We shall ever be learning new lessons of heavenly truth, and growing into the image of His purity. Thus shall we "be taught of the Lord"; and in the lot wherein we are called, we shall "abide with God." Isaiah 54:13; 1 Corinthians 7:24.

2
"The Sower Went Forth to Sow"

Based on Matthew 13:1–9, 18–23; Mark 4:1–20; Luke 8:4–15

The Sower and the Seed

By the parable of the sower, Christ illustrates the things of the kingdom of heaven, and the work of the great Husbandman for His people. Like a sower in the field, He came to scatter the heavenly grain of truth. And His parable teaching itself was the seed with which the most precious truths of His grace were sown. Because of its simplicity the parable of the sower has not been valued as it should be. From the natural seed cast into the soil, Christ desires to lead our minds to the gospel seed, the sowing of which results in bringing man back to his loyalty to God. He who gave the parable of the tiny seed is the Sovereign of heaven, and the same laws that govern earthly seed sowing govern the sowing of the seeds of truth.

By the Sea of Galilee a company had gathered to see and hear Jesus—an eager, expectant throng. The sick were there, lying on their mats, waiting to present their cases before Him. It was Christ's God-given right to heal the woes of a sinful race, and He now rebuked disease, and diffused around Him life and health and peace.

As the crowd continued to increase, the people pressed close about Christ until there was no room to receive them. Then, speaking a word to the men in their fishing boats, He stepped into the boat that was waiting to take Him across the lake, and bidding His disciples push off a little from the land, He spoke to the multitude upon the shore.

Beside the sea lay the beautiful plain of Gennesaret, beyond rose the hills, and upon hillside and plain both sowers and reapers were busy, the one casting seed and the other harvesting the early grain. Looking upon the scene, Christ said—

"Behold, the sower went forth to sow; and as he sowed, some seeds fell by the wayside, and the birds came and devoured them" (R.V.); "some fell upon stony places, where they had not much earth; and forthwith they sprung up, because they had no deepness of earth: and when the sun was up, they were scorched; and because they had no root, they withered away. And some fell among thorns; and the thorns sprung up, and choked them: but other fell into good ground, and brought forth fruit, some an hundredfold, some sixty-fold, some thirtyfold."

Christ's mission was not understood by the people of His time. The manner of His coming was not in accordance with their expectations. The

Lord Jesus was the foundation of the whole Jewish economy. Its imposing services were of divine appointment. They were designed to teach the people that at the time appointed One would come to whom those ceremonies pointed. But the Jews had exalted the forms and ceremonies and had lost sight of their object. The traditions, maxims, and enactments of men hid from them the lessons which God intended to convey. These maxims and traditions became an obstacle to their understanding and practice of true religion. And when the Reality came, in the person of Christ, they did not recognize in Him the fulfillment of all their types, the substance of all their shadows. They rejected the antitype, and clung to their types and useless ceremonies. The Son of God had come, but they continued to ask for a sign. The message, "Repent ye; for the kingdom of heaven is at hand," they answered by demands for a miracle. Matthew 3:2. The gospel of Christ was a stumbling block to them because they demanded signs instead of a Saviour. They expected the Messiah to prove His claims by mighty deeds of conquest, to establish His empire on the ruins of earthly kingdoms. This expectation Christ answered in the parable of the sower. Not by force of arms, not by violent interpositions, was the kingdom of God to prevail, but by the implanting of a new principle in the hearts of men.

"He that soweth the good seed is the Son of man." Matthew 13:37. Christ had come, not as a king, but as a sower; not for the overthrow of kingdoms, but for the scattering of seed; not to point His followers to earthly triumphs and national greatness, but to a harvest to be gathered after patient toil and through losses and disappointments.

The Pharisees perceived the meaning of Christ's parable, but to them its lesson was unwelcome. They affected not to understand it. To the multitude it involved in still greater mystery the purpose of the new teacher, whose words had so strangely moved their hearts and so bitterly disappointed their ambitions. The disciples themselves had not understood the parable, but their interest was awakened. They came to Jesus privately and asked for an explanation.

This was the desire which Christ wished to arouse, that He might give them more definite instruction. He explained the parable to them, as He will make plain His word to all who seek Him in sincerity of heart. Those who study the word of God with hearts open to the enlightenment of the Holy Spirit, will not remain in darkness as to the meaning of the word. "If any man willeth to do His will," Christ said, "he shall know of the teaching whether it be of God, or whether I speak from Myself." John 7:17, R.V. All who come to Christ for a clearer knowledge of the truth will receive it. He will unfold to them the mysteries of the kingdom of heaven, and these mysteries will be understood by the heart that longs to know the truth. A heavenly light will shine into the soul temple, and will be revealed to others as the bright shining of a lamp on a dark path.

"The sower went forth to sow" (R.V.). In the East the state of affairs was so unsettled, and there was so great danger from violence that the people dwelt chiefly in walled towns, and the husbandmen went forth daily to their labor outside the walls. So Christ, the heavenly Sower, went forth to sow. He left His home of security and peace, left the glory that He had with the Father before the world was, left His position upon the throne of the universe. He went forth, a suffering, tempted man; went forth in solitude, to sow in tears, to water with His blood, the seed of life for a world lost.

His servants in like manner must go forth to sow. When called to become a sower of the seed of truth, Abraham was bidden, "Get thee out of thy country, and from thy kindred, and from thy father's house, unto a land that I will show thee." Genesis 12:1. "And he went out, not knowing whither he went." Hebrews 11:8. So to the apostle Paul, praying in the temple at Jerusalem, came the message from God, "Depart; for I will send thee far hence unto the Gentiles." Acts 22:21. So those who are called to unite with Christ must leave all, in order to follow Him. Old associations must be broken up, plans of life relinquished, earthly hopes surrendered. In toil and tears, in solitude, and through sacrifice, must the seed be sown.

"The sower soweth the word." Christ came to sow the world with truth. Ever since the fall of man, Satan has been sowing the seeds of error. It was by a lie that he first gained control over men, and thus he still works to overthrow God's kingdom in the earth and to bring men under his power. A sower from a higher world, Christ came to sow the seeds of truth. He who had stood in the councils of God, who had dwelt in the innermost sanctuary of the Eternal, could bring to men the pure principles of truth. Ever since the fall of man, Christ had been the Revealer of truth to the world. By Him the incorruptible seed, "the word of God, which liveth and abideth forever," is communicated to men. 1 Peter 1:23. In that first promise spoken to our fallen race in Eden, Christ was sowing the gospel seed. But it is to His personal ministry among men and to the work which He thus established that the parable of the sower especially applies.

The word of God is the seed. Every seed has in itself a germinating principle. In it the life of the plant is enfolded. So there is life in God's word. Christ says, "The words that I speak unto you, they are Spirit, and they are life." John 6:63. "He that heareth My word, and believeth on Him that sent Me, hath everlasting life." John 5:24. In every command and in every promise of the word of God is the power, the very life of God, by which the command may be fulfilled and the promise realized. He who by faith receives the word is receiving the very life and character of God.

Every seed brings forth fruit after its kind. Sow the seed under right conditions, and it will develop its own life in the plant. Receive into the soul by faith the incorruptible seed of the word, and it will bring forth a character and a life after the similitude of the character and the life of God.

The teachers of Israel were not sowing the seed of the word of God. Christ's work as a teacher of truth was in marked contrast to that of the rabbis of His time. They dwelt upon traditions, upon human theories and speculations. Often that which man had taught and written about the word, they put in place of the word itself. Their teaching had no power to quicken the soul. The subject of Christ's teaching and preaching was the word of God. He met questioners with a plain, "It is written." "What saith the Scriptures?" "How readest thou?" At every opportunity, when an interest was awakened by either friend or foe, He sowed the seed of the word. He who is the Way, the Truth, and the Life, Himself the living Word, points to the Scriptures, saying, "They are they which testify of Me." And "beginning at Moses and all the prophets," He opened to His disciples "in all the Scriptures the things concerning Himself." John 5:39; Luke 24:27.

Christ's servants are to do the same work. In our day, as of old, the vital truths of God's word are set aside for human theories and speculations. Many professed ministers of the gospel do not accept the whole Bible as the inspired word. One wise man rejects one portion; another questions another part. They set up their judgment as superior to the word; and the Scripture which they do teach rests upon their own authority. Its divine authenticity is destroyed. Thus the seeds of infidelity are sown broadcast; for the people become confused and know not what to believe. There are many beliefs that the mind has no right to entertain. In the days of Christ the rabbis put a forced, mystical construction upon many portions of Scripture. Because the plain teaching of God's word condemned their practices, they tried to destroy its force. The same thing is done today. The word of God is made to appear mysterious and obscure in order to excuse transgression of His law. Christ rebuked these practices in His day. He taught that the word of God was to be understood by all. He pointed to the Scriptures as of unquestionable authority, and we should do the same. The Bible is to be presented as the word of the infinite God, as the end of all controversy and the foundation of all faith.

The Bible has been robbed of its power, and the results are seen in a lowering of the tone of spiritual life. In the sermons from many pulpits of today there is not that divine manifestation which awakens the conscience and brings life to the soul. The hearers can not say, "Did not our heart burn within us, while He talked with us by the way, and while He opened to us the Scriptures?" Luke 24:32. There are many who are crying out for the living God, longing for the divine presence. Philosophical theories or literary essays, however brilliant, cannot satisfy the heart. The assertions and inventions of men are of no value. Let the word of God speak to the people. Let those who have heard only traditions and human theories and maxims hear the voice of Him whose word can renew the soul unto everlasting life.

Christ's favorite theme was the paternal tenderness and abundant grace of God; He dwelt much upon the holiness of His character and His law; He presented Himself to the people as the Way, the Truth, and the Life. Let these be the themes of Christ's ministers. Present the truth as it is in Jesus. Make plain the requirements of the law and the gospel. Tell the people of Christ's life of self-denial and sacrifice; of His humiliation and death; of His resurrection and ascension; or His intercession for them in the courts of God; of His promise, "I will come again, and receive you unto Myself." John 14:3.

Instead of discussing erroneous theories, or seeking to combat the opponents of the gospel, follow the example of Christ. Let fresh truths from God's treasure house flash into life. "Preach the word." "Sow beside all waters." "Be instant in season, out of season." "He that hath My word, let him speak My word faithfully. What is the chaff to the wheat? saith the Lord." "Every word of God is pure.... Add thou not unto His words, lest He reprove thee, and thou be found a liar." 2 Timothy 4:2; Isaiah 32:20; Jeremiah 23:28; Proverbs 30:5, 6.

"The sower soweth the word." Here is presented the great principle which should underlie all educational work. "The seed is the word of God." But in too many schools of our day God's word is set aside. Other subjects occupy the mind. The study of infidel authors holds a large place in the educational system. Skeptical sentiments are interwoven in the matter placed in school books. Scientific research becomes misleading, because its discoveries are misinterpreted and perverted. The word of God is compared with the supposed teachings of science, and is made to appear uncertain and untrustworthy. Thus the seeds of doubt are planted in the minds of the youth, and in time of temptation they spring up. When faith in God's word is lost, the soul has no guide, no safeguard. The youth are drawn into paths which lead away from God and from everlasting life.

To this cause may in great degree be attributed the widespread iniquity in our world today. When the word of God is set aside, its power to restrain the evil passions of the natural heart is rejected. Men sow to the flesh, and of the flesh they reap corruption.

And here, too, is the great cause of mental weakness and inefficiency. In turning from God's word to feed on the writings of uninspired men, the mind becomes dwarfed and cheapened. It is not brought in contact with deep, broad principles of eternal truth. The understanding adapts itself to the comprehension of the things with which it is familiar, and in this devotion to finite things it is weakened, its power is contracted, and after a time it becomes unable to expand.

All this is false education. The work of every teacher should be to fasten the mind of the youth upon the grand truths of the word of Inspiration. This is the education essential for this life and for the life to come.

And let it not be thought that this will prevent the study of the sciences, or cause a lower standard in education. The knowledge of God is as high as heaven and as broad as the universe. There is nothing so ennobling and invigorating as a study of the great themes which concern our eternal life. Let the youth seek to grasp these God-given truths, and their minds will expand and grow strong in the effort. It will bring every student who is a doer of the word into a broader field of thought, and secure for him a wealth of knowledge that is imperishable.

The education to be secured by searching the Scriptures is an experimental knowledge of the plan of salvation. Such an education will restore the image of God in the soul. It will strengthen and fortify the mind against temptation, and fit the learner to become a co-worker with Christ in His mission of mercy to the world. It will make him a member of the heavenly family; and prepare him to share the inheritance of the saints in light.

But the teacher of sacred truth can impart only that which he himself knows by experience. "The sower sowed *his* seed." Christ taught the truth because He was the truth. His own thought, His character, His life-experience, were embodied in His teaching. So with His servants: those who would teach the word are to make it their own by a personal experience. They must know what it is to have Christ made unto them wisdom and righteousness and sanctification and redemption. In presenting the word of God to others, they are not to make it a suppose-so or a may-be. They should declare with the apostle Peter, "We have not followed cunningly devised fables when we made known unto you the power and coming of our Lord Jesus Christ, but were eye-witnesses of His majesty." 2 Peter 1:16. Every minister of Christ and every teacher should be able to say with the beloved John, "The life was manifested, and we have seen it, and bear witness, and show unto you that eternal life which was with the Father, and was manifested unto us." 1 John 1:2.

The Soil—by the Wayside

That with which the parable of the sower chiefly deals is the effect produced on the growth of the seed by the soil into which it is cast. By this parable Christ was virtually saying to His hearers, It is not safe for you to stand as critics of My work, or to indulge disappointment because it does not meet your ideas. The question of greatest importance to you is, How do you treat My message? Upon your reception or rejection of it your eternal destiny depends.

Explaining the seed that fell by the wayside, He said, "When any one heareth the word of the kingdom, and understandeth it not, then cometh the wicked one, and catcheth away that which was sown in his heart. This is he which received seed by the wayside."

The seed sown by the wayside represents the word of God as it falls upon the heart of an inattentive hearer. Like the hard-beaten path, trodden down by the feet of men and beasts, is the heart that becomes a highway for the world's traffic, its pleasures and sins. Absorbed in selfish aims and sinful indulgences, the soul is "hardened through the deceitfulness of sin." Hebrews 3:13. The spiritual faculties are paralyzed. Men hear the word, but understand it not. They do not discern that it applies to themselves. They do not realize their need or their danger. They do not perceive the love of Christ, and they pass by the message of His grace as something that does not concern them.

As the birds are ready to catch up the seed from the wayside, so Satan is ready to catch away the seeds of divine truth from the soul. He fears that the word of God may awaken the careless, and take effect upon the hardened heart. Satan and his angels are in the assemblies where the gospel is preached. While angels of heaven endeavor to impress hearts with the word of God, the enemy is on the alert to make the word of no effect. With an earnestness equaled only by his malice, he tries to thwart the work of the Spirit of God. While Christ is drawing the soul by His love, Satan tries to turn away the attention of the one who is moved to seek the Saviour. He engages the mind with worldly schemes. He excites criticism, or insinuates doubt and unbelief. The speaker's choice of language or his manner may not please the hearers, and they dwell upon these defects. Thus the truth they need, and which God has graciously sent them, makes no lasting impression.

Satan has many helpers. Many who profess to be Christians are aiding the tempter to catch away the seeds of truth from other hearts. Many who listen to the preaching of the word of God make it the subject of criticism at home. They sit in judgment on the sermon as they would on the words of a lecturer or a political speaker. The message that should be regarded as the word of the Lord to them is dwelt upon with trifling or sarcastic comment. The minister's character, motives, and actions, and the conduct of fellow members of the church, are freely discussed. Severe judgment is pronounced, gossip or slander repeated, and this in the hearing of the unconverted. Often these things are spoken by parents in the hearing of their own children. Thus are destroyed respect for God's messengers, and reverence for their message. And many are taught to regard lightly God's word itself.

Thus in the homes of professed Christians many youth are educated to be infidels. And the parents question why their children are so little interested in the gospel, and so ready to doubt the truth of the Bible. They wonder that it is so difficult to reach them with moral and religious influences. They do not see that their own example has hardened the hearts of their children. The good seed finds no place to take root, and Satan catches it away.

In Stony Places

"He that receiveth the seed into stony places, the same is he that heareth the word, and anon with joy receiveth it; yet hath he not root in himself, but dureth for a while; for when tribulation or persecution ariseth because of the word, by and by he is offended."

The seed sown upon stony ground finds little depth of soil. The plant springs up quickly, but the root cannot penetrate the rock to find nutriment to sustain its growth, and it soon perishes. Many who make a profession of religion are stony-ground hearers. Like the rock underlying the layer of earth, the selfishness of the natural heart underlies the soil of their good desires and aspirations. The love of self is not subdued. They have not seen the exceeding sinfulness of sin, and the heart has not been humbled under a sense of its guilt. This class may be easily convinced, and appear to be bright converts, but they have only a superficial religion.

It is not because men receive the word immediately, nor because they rejoice in it, that they fall away. As soon as Matthew heard the Saviour's call, immediately he rose up, left all, and followed Him. As soon as the divine word comes to our hearts, God desires us to receive it; and it is right to accept it with joy. "Joy shall be in heaven over one sinner that repenteth." Luke 15:7. And there is joy in the soul that believes on Christ.

But those who in the parable are said to receive the word immediately, do not count the cost. They do not consider what the word of God requires of them. They do not bring it face to face with all their habits of life, and yield themselves fully to its control.

The roots of the plant strike down deep into the soil, and hidden from sight nourish the life of the plant. So with the Christian; it is by the invisible union of the soul with Christ, through faith, that the spiritual life is nourished. But the stony-ground hearers depend upon self instead of Christ. They trust in their good works and good impulses, and are strong in their own righteousness. They are not strong in the Lord, and in the power of His might. Such a one "hath not root in himself"; for he is not connected with Christ.

The hot summer sun, that strengthens and ripens the hardy grain, destroys that which has no depth of root. So he who "hath not root in himself," "dureth for a while"; but "when tribulation or persecution ariseth because of the word, by and by he is offended." Many receive the gospel as a way of escape from suffering, rather than as a deliverance from sin. They rejoice for a season, for they think that religion will free them from difficulty and trial. While life moves smoothly with them, they may appear to be consistent Christians. But they faint beneath the fiery test of temptation. They cannot bear reproach for Christ's sake. When the word of God points out some cherished sin, or requires self-denial or sacrifice, they are offended. It would cost them too much effort to make a radical change in their life. They look at the present inconvenience and trial, and forget the eternal realities. Like the disciples who left Jesus, they are ready to say, "This is an hard saying; who can hear it?" John 6:60.

There are very many who claim to serve God, but who have no experimental knowledge of Him. Their desire to do His will is based upon their own inclination, not upon the deep conviction of the Holy Spirit. Their conduct is not brought into harmony with the law of God. They profess to accept Christ as their Saviour, but they do not believe that He will give them power to overcome their sins. They have not a personal relation with a living Saviour, and their characters reveal defects both hereditary and cultivated.

It is one thing to assent in a general way to the agency of the Holy Spirit, and another thing to accept His work as a reprover calling to repentance. Many feel a sense of estrangement from God, a realization of their bondage to self and sin; they make efforts for reform; but they do not crucify self. They do not give themselves entirely into the hands of Christ, seeking for divine power to do His will. They are not willing to be molded after the divine similitude. In a general way they acknowledge their imperfections, but they do not give up their particular sins. With each wrong act the old selfish nature is gaining strength.

The only hope for these souls is to realize in themselves the truth of Christ's words to Nicodemus, "Ye must be born again." "Except a man be born from above, he can not see the kingdom of God." John 3:7, 3, margin.

True holiness is wholeness in the service of God. This is the condition of true Christian living. Christ asks for an unreserved consecration, for undivided service. He demands the heart, the mind, the soul, the strength. Self is not to be cherished. He who lives to himself is not a Christian.

Love must be the principle of action. Love is the underlying principle of God's government in heaven and earth, and it must be the foundation of the Christian's character. This alone can make and keep him steadfast. This alone can enable him to withstand trial and temptation.

And love will be revealed in sacrifice. The plan of redemption was laid in sacrifice—a sacrifice so broad and deep and high that it is immeasurable. Christ gave all for us, and those who receive Christ will be ready to sacrifice all for the sake of their Redeemer. The thought of His honor and glory will come before anything else.

If we love Jesus, we shall love to live for Him, to present our thank offerings to Him, to labor for Him. The very labor will be light. For His sake we shall covet pain and toil and sacrifice. We shall sympathize with His longing for the salvation of men. We shall feel the same tender craving for souls that He has felt.

This is the religion of Christ. Anything short of it is a deception. No mere theory of truth or profession of discipleship will save any soul. We do not belong to Christ unless we are His wholly. It is by halfheartedness in the Christian life that men become feeble in purpose and changeable in desire. The effort to serve both self and Christ makes one a stony-ground hearer, and he will not endure when the test comes upon him.

Among Thorns

"He also that received seed among the thorns is he that heareth the word; and the care of this world, and the deceitfulness of riches, choke the word, and he becometh unfruitful."

The gospel seed often falls among thorns and noxious weeds; and if there is not a moral transformation in the human heart, if old habits and practices and the former life of sin are not left behind, if the attributes of Satan are not expelled from the soul, the wheat crop will be choked. The thorns will come to be the crop, and will kill out the wheat.

Grace can thrive only in the heart that is being constantly prepared for the precious seeds of truth. The thorns of sin will grow in any soil; they need no cultivation; but grace must be carefully cultivated. The briers and thorns are always ready to spring up, and the work of purification must advance continually. If the heart is not kept under the control of God, if the Holy Spirit does not work unceasingly to refine and ennoble the character, the old habits will reveal themselves in the life. Men may profess to believe the gospel; but unless they are sanctified by the gospel their profession is of no avail. If they do not gain the victory over sin, then sin is gaining the victory over them. The thorns that have been cut off but not uprooted grow apace, until the soul is overspread with them.

Christ specified the things that are dangerous to the soul. As recorded by Mark He mentions the cares of this world, the deceitfulness of riches, and the lusts of other things. Luke specifies the cares, riches, and pleasures of this life. These are what choke the word, the growing spiritual seed. The soul ceases to draw nourishment from Christ, and spirituality dies out of the heart.

"The cares of this world." No class is free from the temptation to worldly care. To the poor, toil and deprivation and the fear of want bring perplexities and burdens. To the rich come fear of loss and a multitude of anxious cares. Many of Christ's followers forget the lesson He has bidden us learn from the flowers of the field. They do not trust to His constant care. Christ cannot carry their burden, because they do not cast it upon Him. Therefore the cares of life, which should drive them to the Saviour for help and comfort, separate them from Him.

Many who might be fruitful in God's service become bent on acquiring wealth. Their whole energy is absorbed in business enterprises, and they feel obliged to neglect things of a spiritual nature. Thus they separate themselves from God. We are enjoined in the Scriptures to be "not slothful in business." Romans 12:11. We are to labor that we may impart to him who needs. Christians must work, they must engage in business, and they can do this without committing sin. But many become so absorbed in business that they have no time for prayer, no time for the study of the Bible, no time to seek and serve God. At times the longings of the soul go out for holiness and heaven; but there is no time to turn aside from the din of the world to listen to the majestic and authoritative utterances of the Spirit of God. The things of eternity are made subordinate, the things of the world supreme. It is impossible for the seed of the word to bring forth fruit; for the life of the soul is given to nourish the thorns of worldliness.

And many who are working with a very different purpose, fall into a like error. They are working for others' good; their duties are pressing, their responsibilities are many, and they allow their labor to crowd out devotion. Communion with God through prayer and a study of His word is neglected. They forget that Christ has said, "Without Me ye can do nothing." John 15:5. They walk apart from Christ, their life is not pervaded by His grace, and the characteristics of self are revealed. Their service is marred by desire for supremacy, and the harsh, unlovely traits of the unsubdued heart. Here is one of the chief secrets of failure in Christian work. This is why its results are often so meager.

"The deceitfulness of riches." The love of riches has an infatuating, deceptive power. Too often those who possess worldly treasure forget that it is God who gives them power to get wealth. They say, "My power and the might of mine hand hath gotten me this wealth." Deuteronomy 8:17. Their riches, instead of awakening gratitude to God, lead to the exaltation of self. They lose the sense of their dependence upon God and their obligation to their fellow men. Instead of regarding wealth as a talent to be employed for the glory of God and the uplifting of humanity, they look upon it as a means of serving themselves. Instead of developing in man the attributes of God, riches thus used are developing in him the attributes of Satan. The seed of the word is choked with thorns.

"And pleasures of this life." There is danger in amusement that is sought merely for self-gratification. All habits of indulgence that weaken the physical powers, that becloud the mind, or that benumb the spiritual perceptions, are "fleshly lusts, which war against the soul." 1 Peter 2:11.

"And the lusts of other things." These are not necessarily things sinful in themselves, but something that is made first instead of the kingdom of God. Whatever attracts the mind from God, whatever draws the affections away from Christ, is an enemy to the soul.

When the mind is youthful and vigorous and susceptible of rapid development, there is great temptation to be ambitious for self, to serve self. If worldly schemes are successful, there is an inclination to continue in a line that deadens conscience, and prevents a correct estimate as to what constitutes real excellence of character. When circumstances favor this development, growth will be seen in a direction prohibited by the word of God.

In this formative period of their children's life, the responsibility of parents is very great. It should be their study to surround the youth with right influences, influences that will give them correct views of life and its true success. Instead of this, how many parents make it their first object to secure for their children worldly prosperity. All their associations are chosen with reference to this object. Many parents make their home in some large city, and introduce their children into fashionable society. They surround them with influences that encourage worldliness and pride. In this atmosphere the mind and soul are dwarfed. The high and noble aims of life are lost sight of. The privilege of being sons of God, heirs of eternity, is bartered for worldly gain.

Many parents seek to promote the happiness of their children by gratifying their love of amusement. They allow them to engage in sports, and to attend parties of pleasure, and provide them with money to use freely in display and self-gratification. The more the desire for pleasure is indulged, the stronger it becomes. The interest of these youth is more and more absorbed in amusement, until they come to look upon it as the great object of life. They form habits of idleness and self-indulgence that make it almost impossible for them ever to become steadfast Christians.

Even the church, which should be the pillar and ground of the truth, is found encouraging the selfish love of pleasure. When money is to be raised for religious purposes, to what means do many churches resort? To bazaars, suppers, fancy fairs, even to lotteries, and like devices. Often the place set apart for God's worship is desecrated by feasting and drinking, buying, selling, and merrymaking. Respect for the house of God and reverence for His worship are lessened in the minds of the youth. The barriers of self-restraint are weakened. Selfishness, appetite, the love of display, are appealed to, and they strengthen as they are indulged.

The pursuit of pleasure and amusement centers in the cities. Many parents who choose a city home for their children, thinking to give them greater advantages, meet with disappointment, and too late repent their terrible mistake. The cities of today are fast becoming like Sodom and Gomorrah. The many holidays encourage idleness. The exciting sports—theatergoing, horse racing, gambling, liquor-drinking, and reveling—stimulate every passion to intense activity. The youth are swept away by the popular current. Those who learn to love amusement for its own sake open the door to a flood of temptations. They give themselves up to social gaiety and thoughtless mirth, and their intercourse with pleasure lovers has an intoxicating effect upon the mind. They are led on from one form of dissipation to another, until they lose both the desire and the capacity for a life of usefulness. Their religious aspirations are chilled; their spiritual life is darkened. All the nobler faculties of the soul, all that link man with the spiritual world, are debased.

It is true that some may see their folly and repent. God may pardon them. But they have wounded their own souls, and brought upon themselves a lifelong peril. The power of discernment, which ought ever to be kept keen and sensitive to distinguish between right and wrong, is in a great measure destroyed. They are not quick to recognize the guiding voice of the Holy Spirit, or to discern the devices of Satan. Too often in time of danger they fall under temptation, and are led away from God. The end of their pleasure-loving life is ruin for this world and for the world to come.

Cares, riches, pleasures, all are used by Satan in playing the game of life for the human soul. The warning is given, "Love not the world, neither the things that are in the world. If any man love the world, the love of the Father is not in him. For all that is in the world, the lust of the flesh, and the lust of the eyes, and the pride of life, is not of the Father, but is of the world." 1 John 2:15, 16. He who reads the hearts of men as an open book says, "Take heed to yourselves, lest at any time your hearts be overcharged with surfeiting and drunkenness and cares of this life." Luke 21:34. And the apostle Paul by the Holy Spirit writes, "They that will be rich fall into temptation and a snare, and into many foolish and hurtful lusts, which drown men in destruction and perdition. For the love of money is the root of all evil; which, while some coveted after, they have erred from the faith, and pierced themselves through with many sorrows." 1 Timothy 6:9, 10.

Preparation of the Soil

Throughout the parable of the sower, Christ represents the different results of the sowing as depending upon the soil. In every case the sower and the seed are the same. Thus He teaches that if the word of God fails of accomplishing its work in our hearts and lives, the reason is to be found in ourselves. But the result is not beyond our control. True, we cannot change ourselves; but the power of choice is ours, and it rests with us to determine what we will become. The wayside, the stony-ground, the thorny-ground hearers need not remain such. The Spirit of God is ever seeking to break the spell of infatuation that holds men absorbed in worldly things, and to awaken a desire for the imperishable treasure. It is by resisting the Spirit that men become inattentive to or neglectful of God's word. They are themselves responsible for the hardness of heart that prevents the good seed from taking root, and for the evil growths that check its development.

The garden of the heart must be cultivated. The soil must be broken up by deep repentance for sin. Poisonous, Satanic plants must be uprooted. The soil once overgrown by thorns can be reclaimed only by diligent labor. So the evil tendencies of the natural heart can be overcome only by earnest effort in the name and strength of Jesus. The Lord bids us by His prophet, "Break up your fallow ground, and sow not among thorns." "Sow to yourselves in righteousness; reap in mercy." Jeremiah 4:3; Hosea 10:12. This work He desires to accomplish for us, and He asks us to co-operate with Him.

The sowers of the seed have a work to do in preparing hearts to receive the gospel. In the ministry of the word there is too much sermonizing, and too little of real heart-to-heart work. There is need of personal labor for the souls of the lost. In Christlike sympathy we should come close to men individually, and seek to awaken their interest in the great things of eternal life. Their hearts may be as hard as the beaten highway, and apparently it may be a useless effort to present the Saviour to them; but while logic may fail to move, and argument be powerless to convince, the love of Christ, revealed in personal ministry, may soften the stony heart, so that the seed of truth can take root.

So the sowers have something to do that the seed may not be choked with thorns or perish because of shallowness of soil. At the very outset of the Christian life every believer should be taught its foundation principles. He should be taught that he is not merely to be saved by Christ's sacrifice, but that he is to make the life of Christ his life and the character of Christ his character. Let all be taught that they are to bear burdens and to deny natural inclination. Let them learn the blessedness of working for Christ, following Him in self-denial, and enduring hardness as good soldiers. Let them learn to trust His love and to cast on Him their cares. Let them taste the joy of winning souls for Him. In their love and interest for the lost, they will lose sight of self. The pleasures of the world will lose their power to attract and its burdens to dishearten. The plowshare of truth will do its work. It will break up the fallow ground. It will not merely cut off the tops of the thorns, but will take them out by the roots.

In Good Ground

The sower is not always to meet with disappointment. Of the seed that fell into good ground the Saviour said, This "is he that heareth the word, and understandeth it; which also beareth fruit, and bringeth forth, some an hundredfold, some sixty, some thirty." "That on the good ground are they, which, in an honest and good heart, having heard the word, keep it, and bring forth fruit with patience."

The "honest and good heart" of which the parable speaks, is not a heart without sin; for the gospel is to be preached to the lost. Christ said, "I came not to call the righteous, but sinners to repentance." Mark 2:17. He has an honest heart who yields to the conviction of the Holy Spirit. He confesses his guilt, and feels his need of the mercy and love of God. He has a sincere desire to know the truth, that he may obey it. The good heart is a believing heart, one that has faith in the word of God. Without faith it is impossible to receive the word. "He that cometh to God must believe that He is, and that He is a rewarder of them that diligently seek Him." Hebrews 11:6.

This "is he that heareth the word, and understandeth it." The Pharisees of Christ's day closed their eyes lest they should see, and their ears lest they should hear; therefore the truth could not reach their hearts. They were to suffer retribution for their willful ignorance and self-imposed blindness. But Christ taught His disciples that they were to open their minds to instruction, and be ready to believe. He pronounced a blessing upon them because they saw and heard with eyes and ears that believed.

The good-ground hearer receives the word "not as the word of men, but as it is in truth, the word of God." 1 Thessalonians 2:13. Only he who receives the Scriptures as the voice of God speaking to himself is a true learner. He trembles at the word; for to him it is a living reality. He opens his understanding and his heart to receive it. Such hearers were Cornelius and his friends, who said to the apostle Peter, "Now therefore are we all here present before God, to hear all things that are commanded thee of God." Acts 10:33.

A knowledge of the truth depends not so much upon strength of intellect as upon pureness of purpose, the simplicity of an earnest, dependent faith. To those who in humility of heart seek for divine guidance, angels of God draw near. The Holy Spirit is given to open to them the rich treasures of the truth.

The good-ground hearers, having heard the word, keep it. Satan with all his agencies of evil is not able to catch it away.

Merely to hear or to read the word is not enough. He who desires to be profited by the Scriptures must meditate upon the truth that has been presented to him. By earnest attention and prayerful thought he must learn the meaning of the words of truth, and drink deep of the spirit of the holy oracles.

God bids us fill the mind with great thoughts, pure thoughts. He desires us to meditate upon His love and mercy, to study His wonderful work in the great plan of redemption. Then clearer and still clearer will be our perception of truth, higher, holier, our desire for purity of heart and clearness of thought. The soul dwelling in the pure atmosphere of holy thought will be transformed by communion with God through the study of the Scriptures.

"And bring forth fruit." Those who, having heard the word, keep it, will bring forth fruit in obedience. The word of God, received into the soul, will be manifest in good works. Its results will be seen in a Christlike character and life. Christ said of Himself, "I delight to do Thy will, O My God; yea,

Thy law is within My heart." Psalm 40:8. "I seek not Mine own will, but the will of the Father which hath sent Me." John 5:30. And the Scripture says, "He that saith he abideth in Him ought himself also so to walk, even as He walked." 1 John 2:6.

The word of God often comes in collision with man's hereditary and cultivated traits of character and his habits of life. But the good-ground hearer, in receiving the word, accepts all its conditions and requirements. His habits, customs, and practices are brought into submission to God's word. In his view the commands of finite, erring man sink into insignificance beside the word of the infinite God. With the whole heart, with undivided purpose, he is seeking the life eternal, and at the cost of loss, persecution, or death itself, he will obey the truth.

And he brings forth fruit "with patience." None who receive God's word are exempt from difficulty and trial; but when affliction comes, the true Christian does not become restless, distrustful, or despondent. Though we can not see the definite outcome of affairs, or discern the purpose of God's providences, we are not to cast away our confidence. Remembering the tender mercies of the Lord, we should cast our care upon Him, and with patience wait for His salvation.

Through conflict the spiritual life is strengthened. Trials well borne will develop steadfastness of character and precious spiritual graces. The perfect fruit of faith, meekness, and love often matures best amid storm clouds and darkness.

"The husbandman waiteth for the precious fruit of the earth, and hath long patience for it, until he receive the early and latter rain." James 5:7. So the Christian is to wait with patience for the fruition in his life of the word of God. Often when we pray for the graces of the Spirit, God works to answer our prayers by placing us in circumstances to develop these fruits; but we do not understand His purpose, and wonder, and are dismayed. Yet none can develop these graces except through the process of growth and fruit bearing. Our part is to receive God's word and to hold it fast, yielding ourselves fully to its control, and its purpose in us will be accomplished.

"If a man love Me," Christ said, "he will keep My words; and My Father will love him, and we will come unto him, and make our abode with him." John 14:23. The spell of a stronger, a perfect mind will be over us; for we have a living connection with the source of all-enduring strength. In our divine life we shall be brought into captivity to Jesus Christ. We shall no longer live the common life of selfishness, but Christ will live in us. His character will be reproduced in our nature. Thus shall we bring forth the fruits of the Holy Spirit—"some thirty, and some sixty, and some an hundred."

3
"First the Blade, then the Ear"

Based on Mark 4:26–29

The parable of the sower excited much questioning. Some of the hearers gathered from it that Christ was not to establish an earthly kingdom, and many were curious and perplexed. Seeing their perplexity, Christ used other illustrations, still seeking to turn their thoughts from the hope of a worldly kingdom to the work of God's grace in the soul.

"And He said, So is the kingdom of God, as if a man should cast seed into the ground; and should sleep, and rise night and day, and the seed should spring and grow up, he knoweth not how. For the earth bringeth forth fruit of herself; first the blade, then the ear, after that the full corn in the ear. But when the fruit is brought forth, immediately he putteth in the sickle, because the harvest is come."

The husbandman who "putteth in the sickle, because the harvest is come," can be no other than Christ. It is He who at the last great day will reap the harvest of the earth. But the sower of the seed represents those who labor in Christ's stead. The seed is said to "spring and grow up, he knoweth not how," and this is not true of the Son of God. Christ does not sleep over His charge, but watches it day and night. He is not ignorant of how the seed grows.

The parable of the seed reveals that God is at work in nature. The seed has in itself a germinating principle, a principle that God Himself has implanted; yet if left to itself the seed would have no power to spring up. Man has his part to act in promoting the growth of the grain. He must prepare and enrich the soil and cast in the seed. He must till the fields. But there is a point beyond which he can accomplish nothing. No strength or wisdom of man can bring forth from the seed the living plant. Let man put forth his efforts to the utmost limit, he must still depend upon One who has connected the sowing and the reaping by wonderful links of His own omnipotent power.

There is life in the seed, there is power in the soil; but unless an infinite power is exercised day and night, the seed will yield no returns. The showers of rain must be sent to give moisture to the thirsty fields, the sun must impart heat, electricity must be conveyed to the buried seed. The life which the Creator has implanted, He alone can call forth. Every seed grows, every plant develops, by the power of God.

"As the earth bringeth forth her bud, and as the garden causeth the things that are sown in it to spring forth, so the Lord God will cause righteousness and praise to spring forth." Isaiah 61:11. As in the natural, so in the spiritual sowing; the teacher of truth must seek to prepare the soil of the heart; he must sow the seed; but the power that alone can produce life is from God. There is a point beyond which human effort is in vain. While we are to preach the word, we can not impart the power that will quicken the soul, and cause righteousness and praise to spring forth. In the preaching of the word there must be the working of an agency beyond any human power. Only through the divine Spirit will the word be living and powerful to renew the soul unto eternal life. This is what Christ tried to impress upon His disciples. He taught that it was nothing they possessed in themselves which would give success to their labors, but that it is the miracle-working power of God which gives efficiency to His own word.

The work of the sower is a work of faith. The mystery of the germination and growth of the seed he cannot understand. But he has confidence in the agencies by which God causes vegetation to flourish. In casting his seed into the ground, he is apparently throwing away the precious grain that might furnish bread for his family. But he is only giving up a present good for a larger return. He casts the seed away, expecting to gather it manyfold in an abundant harvest. So Christ's servants are to labor, expecting a harvest from the seed they sow.

The good seed may for a time lie unnoticed in a cold, selfish, worldly heart, giving no evidence that it has taken root; but afterward, as the Spirit of God breathes on the soul, the hidden seed springs up, and at last bears fruit to the glory of God. In our lifework we know not which shall prosper, this or that. This is not a question for us to settle. We are to do our work, and leave the results with God. "In the morning sow thy seed, and in the evening withhold not thine hand." Ecclesiastes 11:6. God's great covenant declares that "while the earth remaineth, seed-time and harvest…shall not cease." Genesis 8:22. In the confidence of this promise the husbandman tills and sows. Not less confidently are we in the spiritual sowing to labor, trusting His assurance, "So shall My word be that goeth forth out of My mouth; it shall not return unto Me void, but it shall accomplish that which I please, and it shall prosper in the thing whereto I sent it." Isaiah 55:11. "He that goeth forth and weepeth, bearing precious seed, shall doubtless come again with rejoicing, bringing his sheaves with him." Psalm 126:6.

The germination of the seed represents the beginning of spiritual life, and the development of the plant is a beautiful figure of Christian growth. As in nature, so in grace; there can be no life without growth. The plant must either grow or die. As its growth is silent and imperceptible, but continuous, so is the development of the Christian life. At every stage of development our life may be perfect; yet if God's purpose for us is fulfilled, there will be continual advancement. Sanctification is the work of a lifetime. As our opportunities multiply, our experience will enlarge, and our knowledge increase. We shall become strong to bear responsibility, and our maturity will be in proportion to our privileges.

The plant grows by receiving that which God has provided to sustain its life. It sends down its roots into the earth. It drinks in the sunshine, the dew, and the rain. It receives the life-giving properties from the air. So the Christian is to grow by co-operating with the divine agencies. Feeling our helplessness, we are to improve all the opportunities granted us to gain a fuller experience. As the plant takes root in the soil, so we are to take deep root in Christ. As the plant receives the sunshine, the dew, and the rain, we are to open our hearts to the Holy Spirit. The work is to be done "not by might, nor by power, but by My Spirit, saith the Lord of hosts." Zechariah 4:6. If we keep our minds stayed upon Christ, He will come unto us "as the rain, as the latter and former rain unto the earth." Hosea 6:3. As the Sun of Righteousness, He will arise upon us "with healing in His wings." Malachi 4:2. We shall "grow as the lily." We shall "revive as the corn, and grow as the vine." Hosea 14:5, 7. By constantly relying upon Christ as our personal Saviour, we shall grow up into Him in all things who is our head.

The wheat develops "first the blade, then the ear, after that the full corn in the ear." The object of the husbandman in the sowing of the seed and the culture of the growing plant is the production of grain. He desires bread for the hungry, and seed for future harvests. So the divine Husbandman looks for a harvest as the reward of His labor and sacrifice. Christ is seeking to reproduce Himself in the hearts of men; and He does this through those who believe in Him. The object of the Christian life is fruit bearing—the reproduction of Christ's character in the believer, that it may be reproduced in others.

The plant does not germinate, grow, or bring forth fruit for itself, but to "give seed to the sower, and bread to the eater." Isaiah 55:10. So no man is to live unto himself. The Christian is in the world as a representative of Christ, for the salvation of other souls.

There can be no growth or fruitfulness in the life that is centered in self. If you have accepted Christ as a personal Saviour, you are to forget yourself, and try to help others. Talk of the love of Christ, tell of His goodness. Do every duty that presents itself. Carry the burden of souls upon your heart, and by every means in your power seek to save the lost. As you receive the Spirit of Christ—the Spirit of unselfish love and labor for others—you will grow and bring forth fruit. The graces of the Spirit will ripen in your character. Your faith will increase, your convictions deepen, your love be made perfect. More and more you will reflect the likeness of Christ in all that is pure, noble, and lovely.

"The fruit of the Spirit is love, joy, peace, longsuffering, gentleness, goodness, faith, meekness, temperance." Galations 5:22, 23. This fruit can never perish, but will produce after its kind a harvest unto eternal life.

"When the fruit is brought forth, immediately he putteth in the sickle, because the harvest is come." Christ is waiting with longing desire for the manifestation of Himself in His church. When the character of Christ shall be perfectly reproduced in His people, then He will come to claim them as His own.

It is the privilege of every Christian not only to look for but to hasten the coming of our Lord Jesus Christ, (2 Peter 3:12, margin). Were all who profess His name bearing fruit to His glory, how quickly the whole world would be sown with the seed of the gospel. Quickly the last great harvest would be ripened, and Christ would come to gather the precious grain.

4
Tares

Based on Matthew 13:24–30, 37–43

Another parable put He forth unto them, saying, The kingdom of heaven is likened unto a man which sowed good seed in his field; but while men slept, his enemy came and sowed tares among the wheat, and went his way. But when the blade was sprung up, and brought forth fruit, then appeared the tares also."

"The field," Christ said, "is the world." But we must understand this as signifying the church of Christ in the world. The parable is a description of that which pertains to the kingdom of God, His work of salvation of men; and this work is accomplished through the church. True, the Holy Spirit has gone out into all the world; everywhere it is moving upon the hearts of men; but it is in the church that we are to grow and ripen for the garner of God.

"He that sowed the good seed is the Son of man.... The good seed are the children of the kingdom; but the tares are the children of the wicked one." The good seed represents those who are born of the word of God, the truth. The tares represent a class who are the fruit or embodiment of error, of false principles. "The enemy that sowed them is the devil." Neither God nor His angels ever sowed a seed that would produce a tare. The tares are always sown by Satan, the enemy of God and man.

In the East, men sometimes took revenge upon an enemy by strewing his newly sown fields with the seeds of some noxious weed that, while growing, closely resembled wheat. Springing up with the wheat, it injured the crop and brought trouble and loss to the owner of the field. So it is from enmity to Christ that Satan scatters his evil seed among the good grain of the kingdom. The fruit of his sowing he attributes to the Son of God. By bringing into the church those who bear Christ's name while they deny His character, the wicked one causes that God shall be dishonored, the work of salvation misrepresented, and souls imperiled.

Christ's servants are grieved as they see true and false believers mingled in the church. They long to do something to cleanse the church. Like the servants of the householder, they are ready to uproot the tares. But Christ says to them, "Nay; lest while ye gather up the tares, ye root up also the wheat with them. Let both grow together until the harvest."

Christ has plainly taught that those who persist in open sin must be separated from the church, but He has not committed to us the work of judging character and motive. He knows our nature too well to entrust this work to us. Should we try to uproot from the church those whom we suppose to be spurious Christians, we should be sure to make mistakes. Often we regard as hopeless subjects the very ones whom Christ is drawing to Himself. Were we to deal with these souls according to our imperfect judgment, it would perhaps extinguish their last hope. Many who think themselves Christians will at last be found wanting. Many will be in heaven who their neighbors supposed would never enter there. Man judges from appearance, but God judges the heart. The tares and the wheat are to grow together until the harvest; and the harvest is the end of probationary time.

There is in the Saviour's words another lesson, a lesson of wonderful forbearance and tender love. As the tares have their roots closely intertwined with those of the good grain, so false brethren in the church may be closely linked with true disciples. The real character of these pretended believers is not fully manifested. Were they to be separated from the church, others might be caused to stumble, who but for this would have remained steadfast.

The teaching of this parable is illustrated in God's own dealing with men and angels. Satan is a deceiver. When he sinned in heaven, even the loyal angels did not fully discern his character. This was why God did not at once destroy Satan. Had He done so, the holy angels would not have perceived the justice and love of God. A doubt of God's goodness would have been as evil seed that would yield the bitter fruit of sin and woe. Therefore the author of evil was spared, fully to develop his character. Through long ages God has borne the anguish of beholding the work of evil, He has given the infinite Gift of Calvary, rather than leave any to be deceived by the misrepresentations of the wicked one; for the tares could not be plucked up without danger of uprooting the precious grain. And shall we not be as forbearing toward our fellow men as the Lord of heaven and earth is toward Satan?

The world has no right to doubt the truth of Christianity because there are unworthy members in the church, nor should Christians become disheartened because of these false brethren. How was it with the early church? Ananias and Sapphira joined themselves to the disciples. Simon Magus was baptized. Demas, who forsook Paul, had been counted a believer. Judas Iscariot was numbered with the apostles. The Redeemer does not want to lose one soul; His experience with Judas is recorded to show His long patience with perverse human nature; and He bids us bear with it as He has borne. He has said that false brethren will be found in the church till the close of time.

Notwithstanding Christ's warning, men have sought to uproot the tares. To punish those who were supposed to be evildoers, the church has had recourse to the civil power. Those who differed from the established doctrines have been imprisoned, put to torture and to death, at the instigation of men who claimed to be acting under the sanction of Christ. But it is the spirit of Satan, not the Spirit of Christ, that inspires such acts. This is Satan's own method of bringing the world under his dominion. God has been misrepresented through the church by this way of dealing with those supposed to be heretics.

Not judgment and condemnation of others, but humility and distrust of self, is the teaching of Christ's parable. Not all that is sown in the field is good grain. The fact that men are in the church does not prove them Christians.

The tares closely resembled the wheat while the blades were green; but when the field was white for the harvest, the worthless weeds bore no likeness to the wheat that bowed under the weight of its full, ripe heads. Sinners who make a pretension of piety mingle for a time with the true followers of Christ, and the semblance of Christianity is calculated to deceive many; but in the harvest of the world there will be no likeness between good and evil. Then those who have joined the church, but who have not joined Christ, will be manifest.

The tares are permitted to grow among the wheat, to have all the advantage of sun and shower; but in the time of harvest ye shall "return, and discern between the righteous and the wicked, between him that serveth God and him that serveth Him not." Malachi 3:18. Christ Himself will decide who are worthy to dwell with the family of heaven. He will judge every man according to his words and his works. Profession is as nothing in the scale. It is character that decides destiny.

The Saviour does not point forward to a time when all the tares become wheat. The wheat and tares grow together until the harvest, the end of the world. Then the tares are bound in bundles to be burned, and the wheat is gathered into the garner of God. "Then shall the righteous shine forth as the sun in the kingdom of their Father." Then "the Son of man shall send forth His angels, and they shall gather out of His kingdom all things that offend, and them which do iniquity; and shall cast them into a furnace of fire; there shall be wailing and gnashing of teeth."

5
"Like a Grain of Mustard Seed"

Based on Matthew 13:31, 32; Mark 4:30–32; Luke 13:18, 19

In the multitude that listened to Christ's teaching there were many Pharisees. These noted contemptuously how few of His hearers acknowledged Him as the Messiah. And they questioned with themselves how this unpretending teacher could exalt Israel to universal dominion. Without riches, power, or honor, how was He to establish the new kingdom? Christ read their thoughts and answered them:

"Whereunto shall we liken the kingdom of God? or with what comparison shall we compare it?" In earthly governments there was nothing that could serve for a similitude. No civil society could afford Him a symbol. "It is like a grain of mustard seed," He said, "which, when it is sown upon the earth, though it be less than all the seeds that are upon the earth, yet when it is sown, groweth up, and becometh greater than all the herbs, and putteth out great branches; so that the birds of the heaven can lodge under the shadow thereof." (R.V.)

The germ in the seed grows by the unfolding of the life-principle which God has implanted. Its development depends upon no human power. So it is with the kingdom of Christ. It is a new creation. Its principles of development are the opposite of those that rule the kingdoms of this world. Earthly governments prevail by physical force; they maintain their dominion by war; but the founder of the new kingdom is the Prince of Peace. The Holy Spirit represents worldly kingdoms under the symbol of fierce beasts of prey; but Christ is "the Lamb of God, which taketh away the sin of the world." John 1:29. In His plan of government there is no employment of brute force to compel the conscience. The Jews looked for the kingdom of God to be established in the same way as the kingdoms of the world. To promote righteousness they resorted to external measures. They devised methods and plans. But Christ implants a principle. By implanting truth and righteousness, He counterworks error and sin.

As Jesus spoke this parable, the mustard plant could be seen far and near, lifting itself above the grass and grain, and waving its branches lightly in the air. Birds flitted from twig to twig, and sang amid the leafy foliage. Yet the seed from which sprang this giant plant was among the least of all seeds. At first it sent up a tender shoot, but it was of strong vitality, and grew and flourished until it reached its present great size. So the kingdom of Christ in its beginning seemed humble and insignificant. Compared with earthly kingdoms it appeared to be the least of all. By the rulers of this world Christ's claim to be a king was ridiculed. Yet in the mighty truths committed to His followers the kingdom of the gospel possessed a divine life. And how rapid was its growth, how widespread its influence! When Christ spoke this parable, there were only a few Galilean peasants to represent the new kingdom. Their poverty, the fewness of their numbers, were urged over and over again as a reason why men should not connect themselves with these simple-minded fishermen who followed Jesus. But the mustard seed was to grow and spread forth its branches throughout the world. When the earthly kingdoms whose glory then filled the hearts of men should perish, the kingdom of Christ would remain, a mighty and far-reaching power.

So the work of grace in the heart is small in its beginning. A word is spoken, a ray of light is shed into the soul, an influence is exerted that is the beginning of the new life; and who can measure its results?

Not only is the growth of Christ's kingdom illustrated by the parable of the mustard seed, but in every stage of its growth the experience represented in the parable is repeated. For His church in every generation God has a special truth and a special work. The truth that is hid from the worldly wise and prudent is revealed to the child-like and humble. It calls for self-sacrifice. It has battles to fight and victories to win. At the outset its advocates are few. By the great men of the world and by a world-conforming church, they are opposed and despised. See John the Baptist, the forerunner of Christ, standing alone to rebuke the pride and formalism of the Jewish nation. See the first bearers of the gospel into Europe. How obscure, how hopeless, seemed the mission of Paul and Silas, the two tentmakers, as they with their companions took ship at Troas for Philippi. See "Paul the aged," in chains, preaching Christ in the stronghold of the Caesars. See the little communities of slaves and peasants in conflict with the heathenism of imperial Rome. See Martin Luther withstanding that mighty church which is the masterpiece of the world's wisdom. See him holding fast God's word against emperor and pope, declaring, "Here I take my stand; I can not do otherwise. God be my help." See John Wesley preaching Christ and His righteousness in the midst of formalism, sensualism, and infidelity. See one burdened with the woes of the heathen world, pleading for the privilege of carrying to them Christ's message of love. Hear the response of ecclesiasticism: "Sit down, young man. When God wants to convert the heathen, He will do it without your help or mine."

The great leaders of religious thought in this generation sound the praises and build the monuments of those who planted the seed of truth centuries ago. Do not many turn from this work to trample down the growth springing from the same seed today? The old cry is repeated, "We *know* that God spake unto Moses; as for this fellow [Christ in the messenger He sends], we know not from whence he is." John 9:29. As in earlier ages, the special truths for this time are found, not with the ecclesiastical authorities, but with men and women who are not too learned or too wise to believe the word of God.

"For ye see your calling, brethren, how that not many wise men after the flesh, not many mighty, not many noble, are called; but God hath chosen the foolish things of the world to confound the wise; and God hath chosen the weak things of the world to confound the things which are mighty. And base things of the world, and things which are despised, hath God chosen, yea, and things which are not, to bring to naught things that are" (1 Corinthians 1:26–28); "that your faith should not stand in the wisdom of men, but in the power of God" (1 Corinthians 2:5).

And in this last generation the parable of the mustard seed is to reach a signal and triumphant fulfillment. The little seed will become a tree. The last message of warning and mercy is to go to "every nation and kindred and tongue" (Revelation 14:6–14), "to take out of them a people for His name" (Acts 15:14; Revelation 18:1). And the earth shall be lightened with His glory.

6
Other Lessons from Seed-Sowing

From the work of seed sowing and the growth of the plant from the seed, precious lessons may be taught in the family and the school. Let the children and youth learn to recognize in natural things the working of divine agencies, and they will be enabled to grasp by faith unseen benefits. As they come to understand the wonderful work of God in supplying the wants of His great family, and how we are to co-operate with Him, they will have more faith in God, and will realize more of His power in their own daily life.

God created the seed, as He created the earth, by His word. By His word He gave it power to grow and multiply. He said, "Let the earth bring forth grass, the herb yielding seed, and the fruit tree yielding fruit after his kind, whose seed is in itself, upon the earth; and it was so...: And God saw that it was good." Genesis 1:11, 12. It is that word which still causes the seed to grow. Every seed that sends up its green blade to the sunlight declares the wonder-working power of that word uttered by Him who "spake, and it was"; who "commanded, and it stood fast." Psalm 33:9.

Christ taught His disciples to pray "Give us this day our daily bread." And pointing to the flowers He gave them the assurance, "If God so clothe the grass of the field,...shall He not much more clothe you?" Matthew 6:11, 30. Christ is constantly working to answer this prayer, and to make good this assurance. There is an invisible power constantly at work as man's servant to feed and to clothe him. Many agencies our Lord employs to make the seed, apparently thrown away, a living plant. And He supplies in due proportion all that is required to perfect the harvest. In the beautiful words of the psalmist:

"Thou visitest the earth, and waterest it;
Thou greatly enrichest it;
The river of God is full of water;
Thou providest them corn when Thou hast so prepared the earth.
Thou waterest her furrows abundantly;
Thou settlest the ridges thereof;
Thou makest it soft with showers;
Thou blessest the springing thereof.
Thou crownest the year with Thy goodness;
And Thy paths drop fatness."

Psalm 65:9–11, R.V.

The material world is under God's control. The laws of nature are obeyed by nature. Everything speaks and acts the will of the Creator. Cloud and sunshine, dew and rain, wind and storm, all are under the supervision of God, and yield implicit obedience to His command. It is in obedience to the law of God that the spire of grain bursts through the ground, "first the blade, then the ear, after that the full corn in the ear." Mark 4:28. These the Lord develops in their proper season because they do not resist His working. And can it be that man, made in the image of God, endowed with reason and speech, shall alone be unappreciative of His gifts and disobedient to His will? Shall rational beings alone cause confusion in our world?

In everything that tends to the sustenance of man is seen the concurrence of divine and human effort. There can be no reaping unless the human hand acts its part in the sowing of the seed. But without the agencies which God provides in giving sunshine and showers, dew and clouds, there would be no increase. Thus it is in every business pursuit, in every department of study and science. Thus it is in spiritual things, in the formation of the character, and in every line of Christian work. We have a part to act, but we must have the power of divinity to unite with us, or our efforts will be in vain.

Whenever man accomplishes anything, whether in spiritual or in temporal lines, he should bear in mind that he does it through co-operation with his Maker. There is great necessity for us to realize our dependence on God. Too much confidence is placed in man, too much reliance on human inventions. There is too little confidence in the power which God stands ready to give. "We are laborers together with God." 1 Corinthians 3:9. Immeasurably inferior is the part which the human agent sustains; but if he is linked with the divinity of Christ, he can do all things through the strength that Christ imparts.

The gradual development of the plant from the seed is an object lesson in child training. There is "first the blade, then the ear, after that the full corn in the ear." He who gave this parable created the tiny seed, gave it its vital properties, and ordained the laws that govern its growth. And the truths which the parable teaches were made a living reality in His own life. In both His physical and His spiritual nature He followed the divine order of growth illustrated by the plant, as He wishes all youth to do. Although He was the

Majesty of heaven, the King of glory, He became a babe in Bethlehem, and for a time represented the helpless infant in its mother's care. In childhood He did the works of an obedient child. He spoke and acted with the wisdom of a child and not of a man, honoring His parents and carrying out their wishes in helpful ways, according to the ability of a child. But at each stage of His development He was perfect, with the simple, natural grace of a sinless life. The sacred record says of His childhood, "The child grew, and waxed strong in spirit, filled with wisdom; and the grace of God was upon Him." And of His youth it is recorded, "Jesus increased in wisdom and stature, and in favor with God and man." Luke 2:40, 52.

The work of parents and teachers is here suggested. They should aim so to cultivate the tendencies of the youth that at each stage of their life they may represent the natural beauty appropriate to that period, unfolding naturally, as do the plants in the garden.

Those children are most attractive who are natural, unaffected. It is not wise to give them special notice, and repeat their clever sayings before them. Vanity should not be encouraged by praising their looks, their words, or their actions. Nor should they be dressed in an expensive or showy manner. This encourages pride in them, and awakens envy in the hearts of their companions.

The little ones should be educated in childlike simplicity. They should be trained to be content with the small, helpful duties and the pleasures and experiences natural to their years. Childhood answers to the blade in the parable, and the blade has a beauty peculiarly its own. The children should not be forced into a precocious maturity but should retain as long as possible the freshness and grace of their early years.

The little children may be Christians, having an experience in accordance with their years. This is all that God expects of them. They need to be educated in spiritual things; and parents should give them every advantage that they may form characters after the similitude of the character of Christ.

In the laws of God in nature, effect follows cause with unerring certainty. The reaping will testify as to what the sowing has been. The slothful worker is condemned by his work. The harvest bears witness against him. So in spiritual things: the faithfulness of every worker is measured by the results of his work. The character of his work, whether diligent or slothful, is revealed by the harvest. It is thus that his destiny for eternity is decided.

Every seed sown produces a harvest of its kind. So it is in human life. We all need to sow the seeds of compassion, sympathy, and love; for we shall reap what we sow. Every characteristic of selfishness, self-love, self-esteem, every act of self-indulgence, will bring forth a like harvest. He who lives for self is sowing to the flesh, and of the flesh he will reap corruption.

God destroys no man. Everyone who is destroyed will have destroyed himself. Everyone who stifles the admonitions of conscience is sowing the seeds of unbelief, and these will produce a sure harvest. By rejecting the first warning from God, Pharaoh of old sowed the seeds of obstinacy, and he reaped obstinacy. God did not compel him to disbelieve. The seed of unbelief which he sowed produced a harvest of its kind. Thus his resistance continued, until he looked upon his devastated land, upon the cold, dead form of his first-born, and the first-born of all in his house and of all the families in his kingdom, until the waters of the sea closed over his horses and his chariots and his men of war. His history is a fearful illustration of the truth of the words that "whatsoever a man soweth, that shall he also reap." Galations 6:7. Did men but realize this, they would be careful what seed they sow.

As the seed sown produces a harvest, and this in turn is sown, the harvest is multiplied. In our relation to others, this law holds true. Every act, every word, is a seed that will bear fruit. Every deed of thoughtful kindness, of obedience, or of self-denial, will reproduce itself in others, and through them in still others. So every act of envy, malice, or dissension is a seed that will spring up in a "root of bitterness" (Hebrews 12:15), whereby many shall be defiled. And how much larger number will the "many" poison. Thus the sowing of good and evil goes on for time and for eternity.

Liberality both in spiritual and in temporal things is taught in the lesson of seed sowing. The Lord says, "Blessed are ye that sow beside all waters." Isaiah 32:20. "This I say, He which soweth sparingly shall reap also sparingly; and he which soweth bountifully shall reap also bountifully." 2 Corinthians 9:6. To sow beside all waters means a continual imparting of God's gifts. It means giving wherever the cause of God or the needs of humanity demand our aid. This will not tend to poverty. "He which soweth bountifully shall reap also bountifully." The sower multiplies his seed by casting it away. So it is with those who are faithful in distributing God's gifts. By imparting they increase their blessings. God has promised them a sufficiency that they may continue to give. "Give, and it shall be given unto you; good measure, pressed down, and shaken together, and running over, shall men give into your bosom." Luke 6:38.

And more than this is wrapped up in the sowing and the reaping. As we distribute God's temporal blessings, the evidence of our love and sympathy awakens in the receiver gratitude and thanksgiving to God. The soil of the heart is prepared to receive the seeds of spiritual truth. And He who ministers seed to the sower will cause the seed to germinate and bear fruit unto eternal life.

By the casting of the grain into the soil, Christ represents the sacrifice of Himself for our redemption. "Except a corn of wheat fall into the ground and die," He says, "it abideth alone; but if it die, it bringeth forth much fruit." John 12:24. So the death of Christ will result in fruit for the kingdom of God. In accordance with the law of the vegetable kingdom, life will be the result of His death.

And all who would bring forth fruit as workers together with Christ must first fall into the ground and die. The life must be cast into the furrow of the world's need. Self-love, self-interest, must perish. But the law of self-sacrifice is the law of self-preservation. The seed buried in the ground produces fruit, and in turn this is planted. Thus the harvest is multiplied. The husbandman preserves his grain by casting it away. So in human life, to give is to live. The life that will be preserved is the life that is freely given in service to God and man. Those who for Christ's sake sacrifice their life in this world, will keep it unto life eternal.

The seed dies to spring forth into new life, and in this we are taught the lesson of the resurrection. All who love God will live again in the Eden above. Of the human body laid away to molder in the grave God has said, "It is sown in corruption; it is raised in incorruption: it is sown in dishonor; it is raised in glory: it is sown in weakness; it is raised in power." 1 Corinthians 15:42, 43.

Such are a few of the many lessons taught by nature's living parable of the sower and the seed. As parents and teachers try to teach these lessons, the work should be made practical. Let the children themselves prepare the soil and sow the seed. As they work, the parent or teacher can explain the garden of the heart with the good or bad seed sown there, and that as the garden must be prepared for the natural seed, so the heart must be prepared for the seed of truth. As the seed is cast into the ground, they can teach the lesson of Christ's death; and as the blade springs up, they can teach the lesson of the truth of the resurrection. As the plants grow, the correspondence between the natural and the spiritual sowing may be continued.

The youth should be instructed in a similar way. They should be taught to till the soil. It would be well if there were, connected with every school, lands for cultivation. Such lands should be regarded as God's own schoolroom. The things of nature should be looked upon as a lesson book which His children are to study, and from which they may obtain knowledge as to the culture of the soul.

In tilling the soil, in disciplining and subduing the land, lessons may constantly be learned. No one would think of settling upon a raw piece of land, expecting it at once to yield a harvest. Earnestness, diligence, and persevering labor are to be put forth in treating the soil preparatory to sowing the seed. So it is in the spiritual work in the human heart. Those who would be benefited by the tilling of the soil must go forth with the word of God in their hearts. They will then find the fallow ground of the heart broken by the softening, subduing influence of the Holy Spirit. Unless hard work is bestowed on the soil, it will not yield a harvest. So with the soil of the heart: the Spirit of God must work upon it to refine and discipline it before it can bring forth fruit to the glory of God.

The soil will not produce its riches when worked by impulse. It needs thoughtful, daily attention. It must be plowed often and deep, with a view to keeping out the weeds that take nourishment from the good seed planted. Thus those who plow and sow prepare for the harvest. None need stand in the field amid the sad wreck of their hopes.

The blessing of the Lord will rest upon those who thus work the land, learning spiritual lessons from nature. In cultivating the soil the worker knows little what treasures will open up before him. While he is not to despise the instruction he may gather from minds that have had an experience, and from the information that intelligent men may impart, he should gather lessons for himself. This is a part of his training. The cultivation of the soil will prove an education to the soul.

He who causes the seed to spring up, who tends it day and night, who gives it power to develop, is the Author of our being, the King of heaven, and He exercises still greater care and interest in behalf of His children. While the human sower is planting the seed to sustain our earthly life, the Divine Sower will plant in the soul the seed that will bring forth fruit unto life everlasting.

7
"Like unto Leaven"

Based on Matthew 13:33; Luke 13:20, 21

Many educated and influential men had come to hear the Prophet of Galilee. Some of these looked with curious interest upon the multitude that had gathered about Christ as He taught by the sea. In this great throng all classes of society were represented. There were the poor, the illiterate, the ragged beggar, the robber with the seal of guilt upon his face, the maimed, the dissipated, the merchant and the man of leisure, high and low, rich and poor, all crowding upon one another for a place to stand and hear the words of Christ. As these cultured men gazed upon the strange assembly, they asked themselves, Is the kingdom of God composed of such material as this? Again the Saviour replied by a parable:

"The kingdom of heaven is like unto leaven, which a woman took, and hid in three measures of meal, till the whole was leavened."

Among the Jews leaven was sometimes used as an emblem of sin. At the time of the Passover the people were directed to remove all the leaven from their houses as they were to put away sin from their hearts. Christ warned His disciples, "Beware ye of the leaven of the Pharisees, which is hypocrisy." Luke 12:1. And the apostle Paul speaks of the "leaven of malice and wickedness." I Corinthians 5:8. But in the Saviour's parable, leaven is used to represent the kingdom of heaven. It illustrates the quickening, assimilating power of the grace of God.

None are so vile, none have fallen so low, as to be beyond the working of this power. In all who will submit themselves to the Holy Spirit a new principle of life is to be implanted; the lost image of God is to be restored in humanity.

But man cannot transform himself by the exercise of his will. He possesses no power by which this change can be effected. The leaven—something wholly from without—must be put into the meal before the desired change can be wrought in it. So the grace of God must be received by the sinner before he can be fitted for the kingdom of glory. All the culture and education which the world can give will fail of making a degraded child of sin a child of heaven. The renewing energy must come from God. The change can be made only by the Holy Spirit. All who would be saved, high or low, rich or poor, must submit to the working of this power.

As the leaven, when mingled with the meal, works from within outward, so it is by the renewing of the heart that the grace of God works to transform the life. No mere external change is sufficient to bring us into harmony with

God. There are many who try to reform by correcting this or that bad habit, and they hope in this way to become Christians, but they are beginning in the wrong place. Our first work is with the heart.

A profession of faith and the possession of truth in the soul are two different things. The mere knowledge of truth is not enough. We may possess this, but the tenor of our thoughts may not be changed. The heart must be converted and sanctified.

The man who attempts to keep the commandments of God from a sense of obligation merely—because he is required to do so—will never enter into the joy of obedience. He does not obey. When the requirements of God are accounted a burden because they cut across human inclination, we may know that the life is not a Christian life. True obedience is the outworking of a principle within. It springs from the love of righteousness, the love of the law of God. The essence of all righteousness is loyalty to our Redeemer. This will lead us to do right because it is right—because right doing is pleasing to God.

The great truth of the conversion of the heart by the Holy Spirit is presented in Christ's words to Nicodemus: "Verily, verily, I say unto thee, Except a man be born from above, he can not see the kingdom of God.... That which is born of the flesh is flesh, and that which is born of the Spirit is spirit. Marvel not that I said unto thee, Ye must be born again. The wind bloweth where it listeth, and thou hearest the sound thereof, but canst not tell whence it cometh and whither it goeth. So is every one that is born of the Spirit." John 3:3–8, margin.

The apostle Paul, writing by the Holy Spirit, says, "God, who is rich in mercy, for His great love wherewith He loved us, even when we were dead in sins, hath quickened us together with Christ, (by grace ye are saved;) and hath raised us up together, and made us sit together in heavenly places in Christ Jesus: that in the ages to come He might show the exceeding riches of His grace in His kindness toward us through Christ Jesus. For by grace are ye saved through faith; and that not of yourselves; it is the gift of God." Ephesians 2:4–8.

The leaven hidden in the flour works invisibly to bring the whole mass under its leavening process; so the leaven of truth works secretly, silently, steadily, to transform the soul. The natural inclinations are softened and subdued. New thoughts, new feelings, new motives, are implanted. A new standard of character is set up—the life of Christ. The mind is changed; the faculties are roused to action in new lines. Man is not endowed with new faculties, but the faculties he has are sanctified. The conscience is awakened. We are endowed with traits of character that enable us to do service for God.

Often the question arises, Why, then, are there so many, claiming to believe God's word, in whom there is not seen a reformation in words, in spirit, and in character? Why are there so many who cannot bear opposition to their purposes and plans, who manifest an unholy temper, and whose words are harsh, overbearing, and passionate? There is seen in their lives the same love of self, the same selfish indulgence, the same temper and hasty speech, that is seen in the life of the worldling. There is the same sensitive pride, the same yielding to natural inclination, the same perversity of character, as if the truth were wholly unknown to them. The reason is that they are not converted. They have not hidden the leaven of truth in the heart. It has not had opportunity to do its work. Their natural and cultivated tendencies to evil have not been submitted to its transforming power. Their lives reveal the absence of the grace of Christ, an unbelief in His power to transform the character.

"Faith cometh by hearing, and hearing by the word of God." Romans 10:17. The Scriptures are the great agency in the transformation of character. Christ prayed, "Sanctify them through Thy truth; Thy word is truth." John 17:17. If studied and obeyed, the word of God works in the heart, subduing every unholy attribute. The Holy Spirit comes to convict of sin, and the faith that springs up in the heart works by love to Christ, conforming us in body, soul, and spirit to His own image. Then God can use us to do His will. The power given us works from within outwardly, leading us to communicate to others the truth that has been communicated to us.

The truths of the word of God meet man's great practical necessity—the conversion of the soul through faith. These grand principles are not to be thought too pure and holy to be brought into the daily life. They are truths which reach to heaven and compass eternity, yet their vital influence is to be woven into human experience. They are to permeate all the great things and all the little things of life.

Received into the heart, the leaven of truth will regulate the desires, purify the thoughts, and sweeten the disposition. It quickens the faculties of the mind and the energies of the soul. It enlarges the capacity for feeling, for loving.

The world regards as a mystery the man who is imbued with this principle. The selfish, money-loving man lives only to secure for himself the riches, honors, and pleasures of this world. He loses the eternal world from his reckoning. But with the follower of Christ these things will not be all-absorbing. For Christ's sake he will labor and deny self, that he may aid in the great work of saving souls who are without Christ and without hope in the world. Such a man the world cannot understand; for he is keeping in view eternal realities. The love of Christ with its redeeming power has come into the heart. This love masters every other motive, and raises its possessor above the corrupting influence of the world.

The word of God is to have a sanctifying effect on our association with every member of the human family. The leaven of truth will not produce the spirit of rivalry, the love of ambition, the desire to be first. True, heaven-born love is not selfish and changeable. It is not dependent on human praise. The heart of him who receives the grace of God overflows with love for God and for those for whom Christ died. Self is not struggling for recognition. He does not love others because they love and please him, because they appreciate his merits, but because they are Christ's purchased possession. If his motives, words, or actions are misunderstood or misrepresented, he takes no offense, but pursues the even tenor of his way. He is kind and thoughtful, humble in his opinion of himself, yet full of hope, always trusting in the mercy and love of God.

The apostle exhorts us, "As He which hath called you is holy, so be ye holy in all manner of conversation; because it is written, Be ye holy; for I am holy." 1 Peter 1:15, 16. The grace of Christ is to control the temper and the voice. Its working will be seen in politeness and tender regard shown by brother for brother, in kind, encouraging words. An angel presence is in the home. The life breathes a sweet perfume, which ascends to God as holy incense. Love is manifested in kindness, gentleness, forbearance, and long-suffering.

The countenance is changed. Christ abiding in the heart shines out in the faces of those who love Him and keep His commandments. Truth is written there. The sweet peace of heaven is revealed. There is expressed a habitual gentleness, a more than human love.

The leaven of truth works a change in the whole man, making the coarse refined, the rough gentle, the selfish generous. By it the impure are cleansed, washed in the blood of the Lamb. Through its life-giving power it brings all there is of mind and soul and strength into harmony with the divine life. Man with his human nature becomes a partaker of divinity. Christ is honored in excellence and perfection of character. As these changes are effected, angels break forth in rapturous song, and God and Christ rejoice over souls fashioned after the divine similitude.

8
Hidden Treasure

Based on Matthew 13:44

Again, the kingdom of heaven is like unto treasure hid in a field; the which when a man hath found, he hideth, and for joy thereof goeth and selleth all that he hath, and buyeth that field."

In ancient times it was customary for men to hide their treasures in the earth. Thefts and robberies were frequent. And whenever there was a change in the ruling power, those who had large possessions were liable to be put under heavy tribute. Moreover the country was in constant danger of invasion by marauding armies. As a consequence, the rich endeavored to preserve their wealth by concealing it, and the earth was looked upon as a safe hiding place. But often the place of concealment was forgotten; death might claim the owner, imprisonment or exile might separate him from his treasure, and the wealth he had taken such pains to preserve was left for the fortunate finder. In Christ's day it was not uncommon to discover in neglected land old coins and ornaments of gold and silver.

A man hires land to cultivate, and as the oxen plow the soil, buried treasure is unearthed. As the man discovers this treasure, he sees that a fortune is within his reach. Restoring the gold to its hiding place, he returns to his home and sells all that he has, in order to purchase the field containing the treasure. His family and his neighbors think that he is acting like a madman. Looking on the field, they see no value in the neglected soil. But the man knows what he is doing; and when he has a title to the field, he searches every part of it to find the treasure that he has secured.

This parable illustrates the value of the heavenly treasure, and the effort that should be made to secure it. The finder of the treasure in the field was ready to part with all that he had, ready to put forth untiring labor, in order to secure the hidden riches. So the finder of heavenly treasure will count no labor too great and no sacrifice too dear, in order to gain the treasures of truth.

In the parable the field containing the treasure represents the Holy Scriptures. And the gospel is the treasure. The earth itself is not so interlaced with golden veins and filled with precious things as is the word of God.

How Hidden

The treasures of the gospel are said to be hidden. By those who are wise in their own estimation, who are puffed up by the teaching of vain philosophy, the beauty and power and mystery of the plan of redemption are not perceived. Many have eyes, but they see not; they have ears, but they hear not; they have intellect, but they discern not the hidden treasure.

A man might pass over the place where treasure had been concealed. In dire necessity he might sit down to rest at the foot of a tree, not knowing of the riches hidden at its roots. So it was with the Jews. As a golden treasure, truth had been intrusted to the Hebrew people. The Jewish economy, bearing the signature of Heaven, had been instituted by Christ Himself. In types and symbols the great truths of redemption were veiled. Yet when Christ came, the Jews did not recognize Him to whom all these symbols pointed. They had the word of God in their hands; but the traditions which had been handed down from generation to generation, and the human interpretation of the Scriptures, hid from them the truth as it is in Jesus. The spiritual import of the sacred writings was lost. The treasure house of all knowledge was open to them, but they knew it not.

God does not conceal His truth from men. By their own course of action they make it obscure to themselves. Christ gave the Jewish people abundant evidence that He was the Messiah; but His teaching called for a decided change in their lives. They saw that if they received Christ, they must give up their cherished maxims and traditions, their selfish, ungodly practices. It required a sacrifice to receive changeless, eternal truth. Therefore they would not admit the most conclusive evidence that God could give to establish faith in Christ. They professed to believe the Old Testament Scriptures, yet they refused to accept the testimony contained therein concerning Christ's life and character. They were afraid of being convinced lest they should be converted and be compelled to give up their preconceived opinions. The treasure of the gospel, the Way, the Truth, and the Life, was among them, but they rejected the greatest gift that Heaven could bestow.

"Among the chief rulers also many believed on Him," we read; "but because of the Pharisees they did not confess Him, lest they should be put out of the synagogue." John 12:42. They were convinced; they believed Jesus to be the Son of God; but it was not in harmony with their ambitious desires to confess Him. They had not the faith that would have secured for them the heavenly treasure. They were seeking worldly treasure.

And today men are eagerly seeking for earthly treasure. Their minds are filled with selfish, ambitious thoughts. For the sake of gaining worldly riches, honor, or power, they place the maxims, traditions, and requirements of men above the requirements of God. From them the treasures of His word are hidden.

"The natural man receiveth not the things of the Spirit of God; for they are foolishness unto him; neither can he know them, because they are spiritually discerned," 1 Corinthians 2:14.

"If our gospel be hid, it is hid to them that are lost; in whom the god of this world hath blinded the minds of them which believe not, lest the light of the glorious gospel of Christ, who is the image of God, should shine unto them." 2 Corinthians 4:3, 4.

Value of the Treasure

The Saviour saw that men were absorbed in getting gain, and were losing sight of eternal realities. He undertook to correct this evil. He sought to break the infatuating spell that was paralyzing the soul. Lifting up His voice He cried, "What is a man profited, if he shall gain the whole world, and lose his own soul? or what shall a man give in exchange for his soul?" Matthew 16:26. He presents before fallen humanity the nobler world they have lost sight of, that they may behold eternal realities. He takes them to the threshold of the Infinite, flushed with the indescribable glory of God, and shows them the treasure there.

The value of this treasure is above gold or silver. The riches of earth's mines cannot compare with it.

"The depth saith, It is not in me;
And the sea saith, It is not with me.
It can not be gotten for gold,
Neither shall silver be weighed for the price thereof.
It can not be valued with the gold of Ophir,
With the precious onyx, or the sapphire.
The gold and the crystal can not equal it;
And the exchange of it shall not be for jewels of fine gold.
No mention shall be made of coral or of pearls,
For the price of wisdom is above rubies."

Job 28:14–18.

This is the treasure that is found in the Scriptures. The Bible is God's great lesson book, His great educator. The foundation of all true science is contained in the Bible. Every branch of knowledge may be found by searching the word of God. And above all else it contains the science of all sciences, the science of salvation. The Bible is the mine of the unsearchable riches of Christ.

The true higher education is gained by studying and obeying the word of God. But when God's word is laid aside for books that do not lead to God and the kingdom of heaven, the education acquired is a perversion of the name.

There are wonderful truths in nature. The earth, the sea, and the sky are full of truth. They are our teachers. Nature utters her voice in lessons of heavenly wisdom and eternal truth. But fallen man will not understand. Sin has obscured his vision, and he cannot of himself interpret nature without placing it above God. Correct lessons cannot impress the minds of those who reject the word of God. The teaching of nature is by them so perverted that it turns the mind away from the Creator.

By many, man's wisdom is thought to be higher than the wisdom of the divine Teacher, and God's lesson book is looked upon as old-fashioned, stale, and uninteresting. But by those who have been vivified by the Holy Spirit it is not so regarded. They see the priceless treasure, and would sell all to buy the field that contains it. Instead of books containing the suppositions of reputedly great authors, they choose the word of Him who is the greatest author and the greatest teacher the world has ever known, who gave His life for us, that through Him we might have everlasting life.

Results of Neglecting the Treasure

Satan works on human minds, leading them to think that there is wonderful knowledge to be gained apart from God. By deceptive reasoning he led Adam and Eve to doubt God's word, and to supply its place with a theory that led to disobedience. And his sophistry is doing today what it did in Eden. Teachers who mingle the sentiments of infidel authors with the education they are giving, plant in the minds of youth thoughts that will lead to distrust of God and transgression of His law. Little do they know what they are doing. Little do they realize what will be the result of their work.

A student may go through all the grades of the schools and colleges of today. He may devote all his powers to acquiring knowledge. But unless he has a knowledge of God, unless he obeys the laws that govern his being, he will destroy himself. By wrong habits he loses his power of self-appreciation. He loses self-control. He cannot reason correctly about matters that concern him most closely. He is reckless and irrational in his treatment of mind and body. By wrong habits he makes of himself a wreck. Happiness he cannot have; for his neglect to cultivate pure, healthful principles places him under the control of habits that ruin his peace. His years of taxing study are lost, for he has destroyed himself. He has misused his physical and mental powers, and the temple of the body is in ruins. He is ruined for this life and for the life to come. By acquiring earthly knowledge he thought to gain a treasure, but by laying his Bible aside he sacrificed a treasure worth everything else.

Search for the Treasure

The word of God is to be our study. We are to educate our children in the truths found therein. It is an inexhaustible treasure; but men fail to find this treasure because they do not search until it is within their possession. Very many are content with a supposition in regard to the truth. They are content with a surface work, taking for granted that they have all that is essential.

They take the sayings of others for truth, being too indolent to put themselves to diligent, earnest labor, represented in the word as digging for hidden treasure. But man's inventions are not only unreliable, they are dangerous; for they place man where God should be. They place the sayings of men where a "Thus saith the Lord" should be.

Christ is the truth. His words are truth, and they have a deeper significance than appears on the surface. All the sayings of Christ have a value beyond their unpretending appearance. Minds that are quickened by the Holy Spirit will discern the value of these sayings. They will discern the precious gems of truth, though these may be buried treasures.

Human theories and speculations will never lead to an understanding of God's word. Those who suppose that they understand philosophy think that their explanations are necessary to unlock the treasures of knowledge and to prevent heresies from coming into the church. But it is these explanations that have brought in false theories and heresies. Men have made desperate efforts to explain what they thought to be intricate scriptures; but too often their efforts have only darkened that which they tried to make clear.

The priests and Pharisees thought they were doing great things as teachers by putting their own interpretation upon the word of God, but Christ said of them, "Ye know not the scriptures, neither the power of God." Mark 12:24. He charged them with the guilt of "teaching for doctrines the commandments of men." Mark 7:7. Though they were the teachers of the oracles of God, though they were supposed to understand His word, they were not doers of the word. Satan had blinded their eyes that they should not see its true import.

This is the work of many in our day. Many churches are guilty of this sin. There is danger, great danger, that the supposed wise men of today will repeat the experience of the Jewish teachers. They falsely interpret the divine oracles, and souls are brought into perplexity and shrouded in darkness because of their misconception of divine truth.

The Scriptures need not be read by the dim light of tradition or human speculation. As well might we try to give light to the sun with a torch as to explain the Scriptures by human tradition or imagination. God's holy word needs not the torchlight glimmer of earth to make its glories distinguishable. It is light in itself—the glory of God revealed, and beside it every other light is dim.

But there must be earnest study and close investigation. Sharp, clear perceptions of truth will never be the reward of indolence. No earthy blessing can be obtained without earnest, patient, persevering effort. If men attain success in business, they must have a will to do and a faith to look for results. And we cannot expect to gain spiritual knowledge without earnest toil. Those who desire to find the treasures of truth must dig for them as the miner digs for the treasure hidden in the earth. No halfhearted, indifferent work will avail. It is essential for old and young, not only to read God's word, but to study it with wholehearted earnestness, praying and searching for truth as for hidden treasure. Those who do this will be rewarded, for Christ will quicken the understanding.

Our salvation depends on a knowledge of the truth contained in the Scriptures. It is God's will that we should possess this. Search, O search the precious Bible with hungry hearts. Explore God's word as the miner explores the earth to find veins of gold. Never give up the search until you have ascertained your relation to God and His will in regard to you. Christ declared, "Whatsoever ye shall ask in My name, that will I do, that the Father may be glorified in the Son. If ye shall ask anything in My name, I will do it." John 14:13, 14.

Men of piety and talent catch views of eternal realities, but often they fail of understanding, because the things that are seen eclipse the glory of the unseen. He who would seek successfully for the hidden treasure must rise to higher pursuits than the things of this world. His affections and all His capabilities must be consecrated to the search.

Disobedience has closed the door to a vast amount of knowledge that might have been gained from the Scriptures. Understanding means obedience to God's commandments. The Scriptures are not to be adapted to meet the prejudice and jealousy of men. They can be understood only by those who are humbly seeking for a knowledge of the truth that they may obey it.

Do you ask, What shall I do to be saved? You must lay your preconceived opinions, your hereditary and cultivated ideas, at the door of investigation. If you search the Scriptures to vindicate your own opinions, you will never reach the truth. Search in order to learn what the Lord says. If conviction comes as you search, if you see that your cherished opinions are not in harmony with the truth, do not misinterpret the truth in order to suit your own belief, but accept the light given. Open mind and heart that you may behold wondrous things out of God's word.

Faith in Christ as the world's Redeemer calls for an acknowledgment of the enlightened intellect controlled by a heart that can discern and appreciate the heavenly treasure. This faith is inseparable from repentance and transformation of character. To have faith means to find and accept the gospel treasure, with all the obligations which it imposes.

"Except a man be born again, he cannot see the kingdom of God." John 3:3. He may conjecture and imagine, but without the eye of faith he cannot see the treasure. Christ gave His life to secure for us this inestimable treasure; but without regeneration through faith in His blood, there is no remission of sins, no treasure for any perishing soul.

We need the enlightenment of the Holy Spirit in order to discern the truths in God's word. The lovely things of the natural world are not seen until the sun, dispelling the darkness, floods them with its light. So the treasures in the word of God are not appreciated until they are revealed by the bright beams of the Sun of Righteousness.

The Holy Spirit, sent from heaven by the benevolence of infinite love, takes the things of God and reveals them to every soul that has an implicit faith in Christ. By His power the vital truths upon which the salvation of the soul depends are impressed upon the mind, and the way of life is made so plain that none need err therein. As we study the Scriptures, we should pray for the light of God's Holy Spirit to shine upon the word, that we may see and appreciate its treasures.

Reward of Searching

Let none think that there is no more knowledge for them to gain. The depth of human intellect may be measured; the works of human authors may be mastered; but the highest, deepest, broadest flight of the imagination cannot find out God. There is infinity beyond all that we can comprehend. We have seen only the glimmering of divine glory and of the infinitude of knowledge and wisdom; we have, as it were, been working on the surface of the mine, when rich golden ore is beneath the surface, to reward the one who will dig for it. The shaft must be sunk deeper and yet deeper in the mine, and the result will be glorious treasure. Through a correct faith, divine knowledge will become human knowledge.

No one can search the Scriptures in the spirit of Christ without being rewarded. When man is willing to be instructed as a little child, when he submits wholly to God, he will find the truth in His word. If men would be obedient, they would understand the plan of God's government. The heavenly world would open its chambers of grace and glory for exploration. Human beings would be altogether different from what they now are, for by exploring the mines of truth men would be ennobled. The mystery of redemption, the incarnation of Christ, His atoning sacrifice, would not be as they are now, vague in our minds. They would be not only better understood, but altogether more highly appreciated.

In His prayer to the Father, Christ gave to the world a lesson which should be graven on mind and soul. "This is life eternal," He said, "that they might know Thee the only true God, and Jesus Christ, whom Thou hast sent." John 17:3. This is true education. It imparts power. The experimental knowledge of God and of Jesus Christ whom He has sent, transforms man into the image of God. It gives to man the mastery of himself, bringing every impulse and passion of the lower nature under the control of the higher powers of the mind. It makes its possessor a son of God and an heir of heaven. It brings him into communion with the mind of the Infinite, and opens to him the rich treasures of the universe.

This is the knowledge which is obtained by searching the word of God. And this treasure may be found by every soul who will give all to obtain it.

"If thou criest after knowledge, and liftest up thy voice for understanding; if thou seekest her as silver, and searchest for her as for hid treasures; then shalt thou understand the fear of the Lord, and find the knowledge of God." Proverbs 2:3–5.

9
The Pearl

Based on Matthew 13:45, 46

The blessings of redeeming love our Savior compared to a precious pearl. He illustrated His lesson by the parable of the merchantman seeking goodly pearls "who, when he had found one pearl of great price, went and sold all that he had, and bought it." Christ Himself is the pearl of great price. In Him is gathered all the glory of the Father, the fullness of the Godhead. He is the brightness of the Father's glory and the express image of His person. The glory of the attributes of God is expressed in His character. Every page of the Holy Scriptures shines with His light. The righteousness of Christ, as a pure, white pearl, has no defect, no stain. No work of man can improve the great and precious gift of God. It is without a flaw. In Christ are "hid all the treasures of wisdom and knowledge." Colossians 2:3. He is "made unto us wisdom, and righteousness, and sanctification, and redemption." 1 Corinthians 1:30. All that can satisfy the needs and longings of the human soul, for this world and for the world to come, is found in Christ. Our Redeemer is the pearl so precious that in comparison all things else may be accounted loss.

Christ "came unto His own, and His own received Him not." John 1:11. The light of God shone into the darkness of the world, and "the darkness comprehended it not." John 1:5. But not all were found indifferent to the gift of heaven. The merchantman in the parable represents a class who were sincerely desiring truth. In different nations there were earnest and thoughtful men who had sought in literature and science and the religions of the heathen world for that which they could receive as the soul's treasure. Among the Jews there were those who were seeking for that which they had not. Dissatisfied with a formal religion, they longed for that which was spiritual and uplifting. Christ's chosen disciples belonged to the latter class, Cornelius and the Ethiopian eunuch to the former. They had been longing and praying for light from heaven; and when Christ was revealed to them, they received Him with gladness.

In the parable the pearl is not represented as a gift. The merchantman bought it at the price of all that he had. Many question the meaning of this, since Christ is represented in the Scriptures as a gift. He is a gift, but only to those who give themselves, soul, body, and spirit, to Him without reserve. We are to give ourselves to Christ, to live a life of willing obedience to all His requirements. All that we are, all the talents and capabilities we possess, are the Lord's, to be consecrated to His service. When we thus give ourselves wholly to Him, Christ, with all the treasures of heaven, gives Himself to us. We obtain the pearl of great price.

Salvation is a free gift, and yet it is to be bought and sold. In the market of which divine mercy has the management, the precious pearl is represented as being bought without money and without price. In this market all may obtain the goods of heaven. The treasury of the jewels of truth is open to all. "Behold, I have set before thee an open door," the Lord declares, "and no man can shut it." No sword guards the way through this door. Voices from within and at the door say, Come. The Saviour's voice earnestly and lovingly invites us: "I counsel thee to buy of Me gold tried in the fire, that thou mayest be rich." Revelation 3:8, 18.

The gospel of Christ is a blessing that all may possess. The poorest are as well able as the richest to purchase salvation; for no amount of worldly wealth can secure it. It is obtained by willing obedience, by giving ourselves to Christ as His own purchased possession. Education, even of the highest class, cannot of itself bring a man nearer to God. The Pharisees were favored with every temporal and every spiritual advantage, and they said with boastful pride, We are "rich, and increased with goods, and have need of nothing"; yet they were "wretched, and miserable, and poor, and blind, and naked." Revelation 3:17. Christ offered them the pearl of great price; but they disdained to accept it, and He said to them, "The publicans and the harlots go into the kingdom of God before you." Matthew 21:31.

We cannot earn salvation, but we are to seek for it with as much interest and perseverance as though we would abandon everything in the world for it.

We are to seek for the pearl of great price, but not in worldly marts or in worldly ways. The price we are required to pay is not gold or silver, for this belongs to God. Abandon the idea that temporal or spiritual advantages will win for you salvation. God calls for your willing obedience. He asks you to give up your sins. "To him that overcometh," Christ declares, "will I grant to sit with Me in My throne, even as I also overcame, and am set down with My Father in His throne." Revelation 3:21.

There are some who seem to be always seeking for the heavenly pearl. But they do not make an entire surrender of their wrong habits. They do not die to self that Christ may live in them. Therefore they do not find the precious pearl. They have not overcome unholy ambition and their love for worldly attractions. They do not take up the cross and follow Christ in the path of self-denial and sacrifice. Almost Christians, yet not fully Christians, they seem near the kingdom of heaven, but they cannot enter there. Almost but not wholly saved, means to be not almost but wholly lost.

The parable of the merchantman seeking goodly pearls has a double significance: it applies not only to men as seeking the kingdom of heaven, but to Christ as seeking His lost inheritance. Christ, the heavenly merchantman seeking goodly pearls, saw in lost humanity the pearl of price. In man, defiled and ruined by sin, He saw the possibilities of redemption. Hearts that have been the battleground of the conflict with Satan, and that have been rescued by the power of love, are more precious to the Redeemer than are those who have never fallen. God looked upon humanity, not as vile and worthless; He looked upon it in Christ, saw it as it might become through redeeming love. He collected all the riches of the universe, and laid them down in order to buy the pearl. And Jesus, having found it, resets it in His own diadem. "For they shall be as the stones of a crown, lifted up as an ensign upon His land." Zechariah 9:16. "They shall be Mine, saith the Lord of hosts, in that day when I make up My jewels." Malachi 3:17.

But Christ as the precious pearl, and our privilege of possessing this heavenly treasure, is the theme on which we most need to dwell. It is the Holy Spirit that reveals to men the preciousness of the goodly pearl. The time of the Holy Spirit's power is the time when in a special sense the heavenly gift is sought and found. In Christ's day many heard the gospel, but their minds were darkened by false teaching, and they did not recognize in the humble Teacher of Galilee the Sent of God. But after Christ's ascension His enthronement in His mediatorial kingdom was signalized by the outpouring of the Holy Spirit. On the day of Pentecost the Spirit was given. Christ's witnesses proclaimed the power of the risen Saviour. The light of heaven penetrated the darkened minds of those who had been deceived by the enemies of Christ. They now saw Him exalted to be "a Prince and a Saviour, for to give repentance to Israel, and forgiveness of sins." Acts 5:31. They saw Him encircled with the glory of heaven, with infinite treasures in His hands to bestow upon all who would turn from their rebellion. As the apostles set forth the glory of the Only-Begotten of the Father, three thousand souls were convicted. They were made to see themselves as they were, sinful and polluted, and Christ as their friend and Redeemer. Christ was lifted up, Christ was glorified, through the power of the Holy Spirit resting upon men. By faith these believers saw Him as the One who had borne humiliation, suffering, and death that they might not perish but have everlasting life. The revelation of Christ by the Spirit brought to them a realizing sense of His power and majesty, and they stretched forth their hands to Him by faith, saying, "I believe."

Then the glad tidings of a risen Saviour were carried to the uttermost bounds of the inhabited world. The church beheld converts flocking to her from all directions. Believers were reconverted. Sinners united with Christians in seeking the pearl of great price. The prophecy was fulfilled, The weak shall be "as David," and the house of David "as the angel of the Lord." Zechariah 12:8. Every Christian saw in his brother the divine similitude of benevolence and love. One interest prevailed. One object swallowed up all others. All hearts beat in harmony. The only ambition of the believers was to reveal the likeness of Christ's character, and to labor for the enlargement of His kingdom. "The multitude of them that believed were of one heart and of one soul.... With great power gave the apostles witness of the resurrection of the Lord Jesus; and great grace was upon them all." Acts 4:32, 33. "And the Lord added to the church daily such as should be saved." Acts 2:47. The Spirit of Christ animated the whole congregation; for they had found the pearl of great price.

These scenes are to be repeated, and with greater power. The outpouring of the Holy Spirit on the day of Pentecost was the former rain, but the latter rain will be more abundant. The Spirit awaits our demand and reception. Christ is again to be revealed in His fullness by the Holy Spirit's power. Men will discern the value of the precious pearl, and with the apostle Paul they will say, "What things were gain to me, those I counted loss for Christ. Yea doubtless, and I count all things but loss for the excellency of the knowledge of Christ Jesus my Lord." Philippians 3:7, 8.

10
The Net

Based on Matthew 13:47–50

The kingdom of heaven is like unto a net, that was cast into the sea, and gathered of every kind; which, when it was full, they drew to shore, and sat down, and gathered the good into vessels, but cast the bad away. So shall it be at the end of the world: the angels shall come forth, and sever the wicked from among the just, and shall cast them into the furnace of fire: there shall be wailing and gnashing of teeth."

The casting of the net is the preaching of the gospel. This gathers both good and evil into the church. When the mission of the gospel is completed, the judgment will accomplish the work of separation. Christ saw how the existence of false brethren in the church would cause the way of truth to be evil spoken of. The world would revile the gospel because of the inconsistent lives of false professors. Even Christians would be caused to stumble as they saw that many who bore Christ's name were not controlled by His Spirit. Because these sinners were in the church, men would be in danger of thinking that God excused their sins. Therefore Christ lifts the veil from the future and bids all to behold that it is character, not position, which decides man's destiny.

Both the parable of the tares and that of the net plainly teach that there is no time when all the wicked will turn to God. The wheat and the tares grow together until the harvest. The good and the bad fish are together drawn ashore for a final separation.

Again, these parables teach that there is to be no probation after the judgment. When the work of the gospel is completed, there immediately follows the separation between the good and the evil, and the destiny of each class is forever fixed.

God does not desire the destruction of any. "As I live, saith the Lord God, I have no pleasure in the death of the wicked; but that the wicked turn from his way and live. Turn ye, turn ye from your evil ways; for why will ye die?" Ezekiel 33:11. Throughout the period of probationary time His Spirit is entreating men to accept the gift of life. It is only those who reject His pleading that will be left to perish. God has declared that sin must be destroyed as an evil ruinous to the universe. Those who cling to sin will perish in its destruction.

11
"Things New and Old"

Based on Matthew 13:51, 52

While Christ was teaching the people, He was also educating His disciples for their future work. In all His instruction there were lessons for them. After giving the parable of the net, He asked them, "Have ye understood all these things?" They said unto Him, "Yea, Lord." Then in another parable He set before them their responsibility in regard to the truths they had received. "Therefore," He said, "every scribe which is instructed unto the kingdom of heaven is like unto a man that is an householder, which bringeth forth out of his treasure things new and old."

The treasure gained by the householder he does not hoard. He brings it forth to communicate to others. And by use the treasure increases. The householder has precious things both new and old. So Christ teaches that the truth committed to His disciples is to be communicated to the world. And as the knowledge of truth is imparted, it will increase.

All who receive the gospel message into the heart will long to proclaim it. The heaven-born love of Christ must find expression. Those who have put on Christ will relate their experience, tracing step by step the leadings of the Holy Spirit—their hungering and thirsting for the knowledge of God and of Jesus Christ whom He has sent, the results of their searching of the Scriptures, their prayers, their soul agony, and the words of Christ to them, "Thy sins be forgiven thee." It is unnatural for any to keep these things secret, and those who are filled with the love of Christ will not do so. In proportion as the Lord has made them the depositaries of sacred truth will be their desire that others shall receive the same blessing. And as they make known the rich treasures of God's grace, more and still more of the grace of Christ will be imparted to them. They will have the heart of a little child in its simplicity and unreserved obedience. Their souls will pant after holiness, and more and more of the treasures of truth and grace will be revealed to them to be given to the world.

The great storehouse of truth is the word of God-the written word, the book of nature, and the book of experience in God's dealing with human life. Here are the treasures from which Christ's workers are to draw. In the search after truth they are to depend upon God, not upon human intelligences, the great men whose wisdom is foolishness with God. Through His own appointed channels the Lord will impart a knowledge of Himself to every seeker.

If the follower of Christ will believe His word and practice it, there is no science in the natural world that he will not be able to grasp and appreciate.

There is nothing but that will furnish him means for imparting the truth to others. Natural science is a treasure house of knowledge from which every student in the school of Christ may draw. As we contemplate the beauty of nature, as we study its lessons in the cultivation of the soil, in the growth of the trees, in all the wonders of earth and sea and sky, there will come to us a new perception of truth. And the mysteries connected with God's dealings with men, the depths of His wisdom and judgment as seen in human life—these are found to be a storehouse rich in treasure.

But it is in the written word that a knowledge of God is most clearly revealed to fallen man. This is the treasure house of the unsearchable riches of Christ.

The word of God includes the Scriptures of the Old Testament as well as of the New. One is not complete without the other. Christ declared that the truths of the Old Testament are as valuable as those of the New. Christ was as much man's Redeemer in the beginning of the world as He is today. Before He clothed His divinity with humanity and came to our world, the gospel message was given by Adam, Seth, Enoch, Methuselah, and Noah. Abraham in Canaan and Lot in Sodom bore the message, and from generation to generation faithful messengers proclaimed the Coming One. The rites of the Jewish economy were instituted by Christ Himself. He was the foundation of their system of sacrificial offerings, the great antitype of all their religious service. The blood shed as the sacrifices were offered pointed to the sacrifice of the Lamb of God. All the typical offerings were fulfilled in Him.

Christ as manifested to the patriarchs, as symbolized in the sacrificial service, as portrayed in the law, and as revealed by the prophets, is the riches of the Old Testament. Christ in His life, His death, and His resurrection, Christ as He is manifested by the Holy Spirit, is the treasure of the New Testament. Our Saviour, the outshining of the Father's glory, is both the Old and the New.

Of Christ's life and death and intercession, which prophets had foretold, the apostles were to go forth as witnesses. Christ in His humiliation, in His purity and holiness, in His matchless love, was to be their theme. And in order to preach the gospel in its fullness, they must present the Saviour not only as revealed in His life and teachings, but as foretold by the prophets of the Old Testament and as symbolized by the sacrificial service.

Christ in His teaching presented old truths of which He Himself was the originator, truths which He had spoken through patriarchs and prophets; but He now shed upon them a new light. How different appeared their meaning! A flood of light and spirituality was brought in by His explanation. And He promised that the Holy Spirit should enlighten the disciples, that the word of God should be ever unfolding to them. They would be able to present its truths in new beauty.

Ever since the first promise of redemption was spoken in Eden, the life, the character, and the mediatorial work of Christ have been the study of human minds. Yet every mind through whom the Holy Spirit has worked has presented these themes in a light that is fresh and new. The truths of redemption are capable of constant development and expansion. Though old, they are ever new, constantly revealing to the seeker for truth a greater glory and a mightier power.

In every age there is a new development of truth, a message of God to the people of that generation. The old truths are all essential; new truth is not independent of the old, but an unfolding of it. It is only as the old truths are understood that we can comprehend the new. When Christ desired to open to His disciples the truth of His resurrection, He began "at Moses and all the prophets" and "expounded unto them in all the scriptures the things concerning Himself." Luke 24:27. But it is the light which shines in the fresh unfolding of truth that glorifies the old. He who rejects or neglects the new does not really possess the old. For him it loses its vital power and becomes but a lifeless form.

There are those who profess to believe and to teach the truths of the Old Testament, while they reject the New. But in refusing to receive the teachings of Christ, they show that they do not believe that which patriarchs and prophets have spoken. "Had ye believed Moses," Christ said, "ye would have believed Me; for he wrote of Me." John 5:46. Hence there is no real power in their teaching of even the Old Testament.

Many who claim to believe and to teach the gospel are in a similar error. They set aside the Old Testament Scriptures, of which Christ declared, "They are they which testify of Me." John 5:39. In rejecting the Old, they virtually reject the New; for both are parts of an inseparable whole. No man can rightly present the law of God without the gospel, or the gospel without the law. The law is the gospel embodied, and the gospel is the law unfolded. The law is the root, the gospel is the fragrant blossom and fruit which it bears.

The Old Testament sheds light upon the New, and the New upon the Old. Each is a revelation of the glory of God in Christ. Both present truths that will continually reveal new depths of meaning to the earnest seeker.

Truth in Christ and through Christ is measureless. The student of Scripture looks, as it were, into a fountain that deepens and broadens as he gazes into its depths. Not in this life shall we comprehend the mystery of God's love in giving His Son to be the propitiation for our sins. The work of our Redeemer on this earth is and ever will be a subject that will put to the stretch our highest imagination. Man may tax every mental power in the endeavor to fathom this mystery, but his mind will become faint and weary. The most diligent searcher will see before him a boundless, shoreless sea.

The truth as it is in Jesus can be experienced, but never explained. Its height and breadth and depth pass our knowledge. We may task our imagination to the utmost, and then we shall see only dimply the outlines of a love that is unexplainable, that is as high as heaven, but that stooped to the earth to stamp the image of God on all mankind.

Yet it is possible for us to see all that we can bear of the divine compassion. This is unfolded to the humble, contrite soul. We shall understand God's compassion just in proportion as we appreciate His sacrifice for us. As we search the word of God in humility of heart, the grand theme of redemption will open to our research. It will increase in brightness as we behold it, and as we aspire to grasp it, its height and depth will ever increase.

Our life is to be bound up with the life of Christ; we are to draw constantly from Him, partaking of Him, the living Bread that came down from heaven, drawing from a fountain ever fresh, ever giving forth its abundant treasures. If we keep the Lord ever before us, allowing our hearts to go out in thanksgiving and praise to Him, we shall have a continual freshness in our religious life. Our prayers will take the form of a conversation with God as we would talk with a friend. He will speak His mysteries to us personally. Often there will come to us a sweet joyful sense of the presence of Jesus. Often our hearts will burn within us as He draws nigh to commune with us as He did with Enoch. When this is in truth the experience of the Christian, there is seen in his life a simplicity, a humility, meekness, and lowliness of heart, that show to all with whom he associates that he has been with Jesus and learned of Him.

In those who possess it, the religion of Christ will reveal itself as a vitalizing, pervading principle, a living, working, spiritual energy. There will be manifest the freshness and power and joyousness of perpetual youth. The heart that receives the word of God is not as a pool that evaporates, not like a broken cistern that loses its treasure. It is like the mountain stream fed by unfailing springs, whose cool, sparkling waters leap from rock to rock, refreshing the weary, the thirsty, the heavy laden.

This experience gives every teacher of truth the very qualifications that will make him a representative of Christ. The spirit of Christ's teaching will give a force and directness to his communications and to his prayers. His witness to Christ will not be a narrow, lifeless testimony. The minister will not preach over and over the same set discourses. His mind will be open to the constant illumination of the Holy Spirit.

Christ said, "Whoso eateth My flesh, and drinketh My blood, hath eternal life.... As the living Father hath sent Me, and I live by the Father; so he that eateth Me, even he shall live by Me.... It is the Spirit that quickeneth;...the words that I speak unto you, they are spirit, and they are life." John 6:54–63.

When we eat Christ's flesh and drink His blood, the element of eternal life will be found in the ministry. There will not be a fund of stale, oft-repeated ideas. The tame, dull sermonizing will cease. The old truths will be presented, but they will be seen in a new light. There will be a new perception of truth, a clearness and a power that all will discern. Those who have the privilege of sitting under such a ministry will, if susceptible to the Holy Spirit's influence, feel the energizing power of a new life. The fire of God's love will be kindled within them. their perceptive faculties will be quickened to discern the beauty and majesty of truth.

The faithful householder represents what every teacher of the children and youth should be. If he makes the word of God his treasure, he will continually bring forth new beauty and new truth. When the teacher will rely upon God in prayer, the Spirit of Christ will come upon him, and God will work through him by the Holy Spirit upon the minds of others. The Spirit fills the mind and heart with sweet hope and courage and Bible imagery, and all this will be communicated to the youth under his instruction.

The springs of heavenly peace and joy, unsealed in the soul of the teacher by the words of Inspiration, will become a mighty river of influence to bless all who connect with him. The Bible will not become a tiresome book to the student. Under a wise instructor the word will become more and more desirable. It will be as the bread of life, and will never grow old. Its freshness and beauty will attract and charm the children and youth. It is like the sun shining upon the earth, perpetually imparting brightness and warmth, yet never exhausted.

God's holy, educating Spirit is in His word. A light, a new and precious light, shines forth from every page. Truth is there revealed, and words and sentences are made bright and appropriate for the occasion, as the voice of God speaking to the soul.

The Holy Spirit loves to address the youth, and to discover to them the treasures and beauties of God's word. The promises spoken by the great Teacher will captivate the senses and animate the soul with aspiritual power that is divine. There will grow in the fruitful mind a familiarity with divine things that will be as a barricade against temptation.

The words of truth will grow in importance, and assume a breadth and fullness of meaning of which we have never dreamed. The beauty and riches of the word have a transforming influence on mind and character. The light of heavenly love will fall upon the heart as an inspiration.

The appreciation of the Bible grows with its study. Whichever way the student may turn, he will find displayed the infinite wisdom and love of God.

The significance of the Jewish economy is not yet fully comprehended. Truths vast and profound are shadowed forth in its rites and symbols. The gospel is the key that unlocks its mysteries. Through a knowledge of the plan of redemption, its truths are opened to the understanding. Far more than we do, it is our privilege to understand these wonderful themes. We are to comprehend the deep things of God. Angels desire to look into the truths that are revealed to the people who with contrite hearts are searching the word of God, and praying for greater lengths and breadths and depths and heights of the knowledge which He alone can give.

As we near the close of this world's history, the prophecies relating to the last days especially demand our study. The last book of the New Testament scriptures is full of truth that we need to understand. Satan has blinded the minds of many, so that they have been glad of any excuse for not making the Revelation their study. But Christ through His servant John has here declared what shall be in the last days, and He says, "Blessed is he that readeth, and they that hear the words of this prophecy, and keep those things which are written therein." Revelation 1:3.

"This is life eternal," Christ said, "that they might know Thee the only true God, and Jesus Christ, whom Thou hast sent." John 17:3. Why is it that we do not realize the value of this knowledge? Why are not these glorious truths glowing in our hearts, trembling upon our lips, and pervading our whole being?

In giving us His word, God has put us in possession of every truth essential for our salvation. Thousands have drawn water from these wells of life, yet there is no diminishing of the supply. Thousands have set the Lord before them, and by beholding have been changed into the same image. Their spirit burns within them as they speak of His character, telling what Christ is to them, and what they are to Christ. But these searchers have not exhausted these grand and holy themes. Thousands more may engage in the work of searching out the mysteries of salvation. As the life of Christ and the character of His mission are dwelt upon, rays of light will shine forth more distinctly at every attempt to discover truth. Each fresh search will reveal something more deeply interesting than has yet been unfolded. The subject is inexhaustible. The study of the incarnation of Christ, His atoning sacrifice and mediatorial work, will employ the mind of the diligent student as long as time shall last; and looking to heaven with its unnumbered years he will exclaim, "Great is the mystery of godliness."

In eternity we shall learn that which, had we received the enlightenment it was possible to obtain here, would have opened our understanding. The themes of redemption will employ the hearts and minds and tongues of the redeemed through the everlasting ages. They will understand the truths which Christ longed to open to His disciples, but which they did not have faith to grasp. Forever and forever new views of the perfection and glory of Christ will appear. Through endless ages will the faithful Householder bring forth from His treasure things new and old.

12
Asking to Give

Based on Luke 11:1–13

Christ was continually receiving from the Father that He might communicate to us. "The word which ye hear," He said, "is not Mine, but the Father's which sent Me." John 14:24. "The Son of man came not to be ministered unto, but to minister." Matthew 20:28. Not for Himself, but for others, He lived and thought and prayed. From hours spent with God He came forth morning by morning, to bring the light of heaven to men. Daily He received a fresh baptism of the Holy Spirit. In the early hours of the new day the Lord awakened Him from His slumbers, and His soul and His lips were anointed with grace, that He might impart to others. His words were given Him fresh from the heavenly courts, words that He might speak in season to the weary and oppressed. "The Lord God hath given Me," He said, "the tongue of the learned, that I should know how to speak a word in season to him that is weary: He wakeneth morning by morning, He wakeneth Mine ear to hear as the learned." Isaiah 50:4.

Christ's disciples were much impressed by His prayers and by His habit of communion with God. One day after a short absence from their Lord, they found Him absorbed in supplication. Seeming unconscious of their presence, He continued praying aloud. The hearts of the disciples were deeply moved. As He ceased praying, they exclaimed, "Lord, teach us to pray."

In answer, Christ repeated the Lord's prayer, as He had given it in the sermon on the mount. Then in a parable He illustrated the lesson He desired to teach them.

"Which of you," He said, "shall have a friend, and shall go unto him at midnight, and say unto him, Friend, lend me three loaves; for a friend of mine in his journey is come to me, and I have nothing to set before him? And he from within shall answer and say, Trouble me not; the door is now shut, and my children are with me in bed: I cannot rise and give thee. I say unto you, Though he will not rise and give him because he is his friend, yet because of his importunity he will rise and give him as many as he needeth."

Here Christ represents the petitioner as asking that he may give again. He must obtain the bread, else he cannot supply the necessities of a weary, belated wayfarer. Though his neighbor is unwilling to be troubled, he will not desist his pleading; his friend must be relieved; and at last his importunity is rewarded, his wants are supplied.

In like manner the disciples were to seek blessings from God. In the feeding of the multitude and in the sermon on the bread from heaven, Christ had opened to them their work as His representatives. They were to give the bread of life to the people. He who had appointed their work, saw how often their faith would be tried. Often they would be thrown into unexpected positions, and would realize their human insufficiency. Souls that were hungering for the bread of life would come to them, and they would feel themselves to be destitute and helpless. They must receive spiritual food, or they would have nothing to impart. But they were not to turn one soul away unfed. Christ directs them to the source of supply. The man whose friend came to him for entertainment, even at the unseasonable hour of midnight, did not turn him away. He had nothing to set before him, but he went to one who had food and pressed his request until the neighbor supplied his need. And would not God, who had sent His servants to feed the hungry, supply their need for His own work?

But the selfish neighbor in the parable does not represent the character of God. The lesson is drawn, not by comparison, but by contrast. A selfish man will grant an urgent request, in order to rid himself of one who disturbs his rest. But God delights to give. He is full of compassion, and He longs to grant the requests of those who come unto Him in faith. He gives to us that we may minister to others and thus become like Himself.

Christ declares, "Ask, and it shall be given you; seek, and ye shall find; knock, and it shall be opened unto you. For every one that asketh receiveth; and he that seeketh findeth; and to him that knocketh it shall be opened."

The Saviour continues: "If a son shall ask bread of any of you that is a father, will he give him a stone? or if he ask a fish, will he for a fish give him a serpent? or if he shall ask an egg, will he offer him a scorpion? If ye then, being evil, know how to give good gifts unto your children, how much more shall your heavenly Father give the Holy Spirit to them that ask Him?"

In order to strengthen our confidence in God, Christ teaches us to address Him by a new name, a name entwined with the dearest associations of the human heart. He gives us the privilege of calling the infinite God our Father. This name, spoken to Him and of Him, is a sign of our love and trust toward Him, and a pledge of His regard and relationship to us. Spoken when asking His favor or blessing, it is as music in His ears. That we might not think it presumption to call Him by this name, He has repeated it again and again. He desires us to become familiar with the appellation.

God regards us as His children. He has redeemed us out of the careless world and has chosen us to become members of the royal family, sons and daughters of the heavenly King. He invites us to trust in Him with a trust deeper and stronger than that of a child in his earthly father. Parents love their children, but the love of God is larger, broader, deeper, than human love can possibly be. It is immeasurable. Then if earthly parents know how to give good gifts to their children, how much more shall our Father in heaven give the Holy Spirit to those who ask Him?

Christ's lessons in regard to prayer should be carefully considered. There is a divine science in prayer, and His illustration brings to view principles that all need to understand. He shows what is the true spirit of prayer, He teaches the necessity of perseverance in presenting our requests to God, and assures us of His willingness to hear and answer prayer.

Our prayers are not to be a selfish asking, merely for our own benefit. We are to ask that we may give. The principle of Christ's life must be the principle of our lives. "For their sakes," He said, speaking of His disciples, "I sanctify Myself, that they also might be sanctified." John 17:19. The same devotion, the same self-sacrifice, the same subjection to the claims of the word of God, that were manifest in Christ, must be seen in His servants. Our mission to the world is not to serve or please ourselves; we are to glorify God by co-operating with Him to save sinners. We are to ask blessings from God that we may communicate to others. The capacity for receiving is preserved only by imparting. We cannot continue to receive heavenly treasure without communicating to those around us.

In the parable the petitioner was again and again repulsed, but he did not relinquish his purpose. So our prayers do not always seem to receive an immediate answer; but Christ teaches that we should not cease to pray. Prayer is not to work any change in God; it is to bring us into harmony with God. When we make request of Him, He may see that it is necessary for us to search our hearts and repent of sin. Therefore He takes us through test and trial, He brings us through humiliation, that we may see what hinders the working of His Holy Spirit through us.

There are conditions to the fulfillment of God's promises, and prayer can never take the place of duty. "If ye love Me," Christ says, "Keep My commandments." "He that hath My commandments, and keepeth them, he it is that loveth Me; and he that loveth Me shall be loved of My Father, and I will love him, and will manifest Myself to him." John 14:15, 21. Those who bring their petitions to God, claiming His promise while they do not comply with the conditions, insult Jehovah. They bring the name of Christ as their authority for the fulfillment of the promise, but they do not those things that would show faith in Christ and love for Him.

Many are forfeiting the condition of acceptance with the Father. We need to examine closely the deed of trust wherewith we approach God. If we are disobedient, we bring to the Lord a note to be cashed when we have not fulfilled the conditions that would make it payable to us. We present to God His promises, and ask Him to fulfill them, when by so doing He would dishonor His own name.

The promise is "If ye abide in Me, and My words abide in you, ye shall ask what ye will, and it shall be done unto you." John 15:7. And John declares: "Hereby we do know that we know Him, if we keep His commandments. He that saith, I know Him, and keepeth not His commandments, is a liar, and the truth is not in him. But whoso keepeth His word, in him verily is the love of God perfected." 1 John 2:3–5.

One of Christ's last commands to His disciples was "Love one another as I have loved you." John 13:34. Do we obey this command, or are we indulging sharp, unchristlike traits of character? If we have in any way grieved or wounded others, it is our duty to confess our fault and seek for reconciliation. This is an essential preparation that we may come before God in faith, to ask His blessing.

There is another matter too often neglected by those who seek the Lord in prayer. Have you been honest with God? By the prophet Malachi the Lord declares, "Even from the days of your fathers ye are gone away from Mine ordinances, and have not kept them. Return unto Me, and I will return unto you, saith the Lord of hosts. But ye said, Wherein shall we return? Will a man rob God? Yet ye have robbed Me. But ye say, Wherein have we robbed Thee? In tithes and offerings." Malachi 3:7, 8.

As the Giver of every blessing, God claims a certain portion of all we possess. This is His provision to sustain the preaching of the gospel. And by making this return to God, we are to show our appreciation of His gifts. But if we withhold from Him that which is His own, how can we claim His blessing? If we are unfaithful stewards of earthly things, how can we expect Him to entrust us with the things of heaven? It may be that here is the secret of unanswered prayer.

But the Lord in His great mercy is ready to forgive, and He says, "Bring ye all the tithes into the storehouse, that there may be meat in Mine house, and prove Me now herewith,...if I will not open you the windows of heaven, and pour you out a blessing, that there shall not be room enough to receive it. And I will rebuke the devourer for your sakes, and he shall not destroy the fruits of your ground; neither shall your vine cast her fruit before the time in the field.... And all nations shall call you blessed; for ye shall be a delightsome land, saith the Lord of hosts." Malachi 3:10–12.

So it is with every other one of God's requirements. All His gifts are promised on condition of obedience. God has a heaven full of blessings for those who will co-operate with Him. All who obey Him may with confidence claim the fulfillment of His promises.

But we must show a firm, undeviating trust in God. Often He delays to answer us in order to try our faith or test the genuineness of our desire. Having asked according to His word, we should believe His promise and press our petitions with a determination that will not be denied.

God does not say, Ask once, and you shall receive. He bids us ask. Unwearyingly persist in prayer. The persistent asking brings the petitioner into a more earnest attitude, and gives him an increased desire to receive the things for which he asks. Christ said to Martha at the grave of Lazarus, "If thou wouldest believe, thou shouldest see the glory of God." John 11:40.

But many have not a living faith. This is why they do not see more of the power of God. Their weakness is the result of their unbelief. They have more faith in their own working than in the working of God for them. They take themselves into their own keeping. They plan and devise, but pray little, and have little real trust in God. They think they have faith, but it is only the impulse of the moment. Failing to realize their own need, or God's willingness to give, they do not persevere in keeping their requests before the Lord.

Our prayers are to be as earnest and persistent as was the petition of the needy friend who asked for the loaves at midnight. The more earnestly and steadfastly we ask, the closer will be our spiritual union with Christ. We shall receive increased blessings because we have increased faith.

Our part is to pray and believe. Watch unto prayer. Watch, and co-operate with the prayer-hearing God. Bear in mind that "we are labourers together with God." I Corinthians 3:9. Speak and act in harmony with your prayers. It will make an infinite difference with you whether trial shall prove your faith to be genuine, or show that your prayers are only a form.

When perplexities arise, and difficulties confront you, look not for help to humanity. Trust all with God. The practice of telling our difficulties to others only makes us weak, and brings no strength to them. It lays upon them the burden of our spiritual infirmities, which they cannot relieve. We seek the strength of erring, finite man, when we might have the strength of the unerring, infinite God.

You need not go to the ends of the earth for wisdom, for God is near. It is not the capabilities you now possess or ever will have that will give you success. It is that which the Lord can do for you. We need to have far less confidence in what man can do and far more confidence in what God can do for every believing soul. He longs to have you reach after Him by faith. He longs to have you expect great things from Him. He longs to give you understanding in temporal as well as in spiritual matters. He can sharpen the intellect. He can give tact and skill. Put your talents into the work, ask God for wisdom, and it will be given you.

Take the word of Christ as your assurance. Has He not invited you to come unto Him? Never allow yourself to talk in a hopeless, discouraged way. If you do you will lose much. By looking at appearances and complaining when difficulties and pressure come, you give evidence of a sickly, enfeebled faith. Talk and act as if your faith was invincible. The Lord is rich in resources; He owns the world. Look heavenward in faith. Look to Him who has light and power and efficiency.

There is in genuine faith a buoyancy, a steadfastness of principle, and a fixedness of purpose that neither time nor toil can weaken. "Even the youths shall faint and be weary, and the young men shall utterly fall: but they that wait upon the Lord shall renew their strength; they shall mount up with wings as eagles; they shall run, and not be weary; and they shall walk, and not faint." Isaiah 40:30, 31.

There are many who long to help others, but they feel that they have no spiritual strength or light to impart. Let them present their petitions at the throne of grace. Plead for the Holy Spirit. God stands back of every promise He has made. With your Bible in your hands say, I have done as Thou hast said. I present Thy promise, "Ask, and it shall be given you; seek, and ye shall find; knock, and it shall be opened unto you."

We must not only pray in Christ's name, but by the inspiration of the Holy Spirit. This explains what is meant when it is said that the Spirit "maketh intercession for us, with groanings which cannot be uttered." Romans 8:26. Such prayer God delights to answer. When with earnestness and intensity we breathe a prayer in the name of Christ, there is in that very intensity a pledge from God that He is about to answer our prayer "exceeding abundantly above all that we ask or think." Ephesians 3:20.

Christ has said, "What things soever ye desire, when ye pray, believe that ye receive them, and ye shall have them." Mark 11:24. "Whatsoever ye shall ask in My name, that will I do, that the Father may be glorified in the Son." John 14:13. And the beloved John, under the inspiration of the Holy Spirit, speaks with great plainness and assurance: "If we ask anything according to His will, He heareth us: and if we know that He hear us, whatsoever we ask, we know that we have the petitions that we desired of Him." I John 5:14, 15. Then press your petition to the Father in the name of Jesus. God will honor that name.

The rainbow round about the throne is an assurance that God is true, that in Him is no variableness, neither shadow of turning. We have sinned against Him, and are undeserving of His favor; yet He Himself has put into our lips that most wonderful of pleas, "Do not abhor us, for Thy name's sake; do not disgrace the throne of Thy glory; remember, break not Thy covenant with us." Jeremiah 14:21. When we come to him confessing our unworthiness and sin, He has pledged Himself to give heed to our cry. The honor of His throne is staked for the fulfillment of His word unto us.

Like Aaron, who symbolized Christ, our Saviour bears the names of all His people on His heart in the holy place. Our great High Priest remembers all the words by which He has encouraged us to trust. He is ever mindful of His covenant.

All who seek of Him shall find. All who knock will have the door opened to them. The excuse will not be made, Trouble Me not; the door is closed; I do not wish to open it. Never will one be told, I cannot help you. Those who beg at midnight for loaves to feed the hungry souls will be successful.

In the parable, he who asks bread for the stranger, receives "as many as he needeth." And in what measure will God impart to us that we may impart to others? "According to the measure of the gift of Christ." Ephesians 4:7. Angels are watching with intense interest to see how man is dealing with his fellow men. When they see one manifest Christlike sympathy for the erring, they press to his side and bring to his remembrance words to speak that will be as the bread of life to the soul. So "God shall supply all your need according to His riches in glory by Christ Jesus." Philippians 4:19. Your testimony in its genuineness and reality He will make powerful in the power of the life to come. The word of the Lord will be in your mouth as truth and righteousness.

Personal effort for others should be preceded by much secret prayer; for it requires great wisdom to understand the science of saving souls. Before communicating with men, commune with Christ. At the throne of heavenly grace obtain a preparation for ministering to the people.

Let your heart break for the longing it has for God, for the living God. The life of Christ has shown what humanity can do by being partaker of the divine nature. All that Christ received from God we too may have. Then ask and receive. With the persevering faith of Jacob, with the unyielding persistence of Elijah, claim for yourself all that God has promised.

Let the glorious conceptions of God possess your mind. Let your life be knit by hidden links to the life of Jesus. He who commanded the light to shine out of darkness is willing to shine in your heart, to give the light of the knowledge of the glory of God in the face of Jesus Christ. The Holy Spirit will take the things of God and show them unto you, conveying them as a living power into the obedient heart. Christ will lead you to the threshold of the Infinite. You may behold the glory beyond the veil, and reveal to men the sufficiency of Him who ever liveth to make intercession for us.

13
Two Worshipers

Based on Luke 18:9–14

Unto certain which trusted in themselves that they were righteous, and despised others," Christ spoke the parable of the Pharisee and the publican. The Pharisee goes up to the temple to worship, not because he feels that he is a sinner in need of pardon, but because he thinks himself righteous and hopes to win commendation. His worship he regards as an act of merit that will recommend him to God. At the same time it will give the people a high opinion of his piety. He hopes to secure favor with both God and man. His worship is prompted by self-interest.

And he is full of self-praise. He looks it, he walks it, he prays it. Drawing apart from others as if to say, "Come not near to me; for I am holier than thou" (Isaiah 65:5), he stands and prays "with himself." Wholly self-satisfied, he thinks that God and men regard him with the same complacency.

"God, I thank thee," he says, "that I am not as other men are, extortioners, unjust, adulterers, or even as this publican." He judges his character, not by the holy character of God, but by the character of other men. His mind is turned away from God to humanity. This is the secret of his self-satisfaction.

He proceeds to recount his good deeds: "I fast twice in the week, I give tithes of all that I possess." The religion of the Pharisee does not touch the soul. He is not seeking Godlikeness of character, a heart filled with love and mercy. He is satisfied with a religion that has to do only with the outward life. His righteousness is his own—the fruit of his own works—and judged by a human standard.

Whoever trusts in himself that he is righteous, will despise others. As the Pharisee judges himself by other men, so he judges other men by himself. His righteousness is estimated by theirs, and the worse they are the more righteous by contrast he appears. His self-righteousness leads to accusing. "Other men" he condemns as transgressors of God's law. Thus he is making manifest the very spirit of Satan, the accuser of the brethren. With this spirit it is impossible for him to enter into communion with God. He goes down to his house destitute of the divine blessing.

The publican had gone to the temple with other worshipers, but he soon drew apart from them as unworthy to unite in their devotions. Standing afar off, he "would not lift up so much as his eyes unto heaven, but smote upon his breast," in bitter anguish and self-abhorrence. He felt that he had transgressed against God, that he was sinful and polluted. He could not expect even pity from those around him, for they looked upon him with contempt. He knew that he had no merit to commend him to God, and in utter self-despair he cried, "God be merciful to me, a sinner." He did not compare himself with others. Overwhelmed with a sense of guilt, he stood as if alone in God's presence. His only desire was for pardon and peace, his only plea was the mercy of God. And he was blessed. "I tell you," Christ said, "this man went down to his house justified rather than the other."

The Pharisee and the publican represent two great classes into which those who come to worship God are divided. Their first two representatives are found in the first two children that were born into the world. Cain thought himself righteous, and he came to God with a thank offering only. He made no confession of sin, and acknowledged no need of mercy. But Abel came with the blood that pointed to the Lamb of God. He came as a sinner, confessing himself lost; his only hope was the unmerited love of God. The Lord had respect to his offering, but to Cain and his offering He had not respect. The sense of need, the recognition of our poverty and sin, is the very first condition of acceptance with God. "Blessed are the poor in spirit; for theirs is the kingdom of heaven." Matthew 5:3.

For each of the classes represented by the Pharisee and the publican there is a lesson in the history of the apostle Peter. In his early discipleship Peter thought himself strong. Like the Pharisee, in his own estimation he was "not as other men are." When Christ on the eve of His betrayal forewarned His disciples, "All ye shall be offended because of Me this night," Peter confidently declared, "Although all shall be offended, yet will not I." Mark 14:27, 29. Peter did not know his own danger. Self-confidence misled him. He thought himself able to withstand temptation; but in a few short hours the test came, and with cursing and swearing he denied his Lord.

When the crowing of the cock reminded him of the words of Christ, surprised and shocked at what he had just done he turned and looked at his Master. At that moment Christ looked at Peter, and beneath that grieved look, in which compassion and love for him were blended, Peter understood himself. He went out and wept bitterly. That look of Christ's broke his heart. Peter had come to the turning point, and bitterly did he repent his sin. He was like the publican in his contrition and repentance, and like the publican he found mercy. The look of Christ assured him of pardon.

Now his self-confidence was gone. Never again were the old boastful assertions repeated.

Christ after His resurrection thrice tested Peter. "Simon, son of Jonas," He said, "lovest thou Me more than these?" Peter did not now exalt himself above his brethren. He appealed to the One who could read His heart. "Lord," he said, "Thou knowest all things; Thou knowest that I love Thee." John 21:15, 17.

Then he received his commission. A work broader and more delicate than had heretofore been his was appointed him. Christ bade him feed the sheep and the lambs. In thus committing to his stewardship the souls for whom the Saviour had laid down his own life, Christ gave to Peter the strongest proof of confidence in his restoration. The once restless, boastful, self-confident disciple had become subdued and contrite. Henceforth he followed his Lord in self-denial and self-sacrifice. He was a partaker of Christ's sufferings; and when Christ shall sit upon the throne of His glory, Peter will be a partaker in His glory.

The evil that led to Peter's fall and that shut out the Pharisee from communion with God is proving the ruin of thousands today. There is nothing so offensive to God or so dangerous to the human soul as pride and self-sufficiency. Of all sins it is the most hopeless, the most incurable.

Peter's fall was not instantaneous, but gradual. Self-confidence led him to the belief that he was saved, and step after step was taken in the downward path, until he could deny his Master. Never can we safely put confidence in self or feel, this side of heaven, that we are secure against temptation. Those who accept the Saviour, however sincere their conversion, should never be taught to say or to feel that they are saved. This is misleading. Every one should be taught to cherish hope and faith; but even when we give ourselves to Christ and know that He accepts us, we are not beyond the reach of temptation. God's word declares, "Many shall be purified, and made white, and tried." Daniel 12:10. Only he who endures the trial will receive the crown of life. (James 1:12.)

Those who accept Christ, and in their first confidence say, I am saved, are in danger of trusting to themselves. They lose sight of their own weakness and their constant need of divine strength. They are unprepared for Satan's devices, and under temptation many, like Peter, fall into the very depths of sin. We are admonished, "Let him that thinketh he standeth, take heed lest he fall." 1 Corinthians 10:12. Our only safety is in constant distrust of self, and dependence on Christ.

It was necessary for Peter to learn his own defects of character, and his need of the power and grace of Christ. The Lord could not save him from trial, but He could have saved him from defeat. Had Peter been willing to receive Christ's warning, he would have been watching unto prayer. He would have walked with fear and trembling lest his feet should stumble. And he would have received divine help so that Satan could not have gained the victory.

It was through self-sufficiency that Peter fell; and it was through repentance and humiliation that his feet were again established. In the record of his experience every repenting sinner may find encouragement. Though Peter had grievously sinned, he was not forsaken. The words of Christ were written upon his soul, "I have prayed for thee, that thy faith fail not." Luke 22:32. In his bitter agony of remorse, this prayer, and the memory of Christ's look of love and pity, gave him hope. Christ after His resurrection remembered Peter, and gave the angel the message for the women, "Go your way, tell His disciples and Peter that He goeth before you into Galilee; there shall ye see Him." Mark 16:7. Peter's repentance was accepted by the sin-pardoning Saviour.

And the same compassion that reached out to rescue Peter is extended to every soul who has fallen under temptation. It is Satan's special device to lead man into sin, and then leave him, helpless and trembling, fearing to seek for pardon. But why should we fear, when God has said, "Let him take hold of My strength, that he may make peace with Me; and he shall make peace with Me?" Isaiah 27:5. Every provision has been made for our infirmities, every encouragement offered us to come to Christ.

Christ offered up His broken body to purchase back God's heritage, to give man another trial. "Wherefore He is able also to save them to the uttermost that come unto God by Him, seeing He ever liveth to make intercession for them." Hebrews 7:25. By His spotless life, His obedience, His death on the cross of Calvary, Christ interceded for the lost race. And now, not as a mere petitioner does the Captain of our salvation intercede for us, but as a Conqueror claiming His victory. His offering is complete, and as our Intercessor He executes His self-appointed work, holding before God the censer containing His own spotless merits and the prayers, confessions, and thanksgiving of His people. Perfumed with the fragrance of His righteousness, these ascend to God as a sweet savor. The offering is wholly acceptable, and pardon covers all transgression.

Christ has pledged Himself to be our substitute and surety, and He neglects no one. He who could not see human beings exposed to eternal ruin without pouring out His soul unto death in their behalf, will look with pity and compassion upon every soul who realizes that he cannot save himself.

He will look upon no trembling suppliant without raising him up. He who through His own atonement provided for man an infinite fund of moral power, will not fail to employ this power in our behalf. We may take our sins and sorrows to His feet; for He loves us. His every look and word invites our confidence. He will shape and mold our characters according to His own will.

In the whole Satanic force there is not power to overcome one soul who in simple trust casts himself on Christ. "He giveth power to the faint; and to them that have no might He increaseth strength." Isaiah 40:29.

"If we confess our sins, He is faithful and just to forgive us our sins, and to cleanse us from all unrighteousness." The Lord says, "Only acknowledge thine iniquity, that thou hast transgressed against the Lord thy God." "Then will I sprinkle clean water upon you, and ye shall be clean; from all your filthiness and from all your idols will I cleanse you." 1 John 1:9; Jeremiah 3:13; Ezekiel 36:25.

But we must have a knowledge of ourselves, a knowledge that will result in contrition, before we can find pardon and peace. The Pharisee felt no conviction of sin. The Holy Spirit could not work with him. His soul was encased in a self-righteous armor which the arrows of God, barbed and true-aimed by angel hands, failed to penetrate. It is only he who knows himself to be a sinner that Christ can save. He came "to heal the brokenhearted, to preach deliverance to the captives, and recovering of sight to the blind, to set at liberty them that are bruised." Luke 4:18. But "they that are whole need not a physician." Luke 5:31. We must know our real condition, or we shall not feel our need of Christ's help. We must understand our danger, or we shall not flee to the refuge. We must feel the pain of our wounds, or we should not desire healing.

The Lord says, "Because thou sayest, I am rich, and increased with goods, and have need of nothing; and knowest not that thou art wretched, and miserable, and poor, and blind, and naked: I counsel thee to buy of Me gold tried in the fire, that thou mayest be rich; and white raiment, that thou mayest be clothed, and that the shame of thy nakedness do not appear; and anoint thine eyes with eyesalve, that thou mayest see." Revelation 3:17, 18. The gold tried in the fire is faith that works by love. Only this can bring us into harmony with God. We may be active, we may do much work; but without love, such love as dwelt in the heart of Christ, we can never be numbered with the family of heaven.

No man can of himself understand his errors. "The heart is deceitful above all things, and desperately wicked; who can know it?" Jeremiah 17:9. The lips may express a poverty of soul that the heart does not acknowledge. While speaking to God of poverty of spirit, the heart may be swelling with the conceit of its own superior humility and exalted righteousness. In one way only can a true knowledge of self be obtained. We must behold Christ. It is ignorance of Him that makes men so uplifted in their own righteousness. When we contemplate His purity and excellence, we shall see our own weakness and poverty and defects as they really are. We shall see ourselves lost and hopeless, clad in garments of self-righteousness, like every other sinner. We shall see that if we are ever saved, it will not be through our own goodness, but through God's infinite grace.

The prayer of the publican was heard because it showed dependence reaching forth to lay hold upon Omnipotence. Self to the publican appeared nothing but shame. Thus it must be seen by all who seek God. By faith—faith that renounces all self-trust—the needy suppliant is to lay hold upon infinite power.

No outward observances can take the place of simple faith and entire renunciation of self. But no man can empty himself of self. We can only consent for Christ to accomplish the work. Then the language of the soul will be, Lord, take my heart; for I cannot give it. It is Thy property. Keep it pure, for I cannot keep it for Thee. Save me in spite of myself, my weak, unchristlike self. Mold me, fashion me, raise me into a pure and holy atmosphere, where the rich current of Thy love can flow through my soul.

It is not only at the beginning of the Christian life that this renunciation of self is to be made. At every advance step heavenward it is to be renewed. All our good works are dependent on a power outside of ourselves. Therefore there needs to be a continual reaching out of the heart after God, a continual, earnest, heartbreaking confession of sin and humbling of the soul before Him. Only by constant renunciation of self and dependence on Christ can we walk safely.

The nearer we come to Jesus and the more clearly we discern the purity of His character, the more clearly we shall discern the exceeding sinfulness of sin and the less we shall feel like exalting ourselves. Those whom heaven recognizes as holy ones are the last to parade their own goodness. The apostle Peter became a faithful minister of Christ, and he was greatly honored with divine light and power; he had an active part in the upbuilding of Christ's church; but Peter never forgot the fearful experience of his humiliation; his sin was forgiven; yet well he knew that for the weakness of character which had caused his fall only the grace of Christ could avail. He found in himself nothing in which to glory.

None of the apostles or prophets ever claimed to be without sin. Men who have lived nearest to God, men who would sacrifice life itself rather than knowingly commit a wrong act, men whom God had honored with divine light and power, have confessed the sinfulness of their own nature. They have put no confidence in the flesh, have claimed no righteousness of their own, but have trusted wholly in the righteousness of Christ. So will it be with all who behold Christ.

At every advance step in Christian experience our repentance will deepen. It is to those whom the Lord has forgiven, to those whom He acknowledges as His people, that He says, "Then shall ye remember your own evil ways, and your doings that were not good, and shall loathe yourselves in your own sight." Ezekiel 36:31. Again He says, "I will establish My covenant with thee, and thou shalt know that I am the Lord; that thou mayest remember, and be confounded, and never open thy mouth any more because of thy shame, when I am pacified toward thee for all that thou hast done, saith the Lord God." Ezekiel 16:62, 63. Then our lips will not be opened in self-glorification. We shall know that our sufficiency is in Christ alone. We shall make the apostle's confession our own. "I know that in me (that is, in my flesh) dwelleth no good thing." Romans 7:18. "God forbid that I should glory, save in the cross of our Lord Jesus Christ, by whom the world is crucified unto me, and I unto the world." Galations 6:14.

In harmony with this experience is the command, "Work out your own salvation with fear and trembling. For it is God which worketh in you both to will and to do of His good pleasure." Philippians 2:12, 13. God does not bid you fear that He will fail to fulfill His promises, that His patience will weary, or His compassion be found wanting. Fear lest your will shall not be held in subjection to Christ's will, lest your hereditary and cultivated traits of character shall control your life. "It is God which worketh in you both to will and to do of His good pleasure. Fear lest self shall interpose between your soul and the great Master Worker. Fear lest self-will shall mar the high purpose that through you God desires to accomplish. Fear to trust to your own strength, fear to withdraw your hand from the hand of Christ and attempt to walk life's pathway without His abiding presence.

We need to shun everything that would encourage pride and self-sufficiency; therefore we should beware of giving or receiving flattery or praise. It is Satan's work to flatter. He deals in flattery as well as in accusing and condemnation. Thus he seeks to work the ruin of the soul. Those who give praise to men are used by Satan as his agents. Let the workers for Christ direct every word of praise away from themselves. Let self be put out of sight. Christ alone is to be exalted. "Unto Him that loved us, and washed us from our sins in His own blood," let every eye be directed, and praise from every heart ascend. (Revelation 1:5.)

The life in which the fear of the Lord is cherished will not be a life of sadness and gloom. It is the absence of Christ that makes the countenance sad, and the life a pilgrimage of sighs. Those who are filled with self-esteem and self-love do not feel the need of a living, personal union with Christ. The heart that has not fallen on the Rock is proud of its wholeness. Men want a dignified religion. They desire to walk in a path wide enough to take in their own attributes. Their self-love, their love of popularity and love of praise, exclude the Saviour from their hearts, and without Him there is gloom and sadness. But Christ dwelling in the soul is a wellspring of joy. For all who receive Him, the very keynote of the word of God is rejoicing.

"For thus saith the high and lofty One that inhabiteth eternity, whose name is Holy: I dwell in the high and holy place, with him also that is of a contrite and humble spirit, to revive the spirit of the humble, and to revive the heart of the contrite ones." Isaiah 57:15.

It was when Moses was hidden in the cleft of the rock that he beheld the glory of God. It is when we hide in the riven Rock that Christ will cover us with His own pierced hand, and we shall hear what the Lord saith unto His servants. To us as to Moses, God will reveal Himself as "merciful and gracious, long-suffering, and abundant in goodness and truth, keeping mercy for thousands, forgiving iniquity and transgression and sin." Exodus 34:6, 7.

The work of redemption involves consequences of which it is difficult for man to have any conception. "Eye hath not seen, nor ear heard, neither have entered into the heart of man, the things which God hath prepared for them that love Him." 1 Corinthians 2:9. As the sinner, drawn by the power of Christ, approaches the uplifted cross, and prostrates himself before it, there is a new creation. A new heart is given him. He becomes a new creature in Christ Jesus. Holiness finds that it has nothing more to require. God Himself is "the justifier of him which believeth in Jesus." Romans 3:26. And "whom He justified, them He also glorified." Romans 8:30. Great as is the shame and degradation through sin, even greater will be the honor and exaltation through redeeming love. To human beings striving for conformity to the divine image there is imparted an outlay of heaven's treasure, an excellency of power, that will place them higher than even the angels who have never fallen.

"Thus saith the Lord, the Redeemer of Israel, and His Holy One, to him whom man despiseth, to him whom the nation abhorreth,...Kings shall see and arise, princes also shall worship, because of the Lord that is faithful, and the Holy One of Israel, and He shall choose thee." Isaiah 49:7.

"For every one that exalteth himself shall be abased; and he that humbleth himself shall be exalted."

14
"Shall Not God Avenge His Own?"

Based on Luke 18:1–8

Christ had been speaking of the period just before His second coming, and of the perils through which His followers must pass. With special reference to that time He related the parable "to this end, that men ought always to pray, and not to faint."

"There was in a city," He said, "a judge, which feared not God, neither regarded man; and there was a widow in that city; and she came unto him, saying, Avenge me of mine adversary. And he would not for a while; but afterward he said within himself, Though I fear not God, nor regard man; yet because this widow troubleth me, I will avenge her, lest by her continual coming she weary me. And the Lord said, Hear what the unjust judge saith. And shall not God avenge His own elect, which cry day and night unto Him, though He bear long with them? I tell you that He will avenge them speedily."

The judge who is here pictured had no regard for right, nor pity for suffering. The widow who pressed her case before him was persistently repulsed. Again and again she came to him, only to be treated with contempt, and to be driven from the judgment seat. The judge knew that her cause was righteous, and he could have relieved her at once, but he would not. He wanted to show his arbitrary power, and it gratified him to let her ask and plead and entreat in vain. But she would not fail nor become discouraged. Notwithstanding his indifference and hardheartedness, she pressed her petition until the judge consented to attend to her case. "Though I fear not God, nor regard man," he said, "yet because this widow troubleth me, I will avenge her, lest by her continual coming she weary me." To save his reputation, to avoid giving publicity to his partial, one-sided judgment, he avenged the persevering woman.

"And the Lord said, Hear what the unjust judge saith. And shall not God avenge His own elect, which cry day and night unto him, though He bear long with them? I tell you that He will avenge them speedily." Christ here draws a sharp contrast between the unjust judge and God. The judge yielded to the widow's request merely through selfishness, that he might be relieved of her importunity. He felt for her no pity or compassion; her misery was nothing to him. How different is the attitude of God toward those who seek Him. The appeals of the needy and distressed are considered by Him with infinite compassion.

The woman who entreated the judge for justice had lost her husband by death. Poor and friendless, she had no means of retrieving her ruined fortunes. So by sin, man lost his connection with God. Of himself he has no means of salvation. But in Christ we are brought nigh unto the Father. The elect of God are dear to His heart. They are those whom He has called out of darkness into His marvelous light, to show forth His praise, to shine as lights amid the darkness of the world. The unjust judge had no special interest in the widow who importuned him for deliverance; yet in order to rid himself of her pitiful appeals, he heard her plea, and delivered her from her adversary. But God loves His children with infinite love. To Him the dearest object on earth is His church.

"For the Lord's portion is His people; Jacob is the lot of His inheritance. He found him in a desert land, and in the waste, howling wilderness; He led him about, He instructed him, He kept him as the apple of His eye." Deuteronomy 32:9, 10. "For thus saith the Lord of hosts: After the glory hath He sent Me unto the nations which spoiled you; for he that toucheth you toucheth the apple of His eye." Zechariah 2:8.

The widow's prayer, "Avenge me"—"do me justice" (R.V.)—"of mine adversary," represents the prayer of God's children. Satan is their great adversary. He is the "accuser of our brethren," who accuses them before God day and night. (Revelation 12:10.) He is continually working to misrepresent and accuse, to deceive and destroy the people of God. And it is for deliverance from the power of Satan and his agents that in this parable Christ teaches His disciples to pray.

In the prophecy of Zechariah is brought to view Satan's accusing work, and the work of Christ in resisting the adversary of His people. The prophet says, "He showed me Joshua the high priest standing before the angel of the Lord, and Satan standing at his right hand to resist him. And the Lord said unto Satan, The Lord rebuke thee, O Satan; even the Lord that hath chosen Jerusalem rebuke thee: is not this a brand plucked out of the fire? Now Joshua was clothed with filthy garments, and stood before the angel." Zechariah 3:1–3.

The people of God are here represented as a criminal on trial. Joshua, as high priest, is seeking for a blessing for his people, who are in great affliction. While he is pleading before God, Satan is standing at his right hand as his adversary. He is accusing the children of God, and making their case appear as desperate as possible. He presents before the Lord their evil doings and their defects. He shows their faults and failures, hoping they will appear of such a character in the eyes of Christ that He will render them no help in their great need. Joshua, as the representative of God's people, stands under condemnation, clothed with filthy garments. Aware of the sins of his people, he is weighed down with discouragement. Satan is pressing upon his soul a sense of guiltiness that makes him feel almost hopeless. Yet there he stands as a suppliant, with Satan arrayed against him.

The work of Satan as an accuser began in heaven. This has been his work on earth ever since man's fall, and it will be his work in a special sense as we approach nearer to the close of this world's history. As he sees that his time is short, he will work with greater earnestness to deceive and destroy. He is angry when he sees a people on the earth who, even in their weakness and sinfulness, have respect to the law of Jehovah. He is determined that they shall not obey God. He delights in their unworthiness, and has devices prepared for every soul, that all may be ensnared and separated from God. He seeks to accuse and condemn God and all who strive to carry out His purposes in this world in mercy and love, in compassion and forgiveness.

Every manifestation of God's power for His people arouses the enmity of Satan. Every time God works in their behalf, Satan with his angels works with renewed vigor to compass their ruin. He is jealous of all who make Christ their strength. His object is to instigate evil, and when he has succeeded, throw all the blame upon the tempted ones. He points to their filthy garments, their defective characters. He presents their weakness and folly, their sins of ingratitude, their unlikeness to Christ, which have dishonored their Redeemer. All this he urges as an argument proving his right to work his will in their destruction. He endeavors to affright their souls with the thought that their case is hopeless, that the stain of their defilement can never be washed away. He hopes so to destroy their faith that they will yield fully to his temptations, and turn from their allegiance to God.

The Lord's people cannot of themselves answer the charges of Satan. As they look to themselves they are ready to despair. But they appeal to the divine Advocate. They plead the merits of the Redeemer. God can be "just, and the justifier of him which believeth in Jesus." Romans 3:26. With confidence the Lord's children cry unto Him to silence the accusations of Satan, and bring to naught his devices. "Do me justice of mine adversary," they pray; and with the mighty argument of the cross, Christ silences the bold accuser.

"The Lord said unto Satan, The Lord rebuke thee, O Satan, even the Lord that hath chosen Jerusalem rebuke thee: is not this a brand plucked out of the fire?" When Satan seeks to cover the people of God with blackness, and ruin them, Christ interposes. Although they have sinned, Christ has taken the guilt of their sins upon His own soul. He has snatched the race as a brand from the fire. By His human nature He is linked with man, while through His divine nature He is one with the infinite God. Help is brought within the reach of perishing souls. The adversary is rebuked.

"Now Joshua was clothed with filthy garments, and stood before the angel: and he answered and spake unto those that stood before him, saying, Take away the filthy garments from him. And unto him he said, Behold, I have caused thine iniquity to pass from thee, and I will clothe thee with change of raiment. And I said, Let them set a fair miter upon his head. So they set a fair miter upon his head, and clothed him with garments." Then with the authority of the Lord of hosts the angel made a solemn pledge to Joshua, the representative of God's people: "If thou wilt walk in My ways, and if thou wilt keep My charge, then thou shalt also judge My house, and shalt also keep My courts, and I will give thee places to walk among these that stand by"—even among the angels that surround the throne of God. (Zechariah 3:3–7.)

Notwithstanding the defects of the people of God, Christ does not turn away from the objects of His care. He has the power to change their raiment. He removes the filthy garments, He places upon the repenting, believing ones His own robe of righteousness, and writes pardon against their names on the records of heaven. He confesses them as His before the heavenly universe. Satan their adversary is shown to be an accuser and deceiver. God will do justice for His own elect.

The prayer, "Do me justice of mine adversary," applies not only to Satan, but to the agencies whom he instigates to misrepresent, to tempt, and to destroy the people of God. Those who have decided to obey the commandments of God will understand by experience that they have adversaries who are controlled by a power from beneath. Such adversaries beset Christ at every step, how constantly and determinedly no human being can ever know. Christ's disciples, like their Master, are followed by continual temptation.

The Scriptures describe the condition of the world just before Christ's second coming. James the apostle pictures the greed and oppression that will prevail. He says, "Go to now, ye rich men,...ye have heaped treasure together for the last days. Behold, the hire of the labourers who have reaped down your fields, which is of you kept back by fraud, crieth: and the cries of them which have reaped are entered into the ears of the Lord of sabaoth. Ye have lived in pleasure on the earth, and been wanton. Ye have nourished your hearts, as in a day of slaughter. Ye have condemned and killed the just; and he doth not resist you." James 5:1–6. This is a picture of what exists today. By every species of oppression and extortion, men are piling up colossal fortunes, while the cries of starving humanity are coming up before God.

"Judgment is turned away backward, and justice standeth afar off; for truth is fallen in the street, and equity cannot enter. Yea, truth faileth; and he that departeth from evil maketh himself a prey." Isaiah 59:14, 15. This was fulfilled in the life of Christ on earth. He was loyal to God's commandments, setting aside the human traditions and requirements which had been exalted in their place. Because of this He was hated and persecuted. This history is repeated. The laws and traditions of men are exalted above the law of God, and those who are true to God's commandments suffer reproach and persecution. Christ, because of His faithfulness to God, was accused as a Sabbathbreaker and blasphemer. He was declared to be possessed of a devil, and was denounced as Beelzebub. In like manner His followers are accused and misrepresented. Thus Satan hopes to lead them to sin, and cast dishonor upon God.

The character of the judge in the parable, who feared not God nor regarded man, was presented by Christ to show the kind of judgment that was then being executed, and that would soon be witnessed at His trial. He desires His people in all time to realize how little dependence can be placed on earthly rulers or judges in the day of adversity. Often the elect people of God have to stand before men in official positions who do not make the word of God their guide and counselor, but who follow their own unconsecrated, undisciplined impulses.

In the parable of the unjust judge, Christ has shown what we should do. "Shall not God avenge His own elect, which cry day and night unto Him?" Christ, our example, did nothing to vindicate or deliver Himself. He committed His case to God. So His followers are not accuse or condemn, or to resort to force in order to deliver themselves.

When trials arise that seem unexplainable, we should not allow our peace to be spoiled. However unjustly we may be treated, let not passion arise. By indulging a spirit of retaliation we injure ourselves. We destroy our own confidence in God, and grieve the Holy Spirit. There is by our side a witness, a heavenly messenger, who will lift up for us a standard against the enemy. He will shut us in with the bright beams of the Sun of Righteousness. Beyond this Satan cannot penetrate. He cannot pass this shield of holy light.

While the world is progressing in wickedness, none of us need flatter ourselves that we shall have no difficulties. But it is these very difficulties that bring us into the audience chamber of the Most High. We may seek counsel of One who is infinite in wisdom.

The Lord says, "Call upon Me in the day of trouble." Psalm 50:15. He invites us to present to Him our perplexities and necessities, and our need of divine help. He bids us be instant in prayer. As soon as difficulties arise, we are to offer to Him our sincere, earnest petitions. By our importunate prayers we give evidence of our strong confidence in God. The sense of our need leads us to pray earnestly, and our heavenly Father is moved by our supplications.

Often those who suffer reproach or persecution for their faith are tempted to think themselves forsaken by God. In the eyes of men they are in the minority. To all appearance their enemies triumph over them. But let them not violate their conscience. He who has suffered in their behalf, and has borne their sorrows and afflictions, has not forsaken them.

The children of God are not left alone and defenseless. Prayer moves the arm of Omnipotence. Prayer has "subdued kingdoms, wrought righteousness, obtained promises, stopped the mouths of lions, quenched the violence of fire"—we shall know what it means when we hear the reports of the martyrs who died for their faith—"turneth to flight the armies of the aliens." Hebrews 11:33, 34.

If we surrender our lives to His service, we can never be placed in a position for which God has not made provision. Whatever may be our situation, we have a Guide to direct our way; whatever our perplexities, we have a sure Counselor; whatever our sorrow, bereavement, or loneliness, we have a sympathizing Friend. If in our ignorance we make missteps, Christ does not leave us. His voice, clear and distinct, is heard saying, "I am the Way, the Truth, and the Life." John 14:6. "He shall deliver the needy when he crieth; the poor also, and him that hath no helper." Psalm 72:12.

The Lord declares that He will be honored by those who draw nigh to Him, who faithfully do His service. "Thou wilt keep him in perfect peace whose mind is stayed on Thee, because he trusteth in Thee." Isaiah 26:3. The arm of Omnipotence is outstretched to lead us onward and still onward. Go forward, the Lord says; I will send you help. It is for My name's glory that you ask, and you shall receive. I will be honored before those who are watching for your failure. They shall see My word triumph gloriously. "All things, whatsoever ye shall ask in prayer, believing, ye shall receive." Matthew 21:22.

Let all who are afflicted or unjustly used, cry to God. Turn away from those whose hearts are as steel, and make your requests known to your Maker. Never is one repulsed who comes to Him with a contrite heart. Not one sincere prayer is lost. Amid the anthems of the celestial choir, God hears the cries of the weakest human being. We pour out our heart's desire in our closets, we breathe a prayer as we walk by the way, and our words reach the throne of the Monarch of the universe. They may be inaudible to any human ear, but they cannot die away into silence, nor can they be lost through the activities of business that are going on. Nothing can drown the soul's desire. It rises above the din of the street, above the confusion of the multitude, to the heavenly courts. It is God to whom we are speaking, and our prayer is heard.

You who feel the most unworthy, fear not to commit your case to God. When He gave Himself in Christ for the sin of the world, He undertook the case of every soul. "He that spared not His own Son, but delivered Him up for us all, how shall He not with Him also freely give us all things?" Romans 8:32. Will He not fulfill the gracious word given for our encouragement and strength?

Christ desires nothing so much as to redeem His heritage from the dominion of Satan. But before we are delivered from Satan's power without, we must be delivered from his power within. The Lord permits trials in order that we may be cleansed from earthliness, from selfishness, from harsh, unchristlike traits of character. He suffers the deep waters of affliction to go over our souls in order that we may know Him and Jesus Christ whom He has sent, in order that we may have deep heart longings to be cleansed from defilement, and may come forth from the trial purer, holier, happier. Often we enter the furnace of trial with our souls darkened with selfishness; but if patient under the crucial test, we shall come forth reflecting the divine character. When His purpose in the affliction is accomplished, "He shall bring forth thy righteousness as the light, and thy judgment as the noonday." Psalm 37:6.

There is no danger that the Lord will neglect the prayers of His people. The danger is that in temptation and trial they will become discouraged, and fail to persevere in prayer.

The Saviour manifested divine compassion toward the Syrophenician woman. His heart was touched as He saw her grief. He longed to give her an immediate assurance that her prayer was heard; but He desired to teach His disciples a lesson, and for a time He seemed to neglect the cry of her tortured heart. When her faith had been made manifest, He spoke to her words of commendation and sent her away with the precious boon she had asked. The disciples never forgot this lesson, and it is placed on record to show the result of persevering prayer.

It was Christ Himself who put into that mother's heart the persistence which would not be repulsed. It was Christ who gave the pleading widow courage and determination before the judge. It was Christ who, centuries before, in the mysterious conflict by the Jabbok, had inspired Jacob with the same persevering faith. And the confidence which He Himself had implanted, He did not fail to reward.

He who dwells in the heavenly sanctuary judges righteously. His pleasure is more in His people, struggling with temptation in a world of sin, than in the host of angels that surround His throne.

In this speck of a world the whole heavenly universe manifests the greatest interest, for Christ has paid an infinite price for the souls of its inhabitants. The world's Redeemer has bound earth to heaven by ties of intelligence, for the redeemed of the Lord are here. Heavenly beings still visit the earth as in the days when they walked and talked with Abraham and with Moses. Amid the busy activity of our great cities, amid the multitudes that crowd the thoroughfares and fill the marts of trade where from morning till evening the people act as if business and sport and pleasure were all there is to life, where there are so few to contemplate unseen realities—even here heaven has still its watchers and its holy ones. There are invisible agencies observing every word and deed of human beings. In every assembly for business or pleasure, in every gathering for worship, there are more listeners than can be seen with the natural sight. Sometimes the heavenly intelligences draw aside the curtain which hides the unseen world that our thoughts may be withdrawn from the hurry and rush of life to consider that there are unseen witnesses to all we do or say.

We need to understand better than we do the mission of the angel visitants. It would be well to consider that in all our work we have the co-operation and care of heavenly beings. Invisible armies of light and power attend the meek and lowly ones who believe and claim the promises of God. Cherubim and seraphim and angels that excel in strength-ten thousand times ten thousand and thousands of thousands—stand at His right hand, "all ministering spirits, sent forth to minister for them who shall be heirs of salvation." Hebrews 1:14.

By these angel messengers a faithful record is kept of the words and deeds of the children of men. Every act of cruelty or injustice toward God's people, all they are caused to suffer through the power of evil workers, is registered in heaven.

"Shall not God avenge His own elect, which cry day and night unto Him, though He bear long with them? I tell you that He will avenge them speedily."

"Cast not away therefore your confidence, which hath great recompense of reward. For ye have need of patience, that, after ye have done the will of God, ye might receive the promise. For yet a little while, and He that shall come will come, and will not tarry." Hebrews 10:35–37. "Behold, the husbandman waiteth for the precious fruit of the earth, and hath long patience for it, until he receive the early and latter rain. Be ye also patient; stablish your hearts; for the coming of the Lord draweth nigh." James 5:7, 8.

The long-suffering of God is wonderful. Long does justice wait while mercy pleads with the sinner. But "righteousness and judgment are the establishment of His throne." Psalm 97:2, margin. "The Lord is slow to anger;" but He is "great in power, and will not at all acquit the wicked: the Lord hath His way in the whirlwind and in the storm, and the clouds are the dust of His feet." Nahum 1:3.

The world has become bold in transgression of God's law. Because of His long forbearance, men have trampled upon His authority. They have strengthened one another in oppression and cruelty toward His heritage, saying, "How doth God know? and is there knowledge in the Most High?" Psalm 73:11. But there is a line beyond which they cannot pass. The time is near when they will have reached the prescribed limit. Even now they have almost exceeded the bounds of the long-suffering of God, the limits of His grace, the limits of His mercy. The Lord will interpose to vindicate His own honor, to deliver His people, and to repress the swellings of unrighteousness.

In Noah's day, men had disregarded the law of God until almost all remembrance of the Creator had passed away from the earth. Their iniquity reached so great a height that the Lord brought a flood of waters upon the earth, and swept away its wicked inhabitants.

From age to age the Lord has made known the manner of His working. When a crisis has come, He has revealed Himself, and has interposed to hinder the working out of Satan's plans. With nations, with families, and with individuals, He has often permitted matters to come to a crisis, that His interference might become marked. Then He has made manifest that there is a God in Israel who will maintain His law and vindicate His people.

In this time of prevailing iniquity we may know that the last great crisis is at hand. When the defiance of God's law is almost universal, when His people are oppressed and afflicted by their fellow men, the Lord will interpose.

The time is near when He will say, "Come, My people, enter thou into thy chambers, and shut thy doors about thee: hide thyself as it were for a little moment, until the indignation be overpast. For, behold, the Lord cometh out of His place to punish the inhabitants of the earth for their iniquity; the earth also shall disclose her blood, and shall no more cover her slain." Isaiah 26:20, 21. Men who claim to be Christians may now defraud and oppress the poor; they may rob the widow and fatherless; they may indulge their Satanic hatred because they cannot control the consciences of God's people; but for all this God will bring them into judgment. They "shall have judgment without mercy" that have "showed no mercy." (James 2:13.) Not long hence they will stand before the Judge of all the earth, to render an account for the pain they have caused to the bodies and souls of His heritage. They may now indulge in false accusations, they may deride those whom God has appointed to do His work, they may consign His believing ones to prison, to the chain gang, to banishment, to death; but for every pang of anguish, every tear shed, they must answer. God will reward them double for their sins. Concerning Babylon, the symbol of the apostate church, He says to His ministers of judgment, "Her sins have reached unto heaven, and God hath remembered her iniquities. Reward her even as she rewarded you, and double unto her double according to her works: in the cup which she hath filled fill to her double." Revelation 18:5, 6.

From India, from Africa, from China, from the islands of the sea, from the downtrodden millions of so-called Christian lands, the cry of human woe is ascending to God. That cry will not long be unanswered. God will cleanse the earth from it moral corruption, not by a sea of water as in Noah's day, but by a sea of fire that cannot be quenched by any human devising.

"There shall be a time of trouble, such as never was since there was a nation even to that same time; and at that time Thy people shall be delivered, every one that shall be found written in the book." Daniel 12:1.

From garrets, from hovels, from dungeons, from scaffolds, from mountains and deserts, from the caves of the earth and the caverns of the sea, Christ will gather His children to Himself. On earth they have been destitute, afflicted, and tormented. Millions have gone down to the grave loaded with infamy because they refused to yield to the deceptive claims of Satan. By human tribunals the children of God have been adjudged the vilest criminals. But the day is near when "God is judge Himself." (Psalm 50:6). Then the decisions of earth shall be reversed. "The rebuke of His people shall He take away." Isaiah 25:8. White robes will be given to every one of them. (Revelation 6:11.) And "they shall call them the holy people, the redeemed of the Lord." Isaiah 62:12.

Whatever crosses they have been called to bear, whatever losses they have sustained, whatever persecution they have suffered, even to the loss of their temporal life, the children of God are amply recompensed. "They shall see His face; and His name shall be in their foreheads." Revelation 22:4.

15

"This Man Receiveth Sinners"

Based on Luke 15:1–10

As the "publicans and sinners" gathered about Christ, the rabbis expressed their displeasure. "This man receiveth sinners," they said, "and eateth with them."

By this accusation they insinuated that Christ liked to associate with the sinful and vile, and was insensible to their wickedness. The rabbis had been disappointed in Jesus. Why was it that one who claimed so lofty a character did not mingle with them and follow their methods of teaching? Why did He go about so unpretendingly, working among all classes? If He were a true prophet, they said, He would harmonize with them, and would treat the publicans and sinners with the indifference they deserved. It angered these guardians of society that He with whom they were continually in controversy, yet whose purity of life awed and condemned them, should meet, in such apparent sympathy, with social outcasts. They did not approve of His methods. They regarded themselves as educated, refined, and pre-eminently religious; but Christ's example laid bare their selfishness.

It angered them also that those who showed only contempt for the rabbis and who were never seen in the synagogues should flock about Jesus and listen with rapt attention to His words. The scribes and Pharisees felt only condemnation in that pure presence; how was it, then, that publicans and sinners were drawn to Jesus?

They knew not that the explanation lay in the very words they had uttered as a scornful charge, "This man receiveth sinners." The souls who came to Jesus felt in His presence that even for them there was escape from the pit of sin. The Pharisees had only scorn and condemnation for them; but Christ greeted them as children of God, estranged indeed from the Father's house, but not forgotten by the Father's heart. And their very misery and sin made them only the more the objects of His compassion. The farther they had wandered from Him, the more earnest the longing and the greater the sacrifice for their rescue.

All this the teachers of Israel might have learned from the sacred scrolls of which it was their pride to be the keepers and expounders. Had not David written—David, who had fallen into deadly sin—"I have gone astray like a lost sheep, seek Thy servant"? Psalm 119:176. Had not Micah revealed God's love to the sinner, saying, "Who is a God like unto Thee, that pardoneth iniquity, and passeth by the transgression of the remnant of His heritage? He retaineth not His anger forever, because He delighteth in mercy"? Micah 7:18.

The Lost Sheep

Christ did not at this time remind His hearers of the words of Scripture. He appealed to the witness of their own experience. The wide-spreading tablelands on the east of Jordan afforded abundant pasturage for flocks, and through the gorges and over the wooded hills had wandered many a lost sheep, to be searched for and brought back by the shepherd's care. In the company about Jesus there were shepherds, and also men who had money invested in flocks and herds, and all could appreciate His illustration: "What man of *you*, having an hundred sheep, if he lose one of them, doth not leave the ninety and nine in the wilderness, and go after that which is lost, until he find it?"

These souls whom you despise, said Jesus, are the property of God. By creation and by redemption they are His, and they are of value in His sight. As the shepherd loves his sheep, and cannot rest if even one be missing, so, in an infinitely higher degree, does God love every outcast soul. Men may deny the claim of His love, they may wander from Him, they may choose another master; yet they are God's, and He longs to recover His own. He says, "As a shepherd seeketh out his flock in the day that he is among his sheep that are scattered; so will I seek out My sheep, and will deliver them out of all places where they have been scattered in the cloudy and dark day." Ezekiel 34:12.

In the parable the shepherd goes out to search for one sheep—the very least that can be numbered. So if there had been but one lost soul, Christ would have died for that one.

The sheep that has strayed from the fold is the most helpless of all creatures. It must be sought for by the shepherd, for it cannot find its way back. So with the soul that has wandered away from God; he is as helpless as the lost sheep, and unless divine love had come to his rescue he could never find his way to God.

The shepherd who discovers that one of his sheep is missing does not look carelessly upon the flock that is safely housed, and say, "I have ninety and nine, and it will cost me too much trouble to go in search of the straying one. Let him come back, and I will open the door of the sheepfold, and let him in." No; no sooner does the sheep go astray than the shepherd is filled with grief and anxiety. He counts and recounts the flock. When he is sure that one sheep is lost, he slumbers not. He leaves the ninety and nine within the fold, and goes in search of the straying sheep. The darker and more tempestuous the night and the more perilous the way, the greater is the shepherd's anxiety and the more earnest his search. He makes every effort to find that one lost sheep.

With what relief he hears in the distance its first faint cry. Following the sound, he climbs the steepest heights, he goes to the very edge of the precipice, at the risk of his own life. Thus he searches, while the cry, growing fainter, tells him that his sheep is ready to die. At last his effort is rewarded; the lost is found. Then he does not scold it because it has caused him so much trouble. He does not drive it with a whip. He does not even try to lead it home. In his joy he takes the trembling creature upon his shoulders; if it is bruised and wounded, he gathers it in his arms, pressing it close to his bosom, that the warmth of his own heart may give it life. With gratitude that his search has not been in vain, he bears it back to the fold.

Thank God, He has presented to our imagination no picture of a sorrowful shepherd returning without the sheep. The parable does not speak of failure but of success and joy in the recovery. Here is the divine guarantee that not even one of the straying sheep of God's fold is overlooked, not one is left unsuccored. Every one that will submit to be ransomed, Christ will rescue from the pit of corruption and from the briers of sin.

Desponding soul, take courage, even though you have done wickedly. Do not think that *perhaps* God will pardon your transgressions and permit you to come into His presence. God has made the first advance. While you were in rebellion against Him, He went forth to seek you. With the tender heart of the shepherd He left the ninety and nine and went out into the wilderness to find that which was lost. The soul, bruised and wounded and ready to perish, He encircles in His arms of love and joyfully bears it to the fold of safety.

It was taught by the Jews that before God's love is extended to the sinner, he must first repent. In their view, repentance is a work by which men earn the favor of Heaven. And it was this thought that led the Pharisees to exclaim in astonishment and anger. "This man receiveth sinners." According to their ideas He should permit none to approach Him but those who had repented. But in the parable of the lost sheep, Christ teaches that salvation does not come through our seeking after God but through God's seeking after us. "There is none that understandeth, there is none that seeketh after God. They are all gone out of the way." Romans 3:11, 12. We do not repent in order that God may love us, but He reveals to us His love in order that we may repent.

When the straying sheep is at last brought home, the shepherd's gratitude finds expression in melodious songs of rejoicing. He calls upon his friends and neighbors, saying unto them, "Rejoice with me; for I have found my sheep which was lost." So when a wanderer is found by the great Shepherd of the sheep, heaven and earth unite in thanksgiving and rejoicing.

"Joy shall be in heaven over one sinner that repenteth, more than over ninety and nine just persons, which need no repentance." You Pharisees, said Christ, regard yourselves as the favorites of heaven. You think yourselves secure in your own righteousness. Know, then, that if you need no repentance, My mission is not to you. These poor souls who feel their poverty and sinfulness, are the very ones whom I have come to rescue. Angels of heaven are interested in these lost ones whom you despise. You complain and sneer when one of these souls joins himself to Me; but know that angels rejoice, and the song of triumph rings through the courts above.

The rabbis had a saying that there is rejoicing in heaven when one who has sinned against God is destroyed; but Jesus taught that to God the work of destruction is a strange work. That in which all heaven delights is the restoration of God's own image in the souls whom He has made.

When one who has wandered far in sin seeks to return to God, he will encounter criticism and distrust. There are those who will doubt whether his repentance is genuine, or will whisper, "He has no stability; I do not believe that he will hold out." These persons are doing not the work of God but the work of Satan, who is the accuser of the brethren. Through their criticisms the wicked one hopes to discourage that soul, and to drive him still farther from hope and from God. Let the repenting sinner contemplate the rejoicing in heaven over the return of the one that was lost. Let him rest in the love of God and in no case be disheartened by the scorn and suspicion of the Pharisees.

The rabbis understood Christ's parable as applying to the publicans and sinners; but it has also a wider meaning. By the lost sheep Christ represents not only the individual sinner but the one world that has apostatized and has been ruined by sin. This world is but an atom in the vast dominions over which God presides, yet this little fallen world—the one lost sheep—is more precious in His sight that are the ninety and nine that went not astray from the fold. Christ, the loved Commander in the heavenly courts, stooped from His high estate, laid aside the glory that He had with the Father, in order to save the one lost world. For this He left the sinless worlds on high, the ninety and nine that loved Him, and came to this earth, to be "wounded for our transgressions" and "bruised for our iniquities." (Isaiah 53:5.) God gave Himself in His Son that He might have the joy of receiving back the sheep that was lost.

"Behold, what manner of love the Father hath bestowed upon us, that we should be called the sons of God." I John 3:1. And Christ says, "As Thou hast sent Me into the world, even so have I also sent them into the world" (John 17:18)—to "fill up that which is behind of the afflictions of Christ,...-for His body's sake, which is the church." Colossians 1:24. Every soul whom Christ has rescued is called to work in His name for the saving of the lost. This work had been neglected in Israel. Is it not neglected today by those who profess to be Christ's followers?

How many of the wandering ones have you, reader, sought for and brought back to the fold? When you turn from those who seem unpromising and unattractive, do you realize that you are neglecting the souls for whom Christ is seeking? At the very time when you turn from them, they may be in the greatest need of your compassion. In every assembly for worship, there are souls longing for rest and peace. They may appear to be living careless lives, but they are not insensible to the influence of the Holy Spirit. Many among them might be won for Christ.

If the lost sheep is not brought back to the fold, it wanders until it perishes. And many souls go down to ruin for want of a hand stretched out to save. These erring ones may appear hard and reckless; but if they had received the same advantages that others have had, they might have revealed far more nobility of soul, and greater talent for usefulness. Angels pity these wandering ones. Angels weep, while human eyes are dry and hearts are closed to pity.

O the lack of deep, soul-touching sympathy for the tempted and the erring! O for more of Christ's spirit, and for less, far less, of self!

The Pharisees understood Christ's parable as a rebuke to them. Instead of accepting their criticism of His work, He had reproved their neglect of the publicans and sinners. He had not done this openly, lest it should close their hearts against Him; but His illustration set before them the very work which God required of them, and which they had failed to do. Had they been true shepherds, these leaders in Israel would have done the work of a shepherd. They would have manifested the mercy and love of Christ, and would have united with Him in His mission. Their refusal to do this had proved their claims of piety to be false. Now many rejected Christ's reproof; yet to some His words brought conviction. Upon these, after Christ's ascension to heaven, the Holy Spirit came, and they united with His disciples in the very work outlined in the parable of the lost sheep.

The Lost Piece of Silver

After giving the parable of the lost sheep Christ spoke another, saying, "What woman having ten pieces of silver, if she lose one piece, doth not light a candle, and sweep the house, and seek diligently till she find it?"

In the East the houses of the poor usually consisted of but one room, often windowless and dark. The room was rarely swept, and a piece of money falling on the floor would be speedily covered by the dust and rubbish. In order that it might be found, even in the daytime, a candle must be lighted, and the house must be swept diligently.

The wife's marriage portion usually consisted of pieces of money, which she carefully preserved as her most cherished possession, to be transmitted to her own daughters. The loss of one of these pieces would be regarded as a serious calamity, and its recovery would cause great rejoicing, in which the neighboring women would readily share.

"When she hath found it," Christ said, "she calleth her friends and her neighbors together, saying, Rejoice with me, for I have found the piece which I had lost. Likewise, I say unto you, there is joy in the presence of the angels of God over one sinner that repenteth."

This parable, like the preceding, sets forth the loss of something which with proper search may be recovered, and that with great joy. But the two parables represent different classes. The lost sheep knows that it is lost. It has left the shepherd and the flock, and it cannot recover itself. It represents those who realize that they are separated from God and who are in a cloud of perplexity, in humiliation, and sorely tempted. The lost coin represents those who are lost in trespasses and sins, but who have no sense of their condition. They are estranged from God, but they know it not. Their souls are in peril, but they are unconscious and unconcerned. In this parable Christ teaches that even those who are indifferent to the claims of God are the objects of His pitying love. They are to be sought for that they may be brought back to God.

The sheep wandered away from the fold; it was lost in the wilderness or upon the mountains. The piece of silver was lost in the house. It was close at hand, yet it could be recovered only by diligent search.

This parable has a lesson to families. In the household there is often great carelessness concerning the souls of its members. Among their number may be one who is estranged from God; but how little anxiety is felt lest in the family relationship there be lost one of God's entrusted gifts.

The coin, though lying among dust and rubbish, is a piece of silver still. Its owner seeks it because it is of value. So every soul, however degraded by sin, is in God's sight accounted precious. As the coin bears the image and superscription of the reigning power, so man at his creation bore the image and superscription of God; and though now marred and dim through the influence of sin, the traces of this inscription remain upon every soul. God desires to recover that soul and to retrace upon it His own image in righteousness and holiness.

The woman in the parable searches diligently for her lost coin. She lights the candle and sweeps the house. She removes everything that might obstruct her search. Though only one piece is lost, she will not cease her efforts until that piece is found. So in the family if one member is lost to God every means should be used for his recovery. On the part of all the others let there be diligent, careful self-examination. Let the life-practice be investigated. See if there is not some mistake, some error in management, by which that soul is confirmed in impenitence.

If there is in the family one child who is unconscious of his sinful state, parents should not rest. Let the candle be lighted. Search the word of God, and by its light let everything in the home be diligently examined, to see why this child is lost. Let parents search their own hearts, examine their habits and practices. Children are the heritage of the Lord, and we are answerable to Him for our management of His property.

There are fathers and mothers who long to labor in some foreign mission field; there are many who are active in Christian work outside the home, while their own children are strangers to the Saviour and His love. The work of winning their children for Christ many parents trust to the minister or the Sabbath school teacher, but in doing this they are neglecting their own God-given responsibility. The education and training of their children to be Christians is the highest service that parents can render to God. It is a work that demands patient labor, a lifelong diligent and persevering effort. By a neglect of this trust we prove ourselves unfaithful stewards. No excuse for such neglect will be accepted by God.

But those who have been guilty of neglect are not to despair. The woman whose coin was lost searched until she found it. So in love, faith, and prayer let parents work for their households, until with joy they can come to God saying, "Behold, I and the children whom the Lord hath given me." Isaiah 8:18.

This is true home missionary work, and it is as helpful to those who do it as to those for whom it is done. By our faithful interest for the home circle we are fitting ourselves to work for the members of the Lord's family, with whom, if loyal to Christ, we shall live through eternal ages. For our brethren and sisters in Christ we are to show the same interest that as members of one family we have for one another.

And God designs that all this shall fit us to labor for still others. As our sympathies shall broaden and our love increase, we shall find everywhere a work to do. God's great human household embraces the world, and none of its members are to be passed by with neglect.

Wherever we may be, there the lost piece of silver awaits our search. Are we seeking for it? Day by day we meet with those who take no interest in religious things; we talk with them, we visit among them; do we show an interest in their spiritual welfare? Do we present Christ to them as the sin-pardoning Saviour? With our own hearts warm with the love of Christ, do we tell them about that love? If we do not, how shall we meet these souls—lost, eternally lost—when with them we stand before the throne of God?

The value of a soul, who can estimate? Would you know its worth, go to Gethsemane, and there watch with Christ through those hours of anguish, when He sweat as it were great drops of blood. Look upon the Saviour uplifted on the cross. Hear that despairing cry, "My God, My God, why hast Thou forsaken Me?" Mark 15:34. Look upon the wounded head, the pierced side, the marred feet. Remember that Christ risked all. For our redemption, heaven itself was imperiled. At the foot of the cross, remembering that for one sinner Christ would have laid down His life, you may estimate the value of a soul.

If you are in communion with Christ, you will place His estimate upon every human being. You will feel for others the same deep love that Christ has felt for you. Then you will be able to win, not drive, to attract, not repulse, those for whom He died. None would ever have been brought back to God if Christ had not made a personal effort for them; and it is by this personal work that we can rescue souls. When you see those who are going down to death, you will not rest in quiet indifference and ease. The greater their sin and the deeper their misery, the more earnest and tender will be your efforts for their recovery. You will discern the need of those who are suffering, who have been sinning against God, and who are oppressed with a burden of guilt. Your heart will go out in sympathy for them, and you will reach out to them a helping hand. In the arms of your faith and love you will bring them to Christ. You will watch over and encourage them, and your sympathy and confidence will make it hard for them to fall from their steadfastness.

In this work all the angels of heaven are ready to co-operate. All the resources of heaven are at the command of those who are seeking to save the lost. Angels will help you to reach the most careless and the most hardened. And when one is brought back to God, all heaven is made glad; seraphs and cherubs touch their golden harps, and sing praises to God and the Lamb for their mercy and loving-kindness to the children of men.

16
"Lost and Is Found"

Based on Luke 15:11–32

The parables of the lost sheep, the lost coin, and the prodigal son, bring out in distinct lines God's pitying love for those who are straying from Him. Although they have turned away from God, He does not leave them in their misery. He is full of kindness and tender pity toward all who are exposed to the temptations of the artful foe.

In the parable of the prodigal son is presented the Lord's dealing with those who have once known the Father's love, but who have allowed the tempter to lead them captive at his will.

"A certain man had two sons; and the younger of them said to his father, Father, give me the portion of goods that falleth to me. And he divided unto them his living. And not many days after the younger son gathered all together, and took his journey into a far country."

This younger son had become weary of the restraint of his father's house. He thought that his liberty was restricted. His father's love and care for him were misinterpreted, and he determined to follow the dictates of his own inclination.

The youth acknowledges no obligation to his father, and expresses no gratitude; yet he claims the privilege of a child in sharing his father's goods. The inheritance that would fall to him at his father's death he desires to receive now. He is bent on present enjoyment, and cares not for the future.

Having obtained his patrimony, he goes into "a far country," away from his father's home. With money in plenty, and liberty to do as he likes, he flatters himself that the desire of his heart is reached. There is no one to say, Do not do this, for it will be an injury to yourself; or, Do this, because it is right. Evil companions help him to plunge ever deeper into sin, and he wastes his "substance with riotous living."

The Bible tells of men who "professing themselves to be wise" "became fools" (Romans 1:22); and this is the history of the young man of the parable. The wealth which he has selfishly claimed from his father he squanders upon harlots. The treasure of his young manhood is wasted. The precious years of life, the strength of intellect, the bright visions of youth, the spiritual aspirations—all are consumed in the fires of lust.

A great famine arises, he begins to be in want, and he joins himself to a citizen of the country, who sends him into the field to feed swine. To a Jew this was the most menial and degrading of employments. The youth who has boasted of his liberty, now finds himself a slave. He is in the worst of bondage—"holden with the cords of his sins." (Proverbs 5:22.) The glitter and tinsel that enticed him have disappeared, and he feels the burden of his chain. Sitting upon the ground in that desolate and famine-stricken land, with no companions but the swine, he is fain to fill himself with the husks on which the beasts are fed. Of the gay companions who flocked about him in his prosperous days and ate and drank at his expense, there is not one left to befriend him. Where now is his riotous joy? Stilling his conscience, benumbing his sensibilities, he thought himself happy; but now, with money spent, with hunger unsatisfied, with pride humbled, with his moral nature dwarfed, with his will weak and untrustworthy, with his finer feelings seemingly dead, he is the most wretched of mortals.

What a picture here of the sinner's state! Although surrounded with the blessings of His love, there is nothing that the sinner, bent on self-indulgence and sinful pleasure, desires so much as separation from God. Like the ungrateful son, he claims the good things of God as his by right. He takes them as a matter of course, and makes no return of gratitude, renders no service of love. As Cain went out from the presence of the Lord to seek his home; as the prodigal wandered into the "far country," so do sinners seek happiness in forgetfulness of God. (Romans 1:28.)

Whatever the appearance may be, every life centered in self is squandered. Whoever attempts to live apart from God is wasting his substance. He is squandering the precious years, squandering the powers of mind and heart and soul, and working to make himself bankrupt for eternity. The man who separates from God that he may serve himself, is the slave of mammon. The mind that God created for the companionship of angels has become degraded to the service of that which is earthly and bestial. This is the end to which self-serving tends.

If you have chosen such a life, you know that you are spending money for that which is not bread, and labor for that which satisfieth not. There come to you hours when you realize your degradation. Alone in the far country you feel your misery, and in despair you cry, "O wretched man that I am! who shall deliver me from the body of this death?" Romans 7:24. It is the statement of a universal truth which is contained in the prophet's words, "Cursed be the man that trusteth in man, and maketh flesh his arm, and whose heart departeth from the Lord. For he shall be like the heath in the desert, and shall not see when good cometh; but shall inhabit the parched places in the wilderness, in a salt land and not inhabited." Jeremiah 17:5, 6. God "maketh His sun to rise on the evil and on the good, and sendeth rain on the just and on the unjust" (Matthew 5:45); but men have the power to shut themselves away from sunshine and shower. So while the Sun of Righteousness shines, and the showers of grace fall freely for all, we may by separating ourselves from God still "inhabit the parched places in the wilderness."

The love of God still yearns over the one who has chosen to separate from Him, and He sets in operation influences to bring him back to the Father's house. The prodigal son in his wretchedness "came to himself." The deceptive power that Satan had exercised over him was broken. He saw that his suffering was the result of his own folly, and he said, "How many hired servants of my father's have bread enough and to spare, and I perish with hunger! I will arise and go to may father." Miserable as he was, the prodigal found hope in the conviction of his father's love. It was that love which was drawing him toward home. So it is the assurance of God's love that constrains the sinner to return to God. "The goodness of God leadeth thee to repentance." Romans 2:4. A golden chain, the mercy and compassion of divine love, is passed around every imperiled soul. The Lord declares, "I have loved thee with an everlasting love; therefore with loving-kindness have I drawn thee." Jeremiah 31:3.

The son determines to confess his guilt. He will go to his father, saying, "I have sinned against heaven, and before thee, and am no more worthy to be called thy son." But he adds, showing how stinted is his conception of his father's love, "Make me as one of thy hired servants."

The young man turns from the swine herds and the husks, and sets his face toward home. Trembling with weakness and faint from hunger, he presses eagerly on his way. He has no covering to conceal his rags; but his misery has conquered pride ,and he hurries on to beg a servant's place where he was once a child.

Little did the gay, thoughtless youth, as he went out from his father's gate, dream of the ache and longing left in that father's heart. When he danced and feasted with his wild companions, little did he think of the shadow that had fallen on his home. And now as with weary and painful steps he pursues the homeward way, he knows not that one is watching for his return. But while he is yet "a great way off" the father discerns his form. Love is of quick sight. Not even the degradation of the years of sin can conceal the son from the father's eyes. He "had compassion, and ran, and fell on his neck" in a long, clinging, tender embrace.

The father will permit no contemptuous eye to mock at his son's misery and tatters. He takes from his own shoulders the broad, rich mantle, and wraps it around the son's wasted form, and the youth sobs out his repentance, saying, "Father, I have sinned against heaven, and in thy sight, and am no more worthy to be called thy son." The father holds him close to his side, and brings him home. No opportunity is given him to ask a servant's place. He is a son, who shall be honored with the best the house affords, and whom the waiting men and women shall respect and serve.

The father said to his servants, "Bring forth the best robe, and put it on him; and put a ring on his hand, and shoes on his feet; and bring hither the fatted calf, and kill it; and let us eat and be merry; for this my son was dead, and is alive again; he was lost, and is found. And they began to be merry."

In his restless youth the prodigal looked upon his father as stern and severe. How different his conception of him now! So those who are deceived by Satan look upon God as hard and exacting. They regard Him as watching to denounce and condemn, as unwilling to receive the sinner so long as there is a legal excuse for not helping him. His law they regard as a restriction upon men's happiness, a burdensome yoke from which they are glad to escape. But he whose eyes have been opened by the love of Christ will behold God as full of compassion. He does not appear as a tyrannical, relentless being, but as a father longing to embrace his repenting son. The sinner will exclaim with the Psalmist, "Like as a father pitieth his children, so the Lord pitieth them that fear Him." Psalm 103:13.

In the parable there is no taunting, no casting up to the prodigal of his evil course. The son feels that the past is forgiven and forgotten, blotted out forever. And so God says to the sinner, "I have blotted out, as a thick cloud, thy transgressions, and, as a cloud, thy sins," Isaiah 44:22. "I will forgive their iniquity, and I will remember their sin no more." Jeremiah 31:34. "Let the wicked forsake his way, and the unrighteous man his thoughts; and let him return unto the Lord, and He will have mercy upon him; and to our God, for He will abundantly pardon." Isaiah 55:7. "In those days, and in that time, saith the Lord, the iniquity of Israel shall be sought for, and there shall be none; and the sins of Judah, and they shall not be found." Jeremiah 50:20.

What assurance here, of God's willingness to receive the repenting sinner! Have you, reader, chosen your own way? Have you wandered far from God? Have you sought to feast upon the fruits of transgression, only to find them turn to ashes upon your lips? And now, your substance spent, your life-plans thwarted, and your hopes dead, do you sit alone and desolate? Now that voice which has long been speaking to your heart but to which you would not listen comes to you distinct and clear, "Arise ye, and depart; for this is not your rest; because it is polluted, it shall destroy you, even with a sore destruction." Micah 2:10. Return to your Father's house. He invites you, saying, "Return unto Me; for I have redeemed thee." Isaiah 44:22.

Do not listen to the enemy's suggestion to stay away from Christ until you have made yourself better; until you are good enough to come to God. If you wait until then, you will never come. When Satan points to your filthy garments, repeat the promise of Jesus, "Him that cometh to Me I will in no wise cast out." John 6:37. Tell the enemy that the blood of Jesus Christ cleanses from all sin. Make the prayer of David your own, "Purge me with hyssop, and I shall be clean; wash me, and I shall be whiter than snow." Psalm 51:7.

Arise and go to your Father. He will meet you a great way off. If you take even one step toward Him in repentance, He will hasten to enfold you in His arms of infinite love. His ear is open to the cry of the contrite soul. The very first reaching out of the heart after God is known to Him. Never a prayer is offered, however faltering, never a tear is shed, however secret, never a sincere desire after God is cherished, however feeble, but the Spirit of God goes forth to meet it. Even before the prayer is uttered or the yearning of the heart made known, grace from Christ goes forth to meet the grace that is working upon the human soul.

Your heavenly Father will take from you the garments defiled by sin. In the beautiful parabolic prophecy of Zechariah, the high priest Joshua, standing clothed in filthy garments before the angel of the Lord, represents the sinner. And the word is spoken by the Lord, "Take away the filthy garments from him. And unto him He said, Behold, I have caused thine iniquity to pass from thee, and I will clothe thee with change of raiment.... So they set a fair miter upon his head, and clothed him with garments." Zechariah 3:4, 5. Even so God will clothe you with "the garments of salvation," and cover you with "the robe of righteousness." Isaiah 61:10. "Though ye have lien among the pots, yet shall ye be as the wings of a dove covered with silver, and her feathers with yellow gold." Psalm 68:13.

He will bring you into His banqueting house, and His banner over you shall be love. (Song of Solomon 2:4) "If thou wilt walk in My ways," He declares, "I will give thee places to walk among these that stand by"—even among the holy angels that surround His throne. (Zechariah 3:7.)

"As the bridegroom rejoiceth over the bride, so shall thy God rejoice over thee." Isaiah 62:5. "He will save, He will rejoice over thee with joy; He will rest in His love; He will joy over thee with singing." Zephaniah 3:17. And heaven and earth shall unite in the Father's song of rejoicing: "For this My son was dead, and is alive again; he was lost, and is found."

Thus far in the Saviour's parable there is no discordant note to jar the harmony of the scene of joy; but now Christ introduces another element. When the prodigal came home, the elder son "was in the field; and as he came and drew nigh to the house, he heard music and dancing. And he called one of the servants, and asked what these things meant. And he said unto him, Thy brother is come; and thy father hath killed the fatted calf, because he hath received him safe and sound. And he was angry, and would not go in." This elder brother has not been sharing in his father's anxiety and watching for the one that was lost. He shares not, therefore, in the father's joy at the wanderer's return. The sounds of rejoicing kindle no gladness in his heart. He inquires of a servant the reason of the festivity, and the answer excites his jealousy. He will not go in to welcome his lost brother. The favor shown the prodigal he regards as an insult to himself.

When the father comes out to remonstrate with him, the pride and malignity of his nature are revealed. He dwells upon his own life in his father's house as a round of unrequited service, and then places in mean contrast the favor shown to the son just returned. He makes it plain that his own service has been that of a servant rather than a son. When he should have found an abiding joy in his father's presence, his mind has rested upon the profit to accrue from his circumspect life. His words show that it is for this he has foregone the pleasures of sin. Now if this brother is to share in the father's gifts, the elder son counts that he himself has been wronged. He grudges his brother the favor shown him. He plainly shows that had he been in the father's place, he would not have received the prodigal. He does not even acknowledge him as a brother, but coldly speaks of him as "thy son."

Yet the father deals tenderly with him. "Son," he says, "thou art ever with me, and all that I have is thine." Through all these years of your brother's outcast life, have you not had the privilege of companionship with me?

Everything that could minister to the happiness of his children was freely theirs. The son need have no question of gift or reward. "All that I have is thine." You have only to believe my love, and take the gift that is freely bestowed.

One son had for a time cut himself off from the household, not discerning the father's love. But now he has returned, and the tide of joy sweeps away every disturbing thought. "This thy brother was dead, and is alive again; and was lost, and is found."

Was the elder brother brought to see his own mean, ungrateful spirit? Did he come to see that though his brother had done wickedly, he was his brother still? Did the elder brother repent of his jealousy and hardheartedness? Concerning this, Christ was silent. For the parable was still enacting, and it rested with His hearers to determine what the outcome should be.

By the elder son were represented the unrepenting Jews of Christ's day, and also the Pharisees in every age, who look with contempt upon those whom they regard as publicans and sinners. Because they themselves have not gone to great excesses in vice, they are filled with self-righteousness. Christ met these cavilers on their own ground. Like the elder son in the parable, they had enjoyed special privileges from God. They claimed to be sons in God's house, but they had the spirit of the hireling. They were working, not from love, but from hope of reward. In their eyes, God was an exacting taskmaster. They saw Christ inviting publicans and sinners to receive freely the gift of His grace—the gift which the rabbis hoped to secure only by toil and penance—and they were offended. The prodigal's return, which filled the Father's heart with joy, only stirred them to jealousy.

In the parable the father's remonstrance with the elder son was Heaven's tender appeal to the Pharisees. "All that I have is thine"—not as wages, but as a gift. Like the prodigal, you can receive it only as the unmerited bestowal of the Father's love.

Self-righteousness not only leads men to misrepresent God, but makes them cold-hearted and critical toward their brethren. The elder son, in his selfishness and jealousy, stood ready to watch his brother, to criticize every action, and to accuse him for the least deficiency. He would detect every mistake, and make the most of every wrong act. Thus he would seek to justify his own unforgiving spirit. Many today are doing the same thing. While the soul is making its very first struggles against a flood of temptations, they stand by, stubborn, self-willed, complaining, accusing. They may claim to be children of God, but they are acting out the spirit of Satan. By their attitude toward their brethren, these accusers place themselves where God cannot give them the light of His countenance.

Many are constantly questioning, "Wherewith shall I come before the Lord, and bow myself before the high God? Shall I come before Him with burnt-offerings, with calves of a year old? Will the Lord be pleased with thousands of rams, or with ten thousands of rivers of oil?" But "He hath showed thee, O man, what is good; and what doth the Lord require of thee, but to do justly, and to love mercy, and to walk humbly with thy God?" Micah 6:6–8.

This is the service that God has chosen—"to loose the bands of wickedness, to undo the heavy burdens, and to let the oppressed go free, and that ye break every yoke,…and that thou hide not thyself from thine own flesh." Isaiah 58:6, 7. When you see yourselves as sinners saved only by the love of your heavenly Father, you will have tender pity for others who are suffering in sin. You will no longer meet misery and repentance with jealousy and censure. When the ice of selfishness is melted from your hearts, you will be in sympathy with God, and will share His joy in the saving of the lost.

It is true that you claim to be a child of God; but if this claim be true, it is "thy brother" that was "dead, and is alive again; and was lost, and is found." He is bound to you by the closest ties; for God recognizes him as a son. Deny your relationship to him, and you show that you are but a hireling in the household, not a child in the family of God.

Though you will not join in the greeting to the lost, the joy will go on, the restored one will have his place by the Father's side and in the Father's work. He that is forgiven much, the same loves much. But you will be in the darkness without. For "he that loveth not knoweth not God; for God is love." 1 John 4:8.

17
"Spare It This Year Also"

Based on Luke 13:1–9

Christ in His teaching linked with the warning of judgment the invitation of mercy. "The Son of man is not come," He said, "to destroy men's lives, but to save them." Luke 9:56. "God sent not His Son into the world to condemn the world; but that the world through Him might be saved." John 3:17. His mission of mercy in its relation to God's justice and judgment is illustrated in the parable of the barren fig tree.

Christ had been warning the people of the coming of the kingdom of God, and He had sharply rebuked their ignorance and indifference. The signs in the sky, which foretold the weather, they were quick to read; but the signs of the times, which so clearly pointed to His mission, were not discerned.

But men were as ready then as men are now to conclude that they themselves are the favorites of heaven, and that the message of reproof is meant for another. The hearers told Jesus of an event which had just caused great excitement. Some of the measures of Pontius Pilate, the governor of Judea, had given offense to the people. There had been a popular tumult in Jerusalem, and Pilate had attempted to quell this by violence. On one occasion his soldiers had even invaded the precincts of the temple, and had cut down some Galilean pilgrims in the very act of slaying their sacrifices. The Jews regarded calamity as a judgment on account of the sufferer's sin, and those who told of this act of violence did so with secret satisfaction. In their view their own good fortune proved them to be much better, and therefore more favored by God, than were these Galileans. They expected to hear from Jesus words of condemnation for these men, who, they doubted not, richly deserved their punishment.

The disciples of Christ did not venture to express their ideas until they had heard the opinion of their Master. He had given them pointed lessons in reference to judging other men's characters, and measuring retribution according to their finite judgment. Yet they looked for Christ to denounce these men as sinners above others. Great was their surprise at His answer.

Turning to the multitude, the Saviour said, "Suppose ye that these Galileans were sinners above all the Galileans, because they suffered such things? I tell you, Nay; but, except ye repent, ye shall all likewise perish." These startling calamities were designed to lead them to humble their hearts, and to repent of their sins. The storm of vengeance was gathering, which was soon to burst upon all who had not found a refuge in Christ.

As Jesus talked with the disciples and the multitude, He looked forward with prophetic glance and saw Jerusalem besieged with armies. He heard the tramp of the aliens marching against the chosen city and saw the thousands upon thousands perishing in the siege. Many of the Jews were, like those Galileans, slain in the temple courts, in the very act of offering sacrifice. The calamities that had fallen upon individuals were warnings from God to a nation equally guilty. "Except ye repent," said Jesus, "ye shall all likewise perish." For a little time the day of probation lingered for them. There was still time for them to know the things that belonged to their peace.

"A certain man," He continued, "had a fig-tree planted in his vineyard; and he came and sought fruit thereon, and found none. Then said he unto the dresser of his vineyard, Behold, these three years I come seeking fruit on this fig-tree, and find none: cut it down; why cumbereth it the ground?"

Christ's hearers could not misunderstand the application of His words. David had sung of Israel as the vine brought out of Egypt. Isaiah had written, "The vineyard of the Lord of hosts is the house of Israel, and the men of Judah His pleasant plant." Isaiah 5:7. The generation to whom the Saviour had come were represented by the fig tree in the Lord's vineyard—within the circle of His special care and blessing.

God's purpose toward His people, and the glorious possibilities before them, had been set forth in the beautiful words, "That they might be called trees of righteousness, the planting of the Lord, that He might be glorified," Isaiah 61:3. The dying Jacob, under the Spirit of inspiration, had said of his best-loved son, "Joseph is a fruitful bough, even a fruitful bough by a well; whose branches run over the wall." And he said, "The God of thy Father" "shall help thee," the Almighty "shall bless thee with blessings of heaven above, blessings of the deep that lieth under." Genesis 49:22, 25. So God had planted Israel as a goodly vine by the wells of life. He had made His vineyard "in a very fruitful hill." He had "fenced it, and gathered out the stones thereof, and planted it with the choicest vine." Isaiah 5:1, 2.

"And He looked that it should bring forth grapes, and it brought forth wild grapes." Isaiah 5:2. The people of Christ's day made a greater show of piety than did the Jews of earlier ages, but they were even more destitute of the sweet graces of the Spirit of God. The precious fruits of character that made the life of Joseph so fragrant and beautiful, were not manifest in the Jewish nation.

God in His Son had been seeking fruit, and had found none. Israel was a cumberer of the ground. Its very existence was a curse; for it filled the place in the vineyard that a fruitful tree might fill. It robbed the world of the blessings that God designed to give. The Israelites had misrepresented God among the nations. They were not merely useless, but a decided hindrance. To a great degree their religion was misleading, and wrought ruin instead of salvation.

In the parable the dresser of the vineyard does not question the sentence that the tree, if it remained fruitless, should be cut down; but he knows and shares the owner's interest in that barren tree. Nothing could give him greater joy than to see its growth and fruitfulness. He responds to the desire of the owner, saying, "Let it alone this year also, till I shall dig about it and dung it; and if it bear fruit, well."

The gardener does not refuse to minister to so unpromising a plant. He stands ready to give it still greater care. He will make its surroundings most favorable, and will lavish upon it every attention.

The owner and the dresser of the vineyard are one in their interest in the fig tree. So the Father and the Son were one in their love for the chosen people. Christ was saying to His hearers that increased opportunities would be given them. Every means that the love of God could devise would be put in operation that they might become trees of righteousness, bringing forth fruit for the blessing of the world.

Jesus did not in the parable tell the result of the gardener's work. At that point His story was cut short. Its conclusion rested with the generation that heard His words. To them the solemn warning was given. "If not, then after that thou shalt cut it down." Upon them it depended whether the irrevocable words should be spoken. The day of wrath was near. In the calamities that had already befallen Israel, the owner of the vineyard was mercifully forewarning them of the destruction of the unfruitful tree.

The warning sounds down along the line to us in this generation. Are you, O careless heart, a fruitless tree in the Lord's vineyard? Shall the words of doom erelong be spoken of you? How long have you received His gifts? How long has He watched and waited for a return of love? Planted in His vineyard, under the watchful care of the gardener, what privileges are yours! How often has the tender gospel message thrilled your heart! You have taken the name of Christ, you are outwardly a member of the church which is His body, and yet you are conscious of no living connection with the great heart of love. The tide of His life does not flow through you. The sweet graces of His character, "the fruits of the Spirit," are not seen in your life.

The barren tree receives the rain and the sunshine and the gardener's care. It draws nourishment from the soil. But its unproductive boughs only darken the ground, so that fruit-bearing plants cannot flourish in its shadow. So God's gifts, lavished on you, convey no blessing to the world. You are robbing others of privileges that, but for you, might be theirs.

You realize, though it may be but dimly, that you are a cumberer of the ground. Yet in His great mercy God has not cut you down. He does not look coldly upon you. He does not turn away with indifference, or leave you to destruction. Looking upon you He cries, as He cried so many centuries ago concerning Israel, "How shall I give thee up, Ephraim? How shall I deliver thee, Israel?… I will not execute the fierceness of Mine anger. I will not return to destroy Ephraim; for I am God, and not man." Hosea 11:8, 9. The pitying Saviour is saying concerning you, Spare it this year also, till I shall dig about it and dress it.

With what unwearied love did Christ minister to Israel during the period of added probation. Upon the cross He prayed, "Father, forgive them; for they know not what they do." Luke 23:24. After His ascension the gospel was preached first at Jerusalem. There the Holy Spirit was poured out. There the first gospel church revealed the power of the risen Saviour. There Stephen—"his face as it had been the face of an angel" (Acts 6:15)—bore his testimony and laid down his life. All that heaven itself could give was bestowed. "What could have been done more to My vineyard," Christ said, "that I have not done in it?" Isaiah 5:4. So His care and labor for you are not lessened, but increased. Still He says, "I the Lord do keep it; I will water it every moment; lest any hurt it, I will keep it night and day." Isaiah 27:3.

"If it bear fruit, well; and if not, then after that"—

The heart that does not respond to divine agencies becomes hardened until it is no longer susceptible to the influence of the Holy Spirit. Then it is that the word is spoken, "Cut it down; why cumbereth it the ground?"

Today He invites you: "O Israel, return unto the Lord thy God.… I will heal their backsliding, I will love them freely.… I will be as the dew unto Israel; he shall grow as the lily, and cast forth his roots as Lebanon.… They that dwell under his shadow shall return; they shall revive as the corn, and grow as the vine.… From Me is thy fruit found." Hosea 14:1–8.

18
"Go into the Highways and Hedges"

Based on Luke 14:1, 12–24

The Saviour was a guest at the feast of a Pharisee. He accepted invitations from the rich as well as the poor, and according to His custom He linked the scene before Him with His lessons of truth. Among the Jews the sacred feast was connected with all their seasons of national and religious rejoicing. It was to them a type of the blessings of eternal life. The great feast at which they were to sit down with Abraham, Isaac, and Jacob, while the Gentiles stood without, and looked on with longing eyes, was a theme on which they delighted to dwell. The lesson of warning and instruction which Christ desired to give, He now illustrated by the parable of a great supper. The blessings of God, both for the present and for the future life, the Jews thought to shut up to themselves. They denied God's mercy to the Gentiles. By the parable Christ showed that they were themselves at that very time rejecting the invitation of mercy, the call to God's kingdom. He showed that the invitation which they had slighted was to be sent to those whom they despised, those from whom they had drawn away their garments as if they were lepers to be shunned.

In choosing the guests for his feast, the Pharisee had consulted his own selfish interest. Christ said to him, "When thou makest a dinner or a supper, call not thy friends, nor thy brethren, neither thy kinsmen, nor thy rich neighbors, lest they also bid thee again, and a recompense be made thee. But when thou makest a feast, call the poor, the maimed, the lame, the blind: and thou shalt be blessed; for they cannot recompense thee: for thou shalt be recompensed at the resurrection of the just."

Christ was here repeating the instruction He had given to Israel through Moses. At their sacred feasts the Lord had directed that "the stranger, and the fatherless, and the widow, which are within thy gates, shall come, and shall eat, and be satisfied." Deuteronomy 14:29. These gatherings were to be as object lessons to Israel. Being thus taught the joy of true hospitality, the people were throughout the year to care for the bereaved and the poor. And these feasts had a wider lesson. The spiritual blessings given to Israel were not for themselves alone. God had given the bread of life to them, that they might break it to the world.

This work they had not fulfilled. Christ's words were a rebuke to their selfishness. To the Pharisees His words were distasteful. Hoping to turn the conversation into another channel, one of them, with a sanctimonious air, exclaimed, "Blessed is he that shall eat bread in the kingdom of God." This man spoke with great assurance, as if he himself were certain of a place in the kingdom. His attitude was similar to the attitude of those who rejoice that they are saved by Christ, when they do not comply with the conditions upon which salvation is promised. His spirit was like that of Balaam when he prayed, "Let me die the death of the righteous, and let my last end be like his." Numbers 23:10. The Pharisee was not thinking of his own fitness for heaven but of what he hoped to enjoy in heaven. His remark was designed to turn away the minds of the guests at the feast from the subject of their practical duty. He thought to carry them past the present life to the remote time of the resurrection of the just.

Christ read the heart of the pretender, and fastening His eyes upon him He opened before the company the character and value of their present privileges. He showed them that they had a part to act at that very time, in order to share in the blessedness of the future.

"A certain man," He said, "made a great supper, and bade many." When the time of the feast arrived, the host sent his servant to the expected guests with a second message, "Come; for all things are now ready." But a strange indifference was shown. "All with one consent began to make excuse. The first said unto him, I have bought a piece of ground, and I must needs go and see it; I pray thee have me excused. And another said, I have bought five yoke of oxen, and I go to prove them; I pray thee have me excused. And another said, I have married a wife, and therefore I cannot come."

None of the excuses were founded on a real necessity. The man who "must needs go and see" his piece of ground, had already purchased it. His haste to go and see it was due to the fact that his interest was absorbed in his purchase. The oxen, too, had been bought. The proving of them was only to satisfy the interest of the buyer. The third excuse had no more semblance of reason. The fact that the intended guest had married a wife need not have prevented his presence at the feast. His wife also would have been made welcome. But he had his own plans for enjoyment, and these seemed to him more desirable than the feast he had promised to attend. He had learned to find pleasure in other society than that of the host. He did not ask to be excused, made not even a pretense of courtesy in his refusal. The "I cannot" was only a veil for the truth—"I do not care to come."

All the excuses betray a preoccupied mind. To these intended guests other interests had become all-absorbing. The invitation they had pledged themselves to accept was put aside, and the generous friend was insulted by their indifference.

By the great supper, Christ represents the blessings offered through the gospel. The provision is nothing less than Christ Himself. He is the bread that comes down from heaven; and from Him the streams of salvation flow. The Lord's messengers had proclaimed to the Jews the advent of the Saviour; they had pointed to Christ as "the Lamb of God, which taketh away the sin of the world." John 1:29. In the feast He had provided, God offered to them the greatest gift that Heaven can bestow—a gift that is beyond computation. The love of God had furnished the costly banquet, and had provided inexhaustible resources. "If any man eat of this bread," Christ said, "he shall live for ever." John 6:51.

But in order to accept the invitation to the gospel feast, they must make their worldly interests subordinate to the one purpose of receiving Christ and His righteousness. God gave all for man, and He asks him to place His service above every earthly and selfish consideration. He cannot accept a divided heart. The heart that is absorbed in earthly affections cannot be given up to God.

The lesson is for all time. We are to follow the Lamb of God whithersoever He goeth. His guidance is to be chosen, His companionship valued above the companionship of earthly friends. Christ says, "He that loveth father or mother more than Me is not worthy of Me, and he that loveth son or daughter more than Me is not worthy of Me." Matthew 10:37.

Around the family board, when breaking their daily bread, many in Christ's day repeated the words, "Blessed is he that shall eat bread in the kingdom of God." But Christ showed how difficult it was to find guests for the table provided at infinite cost. Those who listened to His words knew that they had slighted the invitation of mercy. To them worldly possessions, riches, and pleasures were all-absorbing. With one consent they had made excuse.

So it is now. The excuses urged for refusing the invitation to the feast cover the whole ground of excuses for refusing the gospel invitation. Men declare that they cannot imperil their worldly prospects by giving attention to the claims of the gospel. They count their temporal interests as of more value than the things of eternity. The very blessings they have received from God become a barrier to separate their souls from their Creator and Redeemer. They will not be interrupted in their worldly pursuits, and they say to the messenger of mercy, "Go thy way for this time; when I have a convenient season, I will call for thee." Acts 24:25. Others urge the difficulties that would arise in their social relations should they obey the call of God. They say they cannot afford to be out of harmony with their relatives and acquaintances. Thus they prove themselves to be the very actors described in the parable. The Master of the feast regards their flimsy excuses as showing contempt for His invitation.

The man who said, "I have married a wife, and therefore I cannot come," represents a large class. Many there are who allow their wives or their husbands to prevent them from heeding the call of God. The husband says, "I cannot obey my convictions of duty while my wife is opposed to it. Her influence would make it exceedingly hard for me to do so." The wife hears the gracious call, "Come; for all things are now ready," and she says, "'I pray thee have me excused.' My husband refuses the invitation of mercy. He says that his business stands in the way. I must go with my husband, and therefore I cannot come." The children's hearts are impressed. They desire to come. But they love their father and mother, and since these do not heed the gospel call, the children think that they cannot be expected to come. They too say, "Have me excused."

All these refuse the Saviour's call because they fear division in the family circle. They suppose that in refusing to obey God they are insuring the peace and prosperity of the home; but this is a delusion. Those who sow selfishness will reap selfishness. In rejecting the love of Christ they reject that which alone can impart purity and steadfastness to human love. They will not only lose heaven, but will fail of the true enjoyment of that for which heaven was sacrificed.

In the parable, the giver of the feast learned how his invitation had been treated, and "being angry, said to his servant, Go out quickly into the streets and lanes of the city, and bring in hither the poor, and the maimed, and the halt, and the blind."

The host turned from those who despised his bounty, and invited a class who were not full, who were not in possession of houses and lands. He invited those who were poor and hungry, and who would appreciate the bounties provided. "The publicans and the harlots," Christ said, "go into the kingdom of God before you." Matthew 21:31. However wretched may be the specimens of humanity that men spurn and turn aside from, they are not too low, too wretched, for the notice and love of God. Christ longs to have careworn, weary, oppressed human beings come to Him. He longs to give them the light and joy and peace that are to be found nowhere else. The veriest sinners are the objects of His deep, earnest pity and love. He sends His Holy Spirit to yearn over them with tenderness, seeking to draw them to Himself.

The servant who brought in the poor and the blind reported to his master, "It is done as thou hast commanded, and yet there is room. And the Lord said unto the servant, Go out into the highways and hedges, and compel them to come in, that my house may be filled." Here Christ pointed to the work of the gospel outside the pale of Judaism, in the highways and byways of the world.

In obedience to this command, Paul and Barnabas declared to the Jews, "It was necessary that the word of God should first have been spoken to you; but seeing ye put it from you, and judge yourselves unworthy of everlasting life, lo, we turn to the Gentiles. For so hath the Lord commanded us, saying, I have set Thee to be a light of the Gentiles, that Thou shouldest be for salvation unto the ends of the earth. And when the Gentiles heard this, they were glad, and glorified the word of the Lord; and as many as were ordained to eternal life believed." Acts 13:46–48.

The gospel message proclaimed by Christ's disciples was the announcement of His first advent to the world. It bore to men the good tidings of salvation through faith in Him. It pointed forward to His second coming in glory to redeem His people, and it set before men the hope, through faith and obedience, of sharing the inheritance of the saints in light. This message is given to men today, and at this time there is coupled with it the announcement of Christ's second coming as at hand. The signs which He Himself gave of His coming have been fulfilled, and by the teaching of God's word we may know that the Lord is at the door.

John in the Revelation foretells the proclamation of the gospel message just before Christ's second coming. He beholds an angel flying "in the midst of heaven, having the everlasting gospel to preach unto them that dwell on the earth, and to every nation, and kindred, and tongue, and people, saying with a loud voice, Fear God, and give glory to Him; for the hour of His judgment is come." Revelation 14:6,7.

In the prophecy this warning of the judgment, with its connected messages, is followed by the coming of the Son of man in the clouds of heaven. The proclamation of the judgment is an announcement of Christ's second coming as at hand. And this proclamation is called the everlasting gospel. Thus the preaching of Christ's second coming, the announcement of its nearness, is shown to be an essential part of the gospel message.

The Bible declares that in the last days men will be absorbed in worldly pursuits, in pleasure and money-getting. They will be blind to eternal realities. Christ says, "As the days of Noah were, so shall also the coming of the Son of man be. For as in the days that were before the flood they were eating and drinking, marrying and giving in marriage, until the day that Noah entered into the ark, and knew not until the flood came, and took them all away; so shall also the coming of the Son of man be." Matthew 24:37–39.

So it is today. Men are rushing on in the chase for gain and selfish indulgence as if there were no God, no heaven, and no hereafter. In Noah's day the warning of the flood was sent to startle men in their wickedness and call them to repentance. So the message of Christ's soon coming is designed to arouse men from their absorption in worldly things. It is intended to awaken them to a sense of eternal realities, that they may give heed to the invitation to the Lord's table.

The gospel invitation is to be given to all the world—"to every nation, and kindred, and tongue, and people." Revelation 14:6. The last message of warning and mercy is to lighten the whole earth with its glory. It is to reach all classes of men, rich and poor, high and low. "Go out into the highways and hedges," Christ says, "and compel them to come in, that My house may be filled."

The world is perishing for want of the gospel. There is a famine for the word of God. There are few who preach the word unmixed with human tradition. Though men have the Bible in their hands, they do not receive the blessing that God has placed in it for them. The Lord calls upon His servants to carry His message to the people. The word of everlasting life must be given to those who are perishing in their sins.

In the command to go into the highways and hedges, Christ sets forth the work of all whom He calls to minister in His name. The whole world is the field for Christ's ministers. The whole human family is comprised in their congregation. The Lord desires that His word of grace shall be brought home to every soul.

To a great degree this must be accomplished by personal labor. This was Christ's method. His work was largely made up of personal interviews. He had a faithful regard for the one-soul audience. Through that one soul the message was often extended to thousands.

We are not to wait for souls to come to us; we must seek them out where they are. When the word has been preached in the pulpit, the work has but just begun. There are multitudes who will never be reached by the gospel unless it is carried to them.

The invitation to the feast was first given to the Jewish people, the people who had been called to stand as teachers and leaders among men, the people in whose hands were the prophetic scrolls foretelling Christ's advent, and to whom was committed the symbolic service foreshadowing His mission. Had priests and people heeded the call, they would have united with Christ's messengers in giving the gospel invitation to the world. The truth was sent to them that they might impart it. When they refused the call, it was sent to the poor, the maimed, the halt, and the blind. Publicans and sinners received the invitation. When the gospel call is sent to the Gentiles, there is the same plan of working. The message is first to be given "in the highways"—to men who have an active part in the world's work, to the teachers and leaders of the people.

Let the Lord's messengers bear this in mind. To the shepherds of the flock, the teachers divinely appointed, it should come as a word to be heeded. Those who belong to the higher ranks of society are to be sought out with tender affection and brotherly regard. Men in business life, in high positions of trust, men with large inventive faculties and scientific insight, men of genius, teachers of the gospel whose minds have not been called to the special truths for this time—these should be the first to hear the call. To them the invitation must be given.

There is a work to be done for the wealthy. They need to be awakened to their responsibility as those entrusted with the gifts of heaven. They need to be reminded that they must give an account to Him who shall judge the living and the dead. The wealthy man needs your labor in the love and fear of God. Too often he trusts in his riches, and feels not his danger. The eyes of his mind need to be attracted to things of enduring value. He needs to recognize the authority of true goodness, which says, "Come unto Me, all ye that labour and are heavy laden, and I will give you rest. Take My yoke upon you, and learn of Me; for I am meek and lowly in heart, and ye shall find rest unto your souls; for My yoke is easy, and My burden is light." Matthew 11:28–30.

Those who stand high in the world for their education, wealth, or calling, are seldom addressed personally in regard to the interests of the soul. Many Christian workers hesitate to approach these classes. But this should not be. If a man were drowning, we would not stand by and see him perish because he was a lawyer, a merchant, or a judge. If we saw persons rushing over a precipice, we would not hesitate to urge them back, whatever might be their position or calling. Neither should we hesitate to warn men of the peril of the soul.

None should be neglected because of their apparent devotion to worldly things. Many in high social positions are heartsore, and sick of vanity. They are longing for a peace which they have not. In the very highest ranks of society are those who are hungering and thirsting for salvation. Many would receive help if the Lord's workers would approach them personally, with a kind manner, a heart made tender by the love of Christ.

The success of the gospel message does not depend upon learned speeches, eloquent testimonies, or deep arguments. It depends upon the simplicity of the message and its adaptation to the souls that are hungering for the bread of life. "What shall I do to be saved?"—this is the want of the soul.

Thousands can be reached in the most simple and humble way. The most intellectual, those who are looked upon as the world's most gifted men and women, are often refreshed by the simple words of one who loves God, and who can speak of that love as naturally as the worldling speaks of the things that interest him most deeply.

Often the words well prepared and studied have but little influence. But the true, honest expression of a son or daughter of God, spoken in natural simplicity, has power to unbolt the door to hearts that have long been closed against Christ and His love.

Let the worker for Christ remember that he is not to labor in his own strength. Let him lay hold of the throne of God with faith in His power to save. Let him wrestle with God in prayer, and then work with all the facilities God has given him. The Holy Spirit is provided as his efficiency. Ministering angels will be by his side to impress hearts.

If the leaders and teachers at Jerusalem had received the truth Christ brought, what a missionary center their city would have been! Backslidden Israel would have been converted. A vast army would have been gathered for the Lord. And how rapidly they could have carried the gospel to all parts of the world. So now, if men of influence and large capacity for usefulness could be won for Christ, then through them what a work could be accomplished in lifting up the fallen, gathering in the outcasts, and spreading far and wide the tidings of salvation. Rapidly the invitation might be given, and the guests be gathered for the Lord's table.

But we are not to think only of great and gifted men, to the neglect of the poorer classes. Christ instructs His messengers to go also to those in the byways and hedges, to the poor and lowly of the earth. In the courts and lanes of the great cities, in the lonely byways of the country, are families and individuals—perhaps strangers in a strange land—who are without church relations, and who, in their loneliness, come to feel that God has forgotten them. They do not understand what they must do to be saved. Many are sunken in sin. Many are in distress. They are pressed with suffering, want, unbelief, despondency. Disease of every type afflicts them, both in body and in soul. They long to find a solace for their troubles, and Satan tempts them to seek it in lusts and pleasures that lead to ruin and death. He is offering them the apples of Sodom, that will turn to ashes upon their lips. They are spending their money for that which is not bread and their labor for that which satisfieth not.

In these suffering ones we are to see those whom Christ came to save. His invitation to them is "Ho, every one that thirsteth, come ye to the waters, and he that hath no money; come ye, buy and eat; yea, come, buy wine and milk without money and without price.... Hearken diligently unto Me, and eat ye that which is good, and let your soul delight itself in fatness. Incline your ear, and come unto Me: hear, and your soul shall live." Isaiah 55:1–3.

God has given a special command that we should regard the stranger, the outcast, and the poor souls who are weak in moral power. Many who appear wholly indifferent to religious things are in heart longing for rest and peace. Although they may have sunken to the very depths of sin, there is a possibility of saving them.

Christ's servants are to follow His example. As He went from place to place, He comforted the suffering and healed the sick. Then He placed before them the great truths in regard to His kingdom. This is the work of His followers. As you relieve the sufferings of the body, you will find ways for ministering to the wants of the soul. You can point to the uplifted Saviour, and tell of the love of the great Physician, who alone has power to restore.

Tell the poor desponding ones who have gone astray that they need not despair. Though they have erred, and have not been building a right character, God has joy to restore them, even the joy of His salvation. He delights to take apparently hopeless material, those through whom Satan has worked, and make them the subjects of His grace. He rejoices to deliver them from the wrath which is to fall upon the disobedient. Tell them there is healing, cleansing for every soul. There is a place for them at the Lord's table. He is waiting to bid them welcome.

Those who go into the byways and hedges will find others of a widely different character, who need their ministry. There are those who are living up to all the light they have, and are serving God the best they know how. But they realize that there is a great work to be done for themselves and for those about them. They are longing for an increased knowledge of God, but they have only begun to see the glimmering of greater light. They are praying with tears that God will send them the blessing which by faith they discern afar off. In the midst of the wickedness of the great cities many of these souls are to be found. Many of them are in very humble circumstances, and because of this they are unnoticed by the world. There are many of whom ministers and churches know nothing. But in lowly, miserable places they are the Lord's witnesses. They may have had little light and few opportunities for Christian training, but in the midst of nakedness, hunger, and cold they are seeking to minister to others. Let the stewards of the manifold grace of God seek out these souls, visit their homes, and through the power of the Holy Spirit minister to their needs. Study the Bible with them and pray with them with that simplicity which the Holy Spirit inspires. Christ will give His servants a message that will be as the bread of heaven to the soul. The precious blessing will be carried from heart to heart, from family to family.

The command given in the parable, to "compel them to come in," has often been misinterpreted. It has been regarded as teaching that we should force men to receive the gospel. But it denotes rather the urgency of the invitation, and the effectiveness of the inducements presented. The gospel never employs force in bringing men to Christ. Its message is "Ho, every one that thirsteth, come ye to the waters." Isaiah 55:I. "The Spirit and the bride say, Come.... And whosoever will, let him take the water of life freely." Revelation 22:17. The power of God's love and grace constrains us to come.

The Saviour says, "Behold, I stand at the door, and knock; if any man hear My voice, and open the door, I will come in to him, and will sup with him, and he with Me." Revelation 3:20. He is not repulsed by scorn or turned aside by threatening, but continually seeks the lost ones, saying, "How shall I give thee up?" Hosea 11:8. Although His love is driven back by the stubborn heart, He returns to plead with greater force, "Behold, I stand at the door, and knock." The winning power of His love compels souls to come in. And to Christ they say, "Thy gentleness hath made me great." Psalm 18:35.

Christ will impart to His messengers the same yearning love that He Himself has in seeking for the lost. We are not merely to say, "Come." There are those who hear the call, but their ears are too dull to take in its meaning. Their eyes are too blind to see anything good in store for them. Many realize their great degradation. They say, I am not fit to be helped; leave me alone.

But the workers must not desist. In tender, pitying love, lay hold of the discouraged and helpless ones. Give them your courage, your hope, your strength. By kindness compel them to come. "Of some have compassion, making a difference; and others save with fear, pulling them out of the fire." Jude 22, 23.

If the servants of God will walk with Him in faith, He will give power to their message. They will be enabled so to present His love and the danger of rejecting the grace of God that men will be constrained to accept the gospel. Christ will perform wonderful miracles if men will but do their God-given part. In human hearts today as great a transformation may be wrought as has ever been wrought in generations past. John Bunyan was redeemed from profanity and reveling, John Newton from slave dealing, to proclaim an uplifted Saviour. A Bunyan and a Newton may be redeemed from among men today. Through human agents who co-operate with the divine, many a poor outcast will be reclaimed, and in his turn will seek to restore the image of God in man. There are those who have had very meager opportunities, who have walked in ways of error because they knew no better way, to whom beams of light will come. As the word of Christ came to Zacchaeus, "Today I must abide at thy house" (Luke 19:5), so the word will come to them; and those who were supposed to be hardened sinners will be found to have hearts as tender as a child's because Christ has deigned to notice them. Many will come from the grossest error and sin, and will take the place of others who have had opportunities and privileges but have not prized them. They will be accounted the chosen of God, elect, precious; and when Christ shall come into His kingdom, they will stand next His throne.

But "see that ye refuse not Him that speaketh." Hebrews 12:25. Jesus said, "None of those men which were bidden shall taste of My supper." They had rejected the invitation, and none of them were to be invited again. In rejecting Christ, the Jews were hardening their hearts, and giving themselves into the power of Satan so that it would be impossible for them to accept His grace. So it is now. If the love of God is not appreciated and does not become an abiding principle to soften and subdue the soul, we are utterly lost. The Lord can give no greater manifestation of His love than He has given. If the love of Jesus does not subdue the heart, there are no means by which we can be reached.

Every time you refuse to listen to the message of mercy, you strengthen yourself in unbelief. Every time you fail to open the door of your heart to Christ, you become more and more unwilling to listen to the voice of Him that speaketh. You diminish your chance of responding to the last appeal of mercy. Let it not be written of you, as of ancient Israel, "Ephraim is joined to idols; let him alone." Hosea 4:17. Let not Christ weep over you as He wept over Jerusalem, saying, "How often would I have gathered thy children together, as a hen doth gather her brood under her wings, and ye would not! Behold, your house is left unto you desolate." Luke 13:34, 35.

We are living in a time when the last message of mercy, the last invitation, is sounding to the children of men. The command, "Go out into the highways and hedges," is reaching its final fulfillment. To every soul Christ's invitation will be given. The messengers are saying, "Come; for all things are now ready." Heavenly angels are still working in co-operation with human agencies. The Holy Spirit is presenting every inducement to constrain you to come. Christ is watching for some sign that will betoken the removing of the bolts and the opening of the door of your heart for His entrance. Angels are waiting to bear the tidings to heaven that another lost sinner has been found. The hosts of heaven are waiting, ready to strike their harps and to sing a song of rejoicing that another soul has accepted the invitation to the gospel feast.

19
The Measure of Forgiveness

Based on Matthew 18:21–35

Peter had come to Christ with the question, "How oft shall my brother sin against me, and I forgive him? till seven times?" The rabbis limited the exercise of forgiveness to three offenses. Peter, carrying out, as he supposed, the teaching of Christ, thought to extend it to seven, the number signifying perfection. But Christ taught that we are never to become weary of forgiving. Not "Until seven times," He said, "but, Until seventy times seven."

Then He showed the true ground upon which forgiveness is to be granted and the danger of cherishing an unforgiving spirit. In a parable He told of a king's dealing with the officers who administered the affairs of his government. Some of these officers were in receipt of vast sums of money belonging to the state. As the king investigated their administration of this trust, there was brought before him one man whose account showed a debt to his lord for the immense sum of ten thousand talents. He had nothing to pay, and according to the custom, the king ordered him to be sold, with all that he had, that payment might be made. But the terrified man fell at his feet and besought him, saying, "Have patience with me, and I will pay thee all. Then the lord of that servant was moved with compassion, and loosed him, and forgave him the debt.

"But the same servant went out, and found one of his fellowservants, which owed him an hundred pence; and he laid hands on him, and took him by the throat, saying, Pay me that thou owest. And his fellowservant fell down at his feet, and besought him, saying, Have patience with me, and I will pay thee all. And he would not; but went and cast him into prison, till he should pay the debt. So when his fellowservants saw what was done, they were very sorry, and came and told unto their lord all that was done. Then his lord, after that he had called him, said unto him, O thou wicked servant, I forgave thee all that debt, because thou desiredst me: shouldest not thou also have had compassion on thy fellowservant, even as I had pity on thee? And his lord was wroth, and delivered him to the tormentors, till he should pay all that was due unto him."

This parable presents details which are needed for the filling out of the picture but which have no counterpart in its spiritual significance. The attention should not be diverted to them. Certain great truths are illustrated, and to these our thought should be given.

The pardon granted by this king represents a divine forgiveness of all sin. Christ is represented by the king, who, moved with compassion, forgave the debt of his servant. Man was under the condemnation of the broken law. He could not save himself, and for this reason Christ came to this world, clothed His divinity with humanity, and gave His life, the just for the unjust. He gave Himself for our sins, and to every soul He freely offers the blood-bought pardon. "With the Lord there is mercy, and with Him is plenteous redemption." Psalm 130:7.

Here is the ground upon which we should exercise compassion toward our fellow sinners. "If God so loved us, we ought also to love one another." John 4:11. "Freely ye have received," Christ says, "freely give." Matthew 10:8.

In the parable, when the debtor pleaded for delay, with the promise, "Have patience with me, and I will pay thee all," the sentence was revoked. The whole debt was canceled. And he was soon given an opportunity to follow the example of the master who had forgiven him. Going out, he met a fellow servant who owed him a small sum. He had been forgiven ten thousand talents; the debtor owed him a hundred pence. But he who had been so mercifully treated, dealt with his fellow laborer in an altogether different manner. His debtor made an appeal similar to that which he himself had made to the king, but without a similar result. He who had so recently been forgiven was not tenderhearted and pitiful. The mercy shown him he did not exercise in dealing with his fellowservant. He heeded not the request to be patient. The small sum owed to him was all that the ungrateful servant would keep in mind. He demanded all that he thought his due, and carried into effect a sentence similar to that which had been so graciously revoked for him.

How many are today manifesting the same spirit. When the debtor pleaded with his lord for mercy, he had no true sense of the greatness of his debt. He did not realize his helplessness. He hoped to deliver himself. "Have patience with me," he said, "and I will pay thee all." So there are many who hope by their own works to merit God's favor. They do not realize their helplessness. They do not accept the grace of God as a free gift, but are trying to build themselves up in self-righteousness. Their own hearts are not broken and humbled on account of sin, and they are exacting and unforgiving toward others. Their own sins against God, compared with their brother's sins against them, are as ten thousand talents to one hundred pence —nearly one million to one; yet they dare to be unforgiving.

In the parable the lord summoned the unmerciful debtor, and "said unto him, O thou wicked servant, I forgave thee all that debt, because thou desiredst me; shouldest not thou also have had compassion on thy fellowservant, even as I had pity on thee? And his lord was wroth, and delivered him to the tormentors, till he should pay all that was due unto him." "So likewise," said Jesus, "shall My Heavenly Father do also unto you, if ye from your hearts forgive not every one his brother their trespasses." He who refuses to forgive is thereby casting away his own hope of pardon.

But the teaching of this parable should not be misapplied. God's forgiveness toward us lessens in no wise our duty to obey Him. So the spirit of forgiveness toward our fellow men does not lessen the claim of just obligation. In the prayer which Christ taught His disciples He said, "Forgive us our debts, as we forgive our debtors." Matthew 6:12. By this He did not mean that in order to be forgiven our sins we must not require our just dues from our debtors. If they cannot pay, even though this may be the result of unwise management, they are not to be cast into prison, oppressed, or even treated harshly; but the parable does not teach us to encourage indolence. The word of God declares that if a man will not work, neither shall he eat. (2 Thessalonians 3:10.) The Lord does not require the hard-working man to support others in idleness. With many there is a waste of time, a lack of effort, which brings to poverty and want. If these faults are not corrected by those who indulge them, all that might be done in their behalf would be like putting treasure into a bag with holes. Yet there is an unavoidable poverty, and we are to manifest tenderness and compassion toward those who are unfortunate. We should treat others just as we ourselves, in like circumstances, would wish to be treated.

The Holy Spirit through the apostle Paul charges us: "If there be therefore any consolation in Christ, if any comfort of love, if any fellowship of the Spirit, if any bowels and mercies, fulfil ye my joy, that ye be likeminded, having the same love, being of one accord, of one mind. Let nothing be done through strife or vainglory; but in lowliness of mind let each esteem other better than themselves. Look not every man on his own things, but every man also on the things of others. Let this mind be in you, which was also in Christ Jesus." Philippians 2:1–5.

But sin is not to be lightly regarded. The Lord has commanded us not to suffer wrong upon our brother. He says, "If thy brother trespass against thee, rebuke him." Luke 17:3. Sin is to be called by its right name, and is to be plainly laid out before the wrongdoer.

In his charge to Timothy, Paul, writing by the Holy Spirit, says, "Be instant in season, out of season; reprove, rebuke, exhort with all longsuffering and doctrine." 2 Timothy 4:2. And to Titus he writes, "There are many unruly and vain talkers and deceivers.... Wherefore rebuke them sharply, that they may be sound in the faith." Titus 1:10–13.

"If thy brother shall trespass against thee," Christ said, "go and tell him his fault between thee and him alone: if he shall hear thee, thou hast gained thy brother. But if he will not hear thee, then take with thee one or two more, that in the mouth of two or three witnesses every word may be established. And if he shall neglect to hear them, tell it unto the church: but if he neglect to hear the church, let him be unto thee as an heathen man and a publican." Matthew 18:15–17.

Our Lord teaches that matters of difficulty between Christians are to be settled within the church. They should not be opened before those who do not fear God. If a Christian is wronged by his brother, let him not appeal to unbelievers in a court of justice. Let him follow out the instruction Christ has given. Instead of trying to avenge himself, let him seek to save his brother. God will guard the interests of those who love and fear Him, and with confidence we may commit our case to Him who judges righteously.

Too often when wrongs are committed again and again, and the wrongdoer confesses his fault, the injured one becomes weary, and thinks he has forgiven quite enough. But the Saviour has plainly told us how to deal with the erring: "If thy brother trespass against thee, rebuke him; and if he repent, forgive him." Luke 17:3. Do not hold him off as unworthy of your confidence. Consider "thyself, lest thou also be tempted." Galations 6:1.

If your brethren err, you are to forgive them. When they come to you with confession, you should not say, I do not think they are humble enough. I do not think they feel their confession. What right have you to judge them, as if you could read the heart? The word of God says, "If he repent, forgive him. And if he trespasses against thee seven times in a day, and seven times in a day turn again to thee, saying, I repent; thou shalt forgive him." Luke 17:3, 4. And not only seven times, but seventy times seven—just as often as God forgives you.

We ourselves owe everything to God's free grace. Grace in the covenant ordained our adoption. Grace in the Saviour effected our redemption, our regeneration, and our exaltation to heirship with Christ. Let this grace be revealed to others.

Give the erring one no occasion for discouragement. Suffer not a Pharisaical hardness to come in and hurt your brother. Let no bitter sneer rise in mind or heart. Let no tinge of scorn be manifest in the voice. If you speak a word of your own, if you take an attitude of indifference, or show suspicion or distrust, it may prove the ruin of a soul. He needs a brother with the Elder Brother's heart of sympathy to touch his heart of humanity. Let him feel the strong clasp of a sympathizing hand, and hear the whisper, Let us pray. God will give a rich experience to you both. Prayer unites us with one another and with God. Prayer brings Jesus to our side, and gives to the fainting, perplexed soul new strength to overcome the world, the flesh, and the devil. Prayer turns aside the attacks of Satan.

When one turns away from human imperfections to behold Jesus, a divine transformation takes place in the character. The Spirit of Christ working upon the heart conforms it to His image. Then let it be your effort to lift up Jesus. Let the mind's eye be directed to "the Lamb of God, which taketh away the sin of the world." John 1:29. And as you engage in this work, remember that "he which converteth the sinner from the error of his way, shall save a soul from death, and shall hide a multitude of sins." James 5:20.

"But if ye forgive not men their trespasses, neither will your Father forgive your trespasses." Matthew 6:15. Nothing can justify an unforgiving spirit. He who is unmerciful toward others shows that he himself is not a partaker of God's pardoning grace. In God's forgiveness the heart of the erring one is drawn close to the great heart of Infinite Love. The tide of divine compassion flows into the sinner's soul, and from him to the souls of others. The tenderness and mercy that Christ has revealed in His own precious life will be seen in those who become sharers of His grace. But "if any man have not the Spirit of Christ, he is none of His." Romans 8:9. He is alienated from God, fitted only for eternal separation from Him.

It is true that he may once have received forgiveness; but his unmerciful spirit shows that he now rejects God's pardoning love. He has separated himself from God, and is in the same condition as before he was forgiven. He has denied his repentance, and his sins are upon him as if he had not repented.

But the great lesson of the parable lies in the contrast between God's compassion and man's hardheartedness; in the fact that God's forgiving mercy is to be the measure of our own. "Shouldest not thou also have had compassion on thy fellowservant, even as I had pity on thee?"

We are not forgiven *because* we forgive, but *as* we forgive. The ground of all forgiveness is found in the unmerited love of God, but by our attitude toward others we show whether we have made that love our own. Wherefore Christ says, "With what judgment ye judge, ye shall be judged; and with what measure ye mete, it shall be measured to you again." Matthew 7:2.

20
Gain That Is Loss

Based on Luke 12:13–21

Christ was teaching, and, as usual, others besides His disciples had gathered about Him. He had been speaking to the disciples of the scenes in which they were soon to act a part. They were to publish abroad the truths He had committed to them, and they would be brought in conflict with the rulers of this world. For His sake they would be called into courts, and before magistrates and kings. He had assured them of wisdom which none could gainsay. His own words, that moved the hearts of the multitude, and brought to confusion His wily adversaries, witnessed to the power of that indwelling Spirit which He had promised to His followers.

But there were many who desired the grace of heaven only to serve their selfish purposes. They recognized the marvelous power of Christ in setting forth the truth in a clear light. They heard the promise to His followers of wisdom to speak before rulers and magistrates. Would He not lend His power for their worldly benefit?

"And one of the company said unto Him, Master, speak to my brother, that he divide the inheritance with me." Through Moses, God had given directions concerning the transmission of property. The eldest son received a double portion of the father's estate (Deuteronomy 21:17), while the younger brothers were to share alike. This man thinks that his brother has defrauded him of his inheritance. His own efforts have failed to secure what he regards as his due, but if Christ will interpose the end will surely be gained. He has heard Christ's stirring appeals, and His solemn denunciations of the scribes and Pharisees. If words of such command could be spoken to this brother, he would not dare to refuse the aggrieved man his portion.

In the midst of the solemn instruction that Christ had given, this man had revealed his selfish disposition. He could appreciate that ability of the Lord which might work for the advancement of his own temporal affairs; but spiritual truths had taken no hold on his mind and heart. The gaining of the inheritance was his absorbing theme. Jesus, the King of glory, who was rich, yet for our sake became poor, was opening to him the treasures of divine love. The Holy Spirit was pleading with him to become an heir of the inheritance that is "incorruptible, and undefiled, and that fadeth not away." 1 Peter 1:4. He had seen evidence of the power of Christ. Now the opportunity was his to speak to the great Teacher, to express the desire uppermost in his heart. But like the man with the muck rake in Bunyan's allegory, his eyes were fixed on the earth. He saw not the crown above his head. Like Simon Magus, he valued the gift of God as a means of worldly gain.

The Saviour's mission on earth was fast drawing to a close. Only a few months remained for Him to complete what He had come to do, in establishing the kingdom of His grace. Yet human greed would have turned Him from His work to take up the dispute over a piece of land. But Jesus was not to be diverted from His mission. His answer was, "Man, who made Me a judge or a divider over you?"

Jesus could have told this man just what was right. He knew the right in the case; but the brothers were in a quarrel because both were covetous. Christ virtually said, It is not My work to settle controversies of this kind. He came for another purpose, to preach the gospel, and thus to arouse men to a sense of eternal realities.

In Christ's treatment of this case is a lesson for all who minister in His name. When He sent forth the twelve, He said, "As ye go, preach, saying, The kingdom of heaven is at hand. Heal the sick, cleanse the lepers, raise the dead, cast out devils: freely ye have received, freely give." Matthew 10:7, 8. They were not to settle the temporal affairs of the people. Their work was to persuade men to be reconciled to God. In this work lay their power to bless humanity. The only remedy for the sins and sorrows of men is Christ. The gospel of His grace alone can cure the evils that curse society. The injustice of the rich toward the poor, the hatred of the poor toward the rich, alike have their root in selfishness, and this can be eradicated only through submission to Christ. He alone, for the selfish heart of sin, gives the new heart of love. Let the servants of Christ preach the gospel with the Spirit sent down from heaven, and work as He did for the benefit of men. Then such results will be manifest in the blessing and uplifting of mankind as are wholly impossible of accomplishment by human power.

Our Lord struck at the root of the affair that troubled this questioner, and of all similar disputes, saying, "Take heed, and beware of covetousness; for a man's life consisteth not in the abundance of the things which he possesseth.

"And He spake a parable unto them, saying, The ground of a certain rich man brought forth plentifully; and he thought within himself, saying, What shall I do, because I have no room where to bestow my fruits? And he said, This will I do: I will pull down my barns, and build greater; and there will I bestow all my fruits and my goods. And I will say to my soul, Soul, thou hast much goods laid up for many years; take thine ease, eat, drink, be merry. But God said unto him, Thou fool, this night thy soul shall be required of thee: then whose shall these things be, which thou hast provided? So is he that layeth up treasure for himself, and is not rich toward God."

By the parable of the foolish rich man, Christ showed the folly of those who make the world their all. This man had received everything from God.

The sun had been permitted to shine upon his land; for its rays fall on the just and on the unjust. The showers of heaven descend on the evil and on the good. The Lord had caused vegetation to flourish, and the fields to bring forth abundantly. The rich man was in perplexity as to what he should do with his produce. His barns were full to overflowing, and he had no place to put the surplus of his harvest. He did not think of God, from whom all his mercies had come. He did not realize that God had made him a steward of His goods that he might help the needy. He had a blessed opportunity of being God's almoner, but he thought only of ministering to his own comfort.

The situation of the poor, the orphan, the widow, the suffering, the afflicted, was brought to this rich man's attention; there were many places in which to bestow his goods. He could easily have relieved himself of a portion of his abundance, and many homes would have been freed from want, many who were hungry would have been fed, many naked clothed, many hearts made glad, many prayers for bread and clothing answered, and a melody of praise would have ascended to heaven. The Lord had heard the prayers of the needy, and of His goodness He had prepared for the poor. (Psalm 68:10.) Abundant provision for the wants of many had been made in the blessings bestowed upon the rich man. But he closed his heart to the cry of the needy, and said to his servants, "This will I do: I will pull down my barns, and build greater; and there will I bestow all my fruits and my goods. And I will say to my soul, Soul, thou hast much goods laid up for many years; take thine ease, eat, drink, and be merry."

This man's aims were no higher than those of the beasts that perish. He lived as if there were no God, no heaven, no future life; as if everything he possessed were his own, and he owed nothing to God or man. The psalmist described this rich man when he wrote, "The fool hath said in his heart, There is no God." Psalm 14:1.

This man has lived and planned for self. He sees that the future is abundantly provided for; there is nothing for him now but to treasure and enjoy the fruits of his labors. He regards himself as favored above other men, and takes credit to himself for his wise management. He is honored by his fellow townsmen as a man of good judgment and a prosperous citizen. For "men will praise thee, when thou doest well to thyself." Psalm 49:18.

But "the wisdom of this world is foolishness with God." 1 Corinthians 3:19. While the rich man is looking forward to years of enjoyment, the Lord is making far different plans. The message comes to this unfaithful steward, "Thou fool, this night thy soul shall be required of thee." Here is a demand that money cannot supply. The wealth he has treasured can purchase no reprieve. In one moment that which he has toiled through his whole life to secure becomes worthless to him. "Then whose shall those things be which thou hast provided?" His broad fields and well-filled granaries pass from under his control. "He heapeth up riches, and knoweth not who shall gather them." Psalm 39:6.

The only thing that would be of value to him now he has not secured. In living for self he has rejected that divine love which would have flowed out in mercy to his fellow men. Thus he has rejected life. For God is love, and love is life. This man has chosen the earthly rather than the spiritual, and with the earthly he must pass away. "Man that is in honour, and understandeth not, is like the beasts that perish." Psalm 49:20.

"So is he that layeth up treasure for himself, and is not rich toward God." The picture is true for all time. You may plan for merely selfish good, you may gather together treasure, you may build mansions great and high, as did the builders of ancient Babylon; but you cannot build wall so high or gate so strong as to shut out the messengers of doom. Belshazzar the king "feasted in his palace," and "praised the gods of gold, and of silver, of brass, of iron, of wood, and of stone." But the hand of One invisible wrote upon his walls the words of doom, and the tread of hostile armies was heard at his palace gates. "In that night was Belshazzar the king of the Chaldeans slain," and an alien monarch sat upon the throne. (Daniel 5:30)

To live for self is to perish. Covetousness, the desire of benefit for self's sake, cuts the soul off from life. It is the spirit of Satan to get, to draw to self. It is the spirit of Christ to give, to sacrifice self for the good of others. "And this is the record, that God hath given to us eternal life, and this life is in His Son. He that hath the Son hath life; and he that hath not the Son of God hath not life." 1 John 5:11, 12.

Wherefore He says, "Take heed, and beware of covetousness; for a man's life consisteth not in the abundance of the things which he possesseth."

21
"A Great Gulf Fixed"

Based on Luke 16:19–31

In the parable of the rich man and Lazarus, Christ shows that in this life men decide their eternal destiny. During probationary time the grace of God is offered to every soul. But if men waste their opportunities in self-pleasing, they cut themselves off from everlasting life. No afterprobation will be granted them. By their own choice they have fixed an impassable gulf between them and their God.

This parable draws a contrast between the rich who have not made God their dependence, and the poor who have made God their dependence. Christ shows that the time is coming when the position of the two classes will be reversed. Those who are poor in this world's goods, yet who trust in God and are patient in suffering, will one day be exalted above those who now hold the highest positions the world can give but who have not surrendered their life to God.

"There was a certain rich man," Christ said, "which was clothed in purple and fine linen, and fared sumptuously every day. And there was a certain beggar named Lazarus, which was laid at his gate, full of sores, and desiring to be fed with the crumbs which fell from the rich man's table."

The rich man did not belong to the class represented by the unjust judge, who openly declared his disregard for God and man. He claimed to be a son of Abraham. He did not treat the beggar with violence or require him to go away because the sight of him was disagreeable. If the poor, loathsome specimen of humanity could be comforted by beholding him as he entered his gates, the rich man was willing that he should remain. But he was selfishly indifferent to the needs of his suffering brother.

There were then no hospitals in which the sick might be cared for. The suffering and needy were brought to the notice of those to whom the Lord had entrusted wealth, that they might receive help and sympathy. Thus it was with the beggar and the rich man. Lazarus was in great need of help; for he was without friends, home, money, or food. Yet he was allowed to remain in this condition day after day, while the wealthy nobleman had every want supplied. The one who was abundantly able to relieve the sufferings of his fellow creature, lived to himself, as many live today.

There are today close beside us many who are hungry, naked, homeless. A neglect to impart of our means to these needy, suffering ones places upon us a burden of guilt which we shall one day fear to meet. All covetousness is condemned as idolatry. All selfish indulgence is an offense in God's sight.

God had made the rich man a steward of His means, and it was his duty to attend to just such cases as that of the beggar. The command had been given, "Thou shalt love the Lord thy God with all thine heart, and with all thy soul, and with all thy might" (Deuteronomy 6:5); and "thou shalt love thy neighbor as thyself" (Leviticus 19:18). The rich man was a Jew, and he was acquainted with the command of God. But he forgot that he was accountable for the use of his entrusted means and capabilities. The Lord's blessings rested upon him abundantly, but he employed them selfishly, to honor himself, not his Maker. In proportion to his abundance was his obligation to use his gifts for the uplifting of humanity. This was the Lord's command, but the rich man had no thought of his obligation to God. He lent money, and took interest for what he loaned; but he returned no interest for what God had lent him. He had knowledge and talents, but did not improve them. Forgetful of his accountability to God, he devoted all his powers to pleasure. Everything with which he was surrounded, his round of amusements, the praise and flattery of his friends, ministered to his selfish enjoyment. So engrossed was he in the society of his friends that he lost all sense of his responsibility to co-operate with God in His ministry of mercy. He had opportunity to understand the word of God, and to practice its teachings; but the pleasure-loving society he chose so occupied his time that he forgot the God of eternity.

The time came when a change took place in the condition of the two men. The poor man had suffered day by day, but he had patiently and quietly endured. In the course of time he died and was buried. There was no one to mourn for him; but by his patience in suffering he had witnessed for Christ, he had endured the test of his faith, and at his death he is represented as being carried by the angels into Abraham's bosom.

Lazarus represents the suffering poor who believe in Christ. When the trumpet sounds and all that are in the graves hear Christ's voice and come forth, they will receive their reward; for their faith in God was not a mere theory, but a reality.

"The rich man also died, and was buried; and in hell he lift up his eyes, being in torments, and seeth Abraham afar off, and Lazarus in his bosom. And he cried and said, Father Abraham, have mercy on me, and send Lazarus, that he may dip the tip of his finger in water, and cool my tongue; for I am tormented in this flame."

In this parable Christ was meeting the people on their own ground. The doctrine of a conscious state of existence between death and the resurrection was held by many of those who were listening to Christ's words. The Saviour knew of their ideas, and He framed His parable so as to inculcate important truths through these preconceived opinions. He held up before His hearers a mirror wherein they might see themselves in their true relation to God. He used the prevailing opinion to convey the idea He wished to make prominent to all—that no man is valued for his possessions; for all he has belongs to him only as lent by the Lord. A misuse of these gifts will place him below the poorest and most afflicted man who loves God and trusts in Him.

Christ desires His hearers to understand that it is impossible for men to secure the salvation of the soul after death. "Son," Abraham is represented as answering, "remember that thou in thy lifetime receivedst thy good things, and likewise Lazarus evil things; but now he is comforted, and thou art tormented. And beside all this, between us and you there is a great gulf fixed; so that they which would pass from hence to you can not; neither can they pass to us, that would come from thence." Thus Christ represented the hopelessness of looking for a second probation. This life is the only time given to man in which to prepare for eternity.

The rich man had not abandoned the idea that he was a child of Abraham, and in his distress he is represented as calling upon him for aid. "Father Abraham," he prayed, "have mercy on me." He did not pray to God, but to Abraham. Thus he showed that he placed Abraham above God, and that he relied on his relationship to Abraham for salvation. The thief on the cross offered his prayer to Christ. "Remember me when Thou comest into Thy kingdom," he said. (Luke 23:42.) And at once the response came, Verily I say unto thee today (as I hang on the cross in humiliation and suffering), thou shalt be with Me in Paradise. But the rich man prayed to Abraham, and his petition was not granted. Christ alone is exalted to be "a Prince and a Saviour, for to give repentance to Israel, and forgiveness of sins." Acts 5:31. "Neither is there salvation in any other." Acts 4:12.

The rich man had spent his life in self-pleasing, and too late he saw that he had made no provision for eternity. He realized his folly, and thought of his brothers, who would go on as he had gone, living to please themselves. Then he made the request, "I pray thee therefore, father, that thou wouldest send him [Lazarus] to my father's house; for I have five brethren; that he may testify unto them, lest they also come into this place of torment." But "Abraham saith unto him, They have Moses and the prophets; let them hear them. And he said, Nay, father Abraham; but if one went unto them from the dead, they will repent. And he said unto him, If they hear not Moses and the prophets, neither will they be persuaded though one rose from the dead."

When the rich man solicited additional evidence for his brothers, he was plainly told that should this evidence be given, they would not be persuaded. His request cast a reflection on God. It was as if the rich man had said, If you had more thoroughly warned me, I should not now be here. Abraham in his answer to this request is represented as saying, Your brothers have been sufficiently warned. Light has been given them, but they would not see; truth has been presented to them, but they would not hear.

"If they hear not Moses and the prophets, neither will they be persuaded, though one rose from the dead." These words were proved true in the history of the Jewish nation. Christ's last and crowning miracle was the raising of Lazarus of Bethany, after he had been dead four days. The Jews were given this wonderful evidence of the Saviour's divinity, but they rejected it. Lazarus rose from the dead and bore his testimony before them, but they hardened their hearts against all evidence, and even sought to take his life. (John 12:9–11.)

The law and the prophets are God's appointed agencies for the salvation of men. Christ said, Let them give heed to these evidences. If they do not listen to the voice of God in His word, the testimony of a witness raised from the dead would not be heeded.

Those who heed Moses and the prophets will require no greater light than God has given; but if men reject the light, and fail to appreciate the opportunities granted them, they would not hear if one from the dead should come to them with a message. They would not be convinced even by this evidence; for those who reject the law and the prophets so harden their hearts that they will reject all light.

The conversation between Abraham and the once-rich man is figurative. The lesson to be gathered from it is that every man is given sufficient light for the discharge of the duties required of him. Man's responsibilities are proportionate to his opportunities and privileges. God gives to every one sufficient light and grace to do the work He has given him to do. If man fails to do that which a little light shows to be his duty, greater light would only reveal unfaithfulness, neglect to improve the blessings given. "He that is faithful in that which is least is faithful also in much; and he that is unjust in the least is unjust also in much." Luke 16:10. Those who refuse to be enlightened by Moses and the prophets and ask for some wonderful miracle to be performed would not be convinced if their wish were granted.

The parable of the rich man and Lazarus shows how the two classes represented by these men are estimated in the unseen world. There is no sin in being rich if riches are not acquired by injustice. A rich man is not condemned for having riches, but condemnation rests upon him if the means entrusted to him is spent in selfishness. Far better might he lay up his money beside the throne of God, by using it to do good. Death cannot make any man poor who thus devotes himself to seeking eternal riches. But the man who hoards his treasure for self can not take any of it to heaven. He has proved himself to be an unfaithful steward. During his lifetime he had his good things, but he was forgetful of his obligation to God. He failed of securing the heavenly treasure.

The rich man who had so many privileges is represented to us as one who should have cultivated his gifts, so that his works should reach to the great beyond, carrying with them improved spiritual advantages. It is the purpose of redemption, not only to blot out sin, but to give back to man those spiritual gifts lost because of sin's dwarfing power. Money cannot be carried into the next life; it is not needed there; but the good deeds done in winning souls to Christ are carried to the heavenly courts. But those who selfishly spend the Lord's gifts on themselves, leaving their needy fellow creatures without aid and doing nothing to advance God's work in the world, dishonor their Maker. Robbery of God is written opposite their names in the books of heaven.

The rich man had all that money could procure, but he did not possess the riches that would have kept his account right with God. He had lived as if all that he possessed were his own. He had neglected the call of God and the claims of the suffering poor. But at length there comes a call which he cannot neglect. By a power which he cannot question or resist he is commanded to quit the premises of which he is no longer steward. The once-rich man is reduced to hopeless poverty. The robe of Christ's righteousness, woven in the loom of heaven, can never cover him. He who once wore the richest purple, the finest linen, is reduced to nakedness. His probation is ended. He brought nothing into the world, and he can take nothing out of it.

Christ lifted the curtain and presented this picture before priests and rulers, scribes and Pharisees. Look at it, you who are rich in this world's goods and are not rich toward God. Will you not contemplate this scene? That which is highly esteemed among men is abhorrent in the sight of God. Christ asks, "What shall it profit a man, if he shall gain the whole world, and lose his own soul? or what shall a man give in exchange for his soul?" Mark 8:36, 37.

Application to the Jewish Nation

When Christ gave the parable of the rich man and Lazarus, there were many in the Jewish nation in the pitiable condition of the rich man, using the Lord's goods for selfish gratification, preparing themselves to hear the sentence, "Thou art weighed in the balances, and art found wanting." Daniel 5:27. The rich man was favored with every temporal and spiritual blessing, but he refused to cooperate with God in the use of these blessings. Thus it was with the Jewish nation. The Lord had made the Jews the depositaries of sacred truth. He had appointed them stewards of His grace. He had given them every spiritual and temporal advantage, and He called upon them to impart these blessings. Special instruction had been given them in regard to their treatment of their brethren who had fallen into decay, of the stranger within their gates, and of the poor among them. They were not to seek to gain everything for their own advantage, but were to remember those in need and share with them. And God promised to bless them in accordance with their deeds of love and mercy. But like the rich man, they put forth no helping hand to relieve the temporal or spiritual necessities of suffering humanity. Filled with pride, they regarded themselves as the chosen and favored people of God; yet they did not serve or worship God. They put their dependence in the fact that they were children of Abraham. "We be Abraham's seed," they said proudly. (John 8:33.) When the crisis came, it was revealed that they had divorced themselves from God, and had placed their trust in Abraham, as if he were God.

Christ longed to let light shine into the darkened minds of the Jewish people. He said to them, "If ye were Abraham's children, ye would do the works of Abraham. But now ye seek to kill Me, a man that hath told you the truth, which I have heard of God. This did not Abraham." John 8:39,40.

Christ recognized no virtue in lineage. He taught that spiritual connection supersedes all natural connection. The Jews claimed to have descended from Abraham; but by failing to do the works of Abraham, they proved that they were not his true children. Only those who prove themselves to be spiritually in harmony with Abraham by obeying the voice of God, are reckoned as of true descent. Although the beggar belonged to the class looked upon by men as inferior, Christ recognized him as one whom Abraham would take into the very closest friendship.

The rich man though surrounded with all the luxuries of life was so ignorant that he put Abraham where God should have been. If he had appreciated his exalted privileges and had allowed God's Spirit to mold his mind and heart, he would have had an altogether different position. So with the nation he represented. If they had responded to the divine call, their future would have been wholly different. They would have shown true spiritual discernment. They had means which God would have increased, making it sufficient to bless and enlighten the whole world. But they had so far separated from the Lord's arrangement that their whole life was perverted. They failed to use their gifts as God's stewards in accordance with truth and righteousness. Eternity was not brought into their reckoning, and the result of their unfaithfulness was ruin to the whole nation.

Christ knew that at the destruction of Jerusalem the Jews would remember His warning. And it was so. When calamity came upon Jerusalem, when starvation and suffering of every kind came upon the people, they remembered these words of Christ and understood the parable. They had brought their suffering upon themselves by their neglect to let their God-given light shine forth to the world.

In the Last Days

The closing scenes of this earth's history are portrayed in the closing of the rich man's history. The rich man claimed to be a son of Abraham, but he was separated from Abraham by an impassable gulf—a character wrongly developed. Abraham served God, following His word in faith and obedience.

But the rich man was unmindful of God and of the needs of suffering humanity. The great gulf fixed between him and Abraham was the gulf of disobedience. There are many today who are following the same course. Though church members, they are unconverted. They may take part in the church service, they may chant the psalm, "As the hart panteth after the water brooks, so panteth my soul after Thee, O God" (Psalm 42:1); but they testify to a falsehood. They are no more righteous in God's sight than is the veriest sinner. The soul that longs after the excitement of worldly pleasure, the mind that is full of love for display, cannot serve God. Like the rich man in the parable, such a one has no inclination to war against the lust of the flesh. He longs to indulge appetite. He chooses the atmosphere of sin. He is suddenly snatched away by death, and he goes down to the grave with the character formed during his lifetime in copartnership with Satanic agencies. In the grave he has no power to choose anything, be it good or evil; for in the day when a man dies, his thoughts perish. (Psalm 146:4; Ecclesiastes 9:5, 6.)

When the voice of God awakes the dead, he will come from the grave with the same appetites and passions, the same likes and dislikes, that he cherished when living. God works no miracle to re-create a man who would not be re-created when he was granted every opportunity and provided with every facility. During his lifetime he took no delight in God, nor found pleasure in His service. His character is not in harmony with God, and he could not be happy in the heavenly family.

Today there is a class in our world who are self-righteous. They are not gluttons, they are not drunkards, they are not infidels; but they desire to live for themselves, not for God. He is not in their thoughts; therefore they are classed with unbelievers. Were it possible for them to enter the gates of the city of God, they could have no right to the tree of life, for when God's commandments were laid before them with all their binding claims they said, No. They have not served God here; therefore they would not serve Him hereafter. They could not live in His presence, and they would feel that any place was preferable to heaven.

To learn of Christ means to receive His grace, which is His character. But those who do not appreciate and utilize the precious opportunities and sacred influences granted them on earth, are not fitted to take part in the pure devotion of heaven. Their characters are not molded according to the divine similitude. By their own neglect they have formed a chasm which nothing can bridge. Between them and the righteous there is a great gulf fixed.

22
Saying and Doing

Based on Matthew 21:23–32

A certain man had two sons; and he came to the first, and said, Son, go work today in my vineyard. He answered and said, I will not; but afterward he repented, and went. And he came to the second, and said likewise. And he answered and said, I go, sir; and went not. Whether of them twain did the will of his father? They say unto him, The first."

In the sermon on the mount Christ said, "Not every one that saith unto Me, Lord, Lord, shall enter into the kingdom of heaven; but he that doeth the will of My Father which is in heaven." Matthew 7:21. The test of sincerity is not in words, but in deeds. Christ does not say to any man, What say ye more than others? but, "What do ye more than others?" Matthew 5:47. Full of meaning are His words, "If ye know these things, happy are ye if ye do them." John 13:17. Words are of no value unless they are accompanied with appropriate deeds. This is the lesson taught in the parable of the two sons.

This parable was spoken at Christ's last visit to Jerusalem before His death. He had driven out the buyers and sellers from the temple. His voice had spoken to their hearts with the power of God. Amazed and terrified, they had obeyed His command without excuse or resistance.

When their terror was abated, the priests and elders, returning to the temple, had found Christ healing the sick and the dying. They had heard the voice of rejoicing and the song of praise. In the temple itself the children who had been restored to health were waving palm branches and singing hosannas to the Son of David. Baby voices were lisping the praises of the mighty Healer. Yet with the priests and elders all this did not suffice to overcome their prejudice and jealousy.

The next day, as Christ was teaching in the temple, the chief priests and elders of the people came to Him and said, "By what authority doest Thou these things? and who gave Thee this authority?"

The priests and elders had had unmistakable evidence of Christ's power. In His cleansing of the temple they had seen Heaven's authority flashing from His face. They could not resist the power by which He spoke. Again in His wonderful deeds of healing He had answered their question. He had given evidence of His authority which could not be controverted. But it was not evidence that was wanted. The priests and elders were anxious for Jesus to proclaim Himself the Messiah that they might misapply His words and stir up the people against Him. They wished to destroy His influence and to put Him to death.

Jesus knew that if they could not recognize God in Him or see in His works the evidence of His divine character, they would not believe His own testimony that He was the Christ. In His answer He evades the issue they hope to bring about and turns the condemnation upon themselves.

"I also will ask you one thing," He said, "which if ye tell Me, I in like wise will tell you by what authority I do these things. The baptism of John, whence was it? from heaven, or of men?"

The priests and rulers were perplexed. "They reasoned with themselves, saying, If we shall say, From heaven, He will say unto us, Why did ye not then believe him? But if we shall say, Of men, we fear the people; for all hold John as a prophet. And they answered Jesus, and said, We can not tell. And He said unto them, Neither tell I you by what authority I do these things."

"We can not tell." This answer was a falsehood. But the priests saw the position they were in, and falsified in order to screen themselves. John the Baptist had come bearing witness of the One whose authority they were now questioning. He had pointed Him out, saying, "Behold the Lamb of God, which taketh away the sin of the world." John 1:29. He had baptized Him, and after the baptism, as Christ was praying, the heavens were opened, and the Spirit of God like a dove rested upon Him, while a voice from heaven was heard saying, "This is My beloved Son, in whom I am well pleased." Matthew 3:17.

Remembering how John had repeated the prophecies concerning the Messiah, remembering the scene at the baptism of Jesus, the priests and rulers dared not say that John's baptism was from heaven. If they acknowledged John to be a prophet, as they believed him to be, how could they deny his testimony that Jesus of Nazareth was the Son of God? And they could not say that John's baptism was of men, because of the people, who believed John to be a prophet. So they said, "We can not tell."

Then Christ gave the parable of the father and the two sons. When the father went to the first son, saying, "Go work today in my vineyard," the son promptly answered, "I will not." He refused to obey, and gave himself up to wicked ways and associations. But afterward he repented, and obeyed the call.

The father went to the second son with the same command, "Go work today in my vineyard." This son made reply, "I go, sir," but he went not.

In this parable the father represents God, the vineyard the church. By the two sons are represented two classes of people. The son who refused to obey the command, saying, "I will not," represented those who were living in open transgression, who made no profession of piety, who openly refused to come under the yoke of restraint and obedience which the law of God imposes. But many of these afterward repented and obeyed the call of God. When the gospel came to them in the message of John the Baptist, "Repent ye; for the kingdom of heaven is at hand," they repented, and confessed their sins. (Matthew 3:2.)

In the son who said, "I go, sir," and went not, the character of the Pharisees was revealed. Like this son, the Jewish leaders were impenitent and self-sufficient. The religious life of the Jewish nation had become a pretense. When the law was proclaimed on Mount Sinai by the voice of God, all the people pledged themselves to obey. They said, "I go, sir," but they went not. When Christ came in person to set before them the principles of the law, they rejected Him. Christ had given the Jewish leaders of His day abundant evidence of His authority and divine power, but although they were convinced, they would not accept the evidence. Christ had shown them that they continued to disbelieve because they had not the spirit which leads to obedience. He had declared to them, "Ye made the commandment of God of none effect by your tradition.... In vain they do worship Me, teaching for doctrines the commandments of men." Matthew 15:6, 9.

In the company before Christ there were scribes and Pharisees, priests and rulers, and after giving the parable of the two sons, Christ addressed to His hearers the question, "Whether of them twain did the will of his father?" Forgetting themselves, the Pharisees answered, "The first." This they said without realizing that they were pronouncing sentence against themselves. Then there fell from Christ's lips the denunciation, "Verily I say unto you, That the publicans and the harlots go into the kingdom of God before you. For John came unto you in the way of righteousness, and ye believed him not; but the publicans and the harlots believed him: and ye, when ye had seen it, repented not afterward, that ye might believe him."

John the Baptist came preaching truth, and by his preaching sinners were convicted and converted. These would go into the kingdom of heaven before the ones who in self-righteousness resisted the solemn warning. The publicans and harlots were ignorant, but these learned men knew the way of truth. Yet they refused to walk in the path which leads to the Paradise of God. The truth that should have been to them a savor of life unto life became a savor of death unto death. Open sinners who loathed themselves had received baptism at the hands of John; but these teachers were hypocrites. Their own stubborn hearts were the obstacle to their receiving the truth. They resisted the conviction of the Spirit of God. They refused obedience to God's commandments.

Christ did not say to them, Ye cannot enter the kingdom of heaven; but He showed that the obstacle which prevented them from entering was of their own creating. The door was still open to these Jewish leaders; the invitation was still held out. Christ longed to see them convicted and converted.

The priests and elders of Israel spent their lives in religious ceremonies, which they regarded as too sacred to be connected with secular business.

Therefore their lives were supposed to be wholly religious. But they performed their ceremonies to be seen by men that they might be thought by the world to be pious and devoted. While professing to obey they refused to render obedience to God. They were not doers of the truth which they professed to teach.

Christ declared John the Baptist to be one of the greatest of the prophets, and He showed His hearers that they had had sufficient evidence that John was a messenger from God. The words of the preacher in the wilderness were with power. He bore his message unflinchingly, rebuking the sins of priests and rulers, and enjoining upon them the works of the kingdom of heaven. He pointed out to them their sinful disregard of their Father's authority in refusing to do the work appointed them. He made no compromise with sin, and many were turned from their unrighteousness.

Had the profession of the Jewish leaders been genuine, they would have received John's testimony and accepted Jesus as the Messiah. But they did not show the fruits of repentance and righteousness. The very ones whom they despised were pressing into the kingdom of God before them.

In the parable the son who said, "I go, sir," represented himself as faithful and obedient; but time proved that his profession was not real. He had no true love for his father. So the Pharisees prided themselves on their holiness, but when tested, it was found wanting. When it was for their interest to do so, they made the requirements of the law very exacting; but when obedience was required from themselves, by cunning sophistries they reasoned away the force of God's precepts. Of them Christ declared, "Do not ye after their works; for they say, and do not." Matthew 23:3. They had no true love for God or man. God called them to be co-workers with Him in blessing the world; but while in profession they accepted the call, in action they refused obedience. They trusted to self, and prided themselves on their goodness; but they set the commands of God at defiance. They refused to do the work which God had appointed them, and because of their transgression the Lord was about to divorce Himself from the disobedient nation.

Self-righteousness is not true righteousness, and those who cling to it will be left to take the consequences of holding a fatal deception. Many today claim to obey the commandments of God, but they have not the love of God in their hearts to flow forth to others. Christ calls them to unite with Him in His work for the saving of the world, but they content themselves with saying, "I go, sir." They do not go. They do not co-operate with those who are doing God's service. They are idlers. Like the unfaithful son, they make false promises to God. In taking upon themselves the solemn covenant of the church they have pledged themselves to receive and obey the word of God, to give themselves to God's service, but they do not do this. In profession they claim to be sons of God, but in life and character they deny the relationship. They do not surrender the will to God. They are living a lie.

The promise of obedience they appear to fulfill when this involves no sacrifice; but when self-denial and self-sacrifice are required, when they see the cross to be lifted, they draw back. Thus the conviction of duty wears away, and known transgression of God's commandments becomes habit. The ear may hear God's word, but the spiritual perceptive powers have departed. The heart is hardened, the conscience seared.

Do not think that because you do not manifest decided hostility to Christ you are doing Him service. We thus deceive our own souls. By withholding that which God has given us to use in His service, be it time or means or any other of His entrusted gifts, we work against Him.

Satan uses the listless, sleepy indolence of professed Christians to strengthen his forces and win souls to his side. Many, who think that though they are doing no actual work for Christ, they are yet on His side, are enabling the enemy to pre-occupy ground and gain advantages. By their failure to be diligent workers for the Master, by leaving duties undone and words unspoken, they have allowed Satan to gain control of souls who might have been won for Christ.

We can never be saved in indolence and inactivity. There is no such thing as a truly converted person living a helpless, useless life. It is not possible for us to drift into heaven. No sluggard can enter there. If we do not strive to gain an entrance into the kingdom, if we do not seek earnestly to learn what constitutes its laws, we are not fitted for a part in it. Those who refuse to co-operate with God on earth would not co-operate with Him in heaven. It would not be safe to take them to heaven.

There is more hope for publicans and sinners than for those who know the word of God but refuse to obey it. He who sees himself a sinner with no cloak for his sin, who knows that he is corrupting soul, body, and spirit before God, becomes alarmed lest he be eternally separated from the kingdom of heaven. He realizes his diseased condition, and seeks healing from the great Physician who has said, "Him that cometh to Me, I will in no wise cast out." John 6:37. These souls the Lord can use as workers in His vineyard.

The son who for a time refused obedience to his father's command was not condemned by Christ; and neither was he commended. The class who act the part of the first son in refusing obedience deserve no credit for holding this position. Their frankness is not to be regarded as a virtue. Sanctified by truth and holiness, it would make men bold witnesses for Christ; but used as it is by the sinner, it is insulting and defiant, and approaches to blasphemy. The fact that a man is not a hypocrite does not make him any the less really a sinner. When the appeals of the Holy Spirit come to the heart, our only safety lies in responding to them without delay. When the call comes, "Go work today in My vineyard," do not refuse the invitation. "Today if ye will hear His voice, harden not your hearts." Hebrews 4:7. It is unsafe to delay obedience. You may never hear the invitation again.

And let none flatter themselves that sins cherished for a time can easily be given up by and by. This is not so. Every sin cherished weakens the character and strengthens habit; and physical, mental, and moral depravity is the result. You may repent of the wrong you have done, and set your feet in right paths; but the mold of your mind and your familiarity with evil will make it difficult for you to distinguish between right and wrong. Through the wrong habits formed, Satan will assail you again and again.

In the command, "Go work today in My vineyard," the test of sincerity is brought to every soul. Will there be deeds as well as words? Will the one called put to use all the knowledge he has, working faithfully, disinterestedly, for the Owner of the vineyard?

The apostle Peter instructs us as to the plan on which we must work. "Grace and peace be multiplied unto you," he says, "through the knowledge of God, and of Jesus our Lord, according as His divine power hath given unto us all things that pertain unto life and godliness, through the knowledge of Him that hath called us to glory and virtue: whereby are given unto us exceeding great and precious promises; that by these ye might be partakers of the divine nature, having escaped the corruption that is in the world through lust.

"And beside this, giving all diligence, add to your faith virtue; and to virtue knowledge; and to knowledge temperance; and to temperance patience; and to patience godliness; and to godliness brotherly kindness; and to brotherly kindness charity." 2 Peter 1:2–7.

If you cultivate faithfully the vineyard of your soul, God is making you a laborer together with Himself. And you will have a work to do not only for yourself, but for others. In representing the church as the vineyard, Christ does not teach that we are to restrict our sympathies and labors to our own numbers. The Lord's vineyard is to be enlarged. In all parts of the earth He desires it to be extended. As we receive the instruction and grace of God, we should impart to others a knowledge of how to care for the precious plants. Thus we may extend the vineyard of the Lord. God is watching for evidence of our faith, love, and patience. He looks to see if we are using every spiritual advantage to become skillful workers in His vineyard on earth, that we may enter the Paradise of God, that Eden home from which Adam and Eve were excluded by transgression.

God stands toward His people in the relation of a father, and He has a father's claim to our faithful service. Consider the life of Christ. Standing at the head of humanity, serving His Father, He is an example of what every son should and may be. The obedience that Christ rendered God requires from human beings today. He served His Father with love, in willingness and freedom. "I delight to do Thy will, O My God," He declared; "yea, Thy law is within My heart." Psalm 40:8. Christ counted no sacrifice too great, no toil too hard, in order to accomplish the work which He came to do. At the age of twelve He said, "Wist ye not that I must be about My Father's business?" Luke 2:49. He had heard the call, and had taken up the work. "My meat," He said, "is to do the will of Him that sent Me, and to finish His work." John 4:34.

Thus we are to serve God. He only serves who acts up to the highest standard of obedience. All who would be sons and daughters of God must prove themselves co-workers with God and Christ and the heavenly angels. This is the test for every soul. Of those who faithfully serve Him the Lord says, "They shall be Mine…in that day when I make up My jewels; and I will spare them, as a man spareth his own son that serveth him." Malachi 3:17.

God's great object in the working out of His providences is to try men, to give them opportunity to develop character. Thus He proves whether they are obedient or disobedient to His commands. Good works do not purchase the love of God, but they reveal that we possess that love. If we surrender the will to God, we shall not work in order to earn God's love. His love as a free gift will be received into the soul, and from love to Him we shall delight to obey His commandments.

There are only two classes in the world today, and only two classes will be recognized in the judgment—those who violate God's law and those who obey it. Christ gives the test by which to prove our loyalty or disloyalty. "If ye love Me," He says, "keep My commandments.… He that hath My commandments, and keepeth them, he it is that loveth Me. And he that loveth Me shall be loved of My Father, and I will love him, and will manifest Myself to him.… He that loveth Me not keepeth not My sayings; and the word which ye hear is not Mine, but the Father's which sent Me." "If ye keep My commandments, ye shall abide in My love; even as I have kept My Father's commandments, and abide in His love." John 14:15–24; 15:10.

23
The Lord's Vineyard

Based on Matthew 21:33–44

The Jewish Nation

The parable of the two sons was followed by the parable of the vineyard. In the one, Christ had set before the Jewish teachers the importance of obedience. In the other, He pointed to the rich blessings bestowed upon Israel, and in these showed God's claim to their obedience. He set before them the glory of God's purpose, which through obedience they might have fulfilled. Withdrawing the veil from the future, He showed how, by failure to fulfill His purpose, the whole nation was forfeiting His blessing, and bringing ruin upon itself.

"There was a certain householder," Christ said, "which planted a vineyard, and hedged it round about, and digged a winepress in it, and built a tower, and let it out to husbandmen, and went into a far country."

A description of this vineyard is given by the prophet Isaiah: "Now will I sing to my wellbeloved a song of my beloved touching His vineyard. My wellbeloved hath a vineyard in a very fruitful hill; and He fenced it, and gathered out the stones thereof, and planted it with the choicest vine, and built a tower in the midst of it, and also made a winepress therein; and He looked that it should bring forth grapes." Isaiah 5:1, 2.

The husbandman chooses a piece of land from the wilderness; he fences, clears, and tills it, and plants it with choice vines, expecting a rich harvest. This plot of ground, in its superiority to the uncultivated waste, he expects to do him honor by showing the results of his care and toil in its cultivation. So God had chosen a people from the world to be trained and educated by Christ. The prophet says, "The vineyard of the Lord of hosts is the house of Israel, and the men of Judah His pleasant plant." Isaiah 5:7. Upon this people God had bestowed great privileges, blessing them richly from His abundant goodness. He looked for them to honor Him by yielding fruit. They were to reveal the principles of His kingdom. In the midst of a fallen, wicked world they were to represent the character of God.

As the Lord's vineyard they were to produce fruit altogether different from that of the heathen nations. These idolatrous peoples had given themselves up to work wickedness. Violence and crime, greed, oppression, and the most corrupt practices, were indulged without restraint. Iniquity, degradation, and misery were the fruits of the corrupt tree. In marked contrast was to be the fruit borne on the vine of God's planting.

It was the privilege of the Jewish nation to represent the character of God as it had been revealed to Moses. In answer to the prayer of Moses, "Show me Thy glory," the Lord promised, "I will make all My goodness pass before thee." Exodus 33:18, 19. "And the Lord passed by before him, and proclaimed, The Lord, the Lord God, merciful and gracious, longsuffering, and abundant in goodness and truth, keeping mercy for thousands, forgiving iniquity and transgression and sin." Exodus 34:6, 7. This was the fruit that God desired from His people. In the purity of their characters, in the holiness of their lives, in their mercy and loving-kindness and compassion, they were to show that "the law of the Lord is perfect, converting the soul." Psalm 19:7.

Through the Jewish nation it was God's purpose to impart rich blessings to all peoples. Through Israel the way was to be prepared for the diffusion of His light to the whole world. The nations of the world, through following corrupt practices, had lost the knowledge of God. Yet in His mercy God did not blot them out of existence. He purposed to give them opportunity for becoming acquainted with Him through His church. He designed that the principles revealed through His people should be the means of restoring the moral image of God in man.

It was for the accomplishment of this purpose that God called Abraham out from his idolatrous kindred and bade him dwell in the land of Canaan. "I will make of thee a great nation," He said, "and I will bless thee, and make thy name great; and thou shalt be a blessing." Genesis 12:2.

The descendants of Abraham, Jacob and his posterity, were brought down to Egypt that in the midst of that great and wicked nation they might reveal the principles of God's kingdom. The integrity of Joseph and his wonderful work in preserving the lives of the whole Egyptian people were a representation of the life of Christ. Moses and many others were witnesses for God.

In bringing forth Israel from Egypt, the Lord again manifested His power and His mercy. His wonderful works in their deliverance from bondage and His dealings with them in their travels through the wilderness were not for their benefit alone. These were to be as an object lesson to the surrounding nations. The Lord revealed Himself as a God above all human authority and greatness. The signs and wonders He wrought in behalf of His people showed His power over nature and over the greatest of those who worshiped nature. God went through the proud land of Egypt as He will go through the earth in the last days. With fire and tempest, earthquake and death, the great I AM redeemed His people. He took them out of the land of bondage. He led them through the "great and terrible wilderness, wherein were fiery serpents, and scorpions, and drought." Deuteronomy 8:15. He brought them forth water out of "the rock and flint," and fed them with "the corn of heaven." Psalm 78:24. "For," said Moses, "the Lord's portion is His people; Jacob is the lot of His inheritance. He found him in a desert land, and in the waste howling wilderness; He led him about, He instructed him, He kept him as the apple of His eye. As an eagle stirreth up her nest, fluttereth over her young, spreadeth abroad her wings, taketh them, beareth them on her wings: so the Lord alone did lead him, and there was no strange god with him." Deuteronomy 32:9–12. Thus He brought them unto Himself, that they might dwell as under the shadow of the Most High.

Christ was the leader of the children of Israel in their wilderness wanderings. Enshrouded in the pillar of cloud by day and the pillar of fire by night, He led and guided them. He preserved them from the perils of the wilderness, He brought them into the land of promise, and in the sight of all the nations that acknowledged not God He established Israel as His own chosen possession, the Lord's vineyard.

To this people were committed the oracles of God. They were hedged about by the precepts of His law, the everlasting principles of truth, justice, and purity. Obedience to these principles was to be their protection, for it would save them from destroying themselves by sinful practices. And as the tower in the vineyard, God placed in the midst of the land His holy temple.

Christ was their instructor. As He had been with them in the wilderness, so He was still to be their teacher and guide. In the tabernacle and the temple His glory dwelt in the holy shekinah above the mercy seat. In their behalf He constantly manifested the riches of His love and patience.

God desired to make of His people Israel a praise and a glory. Every spiritual advantage was given them. God withheld from them nothing favorable to the formation of character that would make them representatives of Himself.

Their obedience to the law of God would make them marvels of prosperity before the nations of the world. He who could give them wisdom and skill in all cunning work would continue to be their teacher, and would ennoble and elevate them through obedience to His laws. If obedient, they would be preserved from the diseases that afflicted other nations, and would be blessed with vigor of intellect. The glory of God, His majesty and power, were to be revealed in all their prosperity. They were to be a kingdom of priests and princes. God furnished them with every facility for becoming the greatest nation on the earth.

In the most definite manner Christ through Moses had set before them God's purpose, and had made plain the terms of their prosperity. "Thou art an holy people unto the Lord thy God," He said; "the Lord thy God hath chosen thee to be a special people unto Himself, above all people that are upon the face of the earth.... Know therefore that the Lord thy God, He is God, the faithful God, which keepeth covenant and mercy with them that love Him and keep His commandments to a thousand generations.... Thou shalt therefore keep the commandments, and the statutes, and the judgments, which I command thee this day, to do them. Wherefore it shall come to pass, if ye hearken to these judgments, and keep, and do them, that the Lord thy God shall keep unto thee the covenant and the mercy which He sware unto thy fathers; and He will love thee, and bless thee, and multiply thee: He will also bless the fruit of thy womb, and the fruit of thy land, thy corn, and thy wine, and thine oil, the increase of thy kine, and the flocks of thy sheep, in the land which He sware unto thy fathers to give thee. Thou shalt be blessed above all people.... And the Lord will take away from thee all sickness, and will put none of the evil diseases of Egypt, which thou knowest, upon thee." Deuteronomy 7:6, 9, 11–15.

If they would keep His commandments, God promised to give them the finest of the wheat, and bring them honey out of the rock. With long life would He satisfy them, and show them His salvation.

Through disobedience to God, Adam and Eve had lost Eden, and because of sin the whole earth was cursed. But if God's people followed His instruction, their land would be restored to fertility and beauty. God Himself gave them directions in regard to the culture of the soil, and they were to co-operate with Him in its restoration. Thus the whole land, under God's control, would become an object lesson of spiritual truth. As in obedience to His natural laws the earth should produce its treasures, so in obedience to His moral law the hearts of the people were to reflect the attributes of His character. Even the heathen would recognize the superiority of those who served and worshiped the living God.

"Behold," said Moses, "I have taught you statutes and judgments, even as the Lord my God commanded me, that ye should do so in the land whither ye go to possess it. Keep therefore and do them; for this is your wisdom and your understanding in the sight of the nations, which shall hear all these statutes, and say, Surely this great nation is a wise and understanding people. For what nation is there so great, who hath God so nigh unto them, as the Lord our God is in all things that we call upon Him for? And what nation is there so great, that hath statutes and judgments so righteous as all this law, which I set before you this day?" Deuteronomy 4:5–8.

The children of Israel were to occupy all the territory which God appointed them. Those nations that rejected the worship and service of the true God were to be dispossessed. But it was God's purpose that by the revelation of His character through Israel men should be drawn unto Him. To all the world the gospel invitation was to be given. Through the teaching of the sacrificial service Christ was to be uplifted before the nations, and all who would look unto Him should live. All who, like Rahab the Canaanite, and Ruth the Moabitess, turned from idolatry to the worship of the true God, were to unite themselves with His chosen people. As the numbers of Israel increased they were to enlarge their borders, until their kingdom should embrace the world.

God desired to bring all peoples under His merciful rule. He desired that the earth should be filled with joy and peace. He created man for happiness, and He longs to fill human hearts with the peace of heaven. He desires that the families below shall be a symbol of the great family above.

But Israel did not fulfill God's purpose. The Lord declared, "I had planted thee a noble vine, wholly a right seed: how then art thou turned into the degenerate plant of a strange vine unto Me?" Jeremiah 2:21. "Israel is an empty vine, he bringeth forth fruit unto himself." Hosea 10:1. "And now, O inhabitants of Jerusalem, and men of Judah, judge, I pray you, betwixt Me and My vineyard. What could have been done more to My vineyard, that I have not done in it? Wherefore when I looked that it should bring forth grapes, brought it forth wild grapes? And now go to; I will tell you what I will do to My vineyard: I will take away the hedge thereof, and it shall be eaten up; and break down the wall thereof, and it shall be trodden down: and I will lay it waste; it shall not be pruned nor digged; but there shall come up briers and thorns: I will also command the clouds that they rain no rain upon it. For…He looked for judgment, but behold oppression; for righteousness, but behold a cry." Isaiah 5:3–7.

The Lord had through Moses set before His people the result of unfaithfulness. By refusing to keep His covenant, they would cut themselves off from the life of God, and His blessing could not come upon them. "Beware," said Moses, "that thou forget not the Lord thy God, in not keeping His commandments, and His judgments, and His statutes, which I command thee this day: lest when thou hast eaten and art full, and hast built goodly houses, and dwelt therein; and when thy herds and thy flocks multiply, and thy silver and thy gold is multiplied, and all that thou hast is multiplied; then thine heart be lifted up, and thou forget the Lord thy God.… And thou say in thine heart, My power and the might of mine hand hath gotten me this wealth.… And it shall be, if thou do at all forget the Lord thy God, and walk after other gods, and serve them, and worship them, I testify against you this day that ye shall surely perish. As the nations which the Lord destroyeth before your face, so shall ye perish; because ye would not be obedient unto the voice of the Lord your God." Deuteronomy 8:11–14, 17, 19, 20.

The warning was not heeded by the Jewish people. They forgot God, and lost sight of their high privilege as His representatives. The blessings they had received brought no blessing to the world. All their advantages were appropriated for their own glorification. They robbed God of the service He required of them, and they robbed their fellow men of religious guidance and a holy example. Like the inhabitants of the antediluvian world, they followed out every imagination of their evil hearts. Thus they made sacred things appear a farce, saying, "The temple of the Lord, the temple of the Lord, are these" (Jeremiah 7:4), while at the same time they were misrepresenting God's character, dishonoring His name, and polluting His sanctuary.

The husbandmen who had been placed in charge of the Lord's vineyard were untrue to their trust. The priests and teachers were not faithful instructors of the people. They did not keep before them the goodness and mercy of God and His claim to their love and service. These husbandmen sought their own glory. They desired to appropriate the fruits of the vineyard. It was their study to attract attention and homage to themselves.

The guilt of these leaders in Israel was not like the guilt of the ordinary sinner. These men stood under the most solemn obligation to God. They had pledged themselves to teach a "Thus saith the Lord" and to bring strict obedience into their practical life. Instead of doing this they were perverting the Scriptures. They laid heavy burdens upon men, enforcing ceremonies that reached to every step in life. The people lived in continual unrest, for they could not fulfill the requirements laid down by the rabbis. As they saw the impossibility of keeping man-made commandments, they became careless in regard to the commandments of God.

The Lord had instructed His people that He was the owner of the vineyard, and that all their possessions were given them in trust to be used for Him. But the priests and teachers did not perform the work of their sacred office as if they were handling the property of God. They were systematically robbing Him of the means and facilities entrusted to them for the advancement of His work. Their covetousness and greed caused them to be despised even by the heathen. Thus the Gentile world was given occasion to misinterpret the character of God and the laws of His kingdom.

With a father's heart, God bore with His people. He pleaded with them by mercies given and mercies withdrawn. Patiently He set their sins before them, and in forbearance waited for their acknowledgment. Prophets and messengers were sent to urge God's claim upon the husbandmen; but instead of being welcomed, they were treated as enemies. The husbandmen persecuted and killed them. God sent still other messengers, but they received the same treatment as the first, only that the husbandmen showed still more determined hatred.

As a last resource, God sent His Son, saying, "They will reverence My Son." But their resistance had made them vindictive, and they said among themselves, "This is the heir; come, let us kill Him, and let us seize on His inheritance." We shall then be left to enjoy the vineyard, and to do as we please with the fruit.

The Jewish rulers did not love God; therefore they cut themselves away from Him, and rejected all His overtures for a just settlement. Christ, the Beloved of God, came to assert the claims of the Owner of the vineyard; but the husbandmen treated Him with marked contempt, saying, We will not have this man to rule over us. They envied Christ's beauty of character. His manner of teaching was far superior to theirs, and they dreaded His success. He remonstrated with them, unveiling their hypocrisy, and showing them the sure results of their course of action. This stirred them to madness. They smarted under the rebukes they could not silence. They hated the high standard of righteousness which Christ continually presented. They saw that His teaching was placing them where their selfishness would be uncloaked, and they determined to kill Him. They hated His example of truthfulness and piety and the elevated spirituality revealed in all He did. His whole life was a reproof to their selfishness, and when the final test came, the test which meant obedience unto eternal life or disobedience unto eternal death, they rejected the Holy One of Israel. When they were asked to choose between Christ and Barabbas, they cried out, "Release unto us Barabbas!" Luke 23:18. And when Pilate asked, "What shall I do then with Jesus?" they cried fiercely, "Let Him be crucified." Matthew 27:22. "Shall I crucify your King?" Pilate asked, and from the priests and rulers came the answer, "We have no king but Caesar." John 19:15. When Pilate washed his hands, saying, "I am innocent of the blood of this just person," the priests joined with the ignorant mob in declaring passionately, "His blood be on us, and on our children." Matthew 27:24, 25.

Thus the Jewish leaders made their choice. Their decision was registered in the book which John saw in the hand of Him that sat upon the throne, the book which no man could open. In all its vindictiveness this decision will appear before them in the day when this book is unsealed by the Lion of the tribe of Judah.

The Jewish people cherished the idea that they were the favorites of heaven, and that they were always to be exalted as the church of God. They were the children of Abraham, they declared, and so firm did the foundation of their prosperity seem to them that they defied earth and heaven to dispossess them of their rights. But by lives of unfaithfulness they were preparing for the condemnation of heaven and for separation from God.

In the parable of the vineyard, after Christ had portrayed before the priests their crowning act of wickedness, He put to them the question, "When the Lord therefore of the vineyard cometh, what will he do unto those husbandmen?" The priests had been following the narrative with deep interest, and without considering the relation of the subject to themselves they joined with the people in answering, "He will miserably destroy those wicked men, and will let out His vineyard unto other husbandmen, which shall render Him the fruits in their seasons."

Unwittingly they had pronounced their own doom. Jesus looked upon them, and under His searching gaze they knew that He read the secrets of their hearts. His divinity flashed out before them with unmistakable power. They saw in the husbandmen a picture of themselves, and they involuntarily exclaimed, "God forbid!"

Solemnly and regretfully Christ asked, "Did ye never read in the scriptures, The stone which the builders rejected, the same is become the head of the corner; this is the Lord's doing, and it is marvelous in our eyes? Therefore say I unto you, The kingdom of God shall be taken from you, and given to a nation bringing forth the fruits thereof. And whosoever shall fall on this stone shall be broken; but on whomsoever it shall fall, it will grind him to powder."

Christ would have averted the doom of the Jewish nation if the people had received Him. But envy and jealousy made them implacable. They determined that they would not receive Jesus of Nazareth as the Messiah. They rejected the Light of the world, and thenceforth their lives were surrounded with darkness as the darkness of midnight. The doom foretold came upon the Jewish nation. Their own fierce passions, uncontrolled, wrought their ruin. In their blind rage they destroyed one another. Their rebellious, stubborn pride brought upon them the wrath of their Roman conquerors. Jerusalem was destroyed, the temple laid in ruins, and its site plowed like a field. The children of Judah perished by the most horrible forms of death. Millions were sold, to serve as bondmen in heathen lands.

As a people the Jews had failed of fulfilling God's purpose, and the vineyard was taken from them. The privileges they had abused, the work they had slighted, was entrusted to others.

The Church of Today

The parable of the vineyard applies not alone to the Jewish nation. It has a lesson for us. The church in this generation has been endowed by God with great privileges and blessings, and He expects corresponding returns.

We have been redeemed by a costly ransom. Only by the greatness of this ransom can we conceive of its results. On this earth, the earth whose soil has been moistened by the tears and blood of the Son of God, are to be brought forth the precious fruits of Paradise. In the lives of God's people the truths of His word are to reveal their glory and excellence. Through His people Christ is to manifest His character and the principles of His kingdom.

Satan seeks to counterwork the work of God, and he is constantly urging men to accept his principles. He represents the chosen people of God as a deluded people. He is an accuser of the brethren, and his accusing power is employed against those who work righteousness. The Lord desires through His people to answer Satan's charges by showing the results of obedience to right principles.

These principles are to be manifest in the individual Christian, in the family, in the church, and in every institution established for God's service.

All are to be symbols of what can be done for the world. They are to be types of the saving power of the truths of the gospel. All are agencies in the fulfillment of God's great purpose for the human race.

The Jewish leaders looked with pride upon their magnificent temple, and the imposing rites of their religious service; but justice, mercy, and the love of God were lacking. The glory of the temple, the splendor of their service, could not recommend them to God; for that which alone is of value in His sight they did not offer. They did not bring Him the sacrifice of a humble and contrite spirit. It is when the vital principles of the kingdom of God are lost that ceremonies become multitudinous and extravagant. It is when the character building is neglected, when the adornment of the soul is lacking, when the simplicity of godliness is lost sight of, that pride and love of display demand magnificent church edifices, splendid adornings, and imposing ceremonials. In all this God is not honored. A fashionable religion that consists of ceremonies, pretense, and display, is not acceptable to Him. Its services call forth no response from the heavenly messengers.

The church is very precious in God's sight. He values it, not for its external advantages, but for the sincere piety which distinguishes it from the world. He estimates it according to the growth of the members in the knowledge of Christ, according to their progress in spiritual experience.

Christ hungers to receive from His vineyard the fruit of holiness and unselfishness. He looks for the principles of love and goodness. Not all the beauty of art can bear comparison with the beauty of temper and character to be revealed in those who are Christ's representatives. It is the atmosphere of grace which surrounds the soul of the believer, the Holy Spirit working upon mind and heart, that makes him a savor of life unto life, and enables God to bless his work.

A congregation may be the poorest in the land. It may be without the attraction of any outward show; but if the members possess the principles of the character of Christ, they will have His joy in their souls. Angels will unite with them in their worship. The praise and thanksgiving from grateful hearts will ascend to God as a sweet oblation.

The Lord desires us to make mention of His goodness and tell of His power. He is honored by the expression of praise and thanksgiving. He says, "Whoso offereth praise glorifieth Me." Psalm 50:23. The people of Israel, as they journeyed through the wilderness, praised God in sacred song. The commandments and promises of the Lord were set to music, and all along the journey these were sung by the pilgrim travelers. And in Canaan as they met at their sacred feasts God's wonderful works were to be recounted, and grateful thanksgiving was to be offered to His name. God desired that the whole life of His people should be a life of praise. Thus His way was to be made "known upon earth," His "saving health among all nations." Psalm 67:2.

So it should be now. The people of the world are worshiping false gods. They are to be turned from their false worship, not by hearing denunciation of their idols, but by beholding something better. God's goodness is to be made known. "Ye are My witnesses, saith the Lord, that I am God." Isaiah 43:12.

The Lord desires us to appreciate the great plan of redemption, to realize our high privilege as the children of God, and to walk before Him in obedience, with grateful thanksgiving. He desires us to serve Him in newness of life, with gladness every day. He longs to see gratitude welling up in our hearts because our names are written in the Lamb's book of life, because we may cast all our care upon Him who cares for us. He bids us rejoice because we are the heritage of the Lord, because the righteousness of Christ is the white robe of His saints, because we have the blessed hope of the soon coming of our Saviour.

To praise God in fullness and sincerity of heart is as much a duty as is prayer. We are to show to the world and to all the heavenly intelligences that we appreciate the wonderful love of God for fallen humanity and that we are expecting larger and yet larger blessings from His infinite fullness. Far more than we do, we need to speak of the precious chapters in our experience. After a special outpouring of the Holy Spirit, our joy in the Lord and our efficiency in His service would be greatly increased by recounting His goodness and His wonderful works in behalf of His children.

These exercises drive back the power of Satan. They expel the spirit of murmuring and complaint, and the tempter loses ground. They cultivate those attributes of character which will fit the dwellers on earth for the heavenly mansions.

Such a testimony will have an influence upon others. No more effective means can be employed for winning souls to Christ.

We are to praise God by tangible service, by doing all in our power to advance the glory of His name. God imparts His gifts to us that we also may give, and thus make known His character to the world. Under the Jewish economy, gifts and offerings formed an essential part of God's worship. The Israelites were taught to devote a tithe of all their income to the service of the sanctuary. Besides this they were to bring sin offerings, free-will gifts, and offerings of gratitude. These were the means for supporting the ministry of the gospel for that time. God expects no less from us than He expected from His people anciently. The great work for the salvation of souls must be carried forward. In the tithe, with gifts and offerings, He has made provision for this work. Thus He intends that the ministry of the gospel shall be sustained. He claims the tithe as His own, and it should ever be regarded as a sacred reserve, to be placed in His treasury for the benefit of His cause. He asks also for our free-will gifts and offerings of gratitude.

All are to be devoted to the sending of the gospel unto the uttermost parts of the earth.

Service to God includes personal ministry. By personal effort we are to co-operate with Him for the saving of the world. Christ's commission, "Go ye into all the world, and preach the gospel to every creature," is spoken to every one of His followers. (Mark 16:15.) All who are ordained unto the life of Christ are ordained to work for the salvation of their fellow men. Their hearts will throb in unison with the heart of Christ. The same longing for souls that He has felt will be manifest in them. Not all can fill the same place in the work, but there is a place and a work for all.

In ancient times, Abraham, Isaac, Jacob, Moses with his meekness and wisdom, and Joshua with his varied capabilities, were all enlisted in God's service. The music of Miriam, the courage and piety of Deborah, the filial affection of Ruth, the obedience and faithfulness of Samuel, the stern fidelity of Elijah, the softening, subduing influence of Elisha—all were needed. So now all upon whom God's blessing has been bestowed are to respond by actual service; every gift is to be employed for the advancement of His kingdom and the glory of His name.

All who receive Christ as a personal Saviour are to demonstrate the truth of the gospel and its saving power upon the life. God makes no requirement without making provision for its fulfillment. Through the grace of Christ we may accomplish everything that God requires. All the riches of heaven are to be revealed through God's people. "Herein is My Father glorified," Christ says, "that ye bear much fruit; so shall ye be My disciples." John 15:8.

God claims the whole earth as His vineyard. Though now in the hands of the usurper, it belongs to God. By redemption no less than by creation it is His. For the world Christ's sacrifice was made. "God so loved the world, that He gave His only begotten Son." John 3:16. It is through that one gift that every other is imparted to men. Daily the whole world receives blessing from God. Every drop of rain, every ray of light shed on our unthankful race, every leaf and flower and fruit, testifies to God's long forbearance and His great love.

And what returns are made to the great Giver? How are men treating the claims of God? To whom are the masses of mankind giving the service of their lives? They are serving mammon. Wealth, position, pleasure in the world, is their aim. Wealth is gained by robbery, not of man only, but of God. Men are using His gifts to gratify their selfishness. Everything they can grasp is made to minister to their greed and their love of selfish pleasure.

The sin of the world today is the sin that brought destruction upon Israel. Ingratitude to God, the neglect of opportunities and blessings, the selfish appropriation of God's gifts—these were comprised in the sin that brought wrath upon Israel. They are bringing ruin upon the world today.

The tears which Christ shed upon Olivet as He stood overlooking the chosen city were not for Jerusalem alone. In the fate of Jerusalem He beheld the destruction of the world.

"If thou hadst known, even thou, at least in this thy day, the things which belong unto thy peace! but now they are hid from thine eyes." Luke 19:42.

"In this thy day." The day is nearing its close. The period of mercy and privilege is well-nigh ended. The clouds of vengeance are gathering. The rejecters of God's grace are about to be involved in swift and irretrievable ruin.

Yet the world is asleep. The people know not the time of their visitation.

In this crisis, where is the church to be found? Are its members meeting the claims of God? Are they fulfilling His commission, and representing His character to the world? Are they urging upon the attention of their fellow men the last merciful message of warning?

Men are in peril. Multitudes are perishing. But how few of the professed followers of Christ are burdened for these souls. The destiny of a world hangs in the balance; but this hardly moves even those who claim to believe the most far-reaching truth ever given to mortals. There is a lack of that love which led Christ to leave His heavenly home and take man's nature that humanity might touch humanity and draw humanity to divinity. There is a stupor, a paralysis, upon the people of God, which prevents them from understanding the duty of the hour.

When the Israelites entered Canaan, they did not fulfill God's purpose by taking possession of the whole land. After making a partial conquest, they settled down to enjoy the fruit of their victories. In their unbelief and love of ease, they congregated in the portions already conquered instead of pushing forward to occupy new territory. Thus they began to depart from God. By their failure to carry out His purpose, they made it impossible for Him to fulfill to them His promise of blessing. Is not the church of today doing the same thing? With the whole world before them in need of the gospel, professed Christians congregate where they themselves can enjoy gospel privileges. They do not feel the necessity of occupying new territory, carrying the message of salvation into regions beyond. They refuse to fulfill Christ's commission, "Go ye into all the world, and preach the gospel to every creature." Mark 16:15. Are they less guilty than was the Jewish church?

The professed followers of Christ are on trial before the heavenly universe; but the coldness of their zeal and the feebleness of their efforts in God's service mark them as unfaithful. If what they are doing were the best they could do, condemnation would not rest upon them; but were their hearts enlisted in the work, they could do much more. They know and the world knows that they have to a great degree lost the spirit of self-denial and cross bearing. Many there are against whose names will be found written in the books of heaven, Not producers, but consumers. By many who bear Christ's name, His glory is obscured, His beauty veiled, His honor withheld.

There are many whose names are on the church books, but who are not under Christ's rule. They are not heeding His instruction or doing His work. Therefore they are under the control of the enemy. They are doing no positive good; therefore they are doing incalculable harm. Because their influence is not a savor of life unto life, it is a savor of death unto death.

The Lord says, "Shall I not visit for these things?" Jeremiah 5:9. Because they failed of fulfilling God's purpose, the children of Israel were set aside, and God's call was extended to other peoples. If these too prove unfaithful, will they not in like manner be rejected?

In the parable of the vineyard it was the husbandmen whom Christ pronounced guilty. It was they who had refused to return to their lord the fruit of his ground. In the Jewish nation it was the priests and teachers who, by misleading the people, had robbed God of the service which He claimed. It was they who turned the nation away from Christ.

The law of God unmixed with human tradition was presented by Christ as the great standard of obedience. This aroused the enmity of the rabbis. They had set human teaching above God's word, and had turned the people away from His precepts. They would not give up their man-made commandments in order to obey the requirements of the word of God. They would not, for the truth's sake, sacrifice the pride of reason and the praise of men. When Christ came, presenting to the nation the claims of God, the priests and elders denied His right to interpose between them and the people. They would not accept His rebukes and warnings, and they set themselves to turn the people against Him and to compass His destruction.

For the rejection of Christ, with the results that followed, they were responsible. A nation's sin and a nation's ruin were due to the religious leaders.

In our day are not the same influences at work? Of the husbandmen of the Lord's vineyard are not many following in the steps of the Jewish leaders? Are not religious teachers turning men away from the plain requirements of the word of God? Instead of educating them in obedience to God's law, are they not educating them in transgression? From many of the pulpits of the churches the people are taught that the law of God is not binding upon them. Human traditions, ordinances, and customs are exalted. Pride and self-satisfaction because of the gifts of God are fostered, while the claims of God are ignored.

In setting aside the law of God, men know not what they are doing. God's law is the transcript of His character. It embodies the principles of His kingdom. He who refuses to accept these principles is placing himself outside the channel where God's blessings flow.

The glorious possibilities set before Israel could be realized only through obedience to God's commandments. The same elevation of character, the same fulness of blessing—blessing on mind and soul and body, blessing on house and field, blessing for this life and for the life to come-is possible for us only through obedience.

In the spiritual as in the natural world, obedience to the laws of God is the condition of fruit bearing. And when men teach the people to disregard God's commandments, they are preventing them from bearing fruit to His glory. They are guilty of withholding from the Lord the fruits of His vineyard.

To us God's messengers come at the bidding of the Master. They come demanding, as did Christ, obedience to the word of God. They present His claim to the fruits of the vineyard, the fruits of love, and humility, and self-sacrificing service. Like the Jewish leaders, are not many of the husbandmen of the vineyard stirred to anger? When the claim of God's law is set before the people, do not these teachers use their influence in leading men to reject it? Such teachers God calls unfaithful servants.

The words of God to ancient Israel have a solemn warning to the church and its leaders today. Of Israel the Lord said, "I have written to him the great things of My law; but they were counted as a strange thing." Hosea 8:12. And to the priests and teachers He declared, "My people are destroyed for lack of knowledge; because thou hast rejected knowledge, I will also reject thee;...seeing thou hast forgotten the law of thy God, I will also forget thy children." Hosea 4:6.

Shall the warnings from God be passed by unheeded? Shall the opportunities for service be unimproved? Shall the world's scorn, the pride of reason, conformity to human customs and traditions, hold the professed followers of Christ from service to Him? Will they reject God's word as the Jewish leaders rejected Christ? The result of Israel's sin is before us. Will the church of today take warning?

"If some of the branches be broken off, and thou, being a wild olive tree, wert graffed in among them, and with them partakest of the root and fatness of the olive tree; boast not.... Because of unbelief they were broken off, and thou standest by faith. Be not highminded, but fear; for if God spared not the natural branches, take heed lest He also spare not thee." Romans 11:17–21.

24
Without a Wedding Garment

Based on Matthew 22:1–14

The parable of the wedding garment opens before us a lesson of the highest consequence. By the marriage is represented the union of humanity with divinity; the wedding garment represents the character which all must possess who shall be accounted fit guests for the wedding.

In this parable, as in that of the great supper, are illustrated the gospel invitation, its rejection by the Jewish people, and the call of mercy to the Gentiles. But on the part of those who reject the invitation, this parable brings to view a deeper insult and a more dreadful punishment. The call to the feast is a king's invitation. It proceeds from one who is vested with power to command. It confers high honor. Yet the honor is unappreciated. The king's authority is despised. While the householder's invitation was regarded with indifference, the king's is met with insult and murder. They treated his servants with scorn, despitefully using them and slaying them.

The householder, on seeing his invitation slighted, declared that none of the men who are bidden should taste of his supper. But for those who had done despite to the king, more than exclusion from his presence and his table is decreed. "He sent forth his armies, and destroyed those murderers, and burned up their city."

In both parables the feast is provided with guests, but the second shows that there is a preparation to be made by all who attend the feast. Those who neglect this preparation are cast out. "The king came in to see the guests," and "saw there a man which had not on a wedding garment; and he saith unto him, Friend, how camest thou in hither not having a wedding garment? And he was speechless. Then said the king to the servants, Bind him hand and foot, and take him away, and cast him into outer darkness; there shall be weeping and gnashing of teeth."

The call to the feast had been given by Christ's disciples. Our Lord had sent out the twelve and afterward the seventy, proclaiming that the kingdom of God was at hand, and calling upon men to repent and believe the gospel. But the call was not heeded. Those who are bidden to the feast did not come. The servants were sent out later to say, "Behold, I have prepared my dinner; my oxen and my fatlings are killed, and all things are ready: come unto the marriage." This was the message borne to the Jewish nation after the crucifixion of Christ; but the nation that claimed to be God's peculiar people rejected the gospel brought to them in the power of the Holy Spirit. Many did this in the most scornful manner. Others were so exasperated by the offer of salvation, the offer of pardon for rejecting the Lord of glory, that they turned upon the bearers of the message. There was "a great persecution." Acts 8:1. Many both of men and women were thrust into prison, and some of the Lord's messengers, as Stephen and James, were put to death.

Thus the Jewish people sealed their rejection of God's mercy. The result was foretold by Christ in the parable. The king "sent forth his armies, and destroyed those murderers, and burned up their city." The judgment pronounced came upon the Jews in the destruction of Jerusalem and the scattering of the nation.

The third call to the feast represents the giving of the gospel to the Gentiles. The king said, "The wedding is ready, but they which were bidden were not worthy. Go ye therefore into the highways, and as many as ye shall find, bid to the marriage."

The king's servants who went out into the highways "gathered together all as many as they found, both bad and good." It was a mixed company. Some of them had no more real regard for the giver of the feast than had the ones who rejected the call. The class first bidden could not afford, they thought, to sacrifice any worldly advantage for the sake of attending the king's banquet. And of those who accepted the invitation, there were some who thought only of benefiting themselves. They came to share the provisions of the feast, but had no desire to honor the king.

When the king came in to view the guests, the real character of all was revealed. For every guest at the feast there had been provided a wedding garment. This garment was a gift from the king. By wearing it the guests showed their respect for the giver of the feast. But one man was clothed in his common citizen dress. He had refused to make the preparation required by the king. The garment provided for him at great cost he disdained to wear. Thus he insulted his lord. To the king's demand, "How camest thou in hither not having a wedding garment?" he could answer nothing. He was self-condemned. Then the king said, "Bind him hand and foot, and take him away, and cast him into outer darkness."

By the king's examination of the guests at the feast is represented a work of judgment. The guests at the gospel feast are those who profess to serve God, those whose names are written in the book of life. But not all who profess to be Christians are true disciples. Before the final reward is given, it must be decided who are fitted to share the inheritance of the righteous. This decision must be made prior to the second coming of Christ in the clouds of heaven; for when He comes, His reward is with Him, "to give every man according as his work shall be." Revelation 22:12. Before His coming, then, the character of every man's work will have been determined, and to every one of Christ's followers the reward will have been apportioned according to his deeds.

It is while men are still dwelling upon the earth that the work of investigative judgment takes place in the courts of heaven. The lives of all His professed followers pass in review before God. All are examined according to the record of the books of heaven, and according to his deeds the destiny of each is forever fixed.

By the wedding garment in the parable is represented the pure, spotless character which Christ's true followers will possess. To the church it is given "that she should be arrayed in fine linen, clean and white," "not having spot, or wrinkle, or any such thing." The fine linen, says the Scripture, "is the righteousness of saints." Revelation 19:8, Ephesians 5:27. It is the righteousness of Christ, His own unblemished character, that through faith is imparted to all who receive Him as their personal Saviour.

The white robe of innocence was worn by our first parents when they were placed by God in holy Eden. They lived in perfect conformity to the will of God. All the strength of their affections was given to their heavenly Father. A beautiful soft light, the light of God, enshrouded the holy pair. This robe of light was a symbol of their spiritual garments of heavenly innocence. Had they remained true to God it would ever have continued to enshroud them. But when sin entered, they severed their connection with God, and the light that had encircled them departed. Naked and ashamed, they tried to supply the place of the heavenly garments by sewing together fig leaves for a covering.

This is what the transgressors of God's law have done ever since the day of Adam and Eve's disobedience. They have sewed together fig leaves to cover the nakedness caused by transgression. They have worn the garments of their own devising, by works of their own they have tried to cover their sins, and make themselves acceptable with God.

But this they can never do. Nothing can man devise to supply the place of his lost robe of innocence. No fig-leaf garment, no worldly citizen dress, can be worn by those who sit down with Christ and angels at the marriage supper of the Lamb.

Only the covering which Christ Himself has provided can make us meet to appear in God's presence. This covering, the robe of His own righteousness, Christ will put upon every repenting, believing soul. "I counsel thee," He says, "to buy of Me…white raiment, that thou mayest be clothed, and that the shame of thy nakedness do not appear." Revelation 3:18.

This robe, woven in the loom of heaven, has in it not one thread of human devising. Christ in His humanity wrought out a perfect character, and this character He offers to impart to us. "All our righteousness are as filthy rags." Isaiah 64:6. Everything that we of ourselves can do is defiled by sin. But the Son of God "was manifested to take away our sins; and in Him is no sin." Sin is defined to be "the transgression of the law." 1 John 3:5, 4. But

Christ was obedient to every requirement of the law. He said of Himself, "I delight to do Thy will, O My God; yea, Thy law is within My heart." Psalm 40:8. When on earth, He said to His disciples, "I have kept My Father's commandments." John 15:10. By His perfect obedience He has made it possible for every human being to obey God's commandments. When we submit ourselves to Christ, the heart is united with His heart, the will is merged in His will, the mind becomes one with His mind, the thoughts are brought into captivity to Him; we live His life. This is what it means to be clothed with the garment of His righteousness. Then as the Lord looks upon us He sees, not the fig-leaf garment, not the nakedness and deformity of sin, but His own robe of righteousness, which is perfect obedience to the law of Jehovah.

The guests at the marriage feast were inspected by the king. Only those were accepted who had obeyed his requirements and put on the wedding garment. So it is with the guests at the gospel feast. All must pass the scrutiny of the great King, and only those are received who have put on the robe of Christ's righteousness.

Righteousness is right doing, and it is by their deeds that all will be judged. Our characters are revealed by what we do. The works show whether the faith is genuine.

It is not enough for us to believe that Jesus is not an impostor, and that the religion of the Bible is no cunningly devised fable. We may believe that the name of Jesus is the only name under heaven whereby man may be saved, and yet we may not through faith make Him our personal Saviour. It is not enough to believe the theory of truth. It is not enough to make a profession of faith in Christ and have our names registered on the church roll. "He that keepeth His commandments dwelleth in Him, and He in him. And hereby we know that He abideth in us, by the Spirit which He hath given us." "Hereby we do know that we know Him if we keep His commandments." 1 John 3:24; 2:3. This is the genuine evidence of conversion. Whatever our profession, it amounts to nothing unless Christ is revealed in works of righteousness.

The truth is to be planted in the heart. It is to control the mind and regulate the affections. The whole character must be stamped with the divine utterances. Every jot and tittle of the word of God is to be brought into the daily practice.

He who becomes a partaker of the divine nature will be in harmony with God's great standard of righteousness, His holy law. This is the rule by which God measures the actions of men. This will be the test of character in the judgment.

There are many who claim that by the death of Christ the law was abrogated; but in this they contradict Christ's own words, "Think not that I am come to destroy the law, or the prophets.... Till heaven and earth pass, one jot or one tittle shall in no wise pass from the law." Matthew 5:17, 18. It was to atone for man's transgression of the law that Christ laid down His life. Could the law have been changed or set aside, then Christ need not have died. By His life on earth He honored the law of God. By His death He established it. He gave His life as a sacrifice, not to destroy God's law, not to create a lower standard, but that justice might be maintained, that the law might be shown to be immutable, that it might stand fast forever.

Satan had claimed that it was impossible for man to obey God's commandments; and in our own strength it is true that we cannot obey them. But Christ came in the form of humanity, and by His perfect obedience He proved that humanity and divinity combined can obey every one of God's precepts.

"As many as received Him, to them gave He power to become the sons of God, even to them that believe on His name." John 1:12. This power is not in the human agent. It is the power of God. When a soul receives Christ, he receives power to live the life of Christ.

God requires perfection of His children. His law is a transcript of His own character, and it is the standard of all character. This infinite standard is presented to all that there may be no mistake in regard to the kind of people whom God will have to compose His kingdom. The life of Christ on earth was a perfect expression of God's law, and when those who claim to be children of God become Christlike in character, they will be obedient to God's commandments. Then the Lord can trust them to be of the number who shall compose the family of heaven. Clothed in the glorious apparel of Christ's righteousness, they have a place at the King's feast. They have a right to join the blood-washed throng.

The man who came to the feast without a wedding garment represents the condition of many in our world today. They profess to be Christians, and lay claim to the blessings and privileges of the gospel; yet they feel no need of a transformation of character. They have never felt true repentance for sin. They do not realize their need of Christ or exercise faith in Him. They have not overcome their hereditary or cultivated tendencies to wrongdoing. Yet they think that they are good enough in themselves, and they rest upon their own merits instead of trusting in Christ. Hearers of the word, they come to the banquet, but they have not put on the robe of Christ's righteousness.

Many who call themselves Christians are mere human moralists. They have refused the gift which alone could enable them to honor Christ by representing Him to the world. The work of the Holy Spirit is to them a strange work. They are not doers of the word. The heavenly principles that distinguish those who are one with Christ from those who are one with the world have become almost indistinguishable. The professed followers of Christ are no longer a separate and peculiar people. The line of demarcation is indistinct. The people are subordinating themselves to the world, to its practices, its customs, its selfishness. The church has gone over to the world in transgression of the law, when the world should have come over to the church in obedience to the law. Daily the church is being converted to the world.

All these expect to be saved by Christ's death, while they refuse to live His self-sacrificing life. They extol the riches of free grace, and attempt to cover themselves with an appearance of righteousness, hoping to screen their defects of character; but their efforts will be of no avail in the day of God.

The righteousness of Christ will not cover one cherished sin. A man may be a law-breaker in heart; yet if he commits no outward act of transgression, he may be regarded by the world as possessing great integrity. But God's law looks into the secrets of the heart. Every act is judged by the motives that prompt it. Only that which is in accord with the principles of God's law will stand in the judgment.

God is love. He has shown that love in the gift of Christ. When "He gave His only begotten Son, that whosoever believeth in Him should not perish, but have everlasting life," He withheld nothing from His purchased possession. (John 3:16.) He gave all heaven, from which we may draw strength and efficiency, that we be not repulsed or overcome by our great adversary. But the love of God does not lead Him to excuse sin. He did not excuse it in Satan; He did not excuse it in Adam or in Cain; nor will He excuse it in any other of the children of men. He will not connive at our sins or overlook our defects of character. He expects us to overcome in His name.

Those who reject the gift of Christ's righteousness are rejecting the attributes of character which would constitute them the sons and daughters of God. They are rejecting that which alone could give them a fitness for a place at the marriage feast.

In the parable, when the king inquired, "How camest thou in hither not having a wedding garment?" the man was speechless. So it will be in the great judgment day. Men may now excuse their defects of character, but in that day they will offer no excuse.

The professed churches of Christ in this generation are exalted to the highest privileges. The Lord has been revealed to us in ever-increasing light. Our privileges are far greater than were the privileges of God's ancient people. We have not only the great light committed to Israel, but we have the increased evidence of the great salvation brought to us through Christ. That which was type and symbol to the Jews is reality to us. They had the Old Testament history; we have that and the New Testament also. We have the assurance of a Saviour who has come, a Saviour who has been crucified, who has risen, and over the rent sepulcher of Joseph has proclaimed, "I am the resurrection and the life." In our knowledge of Christ and His love the kingdom of God is placed in the midst of us. Christ is revealed to us in sermons and chanted to us in songs. The spiritual banquet is set before us in rich abundance. The wedding garment, provided at infinite cost, is freely offered to every soul. By the messengers of God are presented to us the righteousness of Christ, justification by faith, the exceeding great and precious promises of God's word, free access to the Father by Christ, the comfort of the Spirit, the well-grounded assurance of eternal life in the kingdom of God. What could God do for us that He has not done in providing the great supper, the heavenly banquet?

In heaven it is said by the ministering angels: The ministry which we have been commissioned to perform we have done. We pressed back the army of evil angels. We sent brightness and light into the souls of men, quickening their memory of the love of God expressed in Jesus. We attracted their eyes to the cross of Christ. Their hearts were deeply moved by a sense of the sin that crucified the Son of God. They were convicted. They saw the steps to be taken in conversion; they felt the power of the gospel; their hearts were made tender as they saw the sweetness of the love of God. They beheld the beauty of the character of Christ. But with the many it was all in vain. They would not surrender their own habits and character. They would not put off the garments of earth in order to be clothed with the robe of heaven. Their hearts were given to covetousness. They loved the associations of the world more than they loved their God.

Solemn will be the day of final decision. In prophetic vision the apostle John describes it: "I saw a great white throne, and Him that sat on it, from whose face the earth and the heaven fled away; and there was found no place for them. And I saw the dead, small and great, stand before God; and the books were opened; and another book was opened, which is the book of life; and the dead were judged out of those things which were written in the books, according to their works." Revelation 20:11, 12.

Sad will be the retrospect in that day when men stand face to face with eternity. The whole life will present itself just as it has been. The world's pleasures, riches, and honors will not then seem so important. Men will then see that the righteousness they despised is alone of value. They will see that they have fashioned their characters under the deceptive allurements of Satan. The garments they have chosen are the badge of their allegiance to the first great apostate. Then they will see the results of their choice. They will have a knowledge of what it means to transgress the commandments of God.

There will be no future probation in which to prepare for eternity. It is in this life that we are to put on the robe of Christ's righteousness. This is our only opportunity to form characters for the home which Christ has made ready for those who obey His commandments.

The days of our probation are fast closing. The end is near. To us the warning is given, "Take heed to yourselves, lest at any time your hearts be overcharged with surfeiting, and drunkenness, and cares of this life, and so that day come upon you unawares." Luke 21:34. Beware lest it find you unready. Take heed lest you be found at the King's feast without a wedding garment.

"In such an hour as ye think not the Son of man cometh." "Blessed is he that watcheth, and keepeth his garments, lest he walk naked, and they see his shame." Matthew 24:44; Revelation 16:15.

25
Talents

Based on Matthew 25:13–30

Christ on the Mount of Olives had spoken to His disciples of His second advent to the world. He had specified certain signs that were to show when His coming was near, and had bidden His disciples watch and be ready. Again He repeated the warning, "Watch therefore; for ye know neither the day nor the hour wherein the Son of man cometh." Then He showed what it means to watch for His coming. The time is to be spent, not in idle waiting, but in diligent working. This lesson He taught in the parable of the talents.

"The kingdom of heaven," He said, "is as a man traveling into a far country, who called his own servants, and delivered unto them his goods. And unto one he gave five talents, to another two, and to another one; to every man according to his several ability; and straightway took his journey."

The man traveling into a far country represents Christ, who, when speaking this parable, was soon to depart from this earth to heaven. The "bondservants" (R.V.), or slaves, of the parable, represent the followers of Christ. We are not our own. We have been "bought with a price" (1 Corinthians 6:20), not "with corruptible things, as silver and gold,...but with the precious blood of Christ" (1 Peter 1:18, 19); "that they which live should not henceforth live unto themselves, but unto Him which died for them, and rose again" (2 Corinthians 5:15).

All men have been bought with this infinite price. By pouring the whole treasury of heaven into this world, by giving us in Christ all heaven, God has purchased the will, the affections, the mind, the soul, of every human being. Whether believers or unbelievers, all men are the Lord's property. All are called to do service for Him, and for the manner in which they have met this claim, all will be required to render an account at the great judgment day.

But the claims of God are not recognized by all. It is those who profess to have accepted Christ's service who in the parable are represented as His own servants.

Christ's followers have been redeemed for service. Our Lord teaches that the true object of life is ministry. Christ Himself was a worker, and to all His followers He gives the law of service—service to God and to their fellow men. Here Christ has presented to the world a higher conception of life than they had ever known. By living to minister for others, man is brought into connection with Christ. The law of service becomes the connecting link which binds us to God and to our fellow men.

To His servants Christ commits "His goods"—something to be put to use for Him. He gives "to every man his work." Each has his place in the eternal plan of heaven. Each is to work in co-operation with Christ for the salvation of souls. Not more surely is the place prepared for us in the heavenly mansions than is the special place designated on earth where we are to work for God.

Gifts of the Holy Spirit

The talents that Christ entrusts to His church represent especially the gifts and blessings imparted by the Holy Spirit. "To one is given by the Spirit the word of wisdom; to another the word of knowledge by the same Spirit; to another faith by the same Spirit; to another the gifts of healing by the same Spirit; to another the working of miracles; to another prophecy; to another discerning of spirits; to another divers kinds of tongues; to another the interpretation of tongues: but all these worketh that one and the selfsame Spirit, dividing to every man severally as He will." 1 Corinthians 12:8–11. All men do not receive the same gifts, but to every servant of the Master some gift of the Spirit is promised.

Before He left His disciples, Christ "breathed on them, and saith unto them, Receive ye the Holy Ghost." John 20:22. Again He said, "Behold, I send the promise of My Father upon you." Luke 24:29. But not until after the ascension was the gift received in its fullness. Not until through faith and prayer the disciples had surrendered themselves fully for His working was the outpouring of the Spirit received. Then in a special sense the goods of heaven were committed to the followers of Christ. "When He ascended up on high, He led captivity captive, and gave gifts unto men." Ephesians 4:8, 7. "Unto every one of us is given grace, according to the measure of the gift of Christ," the Spirit "dividing to every man severally as He will." 1 Corinthians 12:11. The gifts are already ours in Christ, but their actual possession depends upon our reception of the Spirit of God.

The promise of the Spirit is not appreciated as it should be. Its fulfillment is not realized as it might be. It is the absence of the Spirit that makes the gospel ministry so powerless. Learning, talents, eloquence, every natural or acquired endowment, may be possessed; but without the presence of the Spirit of God, no heart will be touched, no sinner be won to Christ. On the other hand, if they are connected with Christ, if the gifts of the Spirit are theirs, the poorest and most ignorant of His disciples will have a power that will tell upon hearts. God makes them the channel for the outworking of the highest influence in the universe.

Other Talents

The special gifts of the Spirit are not the only talents represented in the parable. It includes all gifts and endowments, whether original or acquired, natural or spiritual. All are to be employed in Christ's service. In becoming His disciples, we surrender ourselves to Him with all that we are and have. These gifts He returns to us purified and ennobled, to be used for His glory in blessing our fellow men.

To every man God has given "according to his several ability." The talents are not apportioned capriciously. He who has ability to use five talents receives five. He who can improve but two, receives two. He who can wisely use only one, receives one. None need lament that they have not received larger gifts; for He who has apportioned to every man is equally honored by the improvement of each trust, whether it be great or small. The one to whom five talents have been committed is to render the improvement of five; he who has but one, the improvement of one. God expects returns "according to that a man hath, and not according to that he hath not." 2 Corinthians 8:12.

In the parable he that had "received the five talents went and traded with the same, and made them other five talents; and likewise he that had received two, he also gained other two."

The talents, however few, are to be put to use. The question that most concerns us is not, How much have I received? but, What am I doing with that which I have? The development of all our powers is the first duty we owe to God and to our fellow men. No one who is not growing daily in capability and usefulness is fulfilling the purpose of life. In making a profession of faith in Christ we pledge ourselves to become all that it is possible for us to be as workers for the Master, and we should cultivate every faculty to the highest degree of perfection, that we may do the greatest amount of good of which we are capable.

The Lord has a great work to be done, and He will bequeath the most in the future life to those who do the most faithful, willing service in the present life. The Lord chooses His own agents, and each day under different circumstances He gives them a trial in His plan of operation. In each true-hearted endeavor to work out His plan, He chooses His agents not because they are perfect but because, through a connection with Him, they may gain perfection.

God will accept only those who are determined to aim high. He places every human agent under obligation to do his best. Moral perfection is required of all. Never should we lower the standard of righteousness in order to accommodate inherited or cultivated tendencies to wrong-doing. We need to understand that imperfection of character is sin. All righteous attributes of character dwell in God as a perfect, harmonious whole, and every one who receives Christ as a personal Saviour is privileged to possess these attributes.

And those who would be workers together with God must strive for perfection of every organ of the body and quality of the mind. True education is the preparation of the physical, mental, and moral powers for the performance of every duty; it is the training of body, mind, and soul for divine service. This is the education that will endure unto eternal life.

Of every Christian the Lord requires growth in efficiency and capability in every line. Christ has paid us our wages, even His own blood and suffering, to secure our willing service. He came to our world to give us an example of how we should work, and what spirit we should bring into our labor. He desires us to study how we can best advance His work and glorify His name in the world, crowning with honor, with the greatest love and devotion, the Father who "so loved the world, that He gave His only begotten Son, that whosoever believeth in Him should not perish, but have everlasting life." John 3:16.

But Christ has given us no assurance that to attain perfection of character is an easy matter. A noble, all-round character is not inherited. It does not come to us by accident. A noble character is earned by individual effort through the merits and grace of Christ. God gives the talents, the powers of the mind; we form the character. It is formed by hard, stern battles with self. Conflict after conflict must be waged against hereditary tendencies. We shall have to criticize ourselves closely, and allow not one unfavorable trait to remain uncorrected.

Let no one say, I cannot remedy my defects of character. If you come to this decision, you will certainly fail of obtaining everlasting life. The impossibility lies in your own will. If you will not, then you can not overcome. The real difficulty arises from the corruption of an unsanctified heart, and an unwillingness to submit to the control of God.

Many whom God has qualified to do excellent work accomplish very little, because they attempt little. Thousands pass through life as if they had no definite object for which to live, no standard to reach. Such will obtain a reward proportionate to their works.

Remember that you will never reach a higher standard than you yourself set. Then set your mark high, and step by step, even though it be by painful effort, by self-denial and sacrifice, ascend the whole length of the ladder of progress. Let nothing hinder you. Fate has not woven its meshes about any human being so firmly that he need remain helpless and in uncertainty. Opposing circumstances should create a firm determination to overcome them. The breaking down of one barrier will give greater ability and courage to go forward. Press with determination in the right direction, and circumstances will be your helpers, not your hindrances.

Be ambitious, for the Master's glory, to cultivate every grace of character. In every phase of your character building you are to please God. This you may do; for Enoch pleased Him though living in a degenerate age. And there are Enochs in this our day.

Stand like Daniel, that faithful statesman, a man whom no temptation could corrupt. Do not disappoint Him who so loved you that He gave His own life to cancel your sins. He says, "Without Me ye can do nothing." John 15:5. Remember this. If you have made mistakes, you certainly gain a victory if you see these mistakes and regard them as beacons of warning. Thus you turn defeat into victory, disappointing the enemy and honoring your Redeemer.

A character formed according to the divine likeness is the only treasure that we can take from this world to the next. Those who are under the instruction of Christ in this world will take every divine attainment with them to the heavenly mansions. And in heaven we are continually to improve. How important, then, is the development of character in this life.

The heavenly intelligences will work with the human agent who seeks with determined faith that perfection of character which will reach out to perfection in action. To everyone engaged in this work Christ says, I am at your right hand to help you.

As the will of man co-operates with the will of God, it becomes omnipotent. Whatever is to be done at His command may be accomplished in His strength. All His biddings are enablings.

Mental Faculties

God requires the training of the mental faculties. He designs that His servants shall possess more intelligence and clearer discernment than the worldling, and He is displeased with those who are too careless or too indolent to become efficient, well-informed workers. The Lord bids us love Him with all the heart, and with all the soul, and with all the strength, and with all the mind. This lays upon us the obligation of developing the intellect to its fullest capacity, that with all the mind we may know and love our Creator.

If placed under the control of His Spirit, the more thoroughly the intellect is cultivated, the more effectively it can be used in the service of God. The uneducated man who is consecrated to God and who longs to bless others can be, and is, used by the Lord in His service. But those who, with the same spirit of consecration, have had the benefit of a thorough education, can do a much more extensive work for Christ. They stand on vantage ground.

The Lord desires us to obtain all the education possible, with the object in view of imparting our knowledge to others. None can know where or how they may be called to labor or to speak for God. Our heavenly Father alone sees what He can make of men. There are before us possibilities which our feeble faith does not discern. Our minds should be so trained that if necessary we can present the truths of His word before the highest earthly authorities in such a way as to glorify His name. We should not let slip even one opportunity of qualifying ourselves intellectually to work for God.

Let the youth who need an education set to work with a determination to obtain it. Do not wait for an opening; make one for yourselves. Take hold in any small way that presents itself. Practice economy. Do not spend your means for the gratification of appetite, or in pleasure seeking. Be determined to become as useful and efficient as God calls you to be. Be thorough and faithful in whatever you undertake. Procure every advantage within your reach for strengthening the intellect. Let the study of books be combined with useful manual labor, and by faithful endeavor, watchfulness, and prayer secure the wisdom that is from above. This will give you an all-round education. Thus you may rise in character, and gain an influence over other minds, enabling you to lead them in the path of uprightness and holiness.

Far more might be accomplished in the work of self-education if we were awake to our own opportunities and privileges. True education means more than the colleges can give. While the study of the sciences is not to be neglected, there is a higher training to be obtained through a vital connection with God. Let every student take his Bible and place himself in communion with the great Teacher. Let the mind be trained and disciplined to wrestle with hard problems in the search for divine truth.

Those who hunger for knowledge that they may bless their fellow men will themselves receive blessing from God. Through the study of His word their mental powers will be aroused to earnest activity. There will be an expansion and development of the faculties, and the mind will acquire power and efficiency.

Self-discipline must be practiced by everyone who would be a worker for God. This will accomplish more than eloquence or the most brilliant talents. An ordinary mind, well disciplined, will accomplish more and higher work than will the most highly educated mind and the greatest talents without self-control.

Speech

The power of speech is a talent that should be diligently cultivated. Of all the gifts we have received from God, none is capable of being a greater blessing than this. With the voice we convince and persuade, with it we offer prayer and praise to God, and with it we tell others of the Redeemer's love. How important, then, that it be so trained as to be most effective for good.

The culture and right use of the voice are greatly neglected, even by persons of intelligence and Christian activity. There are many who read or speak in so low or so rapid a manner that they cannot be readily understood. Some have a thick, indistinct utterance; others speak in a high key, in sharp, shrill tones, that are painful to the hearers. Texts, hymns, and the reports and other papers presented before public assemblies are sometimes read in such a way that they are not understood and often so that their force and impressiveness are destroyed.

This is an evil that can and should be corrected. On this point the Bible gives instruction. Of the Levites who read the Scriptures to the people in the days of Ezra, it is said, "They read in the book in the law of God distinctly, and gave the sense, and caused them to understand the reading." Nehemiah 8:8.

By diligent effort all may acquire the power to read intelligibly, and to speak in a full, clear, round tone, in a distinct and impressive manner. By doing this we may greatly increase our efficiency as workers for Christ.

Every Christian is called to make known to others the unsearchable riches of Christ; therefore he should seek for perfection in speech. He should present the word of God in a way that will commend it to the hearers. God does not design that His human channels shall be uncouth. It is not His will that man shall belittle or degrade the heavenly current that flows through him to the world.

We should look to Jesus, the perfect pattern; we should pray for the aid of the Holy Spirit, and in His strength we should seek to train every organ for perfect work.

Especially is this true of those who are called to public service. Every minister and every teacher should bear in mind that he is giving to the people a message that involves eternal interests. The truth spoken will judge them in the great day of final reckoning. And with some souls the manner of the one delivering the message will determine its reception or rejection. Then let the word be so spoken that it will appeal to the understanding and impress the heart. Slowly, distinctly, and solemnly should it be spoken, yet with all the earnestness which its importance demands.

The right culture and use of the power of speech has to do with every line of Christian work; it enters into the home life, and into all our intercourse with one another. We should accustom ourselves to speak in pleasant tones, to use pure and correct language, and words that are kind and courteous. Sweet, kind words are as dew and gentle showers to the soul. The Scripture says of Christ that grace was poured into His lips that He might "know how to speak a word in season to him that is weary." Psalm 45:2; Isaiah 50:4. And the Lord bids us, "Let your speech be alway with grace" (Colossians 4:6) "that it may minister grace unto the hearers" (Ephesians 4:29).

In seeking to correct or reform others we should be careful of our words. They will be a savor of life unto life or of death unto death. In giving reproof or counsel, many indulge in sharp, severe speech, words not adapted to heal the wounded soul. By these ill-advised expressions the spirit is chafed, and often the erring ones are stirred to rebellion. All who would advocate the principles of truth need to receive the heavenly oil of love. Under all circumstances reproof should be spoken in love. Then our words will reform but not exasperate. Christ by His Holy Spirit will supply the force and the power. This is His work.

Not one word is to be spoken unadvisedly. No evil speaking, no frivolous talk, no fretful repining or impure suggestion, will escape the lips of him who is following Christ. The apostle Paul, writing by the Holy Spirit, says, "Let no corrupt communication proceed out of your mouth." Ephesians 4:29. A corrupt communication does not mean only words that are vile. It means any expression contrary to holy principles and pure and undefiled religion. It includes impure hints and covert insinuations of evil. Unless instantly resisted, these lead to great sin.

Upon every family, upon every individual Christian, is laid the duty of barring the way against corrupt speech. When in the company of those who indulge in foolish talk, it is our duty to change the subject of conversation if possible. By the help of the grace of God we should quietly drop words or introduce a subject that will turn the conversation into a profitable channel.

It is the work of parents to train their children to proper habits of speech. The very best school for this culture is the home life. From the earliest years the children should be taught to speak respectfully and lovingly to their parents and to one another. They should be taught that only words of gentleness, truth, and purity must pass their lips. Let the parents themselves be daily learners in the school of Christ. Then by precept and example they can teach their children the use of "sound speech, that cannot be condemned." Titus 2:8. This is one of the greatest and most responsible of their duties.

As followers of Christ we should make our words such as to be a help and an encouragement to one another in the Christian life. Far more than we do, we need to speak of the precious chapters in our experience. We should speak of the mercy and loving-kindness of God, of the matchless depths of the Saviour's love. Our words should be words of praise and thanksgiving. If the mind and heart are full of the love of God, this will be revealed in the conversation. It will not be a difficult matter to impart that which enters into our spiritual life. Great thoughts, noble aspirations, clear perceptions of truth, unselfish purposes, yearnings for piety and holiness, will bear fruit in words that reveal the character of the heart treasure. When Christ is thus revealed in our speech, it will have power in winning souls to Him.

We should speak of Christ to those who know Him not. We should do as Christ did. Wherever He was, in the synagogue, by the wayside, in the boat thrust out a little from the land, at the Pharisee's feast or the table of the publican, He spoke to men of the things pertaining to the higher life. The things of nature, the events of daily life, were bound up by Him with the words of truth. The hearts of His hearers were drawn to Him; for He had healed their sick, had comforted their sorrowing ones, and had taken their children in His arms and blessed them. When He opened His lips to speak, their attention was riveted upon Him, and every word was to some soul a savor of life unto life.

So it should be with us. Wherever we are, we should watch for opportunities of speaking to others of the Saviour. If we follow Christ's example in doing good, hearts will open to us as they did to Him. Not abruptly, but with tact born of divine love, we can tell them of Him who is the "Chiefest among ten thousand" and the One "altogether lovely." Song of Solomon 5:10, 16. This is the very highest work in which we can employ the talent of speech. It was given to us that we might present Christ as the sin-pardoning Saviour.

Influence

The life of Christ was an ever-widening, shoreless influence, an influence that bound Him to God and to the whole human family. Through Christ, God has invested man with an influence that makes it impossible for him to live to himself. Individually we are connected with our fellow men, a part of God's great whole, and we stand under mutual obligations. No man can be independent of his fellow men; for the well-being of each affects others. It is God's purpose that each shall feel himself necessary to others' welfare, and seek to promote their happiness.

Every soul is surrounded by an atmosphere of its own—an atmosphere, it may be, charged with the life-giving power of faith, courage, and hope, and sweet with the fragrance of love. Or it may be heavy and chill with the gloom of discontent and selfishness, or poisonous with the deadly taint of cherished sin. By the atmosphere surrounding us, every person with whom we come in contact is consciously or unconsciously affected.

This is a responsibility from which we cannot free ourselves. Our words, our acts, our dress, our deportment, even the expression of the countenance, has an influence. Upon the impression thus made there hang results for good or evil which no man can measure. Every impulse thus imparted is seed sown which will produce its harvest. It is a link in the long chain of human events, extending we know not whither. If by our example we aid others in the development of good principles, we give them power to do good. In their turn they exert the same influence upon others, and they upon still others. Thus by our unconscious influence thousands may be blessed.

Throw a pebble into the lake, and a wave is formed, and another and another; and as they increase, the circle widens, until it reaches the very shore. So with our influence. Beyond our knowledge or control it tells upon others in blessing or in cursing.

Character is power. The silent witness of a true, unselfish, godly life carries an almost irresistible influence. By revealing in our own life the character of Christ we co-operate with Him in the work of saving souls. It is only by revealing in our life His character that we can co-operate with Him. And the wider the sphere of our influence, the more good we may do. When those who profess to serve God follow Christ's example, practicing the principles of the law in their daily life; when every act bears witness that they love God supremely and their neighbor as themselves, then will the church have power to move the world.

But never should it be forgotten that influence is no less a power for evil. To lose one's own soul is a terrible thing; but to cause the loss of other souls is still more terrible. That our influence should be a savor of death unto death is a fearful thought; yet this is possible. Many who profess to gather with Christ are scattering from Him. This is why the church is so weak. Many indulge freely in criticism and accusing. By giving expression to suspicion, jealousy, and discontent, they yield themselves as instruments to Satan. Before they realize what they are doing, the adversary has through them accomplished his purpose. The impression of evil has been made, the shadow has been cast, the arrows of Satan have found their mark. Distrust, unbelief, and downright infidelity have fastened upon those who otherwise might have accepted Christ. Meanwhile the workers for Satan look complacently upon those whom they have driven to skepticism, and who are now hardened against reproof and entreaty. They flatter themselves that in comparison with these souls they are virtuous and righteous. They do not realize that these sad wrecks of character are the work of their own unbridled tongues and rebellious hearts. It is through their influence that these tempted ones have fallen.

So frivolity, selfish indulgence, and careless indifference on the part of professed Christians are turning away many souls from the path of life. Many there are who will fear to meet at the bar of God the results of their influence.

It is only through the grace of God that we can make a right use of this endowment. There is nothing in us of ourselves by which we can influence others for good. If we realize our helplessness and our need of divine power, we shall not trust to ourselves. We know not what results a day, an hour, or a moment may determine, and never should we begin the day without committing our ways to our heavenly Father. His angels are appointed to watch over us, and if we put ourselves under their guardianship, then in every time of danger they will be at our right hand. When unconsciously we are in danger of exerting a wrong influence, the angels will be by our side, prompting us to a better course, choosing our words for us, and influencing our actions. Thus our influence may be a silent, unconscious, but mighty power in drawing others to Christ and the heavenly world.

Time

Our time belongs to God. Every moment is His, and we are under the most solemn obligation to improve it to His glory. Of no talent He has given will He require a more strict account than of our time.

The value of time is beyond computation. Christ regarded every moment as precious, and it is thus that we should regard it. Life is too short to be trifled away. We have but a few days of probation in which to prepare for eternity. We have no time to waste, no time to devote to selfish pleasure, no time for the indulgence of sin. It is now that we are to form characters for the future, immortal life. It is now that we are to prepare for the searching judgment.

The human family have scarcely begun to live when they begin to die, and the world's incessant labor ends in nothingness unless a true knowledge in regard to eternal life is gained. The man who appreciates time as his working day will fit himself for a mansion and for a life that is immortal. It is well that he was born.

We are admonished to redeem the time. But time squandered can never be recovered. We cannot call back even one moment. The only way in which we can redeem our time is by making the most of that which remains, by being co-workers with God in His great plan of redemption.

In him who does this, a transformation of character takes place. He becomes a son of God, a member of the royal family, a child of the heavenly King. He is fitted to be the companion of the angels.

Now is our time to labor for the salvation of our fellow men. There are some who think that if they give money to the cause of Christ, this is all they are required to do; the precious time in which they might do personal service for Him passes unimproved. But it is the privilege and duty of all who have health and strength to render to God active service. All are to labor in winning souls to Christ. Donations of money cannot take the place of this.

Every moment is freighted with eternal consequences. We are to stand as minute men, ready for service at a moment's notice. The opportunity that is now ours to speak to some needy soul the word of life may never offer again. God may say to that one, "This night thy soul shall be required of thee," and through our neglect he may not be ready. (Luke 12:20.) In the great judgment day, how shall we render our account to God?

Life is too solemn to be absorbed in temporal and earthly matters, in a treadmill of care and anxiety for the things that are but an atom in comparison with the things of eternal interest. Yet God has called us to serve Him in the temporal affairs of life. Diligence in this work is as much a part of true religion as is devotion. The Bible gives no indorsement to idleness. It is the greatest curse that afflicts our world. Every man and woman who is truly converted will be a diligent worker.

Upon the right improvement of our time depends our success in acquiring knowledge and mental culture. The cultivation of the intellect need not be prevented by poverty, humble origin, or unfavorable surroundings. Only let the moments be treasured. A few moments here and a few there, that might be frittered away in aimless talk; the morning hours so often wasted in bed; the time spent in traveling on trams or railway cars, or waiting at the station; the moments of waiting for meals, waiting for those who are tardy in keeping an appointment—if a book were kept at hand, and these fragments of time were improved in study, reading, or careful thought, what might not be accomplished. A resolute purpose, persistent industry, and careful economy of time, will enable men to acquire knowledge and mental discipline which will qualify them for almost any position of influence and usefulness.

It is the duty of every Christian to acquire habits of order, thoroughness, and dispatch. There is no excuse for slow bungling at work of any character. When one is always at work and the work is never done, it is because mind and heart are not put into the labor. The one who is slow and who works at a disadvantage should realize that these are faults to be corrected. He needs to exercise his mind in planning how to use the time so as to secure the best results. By tact and method, some will accomplish as much in five hours as others do in ten. Some who are engaged in domestic labor are always at work not because they have so much to do but because they do not plan so as to save time. By their slow, dilatory ways they make much work out of very little. But all who will, may overcome these fussy, lingering habits. In their work let them have a definite aim. Decide how long a time is required for a given task, and then bend every effort toward accomplishing the work in the given time. The exercise of the will power will make the hands move deftly.

Through lack of determination to take themselves in hand and reform, persons can become stereotyped in a wrong course of action; or by cultivating their powers they may acquire ability to do the very best of service. Then they will find themselves in demand anywhere and everywhere. They will be appreciated for all that they are worth.

By many children and youth, time is wasted that might be spent in carrying home burdens, and thus showing a loving interest in father and mother. The youth might take upon their strong young shoulders many responsibilities which someone must bear.

The life of Christ from His earliest years was a life of earnest activity. He lived not to please Himself. He was the Son of the infinite God, yet He worked at the carpenter's trade with His father Joseph. His trade was significant. He had come into the world as the character builder, and as such all His work was perfect. Into all His secular labor He brought the same perfection as into the characters He was transforming by His divine power. He is our pattern.

Parents should teach their children the value and right use of time. Teach them that to do something which will honor God and bless humanity is worth striving for. Even in their early years they can be missionaries for God.

Parents cannot commit a greater sin than to allow their children to have nothing to do. The children soon learn to love idleness, and they grow up shiftless, useless men and women. When they are old enough to earn their living, and find employment, they work in a lazy, droning way, yet expect to be paid as much as if they were faithful. There is a world-wide difference between this class of workers and those who realize that they must be faithful stewards.

Indolent, careless habits indulged in secular work will be brought into the religious life and will unfit one to do any efficient service for God. Many who through diligent labor might have been a blessing to the world, have been ruined through idleness. Lack of employment and of steadfast purpose opens the door to a thousand temptations. Evil companions and vicious habits deprave mind and soul, and the result is ruin for this life and for the life to come.

Whatever the line of work in which we engage, the word of God teaches us to be "not slothful in business; fervent in spirit; serving the Lord." "Whatsoever thy hand findeth to do, do it with thy might," "knowing that of the Lord ye shall receive the reward of the inheritance; for ye serve the Lord Christ." Romans 12:11; Ecclesiastes 9:10; Colossians 3:24.

Health

Health is a blessing of which few appreciate the value; yet upon it the efficiency of our mental and physical powers largely depends. Our impulses and passions have their seat in the body, and it must be kept in the best condition physically and under the most spiritual influences in order that our talents may be put to the highest use.

Anything that lessens physical strength enfeebles the mind and makes it less capable of discriminating between right and wrong. We become less capable of choosing the good and have less strength of will to do that which we know to be right.

The misuse of our physical powers shortens the period of time in which our lives can be used for the glory of God. And it unfits us to accomplish the work God has given us to do. By allowing ourselves to form wrong habits, by keeping late hours, by gratifying appetite at the expense of health, we lay the foundation for feebleness. By neglecting physical exercise, by overworking mind or body, we unbalance the nervous system. Those who thus shorten their lives and unfit themselves for service by disregarding nature's laws, are guilty of robbery toward God. And they are robbing their fellow men also. The opportunity of blessing others, the very work for which God sent them into the world, has by their own course of action been cut short. And they have unfitted themselves to do even that which in a briefer period of time they might have accomplished. The Lord holds us guilty when by our injurious habits we thus deprive the world of good.

Transgression of physical law is transgression of the moral law; for God is as truly the author of physical laws as He is the author of the moral law. His law is written with His own finger upon every nerve, every muscle, every faculty, which has been entrusted to man. And every misuse of any part of our organism is a violation of that law.

All should have an intelligent knowledge of the human frame that they may keep their bodies in the condition necessary to do the work of the Lord. The physical life is to be carefully preserved and developed that through humanity the divine nature may be revealed in its fullness. The relation of the physical organism to the spiritual life is one of the most important branches of education. It should receive careful attention in the home and in the school. All need to become acquainted with their physical structure and the laws that control natural life. He who remains in willing ignorance of the laws of his physical being and who violates them through ignorance is sinning against God. All should place themselves in the best possible relation to life and health. Our habits should be brought under the control of a mind that is itself under the control of God.

"Know ye not," says the apostle Paul, "that your body is the temple of the Holy Ghost which is in you, which ye have of God, and ye are not your own? For ye are bought with a price; therefore glorify God in your body, and in your spirit, which are God's." 1 Corinthians 6:19, 20.

Strength

We are to love God, not only with all the heart, mind, and soul, but with all the strength. This covers the full, intelligent use of the physical powers.

Christ was a true worker in temporal as well as in spiritual things, and into all His work He brought a determination to do His Father's will. The things of heaven and earth are more closely connected and are more directly under the supervision of Christ than many realize. It was Christ who planned the arrangement for the first earthly tabernacle. He gave every specification in regard to the building of Solomon's temple. The One who in His earthly life worked as a carpenter in the village of Nazareth was the heavenly architect who marked out the plan for the sacred building where His name was to be honored.

It was Christ who gave to the builders of the tabernacle wisdom to execute the most skillful and beautiful workmanship. He said, "See, I have called by name Bezaleel the son of Uri, the son of Hur, of the tribe of Judah;

and I have filled him with the Spirit of God, in wisdom, and in understanding, and in knowledge, and in all manner of workmanship.... And I, behold, I have given with him Aholiab, the son of Ahisamach, of the tribe of Dan; and in the hearts of all that are wise hearted I have put wisdom, that they may make all that I have commanded thee." Exodus 31:2–6.

God desires that His workers in every line shall look to Him as the Giver of all they possess. All right inventions and improvements have their source in Him who is wonderful in counsel and excellent in working. The skillful touch of the physician's hand, his power over nerve and muscle, his knowledge of the delicate organism of the body, is the wisdom of divine power, to be used in behalf of the suffering. The skill with which the carpenter uses the hammer, the strength with which the blacksmith makes the anvil ring, comes from God. He has entrusted men with talents, and He expects them to look to Him for counsel. Whatever we do, in whatever department of the work we are placed, He desires to control our minds that we may do perfect work.

Religion and business are not two separate things; they are one. Bible religion is to be interwoven with all we do or say. Divine and human agencies are to combine in temporal as well as in spiritual achievements. They are to be united in all human pursuits, in mechanical and agricultural labors, in mercantile and scientific enterprises. There must be co-operation in everything embraced in Christian activity.

God has proclaimed the principles on which alone this co-operation is possible. His glory must be the motive of all who are laborers together with Him. All our work is to be done from love of God and in accordance with His will.

It is just as essential to do the will of God when erecting a building as when taking part in a religious service. And if the workers have brought the right principles into their own character making, then in the erection of every building they will grow in grace and knowledge.

But God will not accept the greatest talents or the most splendid service unless self is laid upon the altar, a living, consuming sacrifice. The root must be holy, else there can be no fruit acceptable to God.

The Lord made Daniel and Joseph shrewd managers. He could work through them because they did not live to please their own inclination but to please God.

The case of Daniel has a lesson for us. It reveals the fact that a businessman is not necessarily a sharp, policy man. He can be instructed by God at every step. Daniel, while prime minister of the kingdom of Babylon, was a prophet of God, receiving the light of heavenly inspiration. Worldly, ambitious statesmen are represented in the word of God as the grass that groweth up and as the flower of the grass that fadeth. Yet the Lord desires to have in His service intelligent men, men qualified for various lines of work. There is need of businessmen who will weave the grand principles of truth into all their transactions. And their talents should be perfected by most thorough study and training. If men in any line of work need to improve their opportunities to become wise and efficient, it is those who are using their ability in building up the kingdom of God in our world. Of Daniel we learn that in all his business transactions, when subjected to the closest scrutiny, not one fault or error could be found. He was a sample of what every businessman may be. His history shows what may be accomplished by one who consecrates the strength of brain and bone and muscle, of heart and life, to the service of God.

Money

God also entrusts men with means. He gives them power to get wealth. He waters the earth with the dews of heaven and with the showers of refreshing rain. He gives the sunlight, which warms the earth, awakening to life the things of nature and causing them to flourish and bear fruit. And He asks for a return of His own.

Our money has not been given us that we might honor and glorify ourselves. As faithful stewards we are to use it for the honor and glory of God. Some think that only a portion of their means is the Lord's. When they have set apart a portion for religious and charitable purposes, they regard the remainder as their own, to be used as they see fit. But in this they mistake. All we possess is the Lord's, and we are accountable to Him for the use we make of it. In the use of every penny, it will be seen whether we love God supremely and our neighbor as ourselves.

Money has great value, because it can do great good. In the hands of God's children it is food for the hungry, drink for the thirsty, and clothing for the naked. It is a defense for the oppressed, and a means of help to the sick. But money is of no more value than sand, only as it is put to use in providing for the necessities of life, in blessing others, and advancing the cause of Christ.

Hoarded wealth is not merely useless, it is a curse. In this life it is a snare to the soul, drawing the affections away from the heavenly treasure. In the great day of God its witness to unused talents and neglected opportunities will condemn its possessor. The Scripture says, "Go to now, ye rich men, weep and howl for your miseries that shall come upon you. Your riches are corrupted, and your garments are motheaten. Your gold and silver is cankered; and the rust of them shall bear witness against you, and shall eat your flesh as it were fire. Ye have heaped treasure together for the last days. Behold, the hire of the labourers who have reaped down your fields, which is of you kept back by fraud, crieth; and the cries of them which have reaped are entered into the ears of the Lord of sabaoth." James 5:1–4.

But Christ sanctions no lavish or careless use of means. His lesson in economy, "Gather up the fragments that remain, that nothing be lost," is for all His followers. (John 6:12.) He who realizes that his money is a talent from God will use it economically, and will feel it a duty to save that he may give.

The more means we expend in display and self-indulgence, the less we can have to feed the hungry and clothe the naked. Every penny used unnecessarily deprives the spender of a precious opportunity of doing good. It is robbing God of the honor and glory which should flow back to Him through the improvement of His entrusted talents.

Kindly Impulses and Affections

Kindly affections, generous impulses, and a quick apprehension of spiritual things are precious talents, and lay their possessor under a weighty responsibility. All are to be used in God's service. But here many err. Satisfied with the possession of these qualities, they fail to bring them into active service for others. They flatter themselves that if they had opportunity, if circumstances were favorable, they would do a great and good work. But they are awaiting the opportunity. They despise the narrowness of the poor niggard who grudges even a pittance to the needy. They see that he is living for self, and that he is responsible for his misused talents. With much complacency they draw the contrast between themselves and such narrow-minded ones, feeling that their own condition is much more favorable than that of their mean-souled neighbors. But they are deceiving themselves. The mere possession of unused qualities only increases their responsibility. Those who possess large affections are under obligation to God to bestow them, not merely on their friends, but on all who need their help. Social advantages are talents, and are to be used for the benefit of all within reach of our influence. The love that gives kindness to only a few is not love, but selfishness. It will not in any way work for the good of souls or the glory of God. Those who thus leave their Master's talents unimproved are even more guilty than are the ones for whom they feel such contempt. To them it will be said, Ye knew your Master's will, but did it not.

Talents Multiplied by Use

Talents used are talents multiplied. Success is not the result of chance or of destiny; it is the outworking of God's own providence, the reward of faith and discretion, of virtue and persevering effort. The Lord desires us to use every gift we have; and if we do this, we shall have greater gifts to use. He does not supernaturally endow us with the qualifications we lack; but while we use that which we have, He will work with us to increase and strengthen every faculty. By every wholehearted, earnest sacrifice for the Master's service our powers will increase. While we yield ourselves as instruments for the Holy Spirit's working, the grace of God works in us to deny old inclinations, to overcome powerful propensities, and to form new habits. As we cherish and obey the promptings of the Spirit, our hearts are enlarged to receive more and more of His power, and to do more and better work. Dormant energies are aroused, and palsied faculties receive new life.

The humble worker who obediently responds to the call of God may be sure of receiving divine assistance. To accept so great and holy a responsibility is itself elevating to the character. It calls into action the highest mental and spiritual powers, and strengthens and purifies the mind and heart. Through faith in the power of God, it is wonderful how strong a weak man may become, how decided his efforts, how prolific of great results. He who begins with a little knowledge, in a humble way, and tells what he knows, while seeking diligently for further knowledge, will find the whole heavenly treasure awaiting his demand. The more he seeks to impart light, the more light he will receive. The more one tries to explain the word of God to others, with a love for souls, the plainer it becomes to himself. The more we use our knowledge and exercise our powers, the more knowledge and power we shall have.

Every effort made for Christ will react in blessing upon ourselves. If we use our means for His glory, He will give us more. As we seek to win others to Christ, bearing the burden of souls in our prayers, our own hearts will throb with the quickening influence of God's grace; our own affections will glow with more divine fervor; our whole Christian life will be more of a reality, more earnest, more prayerful.

The value of man is estimated in heaven according to the capacity of the heart to know God. This knowledge is the spring from which flows all power. God created man that every faculty might be the faculty of the divine mind; and He is ever seeking to bring the human mind into association with the divine. He offers us the privilege of co-operation with Christ in revealing His grace to the world, that we may receive increased knowledge of heavenly things.

Looking unto Jesus we obtain brighter and more distinct views of God, and by beholding we become changed. Goodness, love for our fellow men, becomes our natural instinct. We develop a character which is the counterpart of the divine character. Growing into His likeness, we enlarge our capacity for knowing God. More and more we enter into fellowship with the heavenly world, and we have continually increasing power to receive the riches of the knowledge and wisdom of eternity.

The One Talent

The man who received the one talent "went and digged in the earth, and hid his lord's money."

It was the one with the smallest gift who left his talent unimproved. In this is given a warning to all who feel that the smallness of their endowments excuses them from service for Christ. If they could do some great thing, how gladly would they undertake it; but because they can serve only in little things, they think themselves justified in doing nothing. In this they err. The Lord in His distribution of gifts is testing character. The man who neglected to improve his talent proved himself an unfaithful servant. Had he received five talents, he would have buried them as he buried the one. His misuse of the one talent showed that he despised the gifts of heaven.

"He that is faithful in that which is least is faithful also in much." Luke 16:10. The importance of the little things is often underrated because they are small; but they supply much of the actual discipline of life. There are really no nonessentials in the Christian's life. Our character building will be full of peril while we underrate the importance of the little things.

"He that is unjust in the least is unjust also in much." By unfaithfulness in even the smallest duties, man robs his Maker of the service which is His due. This unfaithfulness reacts upon himself. He fails of gaining the grace, the power, the force of character, which may be received through an unreserved surrender to God. Living apart from Christ he is subject to Satan's temptations, and he makes mistakes in his work for the Master. Because he is not guided by right principles in little things, he fails to obey God in the great matters which he regards as his special work. The defects cherished in dealing with life's minor details pass into more important affairs. He acts on the principles to which he has accustomed himself. Thus actions repeated form habits, habits form character, and by the character our destiny for time and for eternity is decided.

Only by faithfulness in the little things can the soul be trained to act with fidelity under larger responsibilities. God brought Daniel and his fellows into connection with the great men of Babylon, that these heathen men might become acquainted with the principles of true religion. In the midst of a nation of idolaters, Daniel was to represent the character of God. How did he become fitted for a position of so great trust and honor? It was his faithfulness in the little things that gave complexion to his whole life. He honored God in the smallest duties, and the Lord co-operated with him. To Daniel and his companions God gave "knowledge and skill in all learning and wisdom; and Daniel had understanding in all visions and dreams." Daniel 1:17.

As God called Daniel to witness for Him in Babylon, so He calls us to be His witnesses in the world today. In the smallest as well as the largest affairs of life He desires us to reveal to men the principles of His kingdom.

Christ in His life on earth taught the lesson of careful attention to the little things. The great work of redemption weighed continually upon His soul. As He was teaching and healing, all the energies of mind and body were taxed to the utmost; yet He noticed the most simple things in life and in nature. His most instructive lessons were those in which by the simple things of nature He illustrated the great truths of the kingdom of God. He did not overlook the necessities of the humblest of His servants. His ear heard every cry of need. He was awake to the touch of the afflicted woman in the crowd; the very slightest touch of faith brought a response. When He raised from the dead the daughter of Jairus, He reminded her parents that she must have something to eat. When by His own mighty power He rose from the tomb, He did not disdain to fold and put carefully in the proper place the grave-clothes in which He had been laid away.

The work to which as Christians we are called is to co-operate with Christ for the salvation of souls. This work we have entered into covenant with Him to do. To neglect the work is to prove disloyal to Christ. But in order to accomplish this work we must follow His example of faithful, conscientious attention to the little things. This is the secret of success in every line of Christian effort and influence.

The Lord desires His people to reach the highest round of the ladder that they may glorify Him by possessing the ability He is willing to bestow. Through the grace of God every provision has been made for us to reveal that we act upon better plans than those upon which the world acts. We are to show a superiority in intellect, in understanding, in skill and knowledge, because we believe in God and in His power to work upon human hearts.

But those who have not a large endowment of gifts need not become discouraged. Let them use what they have, faithfully guarding every weak point in their characters, seeking by divine grace to make it strong. Into every action of life we are to weave faithfullness and loyalty, cultivating the attributes that will enable us to accomplish the work.

Habits of negligence should be resolutely overcome. Many think it a sufficient excuse for the grossest errors to plead forgetfulness. But do they not, as well as others, possess intellectual faculties? Then they should discipline their minds to be retentive. It is a sin to forget, a sin to be negligent. If you form a habit of negligence, you may neglect your own soul's salvation and at last find that you are unready for the kingdom of God.

Great truths must be brought into little things. Practical religion is to be carried into the lowly duties of daily life. The greatest qualification for any man is to obey implicitly the word of the Lord.

Because they are not connected with some directly religious work, many feel that their lives are useless; that they are doing nothing for the advancement of God's kingdom. But this is a mistake. If their work is that which someone must do, they should not accuse themselves of uselessness in the great household of God. The humblest duties are not to be ignored. Any honest work is a blessing, and faithfulness in it may prove a training for higher trusts.

However lowly, any work done for God with a full surrender of self is as acceptable to Him as the highest service. No offering is small that is given with true-heartedness and gladness of soul.

Wherever we may be, Christ bids us take up the duty that presents itself. If this is in the home, take hold willingly and earnestly to make home a pleasant place. If you are a mother, train your children for Christ. This is as verily a work for God as is that of the minister in the pulpit. If your duty is in the kitchen, seek to be a perfect cook. Prepare food that will be healthful, nourishing, and appetizing. And as you employ the best ingredients in preparing food remember that you are to give your mind the best thoughts. If it is your work to till the soil or to engage in any other trade or occupation, make a success of the present duty. Put your mind on what you are doing. In all your work represent Christ. Do as He would do in your place.

However small your talent, God has a place for it. That one talent, wisely used, will accomplish its appointed work. By faithfulness in little duties, we are to work on the plan of addition, and God will work for us on the plan of multiplication. These littles will become the most precious influences in His work.

Let a living faith run like threads of gold through the performance of even the smallest duties. Then all the daily work will promote Christian growth. There will be a continual looking unto Jesus. Love for Him will give vital force to everything that is undertaken. Thus through the right use of our talents, we may link ourselves by a golden chain to the higher world. This is true sanctification; for sanctification consists in the cheerful performance of daily duties in perfect obedience to the will of God.

But many Christians are waiting for some great work to be brought to them. Because they cannot find a place large enough to satisfy their ambition, they fail to perform faithfully the common duties of life. These seem to them uninteresting. Day by day they let slip opportunities for showing their faithfulness to God. While they are waiting for some great work, life passes away, its purposes unfulfilled, its work unaccomplished.

The Talents Returned

"After a long time the lord of those servants cometh, and reckoneth with them." When the Lord takes account of His servants, the return from every talent will be scrutinized. The work done reveals the character of the worker.

Those who have received the five and the two talents return to the Lord the entrusted gifts with their increase. In doing this they claim no merit for themselves. Their talents are those that have been delivered to them; they have gained other talents, but there could have been no gain without the deposit. They see that they have done only their duty. The capital was the

Lord's; the improvement is His. Had not the Saviour bestowed upon them His love and grace, they would have been bankrupt for eternity.

But when the Master receives the talents, He approves and rewards the workers as though the merit were all their own. His countenance is full of joy and satisfaction. He is filled with delight that He can bestow blessings upon them. For every service and every sacrifice He requites them, not because it is a debt He owes, but because His heart is overflowing with love and tenderness.

"Well done, thou good and faithful servant," He says; "thou hast been faithful over a few things, I will make thee ruler over many things; enter thou into the joy of thy Lord."

It is the faithfulness, the loyalty to God, the loving service, that wins the divine approval. Every impulse of the Holy Spirit leading men to goodness and to God, is noted in the books of heaven, and in the day of God the workers through whom He has wrought will be commended.

They will enter into the joy of the Lord as they see in His kingdom those who have been redeemed through their instrumentality. And they are privileged to participate in His work there, because they have gained a fitness for it by participation in His work here. What we shall be in heaven is the reflection of what we are now in character and holy service. Christ said of Himself, "The Son of man came not to be ministered unto, but to minister." Matthew 20:28. This, His work on earth, is His work in heaven. And our reward for working with Christ in this world is the greater power and wider privilege of working with Him in the world to come.

"Then he which had received the one talent came and said, Lord, I knew thee that thou art an hard man, reaping where thou hast not sown, and gathering where thou hast not strewed; and I was afraid, and went and hid thy talent in the earth; lo, there thou hast that is thine."

Thus men excuse their neglect of God's gifts. They look upon God as severe and tyrannical, as watching to spy out their mistakes and visit them with judgments. They charge Him with demanding what He has never given, with reaping where He has not sown.

There are many who in their hearts charge God with being a hard master because He claims their possessions and their service. But we can bring to God nothing that is not already His. "All things come of Thee," said King David; "and of Thine own have we given Thee." I Chronicles 29:14. All things are God's, not only by creation, but by redemption. All the blessings of this life and of the life to come are delivered to us stamped with the cross of Calvary. Therefore the charge that God is a hard master, reaping where He has not sown, is false.

The master does not deny the charge of the wicked servant, unjust as it is; but taking him on his own ground he shows that his conduct is without excuse. Ways and means had been provided whereby the talent might have been improved to the owner's profit. "Thou oughtest," he said, "to have put my money to the exchangers, and then at my coming I should have received mine own with usury."

Our heavenly Father requires no more nor less than He has given us ability to do. He lays upon His servants no burdens that they are not able to bear. "He knoweth our frame; He remembereth that we are dust." Psalm 103:14. All that He claims from us we through divine grace can render.

"Unto whomsoever much is given, of him shall be much required." Luke 12:48. We shall individually be held responsible for doing one jot less than we have ability to do. The Lord measures with exactness every possibility for service. The unused capabilities are as much brought into account as are those that are improved. For all that we might become through the right use of our talents God holds us responsible. We shall be judged according to what we ought to have done, but did not accomplish because we did not use our powers to glorify God. Even if we do not lose our souls, we shall realize in eternity the result of our unused talents. For all the knowledge and ability that we might have gained and did not, there will be an eternal loss.

But when we give ourselves wholly to God and in our work follow His directions, He makes Himself responsible for its accomplishment. He would not have us conjecture as to the success of our honest endeavors. Not once should we even think of failure. We are to co-operate with One who knows no failure.

We should not talk of our own weakness and inability. This is a manifest distrust of God, a denial of His word. When we murmur because of our burdens, or refuse the responsibilities He calls upon us to bear, we are virtually saying that He is a hard master, that He requires what He has not given us power to do.

The spirit of the slothful servant we are often fain to call humility. But true humility is widely different. To be clothed with humility does not mean that we are to be dwarfs in intellect, deficient in aspiration, and cowardly in our lives, shunning burdens lest we fail to carry them successfully. Real humility fulfills God's purposes by depending upon His strength.

God works by whom He will. He sometimes selects the humblest instrument to do the greatest work, for His power is revealed through the weakness of men. We have our standard, and by it we pronounce one thing great and another small; but God does not estimate according to our rule. We are not to suppose that what is great to us must be great to God, or that what is small to us must be small to Him. It does not rest with us to pass judgment on our talents or to choose our work. We are to take up the burdens that God appoints, bearing them for His sake, and ever going to Him for rest. Whatever our work, God is honored by wholehearted, cheerful service. He is pleased when we take up our duties with gratitude, rejoicing that we are accounted worthy to be co-laborers with Him.

The Talent Removed

Upon the slothful servant the sentence was, "Take therefore the talent from him, and give it unto him which hath ten talents." Here, as in the reward of the faithful worker, is indicated not merely the reward at the final judgment but the gradual process of retribution in this life. As in the natural, so in the spiritual world: every power unused will weaken and decay. Activity is the law of life; idleness is death. "The manifestation of the Spirit is given to every man to profit withal." 1 Corinthians 12:7. Employed to bless others, his gifts increase. Shut up to self-serving they diminish, and are finally withdrawn. He who refuses to impart that which he has received will at last find that he has nothing to give. He is consenting to a process that surely dwarfs and finally destroys the faculties of the soul.

Let none suppose that they can live a life of selfishness, and then, having served their own interests, enter into the joy of their Lord. In the joy of unselfish love they could not participate. They would not be fitted for the heavenly courts. They could not appreciate the pure atmosphere of love that pervades heaven. The voices of the angels and the music of their harps would not satisfy them. To their minds the science of heaven would be as an enigma.

In the great judgment day those who have not worked for Christ, those who have drifted along, carrying no responsibility, thinking of themselves, pleasing themselves, will be placed by the Judge of all the earth with those who did evil. They receive the same condemnation.

Many who profess to be Christians neglect the claims of God, and yet they do not feel that in this there is any wrong. They know that the blasphemer, the murderer, the adulterer, deserves punishment; but as for them, they enjoy the services of religion. They love to hear the gospel preached, and therefore they think themselves Christians. Though they have spent their lives in caring for themselves, they will be as much surprised as was the unfaithful servant in the parable to hear the sentence, "Take the talent from him." Like the Jews, they mistake the enjoyment of their blessings for the use they should make of them.

Many who excuse themselves from Christian effort plead their inability for the work. But did God make them so incapable? No, never. This inability has been produced by their own inactivity and perpetuated by their deliberate choice. Already, in their own characters, they are realizing the result of the sentence, "Take the talent from him." The continual misuse of their talents will effectually quench for them the Holy Spirit, which is the only light. The sentence, "Cast ye the unprofitable servant into outer darkness," sets Heaven's seal to the choice which they themselves have made for eternity.

26
"Friends by the Mammon of Unrighteousness"

Based on Luke 16:1–9

Christ's coming was at a time of intense worldliness. Men were subordinating the eternal to the temporal, the claims of the future to the affairs of the present. They were mistaking phantoms for realities, and realities for phantoms. They did not by faith behold the unseen world. Satan presented before them the things of this life as all-attractive and all-absorbing, and they gave heed to his temptations.

Christ came to change this order of things. He sought to break the spell by which men were infatuated and ensnared. In His teaching He sought to adjust the claims of heaven and earth, to turn men's thoughts from the present to the future. From their pursuit of the things of time, He called them to make provision for eternity.

"There was a certain rich man," He said, "which had a steward; and the same was accused unto him that he had wasted his goods." The rich man had left all his possessions in the hands of this servant; but the servant was unfaithful, and the master was convinced that he was being systematically robbed. He determined to retain him no longer in his service, and he called for an investigation of his accounts. "How is it," he said, "that I hear this of thee? Give an account of thy stewardship; for thou mayest be no longer steward."

With the prospect of discharge before him, the steward saw three paths open to his choice. He must labor, beg, or starve. And he said within himself, "What shall I do? for my lord taketh away from me the stewardship: I cannot dig; to beg I am ashamed. I am resolved what to do, that, when I am put out of the stewardship, they may receive me into their houses. So he called every one of his lord's debtors unto him, and said unto the first, How much owest thou unto my lord? And he said, An hundred measures of oil. And he said unto him, Take thy bill, and sit down quickly, and write fifty. Then said he to another, And how much owest thou? And he said, An hundred measures of wheat. And he said unto him, Take thy bill, and write fourscore".

This unfaithful servant made others sharers with him in his dishonesty. He defrauded his master to advantage them, and by accepting this advantage they placed themselves under obligation to receive him as a friend into their homes.

"And the lord commended the unjust steward, because he had done wisely." The worldly man praised the sharpness of the man who had defrauded him. But the rich man's commendation was not the commendation of God.

Christ did not commend the unjust steward, but He made use of a well-known occurrence to illustrate the lesson He desired to teach. "Make to yourselves friends by means of the mammon of unrighteousness," He said, "that when it shall fail, they may receive you into the eternal tabernacles."

The Saviour had been censured by the Pharisees for mingling with publicans and sinners. But His interest in them was not lessened, nor did His efforts for them cease. He saw that their employment brought them into temptation. They were surrounded by enticements to evil. The first wrong step was easy, and the descent was rapid to greater dishonesty and increased crimes. Christ was seeking by every means to win them to higher aims and nobler principles. This purpose He had in mind in the story of the unfaithful steward. There had been among the publicans just such a case as that represented in the parable, and in Christ's description they recognized their own practices. Their attention was arrested, and from the picture of their own dishonest practices many of them learned a lesson of spiritual truth.

The parable was, however, spoken directly to the disciples. To them first the leaven of truth was imparted, and through them it was to reach others. Much of Christ's teaching the disciples did not at first understand, and often His lessons seemed to be almost forgotten. But under the influence of the Holy Spirit these truths were afterward revived with distinctness, and through the disciples they were brought vividly before the new converts who were added to the church.

And the Saviour was speaking also to the Pharisees. He did not relinquish the hope that they would perceive the force of His words. Many had been deeply convicted, and as they should hear the truth under the dictation of the Holy Spirit, not a few would become believers in Christ.

The Pharisees had tried to bring Christ into disrepute by accusing Him of mingling with publicans and sinners. Now He turns the rebuke on these accusers. The scene known to have taken place among the publicans He holds up before the Pharisees both as representing their course of action and as showing the only way in which they can redeem their errors.

To the unfaithful steward his lord's goods had been entrusted for benevolent purposes; but he had used them for himself. So with Israel. God had chosen the seed of Abraham. With a high arm He had delivered them from bondage in Egypt. He had made them the depositaries of sacred truth for the blessing of the world. He had entrusted to them the living oracles that they might communicate the light to others. But His stewards had used these gifts to enrich and exalt themselves.

The Pharisees, filled with self-importance and self-righteousness, were misapplying the goods lent them by God to use for His glory.

The servant in the parable had made no provision for the future. The goods entrusted to him for the benefit of others he had used for himself; but he had thought only of the present. When the stewardship should be taken from him, he would have nothing to call his own. But his master's goods were still in his hands, and he determined to use them so as to secure himself against future want. To accomplish this he must work on a new plan. Instead of gathering for himself, he must impart to others. Thus he might secure friends, who, when he should be cast out, would receive him. So with the Pharisees. The stewardship was soon to be taken from them, and they were called upon to provide for the future. Only by seeking the good of others could they benefit themselves. Only by imparting God's gifts in the present life could they provide for eternity.

After relating the parable, Christ said, "The children of this world are in their generation wiser than the children of light." That is, worldly-wise men display more wisdom and earnestness in serving themselves than do the professed children of God in their service to Him. So it was in Christ's day. So it is now. Look at the life of many who claim to be Christians. The Lord has endowed them with capabilities, and power, and influence; He has entrusted them with money, that they may be co-workers with Him in the great redemption. All His gifts are to be used in blessing humanity, in relieving the suffering and the needy. We are to feed the hungry, to clothe the naked, to care for the widow and the fatherless, to minister to the distressed and downtrodden. God never meant that the widespread misery in the world should exist. He never meant that one man should have an abundance of the luxuries of life, while the children of others should cry for bread. The means over and above the actual necessities of life are entrusted to man to do good, to bless humanity. The Lord says, "Sell that ye have, and give alms." Luke 12:33. Be "ready to distribute, willing to communicate." 1 Timothy 6:18. "When thou makest a feast, call the poor, the maimed, the lame, the blind." Luke 14:13. "Loose the bands of wickedness," "undo the heavy burdens," "let the oppressed go free," "break every yoke." "Deal thy bread to the hungry," "bring the poor that are cast out to thy house." "When thou seest the naked,…cover him." "Satisfy the afflicted soul." Isaiah 58:6, 7, 10. "Go ye into all the world, and preach the gospel to every creature." Mark 16:15. These are the Lord's commands. Are the great body of professed Christians doing this work?

Alas, how many are appropriating to themselves the gifts of God! How many are adding house to house and land to land. How many are spending their money for pleasure, for the gratification of appetite, for extravagant houses, furniture, and dress. Their fellow beings are left to misery and crime, to disease and death. Multitudes are perishing without one pitying look, one word or deed of sympathy.

Men are guilty of robbery toward God. Their selfish use of means robs the Lord of the glory that should be reflected back to Him in the relief of suffering humanity and the salvation of souls. They are embezzling His entrusted goods. The Lord declares, "I will come near to you to judgment; and I will be a swift witness against…those that oppress the hireling in his wages, the widow, and the fatherless, and that turn aside the stranger from his right." "Will a man rob God? Yet ye have robbed Me. But ye say, Wherein have we robbed Thee? In tithes and offerings. Ye are cursed with a curse; for ye have robbed Me, even this whole nation." Malachi 3:5, 8, 9. "Go to now, ye rich men,…your riches are corrupted, and your garments are motheaten. Your gold and silver is cankered, and the rust of them shall be a witness against you.… Ye have heaped treasure together for the last days." "Ye have lived in pleasure on the earth, and been wanton." "Behold, the hire of the laborers who have reaped down your fields, which is of you kept back by fraud, crieth: and the cries of them which have reaped are entered into the ears of the Lord of sabaoth." James 5:1–3, 5, 4.

Everyone will be required to render up his entrusted gifts. In the day of final judgment men's hoarded wealth will be worthless to them. They have nothing they can call their own.

Those who spend their lives in laying up worldly treasure show less wisdom, less thought and care for their eternal well-being, than did the unjust steward for his earthly support. Less wise than the children of this world in their generation are these professed children of the light. These are they of whom the prophet declared, in his vision of the great judgment day, "A man shall cast the idols of his silver, and the idols of his gold [margin]; which they made each one for himself to worship, to the moles and to the bats; to go into the clefts of the rocks, and into the tops of the ragged rocks, for fear of the Lord, and for the glory of His majesty, when He ariseth to shake terribly the earth." Isaiah 2:20, 21.

"Make to yourselves friends by means of the mammon of unrighteousness," Christ says, "that when it shall fail, they may receive you into the eternal tabernacles." R.V. God and Christ and angels are all ministering to the afflicted, the suffering, and the sinful. Give yourself to God for this work, use His gifts for this purpose, and you enter into partnership with heavenly beings. Your heart will throb in sympathy with theirs. You will be assimilated to them in character. To you these dwellers in the eternal tabernacles will not be strangers. When earthly things shall have passed away, the watchers at heaven's gates will bid you welcome.

And the means used to bless others will bring returns. Riches rightly employed will accomplish great good. Souls will be won to Christ. He who follows Christ's plan of life will see in the courts of God those for whom he has labored and sacrificed on earth. Gratefully will the ransomed ones remember those who have been instrumental in their salvation. Precious will heaven be to those who have been faithful in the work of saving souls.

The lesson of this parable is for all. Everyone will be held responsible for the grace given him through Christ. Life is too solemn to be absorbed in temporal or earthly matters. The Lord desires that we shall communicate to others that which the eternal and unseen communicates to us.

Every year millions upon millions of human souls are passing into eternity unwarned and unsaved. From hour to hour in our varied life opportunities to reach and save souls are opened to us. These opportunities are continually coming and going. God desires us to make the most of them. Days, weeks, and months are passing; we have one day, one week, one month less in which to do our work. A few more years at the longest, and the voice which we cannot refuse to answer will be heard saying, "Give an account of thy stewardship."

Christ calls upon every one to consider. Make an honest reckoning. Put into one scale Jesus, which means eternal treasure, life, truth, heaven, and the joy of Christ in souls redeemed; put into the other every attraction the world can offer. Into one scale put the loss of your own soul, and the souls of those whom you might have been instrumental in saving; into the other, for yourself and for them, a life that measures with the life of God. Weigh for time and for eternity. While you are thus engaged, Christ speaks: "What shall it profit a man, if he shall gain the whole world, and lose his own soul?" Mark 8:36.

God desires us to choose the heavenly in place of the earthly. He opens before us the possibilities of a heavenly investment. He would give encouragement to our loftiest aims, security to our choicest treasure. He declares, "I will make a man more precious than fine gold; even a man than the golden wedge of Ophir." Isaiah 13:12. When the riches that moth devours and rust corrupts shall be swept away, Christ's followers can rejoice in their heavenly treasure, the riches that are imperishable.

Better than all the friendship of the world is the friendship of Christ's redeemed. Better than a title to the noblest palace on earth is a title to the mansions our Lord has gone to prepare. And better than all the words of earthly praise will be the Saviour's words to His faithful servants, "Come, ye blessed of My Father, inherit the kingdom prepared for you from the foundation of the world." Matthew 25:34.

To those who have squandered His goods, Christ still gives opportunity to secure lasting riches. He says, "Give, and it shall be given unto you." "Provide yourselves bags which wax not old, a treasure in the heavens that faileth not, where no thief approacheth, neither moth corrupteth." Luke 6:38; 12:33. "Charge them that are rich in this world,...that they do good, that they be rich in good works, ready to distribute, willing to communicate; laying up in store for themselves a good foundation against the time to come, that they may lay hold on eternal life." 1 Timothy 6:17–19.

Then let your property go beforehand to heaven. Lay up your treasures beside the throne of God. Make sure your title to the unsearchable riches of Christ. "Make to yourselves friends by means of the mammon of unrighteousness, that when it shall fail, they may receive you into the eternal tabernacles." R.V.

27
"Who Is My Neighbor?"

Based on Luke 10:25–37

Among the Jews the question, "Who is my neighbour?" caused endless dispute. They had no doubt as to the heathen and the Samaritans. These were strangers and enemies. But where should the distinction be made among the people of their own nation and among the different classes of society? Whom should the priest, the rabbi, the elder, regard as neighbor? They spent their lives in a round of ceremonies to make themselves pure. Contact with the ignorant and careless multitude, they taught, would cause defilement that would require wearisome effort to remove. Were they to regard the "unclean" as neighbors?

This question Christ answered in the parable of the good Samaritan. He showed that our neighbor does not mean merely one of the church or faith to which we belong. It has no reference to race, color, or class distinction. Our neighbor is every person who needs our help. Our neighbor is every soul who is wounded and bruised by the adversary. Our neighbor is every one who is the property of God.

The parable of the good Samaritan was called forth by a question put to Christ by a doctor of the law. As the Saviour was teaching, "a certain lawyer stood up, and tempted Him, saying, Master, what shall I do to inherit eternal life?" The Pharisees had suggested this question to the lawyer in the hope that they might entrap Christ in His words, and they listened eagerly for His answer. But the Saviour entered into no controversy. He required the answer from the questioner himself. "What is written in the law?" He asked, "How readest thou?" The Jews still accused Jesus of lightly regarding the law given from Sinai, but He turned the question of salvation upon the keeping of God's commandments.

The lawyer said, "Thou shalt love the Lord thy God with all thy heart, and with all thy soul, and with all thy strength, and with all thy mind; and thy neighbour as thyself." "Thou hast answered right," Christ said; this do, and thou shalt live."

The lawyer was not satisfied with the position and works of the Pharisees. He had been studying the scriptures with a desire to learn their real meaning. He had a vital interest in the matter, and he asked in sincerity, "What shall I do?" In his answer as to the requirements of the law, he passed by all the mass of ceremonial and ritualistic precepts. For these he claimed no value, but presented the two great principles on which hang all the law and the prophets. The Saviour's commendation of this answer placed Him on vantage ground with the rabbis. They could not condemn Him for sanctioning that which had been advanced by an expositor of the law.

"This do, and thou shalt live," Christ said. In His teaching He ever presented the law as a divine unity, showing that it is impossible to keep one precept and break another; for the same principle runs through all. Man's destiny will be determined by his obedience to the whole law.

Christ knew that no one could obey the law in his own strength. He desired to lead the lawyer to clearer and more critical research that he might find the truth. Only by accepting the virtue and grace of Christ can we keep the law. Belief in the propitiation for sin enables fallen man to love God with his whole heart and his neighbor as himself.

The lawyer knew that he had kept neither the first four nor the last six commandments. He was convicted under Christ's searching words, but instead of confessing his sin he tried to excuse it. Rather than acknowledge the truth, he endeavored to show how difficult of fulfillment the commandment is. Thus he hoped both to parry conviction and to vindicate himself in the eyes of the people. The Saviour's words had shown that his question was needless, since he was able to answer it himself. Yet he put another question, saying, "Who is my neighbour?"

Again Christ refused to be drawn into controversy. He answered the question by relating an incident, the memory of which was fresh in the minds of His hearers. "A certain man," He said, "went down from Jerusalem to Jericho, and fell among thieves, which stripped him of his raiment, and wounded him, and departed, leaving him half dead."

In journeying from Jerusalem to Jericho, the traveler had to pass through a portion of the wilderness of Judea. The road led down a wild, rocky ravine, which was infested with robbers, and was often the scene of violence. It was here that the traveler was attacked, stripped of all that was valuable, and left half dead by the wayside. As he lay thus, a priest came that way; he saw the man lying wounded and bruised, weltering in his own blood; but he left him without rendering any assistance. He "passed by on the other side." Then a Levite appeared. Curious to know what had happened, he stopped and looked at the sufferer. He was convicted of what he ought to do, but it was not an agreeable duty. He wished that he had not come that way so that he would not have seen the wounded man. He persuaded himself that the case was no concern of his, and he too "passed by on the other side."

But a Samaritan, traveling the same road, saw the sufferer, and he did the work that the others had refused to do. With gentleness and kindness he ministered to the wounded man. "When he saw him, he had compassion on him, and went to him, and bound up his wounds, pouring in oil and wine, and set him on his own beast, and brought him to an inn, and took care of him. And on the morrow when he departed, he took out two pence, and gave them to the host, and said unto him, Take care of him; and whatsoever thou spendest more, when I come again, I will repay thee." The priest and the Levite both professed piety, but the Samaritan showed that he was truly converted. It was no more agreeable for him to do the work than for the priest and the Levite, but in spirit and works he proved himself to be in harmony with God.

In giving this lesson, Christ presented the principles of the law in a direct, forcible way, showing His hearers that they had neglected to carry out these principles. His words were so definite and pointed that the listeners could find no opportunity to cavil. The lawyer found in the lesson nothing that he could criticize. His prejudice in regard to Christ was removed. But he had not overcome his national dislike sufficiently to give credit to the Samaritan by name. When Christ asked, "Which now of these three, thinkest thou, was neighbour unto him that fell among the thieves?" he answered, "He that showed mercy on him."

"Then said Jesus unto him, Go, and do thou likewise." Show the same tender kindness to those in need. Thus you will give evidence that you keep the whole law.

The great difference between the Jews and the Samaritans was a difference in religious belief, a question as to what constitutes true worship. The Pharisees would say nothing good of the Samaritans, but poured their bitterest curses upon them. So strong was the antipathy between the Jews and the Samaritans that to the Samaritan woman it seemed a strange thing for Christ to ask her for a drink. "How is it," she said, "that Thou, being a Jew, askest drink of me, which am a woman of Samaria?" "For," adds the evangelist, "the Jews have no dealings with the Samaritans." John 4:9. And when the Jews were so filled with murderous hatred against Christ that they rose up in the temple to stone Him, they could find no better words by which to express their hatred than, "Say we not well that Thou art a Samaritan, and hast a devil?" John 8:48. Yet the priest and Levite neglected the very work the Lord had enjoined on them, leaving a hated and despised Samaritan to minister to one of their own countrymen.

The Samaritan had fulfilled the command, "Thou shalt love thy neighbour as thyself," thus showing that he was more righteous than those by whom he was denounced. Risking his own life, he had treated the wounded man as his brother. This Samaritan represents Christ. Our Saviour manifested for us a love that the love of man can never equal. When we were bruised and dying, He had pity upon us. He did not pass us by on the other side, and leave us, helpless and hopeless, to perish. He did not remain in His holy, happy home, where He was beloved by all the heavenly host. He beheld our sore need, He undertook our case, and identified His interests with those of humanity. He died to save His enemies. He prayed for His murderers. Pointing to His own example, He says to His followers, "These things I command you, that ye love one another"; "as I have loved you, that ye also love one another." John 15:17; 13:34.

The priest and the Levite had been for worship to the temple whose service was appointed by God Himself. To participate in that service was a great and exalted privilege, and the priest and Levite felt that having been thus honored, it was beneath them to minister to an unknown sufferer by the wayside. Thus they neglected the special opportunity which God had offered them as His agents to bless a fellow being.

Many today are making a similar mistake. They separate their duties into two distinct classes. The one class is made up of great things, to be regulated by the law of God; the other class is made up of so-called little things, in which the command, "Thou shalt love thy neighbour as thyself," is ignored. This sphere of work is left to caprice, subject to inclination or impulse. Thus the character is marred, and the religion of Christ misrepresented.

There are those who would think it lowering to their dignity to minister to suffering humanity. Many look with indifference and contempt upon those who have laid the temple of the soul in ruins. Others neglect the poor from a different motive. They are working, as they believe, in the cause of Christ, seeking to build up some worthy enterprise. They feel that they are doing a great work, and they cannot stop to notice the wants of the needy and distressed. In advancing their supposedly great work they may even oppress the poor. They may place them in hard and trying circumstances, deprive them of their rights, or neglect their needs. Yet they feel that all this is justifiable because they are, as they think, advancing the cause of Christ.

Many will allow a brother or a neighbor to struggle unaided under adverse circumstances. Because they profess to be Christians he may be led to think that in their cold selfishness they are representing Christ. Because the Lord's professed servants are not in co-operation with Him, the love of God, which should flow forth from them, is in great degree cut off from their fellow men. And a large revenue of praise and thanksgiving from human hearts and human lips is prevented from flowing back to God. He is robbed of the glory due to His holy name. He is robbed of the souls for whom Christ died, souls whom He longs to bring into His kingdom to dwell in His presence through endless ages.

Divine truth exerts little influence upon the world, when it should exert much influence through our practice. The mere profession of religion abounds, but it has little weight. We may claim to be followers of Christ, we may claim to believe every truth in the word of God; but this will do our neighbor no good unless our belief is carried into our daily life. Our profession may be as high as heaven, but it will save neither ourselves nor our fellow men unless we are Christians. A right example will do more to benefit the world than all our profession.

By no selfish practices can the cause of Christ be served. His cause is the cause of the oppressed and the poor. In the hearts of His professed followers there is need of the tender sympathy of Christ—a deeper love for those whom He has so valued as to give His own life for their salvation. These souls are precious, infinitely more precious than any other offering we can bring to God. To bend every energy toward some apparently great work, while we neglect the needy or turn the stranger from his right, is not a service that will meet His approval.

The sanctification of the soul by the working of the Holy Spirit is the implanting of Christ's nature in humanity. Gospel religion is Christ in the life—a living, active principle. It is the grace of Christ revealed in character and wrought out in good works. The principles of the gospel cannot be disconnected from any department of practical life. Every line of Christian experience and labor is to be a representation of the life of Christ.

Love is the basis of godliness. Whatever the profession, no man has pure love to God unless he has unselfish love for his brother. But we can never come into possession of this spirit by *trying* to love others. What is needed is the love of Christ in the heart. When self is merged in Christ, love springs forth spontaneously. The completeness of Christian character is attained when the impulse to help and bless others springs constantly from within-when the sunshine of heaven fills the heart and is revealed in the countenance.

It is not possible for the heart in which Christ abides to be destitute of love. If we love God because He first loved us, we shall love all for whom Christ died. We cannot come in touch with divinity without coming in touch with humanity; for in Him who sits upon the throne of the universe, divinity and humanity are combined. Connected with Christ, we are connected with our fellow men by the golden links of the chain of love. Then the pity and compassion of Christ will be manifest in our life. We shall not wait to have the needy and unfortunate brought to us. We shall not need to be entreated to feel for the woes of others. It will be as natural for us to minister to the needy and suffering as it was for Christ to go about doing good.

Wherever there is an impulse of love and sympathy, wherever the heart reaches out to bless and uplift others, there is revealed the working of God's Holy Spirit. In the depths of heathenism, men who have had no knowledge of the written law of God, who have never even heard the name of Christ, have been kind to His servants, protecting them at the risk of their own lives. Their acts show the working of a divine power. The Holy Spirit has implanted the grace of Christ in the heart of the savage, quickening his sympathies contrary to his nature, contrary to his education. The "Light which lighteth every man that cometh into the world" (John 1:9), is shining in his soul; and this light, if heeded, will guide his feet to the kingdom of God.

The glory of heaven is in lifting up the fallen, comforting the distressed. And wherever Christ abides in human hearts, He will be revealed in the same way. Wherever it acts, the religion of Christ will bless. Wherever it works, there is brightness.

No distinction on account of nationality, race, or caste, is recognized by God. He is the Maker of all mankind. All men are of one family by creation, and all are one through redemption. Christ came to demolish every wall of partition, to throw open every compartment of the temple, that every soul may have free access to God. His love is so broad, so deep, so full, that it penetrates everywhere. It lifts out of Satan's circle the poor souls who have been deluded by his deceptions. It places them within reach of the throne of God, the throne encircled by the rainbow of promise.

In Christ there is neither Jew nor Greek, bond nor free. All are brought nigh by His precious blood. (Galations 3:28; Ephesians 2:13.)

Whatever the difference in religious belief, a call from suffering humanity must be heard and answered. Where bitterness of feeling exists because of difference in religion, much good may be done by personal service. Loving ministry will break down prejudice, and win souls to God.

We should anticipate the sorrows, the difficulties, the troubles of others. We should enter into the joys and cares of both high and low, rich and poor. "Freely ye have received," Christ says, "freely give." Matthew 10:8. All around us are poor, tried souls that need sympathizing words and helpful deeds. There are widows who need sympathy and assistance. There are orphans whom Christ has bidden His followers receive as a trust from God. Too often these are passed by with neglect. They may be ragged, uncouth, and seemingly in every way unattractive; yet they are God's property. They have been bought with a price, and they are as precious in His sight as we are. They are members of God's great household, and Christians as His stewards are responsible for them. "Their souls," He says, "will I require at thine hand."

Sin is the greatest of all evils, and it is ours to pity and help the sinner. But not all can be reached in the same way. There are many who hide their soul hunger. These would be greatly helped by a tender word or a kind remembrance. There are others who are in the greatest need, yet they know it not. They do not realize the terrible destitution of the soul. Multitudes are so sunken in sin that they have lost the sense of eternal realities, lost the similitude of God, and they hardly know whether they have souls to be saved or not. They have neither faith in God nor confidence in man. Many of these can be reached only through acts of disinterested kindness. Their physical wants must first be cared for. They must be fed, cleansed, and decently clothed. As they see the evidence of your unselfish love, it will be easier for them to believe in the love of Christ.

There are many who err, and who feel their shame and their folly. They look upon their mistakes and errors until they are driven almost to desperation. These souls we are not to neglect. When one has to swim against the stream, there is all the force of the current driving him back. Let a helping hand then be held out to him as was the Elder Brother's hand to the sinking Peter. Speak to him hopeful words, words that will establish confidence and awaken love.

Thy brother, sick in spirit, needs thee, as thou thyself hast needed a brother's love. He needs the experience of one who has been as weak as he, one who can sympathize with him and help him. The knowledge of our own weakness should help us to help another in his bitter need. Never should we pass by one suffering soul without seeking to impart to him the comfort wherewith we are comforted of God.

It is fellowship with Christ, personal contact with a living Saviour, that enables the mind and heart and soul to triumph over the lower nature. Tell the wanderer of an almighty hand that will hold him up, of an infinite humanity in Christ that pities him. It is not enough for him to believe in law and force, things that have no pity, and never hear the cry for help. He needs to clasp a hand that is warm, to trust in a heart full of tenderness. Keep his mind stayed upon the thought of a divine presence ever beside him, ever looking upon him with pitying love. Bid him think of a Father's heart that ever grieves over sin, of a Father's hand stretched out still, of a Father's voice saying, "Let him take hold of My strength, that he may make peace with Me, and he shall make peace." Isaiah 27:5.

As you engage in this work, you have companions unseen by human eyes. Angels of heaven were beside the Samaritan who cared for the wounded stranger. Angels from the heavenly courts stand by all who do God's service in ministering to their fellow men. And you have the co-operation of Christ Himself. He is the Restorer, and as you work under His supervision, you will see great results.

Upon your faithfulness in this work not only the well-being of others but your own eternal destiny depends. Christ is seeking to uplift all who will be lifted to companionship with Himself, that we may be one with Him as He is one with the Father. He permits us to come in contact with suffering and calamity in order to call us out of our selfishness; He seeks to develop in us the attributes of His character—compassion, tenderness, and love. By accepting this work of ministry we place ourselves in His school, to be fitted for the courts of God. By rejecting it, we reject His instruction, and choose eternal separation from His presence.

"If thou wilt keep My charge," the Lord declares, "I will give thee places to walk among these that stand by"—even among the angels that surround His throne. (Zechariah 3:7.) By co-operating with heavenly beings in their work on earth, we are preparing for their companionship in heaven. "Ministering spirits, sent forth to minister for them who shall be heirs of salvation" (Hebrews 1:14), angels in heaven will welcome those who on earth have lived "not to be ministered unto, but to minister" (Matthew 20:28). In this blessed companionship we shall learn, to our eternal joy, all that is wrapped up in the question, "Who is my neighbour?"

28
The Reward of Grace

Based on Matthew 19:16–30; 20:1–16; Mark 10"17–31; Luke 18:18–30

The truth of God's free grace had been almost lost sight of by the Jews. The rabbis taught that God's favor must be earned. The reward of the righteous they hoped to gain by their own works. Thus their worship was prompted by a grasping, mercenary spirit. From this spirit even the disciples of Christ were not wholly free, and the Saviour sought every opportunity of showing them their error. Just before He gave the parable of the laborers, an event occurred that opened the way for Him to present the right principles.

As He was walking by the way, a young ruler came running to Him, and kneeling, reverently saluted Him. "Good Master," he said, "what good thing shall I do, that I may have eternal life?"

The ruler had addressed Christ merely as an honored rabbi, not discerning in Him the Son of God. The Saviour said, "Why callest thou Me good? There is none good but one, that is, God." On what ground do you call *Me* good? God is the one good. If you recognize Me as such, you must receive Me as His Son and representative.

"If thou wilt enter into life," He added, "keep the commandments." The character of God is expressed in His law; and in order for you to be in harmony with God, the principles of His law must be the spring of your every action.

Christ does not lessen the claims of the law. In unmistakable language He presents obedience to it as the condition of eternal life—the same condition that was required of Adam before his fall. The Lord expects no less of the soul now than He expected of man in Paradise, perfect obedience, unblemished righteousness. The requirement under the covenant of grace is just as broad as the requirement made in Eden—harmony with God's law, which is holy, just, and good.

To the words, "Keep the commandments," the young man answered, "Which?" He supposed that some ceremonial precept was meant, but Christ was speaking of the law given from Sinai. He mentioned several commandments from the second table of the Decalogue, then summed them all up in the precept, "Thou shalt love thy neighbour as thyself."

The young man answered without hesitation, "All these things have I kept from my youth up; what lack I yet?" His conception of the law was external and superficial. Judged by a human standard, he had preserved an unblemished character. To a great degree his outward life had been free from guilt; he verily thought that his obedience had been without a flaw. Yet he had a secret fear that all was not right between his soul and God. This prompted the question, "What lack I yet?"

"If thou wilt be perfect," Christ said, "go and sell that thou hast, and give to the poor, and thou shalt have treasure in heaven, and come and follow Me. But when the young man heard that saying, he went away sorrowful; for he had great possessions."

The lover of self is a transgressor of the law. This Jesus desired to reveal to the young man, and He gave him a test that would make manifest the selfishness of his heart. He showed him the plague spot in his character. The young man desired no further enlightenment. He had cherished an idol in the soul; the world was his god. He professed to have kept the commandments, but he was destitute of the principle which is the very spirit and life of them all. He did not possess true love for God or man. This want was the want of everything that would qualify him to enter the kingdom of heaven. In his love of self and worldly gain he was out of harmony with the principles of heaven.

When this young ruler came to Jesus, his sincerity and earnestness won the Saviour's heart. He "beholding him loved him." In this young man He saw one who might do service as a preacher of righteousness. He would have received this talented and noble youth as readily as He received the poor fishermen who followed Him. Had the young man devoted his ability to the work of saving souls, he might have become a diligent and successful laborer for Christ.

But first he must accept the conditions of discipleship. He must give himself unreservedly to God. At the Saviour's call, John, Peter, Matthew, and their companions "left all, rose up, and followed Him." Luke 5:28. The same consecration was required of the young ruler. And in this Christ did not ask a greater sacrifice than He Himself had made. "He was rich, yet for your sakes He became poor, that ye through His poverty might be rich." 2 Corinthians 8:9. The young man had only to follow where Christ led the way.

Christ looked upon the young man and longed after his soul. He longed to send him forth as a messenger of blessing to men. In the place of that which He called upon him to surrender, Christ offered him the privilege of companionship with Himself. "Follow Me," He said. This privilege had been counted a joy by Peter, James, and John. The young man himself looked upon Christ with admiration. His heart was drawn toward the Saviour. But he was not ready to accept the Saviour's principle of self-sacrifice. He chose his riches before Jesus. He wanted eternal life, but would not receive into the soul that unselfish love which alone is life, and with a sorrowful heart he turned away from Christ.

As the young man turned away, Jesus said to His disciples, "How hardly shall they that have riches enter into the kingdom of God." These words astonished the disciples. They had been taught to look upon the rich as the favorites of heaven; worldly power and riches they themselves hoped to receive in the Messiah's kingdom; if the rich were to fail of entering the kingdom, what hope could there be for the rest of men?

"Jesus answereth again, and saith unto them, Children, how hard is it for them that trust in riches to enter into the kingdom of God! It is easier for a camel to go through the eye of a needle, than for a rich man to enter into the kingdom of God. And they were astonished out of measure." Now they realized that they themselves were included in the solemn warning. In the light of the Saviour's words, their own secret longing for power and riches was revealed. With misgivings for themselves they exclaimed, "Who then can be saved?"

"Jesus looking upon them saith, With men it is impossible, but not with God; for with God all things are possible."

A rich man, as such, cannot enter heaven. His wealth gives him no title to the inheritance of the saints in light. It is only through the unmerited grace of Christ that any man can find entrance into the city of God.

To the rich no less than to the poor are the words of the Holy Spirit spoken, "Ye are not your own; for ye are bought with a price." 1 Corinthians 6:19, 20. When men believe this, their possessions will be held as a trust, to be used as God shall direct, for the saving of the lost, and the comfort of the suffering and the poor. With man this is impossible, for the heart clings to its earthly treasure. The soul that is bound in service to mammon is deaf to the cry of human need. But with God all things are possible. By beholding the matchless love of Christ, the selfish heart will be melted and subdued. The rich man will be led, as was Saul the Pharisee, to say, "What things were gain to me, those I counted loss for Christ. Yea doubtless, and I count all things but loss for the excellency of the knowledge of Christ Jesus my Lord." Philippians 3:7, 8. Then they will not count anything their own. They will joy to regard themselves as stewards of the manifold grace of God, and for His sake servants of all men.

Peter was the first to rally from the secret conviction wrought by the Saviour's words. He thought with satisfaction of what he and his brethren had given up for Christ. "Behold," he said, "we have forsaken all, and followed Thee." Remembering the conditional promise to the young ruler, "Thou shalt have treasure in heaven," he now asked what he and his companions were to receive as a reward for their sacrifices.

The Saviour's answer thrilled the hearts of those Galilean fishermen. It pictured honors that fulfilled their highest dreams: "Verily I say unto you, That ye which have followed Me, in the regeneration when the Son of man shall sit in the throne of His glory, ye also shall sit upon twelve thrones, judging the twelve tribes of Israel." And He added, "There is no man that hath left house, or brethren, or sisters, or father, or mother, or wife, or children, or lands, for My sake, and the gospel's, but he shall receive an hundredfold now in this time, houses, and brethren, and sisters, and mothers, and children, and lands, with persecutions; and in the world to come eternal life."

But Peter's question, "What shall we have therefore?" had revealed a spirit that uncorrected would unfit the disciples to be messengers for Christ; for it was the spirit of a hireling. While they had been attracted by the love of Jesus, the disciples were not wholly free from Pharisaism. They still worked with the thought of meriting a reward in proportion to their labor. They cherished a spirit of self-exaltation and self-complacency, and made comparisons among themselves. When one of them failed in any particular, the others indulged feelings of superiority.

Lest the disciples should lose sight of the principles of the gospel, Christ related to them a parable illustrating the manner in which God deals with His servants, and the spirit in which He desires them to labor for Him.

"The kingdom of heaven," He said, "is like unto a man that is an householder, which went out early in the morning to hire labourers into his vineyard." It was the custom for men seeking employment to wait in the market places, and thither the employers went to find servants. The man in the parable is represented as going out at different hours to engage workmen. Those who are hired at the earliest hours agree to work for a stated sum; those hired later leave their wages to the discretion of the householder.

"So when even was come, the lord of the vineyard saith unto his steward, Call the labourers, and give them their hire, beginning from the last unto the first. And when they came that were hired about the eleventh hour, they received every man a penny. But when the first came, they supposed that they should have received more; and they likewise received every man a penny."

The householder's dealing with the workers in his vineyard represents God's dealing with the human family. It is contrary to the customs that prevail among men. In worldly business, compensation is given according to the work accomplished. The laborer expects to be paid only that which he earns. But in the parable, Christ was illustrating the principles of His kingdom—a kingdom not of this world. He is not controlled by any human standard. The Lord says, "My thoughts are not your thoughts, neither are your ways My ways.... For as the heavens are higher than the earth, so are My ways higher than your ways, and My thoughts than your thoughts." Isaiah 55:8, 9.

In the parable the first laborers agreed to work for a stipulated sum, and they received the amount specified, nothing more. Those later hired believed the master's promise, "Whatsoever is right, that shall ye receive." They showed their confidence in him by asking no question in regard to wages. They trusted to his justice and equity. They were rewarded, not according to the amount of their labor, but according to the generosity of his purpose.

So God desires us to trust in Him who justifieth the ungodly. His reward is given not according to our merit but according to His own purpose, "which He purposed in Christ Jesus our Lord." Ephesians 3:11. "Not by works of righteousness which we have done, but according to His mercy He saved us." Titus 3:5. And for those who trust in Him He will do "exceeding abundantly above all that we ask or think." Ephesians 3:20.

Not the amount of labor performed or its visible results but the spirit in which the work is done makes it of value with God. Those who came into the vineyard at the eleventh hour were thankful for an opportunity to work. Their hearts were full of gratitude to the one who had accepted them; and when at the close of the day the householder paid them for a full day's work, they were greatly surprised. They knew they had not earned such wages. And the kindness expressed in the countenance of their employer filled them with joy. They never forgot the goodness of the householder or the generous compensation they had received. Thus it is with the sinner who, knowing his unworthiness, has entered the Master's vineyard at the eleventh hour. His time of service seems so short, he feels that he is undeserving of reward; but he is filled with joy that God has accepted him at all. He works with a humble, trusting spirit, thankful for the privilege of being a co-worker with Christ. This spirit God delights to honor.

The Lord desires us to rest in Him without a question as to our measure of reward. When Christ abides in the soul, the thought of reward is not uppermost. This is not the motive that actuates our service. It is true that in a subordinate sense we should have respect to the recompense of reward. God desires us to appreciate His promised blessings. But He would not have us eager for rewards nor feel that for every duty we must receive compensation. We should not be so anxious to gain the reward as to do what is right, irrespective of all gain. Love to God and to our fellow men should be our motive.

This parable does not excuse those who hear the first call to labor but who neglect to enter the Lord's vineyard. When the householder went to the market place at the eleventh hour and found men unemployed he said, "Why stand ye here all the day idle?" The answer was, "Because no man hath hired us." None of those called later in the day were there in the morning. They had not refused the call. Those who refuse and afterward repent, do well to repent; but it is not safe to trifle with the first call of mercy.

When the laborers in the vineyard received "every man a penny," those who had begun work early in the day were offended. Had they not worked for twelve hours? they reasoned, and was it not right that they should receive more than those who had worked for only one hour in the cooler part of the day? "These last have wrought but one hour," they said, "and thou hast made them equal unto us, which have borne the burden and heat of the day."

"Friend," the householder replied to one of them, "I do thee no wrong; didst not thou agree with me for a penny? Take that thine is, and go thy way; I will give unto this last, even as unto thee. Is it not lawful for me to do what I will with mine own? Is thine eye evil, because I am good?

"So the last shall be first, and the first last; for many be called, but few chosen."

The first laborers of the parable represent those who, because of their services, claim preference above others. They take up their work in a self-gratulatory spirit, and do not bring into it self-denial and sacrifice. They may have professed to serve God all their lives; they may have been foremost in enduring hardship, privation, and trial, and they therefore think themselves entitled to a large reward. They think more of the reward than of the privilege of being servants of Christ. In their view their labors and sacrifices entitle them to receive honor above others, and because this claim is not recognized, they are offended. Did they bring into their work a loving, trusting spirit, they would continue to be first; but their querulous, complaining disposition is un-Christlike, and proves them to be untrustworthy. It reveals their desire for self-advancement, their distrust of God, and their jealous, grudging spirit toward their brethren. The Lord's goodness and liberality is to them only an occasion of murmuring. Thus they show that there is no connection between their souls and God. They do not know the joy of co-operation with the Master Worker.

There is nothing more offensive to God than this narrow, self-caring spirit. He cannot work with any who manifest these attributes. They are insensible to the working of His Spirit.

The Jews had been first called into the Lord's vineyard, and because of this they were proud and self-righteous. Their long years of service they regarded as entitling them to receive a larger reward than others. Nothing was more exasperating to them than an intimation that the Gentiles were to be admitted to equal privileges with themselves in the things of God.

Christ warned the disciples who had been first called to follow Him, lest the same evil should be cherished among them. He saw that the weakness, the curse of the church, would be a spirit of self-righteousness. Men would think they could do something toward earning a place in the kingdom of heaven. They would imagine that when they had made certain advancement, the Lord would come in to help them. Thus there would be an abundance of self and little of Jesus. Many who had made a little advancement would be puffed up and think themselves superior to others. They would be eager for flattery, jealous if not thought most important. Against this danger Christ seeks to guard His disciples.

All boasting of merit in ourselves is out of place. "Let not the wise man glory in his wisdom, neither let the mighty man glory in his might, let not the rich man glory in his riches; but let him that glorieth, glory in this, that he understandeth and knoweth Me, that I am the Lord which exercise loving kindness, judgment, and righteousness in the earth; for in these things I delight, saith the Lord." Jeremiah 9:23, 24.

The reward is not of works, lest any man should boast; but it is all of grace. "What shall we say then that Abraham our father, as pertaining to the flesh, hath found? For if Abraham were justified by works, he hath whereof to glory; but not before God. For what saith the scripture? Abraham believed God, and it was counted unto him for righteousness. Now to him that worketh is the reward not reckoned of grace, but of debt. But to him that worketh not, but believeth on Him that justifieth the ungodly, his faith is counted for righteousness." Romans 4:1–5. Therefore there is no occasion for one to glory over another or to grudge against another. No one is privileged above another, nor can anyone claim the reward as a right.

The first and the last are to be sharers in the great, eternal reward, and the first should gladly welcome the last. He who grudges the reward to another forgets that he himself is saved by grace alone. The parable of the laborers rebukes all jealousy and suspicion. Love rejoices in the truth and institutes no envious comparisons. He who possesses love compares only the loveliness of Christ and his own imperfect character.

This parable is a warning to all laborers, however long their service, however abundant their labors, that without love to their brethren, without humility before God, they are nothing. There is no religion in the enthronement of self. He who makes self-glorification his aim will find himself destitute of that grace which alone can make him efficient in Christ's service. Whenever pride and self-complacency are indulged, the work is marred.

It is not the length of time we labor but our willingness and fidelity in the work that makes it acceptable to God. In all our service a full surrender of self is demanded. The smallest duty done in sincerity and self-forgetfulness is more pleasing to God than the greatest work when marred with self-seeking. He looks to see how much of the spirit of Christ we cherish, and how much of the likeness of Christ our work reveals. He regards more the love and faithfulness with which we work than the amount we do.

Only when selfishness is dead, when strife for supremacy is banished, when gratitude fills the heart, and love makes fragrant the life—it is only then that Christ is abiding in the soul, and we are recognized as laborers together with God.

However trying their labor, the true workers do not regard it as drudgery. They are ready to spend and to be spent; but it is a cheerful work, done with a glad heart. Joy in God is expressed through Jesus Christ. Their joy is the joy set before Christ—"to do the will of Him that sent Me, and to finish His work." John 4:34. They are in co-operation with the Lord of glory. This thought sweetens all toil, it braces the will, it nerves the spirit for whatever may befall. Working with unselfish heart, ennobled by being partakers of Christ's sufferings, sharing His sympathies, and co-operating with Him in His labor, they help to swell the tide of His joy and bring honor and praise to His exalted name.

This is the spirit of all true service for God. Through a lack of this spirit, many who appear to be first will become last, while those who possess it, though accounted last, will become first.

There are many who have given themselves to Christ, yet who see no opportunity of doing a large work or making great sacrifices in His service. These may find comfort in the thought that it is not necessarily the martyr's self-surrender which is most acceptable to God; it may not be the missionary who has daily faced danger and death that stands highest in heaven's records. The Christian who is such in his private life, in the daily surrender of self, in sincerity of purpose and purity of thought, in meekness under provocation, in faith and piety, in fidelity in that which is least, the one who in the home life represents the character of Christ—such a one may in the sight of God be more precious than even the world-renowned missionary or martyr.

Oh, how different are the standards by which God and men measure character. God sees many temptations resisted of which the world and even near friends never know—temptations in the home, in the heart. He sees the soul's humility in view of its own weakness; the sincere repentance over even a thought that is evil. He sees the wholehearted devotion to His service. He has noted the hours of hard battle with self—battle that won the victory. All this God and angels know. A book of remembrance is written before Him for them that fear the Lord and that think upon His name.

Not in our learning, not in our position, not in our numbers or entrusted talents, not in the will of man, is to be found the secret of success. Feeling our inefficiency we are to contemplate Christ, and through Him who is the strength of all strength, the thought of all thought, the willing and obedient will gain victory after victory.

And however short our service or humble our work, if in simple faith we follow Christ, we shall not be disappointed of the reward. That which even the greatest and wisest cannot earn, the weakest and most humble may receive. Heaven's golden gate opens not to the self-exalted. It is not lifted up to the proud in spirit. But the everlasting portals will open wide to the trembling touch of a little child. Blessed will be the recompense of grace to those who have wrought for God in the simplicity of faith and love.

29
"To Meet the Bridegroom"

Based on Matthew 25:1–13

Christ with His disciples is seated upon the Mount of Olives. The sun has set behind the mountains, and the heavens are curtained with the shades of evening. In full view is a dwelling house lighted up brilliantly as if for some festive scene. The light streams from the openings, and an expectant company wait around, indicating that a marriage procession is soon to appear. In many parts of the East, wedding festivities are held in the evening. The bridegroom goes forth to meet his bride and bring her to his home. By torchlight the bridal party proceed from her father's house to his own, where a feast is provided for the invited guests. In the scene upon which Christ looks, a company are awaiting the appearance of the bridal party, intending to join the procession.

Lingering near the bride's house are ten young women robed in white. Each carries a lighted lamp and a small flagon for oil. All are anxiously watching for the appearance of the bridegroom. But there is a delay. Hour after hour passes; the watchers become weary and fall asleep. At midnight the cry is heard, "Behold, the bridegroom cometh; go ye out to meet him." The sleepers, suddenly awaking, spring to their feet. They see the procession moving on, bright with torches and glad with music. They hear the voice of the bridegroom and the voice of the bride. The ten maidens seize their lamps and begin to trim them, in haste to go forth. But five have neglected to fill their flasks with oil. They did not anticipate so long a delay, and they have not prepared for the emergency. In distress they appeal to their wiser companions saying, "Give us of your oil; for our lamps are going out." (Margin.) But the waiting five, with their freshly trimmed lamps, have emptied their flagons. They have no oil to spare, and they answer, "Not so; lest there be not enough for us and you: but go ye rather to them that sell, and buy for yourselves."

While they went to buy, the procession moved on, and left them behind. The five with lighted lamps joined the throng and entered the house with the bridal train, and the door was shut. When the foolish virgins reached the banqueting hall, they received an unexpected denial. The master of the feast declared, "I know you not." They were left standing without, in the empty street, in the blackness of the night.

As Christ sat looking upon the party that waited for the bridegroom, He told His disciples the story of the ten virgins, by their experience illustrating the experience of the church that shall live just before His second coming.

The two classes of watchers represent the two classes who profess to be waiting for their Lord. They are called virgins because they profess a pure faith. By the lamps is represented the word of God. The psalmist says, "Thy word is a lamp unto my feet, and a light unto may path." Psalm 119:105. The oil is a symbol of the Holy Spirit. Thus the Spirit is represented in the prophecy of Zechariah. "The angel that talked with me came again," he says, "and waked me, as a man that is wakened out of his sleep, and said unto me, What seest thou? And I said, I have looked, and behold a candlestick all of gold, with a bowl upon the top of it, and his seven lamps thereon, and seven pipes to the seven lamps, which are upon the top thereof; and two olive trees by it, one upon the right side of the bowl, and the other upon the left side thereof. So I answered and spake to the angel that talked with me, saying, What are these, my lord?… Then he answered and spake unto me, saying, This is the word of the Lord unto Zerubbabel, saying, Not by might, nor by power, but by My Spirit, saith the Lord of hosts.… And I answered again, and said unto him, What be these two olive branches which through the two golden pipes empty the golden oil out of themselves?… Then said he, These are the two anointed ones, that stand by the Lord of the whole earth." Zechariah 4:1–14.

From the two olive trees the golden oil was emptied through the golden pipes into the bowl of the candlestick, and thence into the golden lamps that gave light to the sanctuary. So from the holy ones that stand in God's presence His Spirit is imparted to the human instrumentalities who are consecrated to His service. The mission of the two anointed ones is to communicate to God's people that heavenly grace which alone can make His word a lamp to the feet and a light to the path. "Not by might, nor by power, but by My Spirit, saith the Lord of hosts." Zechariah 4:6.

In the parable, all the ten virgins went out to meet the bridegroom. All had lamps and vessels for oil. For a time there was seen no difference between them. So with the church that lives just before Christ's second coming. All have a knowledge of the Scriptures. All have heard the message of Christ's near approach, and confidently expect His appearing. But as in the parable, so it is now. A time of waiting intervenes, faith is tried; and when the cry is heard, "Behold, the Bridegroom cometh; go ye out to meet Him," many are unready. They have no oil in their vessels with their lamps. They are destitute of the Holy Spirit.

Without the Spirit of God a knowledge of His word is of no avail. The theory of truth, unaccompanied by the Holy Spirit, cannot quicken the soul or sanctify the heart. One may be familiar with the commands and promises of the Bible; but unless the Spirit of God sets the truth home, the character will not be transformed. Without the enlightenment of the Spirit, men will not be able to distinguish truth from error, and they will fall under the masterful temptations of Satan.

The class represented by the foolish virgins are not hypocrites. They have a regard for the truth, they have advocated the truth, they are attracted to those who believe the truth; but they have not yielded themselves to the Holy Spirit's working. They have not fallen upon the Rock, Christ Jesus, and permitted their old nature to be broken up. This class are represented also by the stony-ground hearers. They receive the word with readiness, but they fail of assimilating its principles. Its influence is not abiding. The Spirit works upon man's heart, according to his desire and consent implanting in him a new nature; but the class represented the foolish virgins have been content with a superficial work. They do not know God. They have not studied His character; they have not held communion with Him; therefore they do not know how to trust, how to look and live. Their service to God degenerates into a form. "They come unto thee as the people cometh, and they sit before thee as My people, and they hear thy words, but they will not do them; for with their mouth they show much love, but their heart goeth after their covetousness." Ezekiel 33:31. The apostle Paul points out that this will be the special characteristic of those who live just before Christ's second coming. He says, "In the last days perilous times shall come: for men shall be lovers of their own selves;... lovers of pleasures more than lovers of God; having a form of godliness, but denying the power thereof." 2 Timothy 3:1–5.

This is the class that in time of peril are found crying, Peace and safety. They lull their hearts into security, and dream not of danger. When startled from their lethargy, they discern their destitution, and entreat others to supply their lack; but in spiritual things no man can make up another's deficiency. The grace of God has been freely offered to every soul. The message of the gospel has been heralded, "Let him that is athirst come. And whosoever will, let him take the water of life freely." Revelation 22:17. But character is not transferable. No man can believe for another. No man can receive the Spirit for another. No man can impart to another the character which is the fruit of the Spirit's working. "Though Noah, Daniel, and Job were in it [the land], as I live, saith the Lord God, they shall deliver neither son nor daughter; they shall but deliver their own souls by their righteousness." Ezekiel 14:20.

It is in a crisis that character is revealed. When the earnest voice proclaimed at midnight, "Behold, the bridegroom cometh; go ye out to meet him," and the sleeping virgins were roused from their slumbers, it was seen who had made preparation for the event. Both parties were taken unawares; but one was prepared for the emergency, and the other was found without preparation. So now, a sudden and unlooked-for calamity, something that brings the soul face to face with death, will show whether there is any real faith in the promises of God. It will show whether the soul is sustained by grace. The great final test comes at the close of human probation, when it will be too late for the soul's need to be supplied.

The ten virgins are watching in the evening of this earth's history. All claim to be Christians. All have a call, a name, a lamp, and all profess to be doing God's service. All apparently wait for Christ's appearing. But five are unready. Five will be found surprised, dismayed, outside the banquet hall.

At the final day, many will claim admission to Christ's kingdom, saying, "We have eaten and drunk in Thy presence, and Thou hast taught in our streets." "Lord, Lord, have we not prophesied in Thy name? and in Thy name have cast out devils? and in Thy name done many wonderful works?" But the answer is, "I tell you, I know you not whence ye are; depart from Me." Luke 13:26, 27; Matthew 7:22. In this life they have not entered into fellowship with Christ; therefore they know not the language of heaven, they are strangers to its joy. "What man knoweth the things of a man, save the spirit of man which is in him? even so the things of God knoweth no man, but the Spirit of God." I Corinthians 2:11.

Saddest of all words that ever fell on mortal ear are those words of doom, "I know you not." The fellowship of the Spirit, which you have slighted, could alone make you one with the joyous throng at the marriage feast. In that scene you cannot participate. Its light would fall on blinded eyes, its melody upon deaf ears. Its love and joy could awake no chord of gladness in the world-benumbed heart. You are shut out from heaven by your own unfitness for its companionship.

We cannot be ready to meet the Lord by waking when the cry is heard, "Behold, the Bridegroom!" and then gathering up our empty lamps to have them replenished. We cannot keep Christ apart from our lives here, and yet be fitted for His companionship in heaven.

In the parable the wise virgins had oil in their vessels with their lamps. Their light burned with undimmed flame through the night of watching. It helped to swell the illumination for the bridegroom's honor. Shining out in the darkness, it helped to illuminate the way to the home of the bridegroom, to the marriage feast.

So the followers of Christ are to shed light into the darkness of the world. Through the Holy Spirit, God's word is a light as it becomes a transforming power in the life of the receiver. By implanting in their hearts the principles of His word, the Holy Spirit develops in men the attributes of God. The light of His glory—His character—is to shine forth in His followers. Thus they are to glorify God, to lighten the path to the Bridegroom's home, to the city of God, to the marriage supper of the Lamb.

The coming of the bridegroom was at midnight—the darkest hour. So the coming of Christ will take place in the darkest period of this earth's history. The days of Noah and Lot pictured the condition of the world just before the coming of the Son of man. The Scriptures pointing forward to this time declare that Satan will work with all power and "with all deceivableness of unrighteousness." 2 Thessalonians 2:9, 10. His working is plainly revealed by the rapidly increasing darkness, the multitudinous errors, heresies, and delusions of these last days. Not only is Satan leading the world captive, but his deceptions are leavening the professed churches of our Lord Jesus Christ. The great apostasy will develop into darkness deep as midnight, impenetrable as sackcloth of hair. To God's people it will be a night of trial, a night of weeping, a night of persecution for the truth's sake. But out of that night of darkness God's light will shine.

He causes "the light to shine out of darkness." 2 Corinthians 4:6. When "the earth was without form, and void, and darkness was upon the face of the deep," "the Spirit of God moved upon the face of the waters. And God said, Let there be light; and there was light." Genesis 1:2,3. So in the night of spiritual darkness, God's word goes forth, "Let there be light." To His people He says, "Arise, shine; for thy light is come, and the glory of the Lord is risen upon thee." Isaiah 60:1.

"Behold," says the Scripture, "the darkness shall cover the earth, and gross darkness the people; but the Lord shall arise upon thee, and His glory shall be seen upon thee." Isaiah 60:2.

It is the darkness of misapprehension of God that is enshrouding the world. Men are losing their knowledge of His character. It has been misunderstood and misinterpreted. At this time a message from God is to be proclaimed, a message illuminating in its influence and saving in its power. His character is to be made known. Into the darkness of the world is to be shed the light of His glory, the light of His goodness, mercy, and truth.

This is the work outlined by the prophet Isaiah in the words, "O Jerusalem, that bringest good tidings, lift up thy voice with strength; lift it up, be not afraid; say unto the cities of Judah, Behold your God! Behold, the Lord God will come with strong hand, and His arm shall rule for Him; behold, His reward is with Him, and His work before Him." Isaiah 40:9,10.

Those who wait for the Bridegroom's coming are to say to the people, "Behold your God." The last rays of merciful light, the last message of mercy to be given to the world, is a revelation of His character of love. The children of God are to manifest His glory. In their own life and character they are to reveal what the grace of God has done for them.

The light of the Sun of Righteousness is to shine forth in good works—in words of truth and deeds of holiness.

Christ, the outshining of the Father's glory, came to the world as its light. He came to represent God to men, and of Him it is written that He was anointed "with the Holy Ghost and with power," and "went about doing good." Acts 10:38. In the synagogue at Nazareth He said, "The Spirit of the Lord is upon Me, because He hath anointed Me to preach the gospel to the poor; He hath sent Me to heal the brokenhearted, to preach deliverance to the captives, and recovering of sight to the blind, to set at liberty them that are bruised, to preach the acceptable year of the Lord." Luke 4:18, 19. This was the work He commissioned His disciples to do. "Ye are the light of the world," He said. "Let your light so shine before men, that they may see your good works, and glorify your Father which is in heaven." Matthew 5:14, 16.

This is the work which the prophet Isaiah describes when he says, "Is it not to deal thy bread to the hungry, and that thou bring the poor that are cast out to thy house? when thou seest the naked, that thou cover him; and that thou hide not thyself from thine own flesh? Then shall thy light break forth as the morning, and thine health shall spring forth speedily; and thy righteousness shall go before thee; the glory of the Lord shall be thy rereward." Isaiah 58:7, 8.

Thus in the night of spiritual darkness God's glory is to shine forth through His church in lifting up the bowed down and comforting those that mourn.

All around us are heard the wails of a world's sorrow. On every hand are the needy and distressed. It is ours to aid in relieving and softening life's hardships and misery.

Practical work will have far more effect than mere sermonizing. We are to give food to the hungry, clothing to the naked, and shelter to the homeless. And we are called to do more than this. The wants of the soul, only the love of Christ can satisfy. If Christ is abiding in us, our hearts will be full of divine sympathy. The sealed fountains of earnest, Christlike love will be unsealed.

God calls not only for our gifts for the needy, but for our cheerful countenance, our hopeful words, our kindly handclasp. When Christ healed the sick, He laid His hands upon them. So should we come in close touch with those whom we seek to benefit.

There are many from whom hope has departed. Bring back the sunshine to them. Many have lost their courage. Speak to them words of cheer. Pray for them. There are those who need the bread of life. Read to them from the word of God. Upon many is a soul sickness which no earthly balm can reach nor physician heal. Pray for these souls, bring them to Jesus. Tell them that there is a balm in Gilead and a Physician there.

Light is a blessing, a universal blessing, pouring forth its treasures on a world unthankful, unholy, demoralized. So it is with the light of the Sun of Righteousness. The whole earth, wrapped as it is in the darkness of sin, and sorrow, and pain, is to be lighted with the knowledge of God's love. From no sect, rank, or class of people is the light shining from heaven's throne to be excluded.

The message of hope and mercy is to be carried to the ends of the earth. Whosoever will, may reach forth and take hold of God's strength and make peace with Him, and he shall make peace. No longer are the heathen to be wrapped in midnight darkness. The gloom is to disappear before the bright beams of the Sun of Righteousness. The power of hell has been overcome.

But no man can impart that which he himself has not received. In the work of God, humanity can originate nothing. No man can by his own effort make himself a light bearer for God. It was the golden oil emptied by the heavenly messengers into the golden tubes, to be conducted from the golden bowl into the lamps of the sanctuary, that produced a continuous bright and shining light. It is the love of God continually transferred to man that enables him to impart light. Into the hearts of all who are united to God by faith the golden oil of love flows freely, to shine out again in good works, in real, heartfelt service for God.

In the great and measureless gift of the Holy Spirit are contained all of heaven's resources. It is not because of any restriction on the part of God that the riches of His grace do not flow earthward to men. If all were willing to receive, all would become filled with His Spirit.

It is the privilege of every soul to be a living channel through which God can communicate to the world the treasures of His grace, the unsearchable riches of Christ. There is nothing that Christ desires so much as agents who will represent to the world His Spirit and character. There is nothing that the world needs so much as the manifestation through humanity of the Saviour's love. All heaven is waiting for channels through which can be poured the holy oil to be a joy and blessing to human hearts.

Christ has made every provision that His church shall be a transformed body, illumined with the Light of the world, possessing the glory of Emmanuel. It is His purpose that every Christian shall be surrounded with a spiritual atmosphere of light and peace. He desires that we shall reveal His own joy in our lives.

The indwelling of the Spirit will be shown by the outflowing of heavenly love. The divine fullness will flow through the consecrated human agent, to be given forth to others.

The Sun of Righteousness has "healing in His wings." Malachi 4:2. So from every true disciple is to be diffused an influence for life, courage, helpfulness, and true healing.

The religion of Christ means more than the forgiveness of sin; it means taking away our sins, and filling the vacuum with the graces of the Holy Spirit. It means divine illumination, rejoicing in God. It means a heart emptied of self, and blessed with the abiding presence of Christ. When Christ reigns in the soul, there is purity, freedom from sin. The glory, the fullness, the completeness of the gospel plan is fulfilled in the life. The acceptance of the Saviour brings a glow of perfect peace, perfect love, perfect assurance. The beauty and fragrance of the character of Christ revealed in the life testifies that God has indeed sent His Son into the world to be its Saviour.

Christ does not bid His followers strive to shine. He says, *Let* your light shine. If you have received the grace of God, the light is in you. Remove the obstructions, and the Lord's glory will be revealed. The light will shine forth to penetrate and dispel the darkness. You cannot help shining within the range of your influence.

The revelation of His own glory in the form of humanity will bring heaven so near to men that the beauty adorning the inner temple will be seen in every soul in whom the Saviour dwells. Men will be captivated by the glory of an abiding Christ. And in currents of praise and thanksgiving from the many souls thus won to God, glory will flow back to the great Giver.

"Arise, shine; for thy light is come, and the glory of the Lord is risen upon thee." Isaiah 60:1. To those who go out to meet the Bridegroom is this message given. Christ is coming with power and great glory. He is coming with His own glory and with the glory of the Father. He is coming with all the holy angels with Him. While all the world is plunged in darkness, there will be light in every dwelling of the saints. They will catch the first light of His second appearing. The unsullied light will shine from His splendor, and Christ the Redeemer will be admired by all who have served Him. While the wicked flee from His presence, Christ's followers will rejoice. The patriarch Job, looking down to the time of Christ's second advent, said, "Whom I shall see for myself, and mine eyes shall behold, and not a stranger." Job 19:27, margin. To His faithful followers Christ has been a daily companion and familiar friend. They have lived in close contact, in constant communion with God. Upon them the glory of the Lord has risen. In them the light of the knowledge of the glory of God in the face of Jesus Christ has been reflected. Now they rejoice in the undimmed rays of the brightness and glory of the King in His majesty. They are prepared for the communion of heaven; for they have heaven in their hearts.

With uplifted heads, with the bright beams of the Sun of Righteousness shining upon them, with rejoicing that their redemption draweth nigh, they go forth to meet the Bridegroom, saying, "Lo, this is our God; we have waited for Him, and He will save us." Isaiah 25:9.

"And I heard as it were the voice of a great multitude, and as the voice of many waters, and as the voice of mighty thunderings, saying, Alleluia; for the Lord God omnipotent reigneth. Let us be glad and rejoice, and give honour to Him; for the marriage of the Lamb is come, and His wife hath made herself ready.... And he saith unto me, Write, Blessed are they which are called unto the marriage supper of the Lamb." "He is Lord of lords, and King of kings; and they that are with Him are called, and chosen, and faithful." Revelation 19:6–9; 17:14.

Index to Scripture References

Page numbers in this index refer to bracketed numbers at the bottom of each page.

Jeremiah

Ezekiel

Daniel

Hosea

Micah

Nahum

Zephaniah

Zechariah

Malachi

Matthew

Mark

Luke

John

Acts

Romans

I Corinthians

II Corinthians

Galatians

Page numbers in this index refer to bracketed numbers at the bottom of each page.

Ephesians

Philippians

Colossians

I Thessalonians

II Thessalonians

I Timothy

II Timothy

Titus

Hebrews

James

I Peter

II Peter

I John

Jude

Revelation

Page numbers in this index refer to bracketed numbers at the bottom of each page.